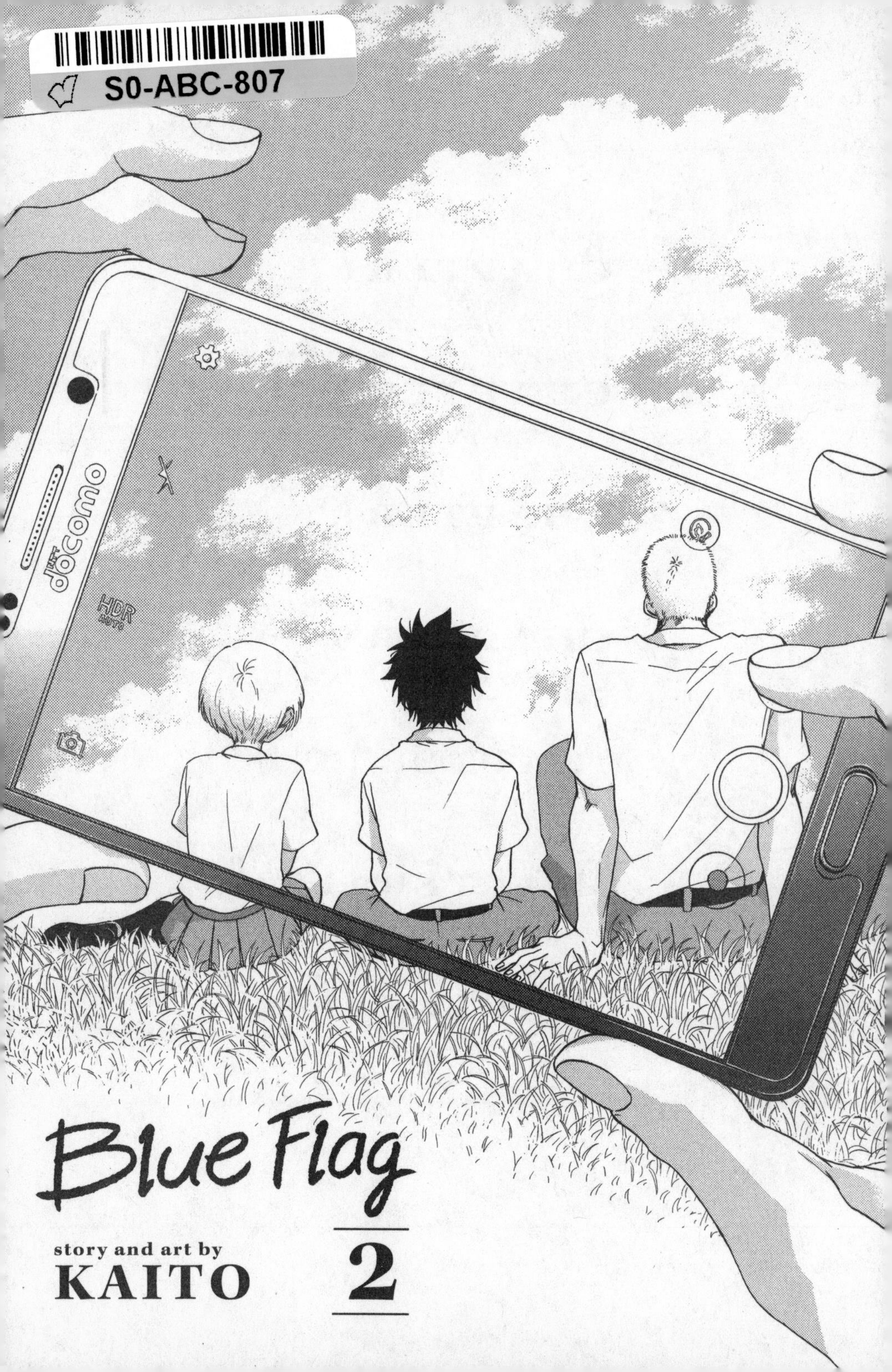
docomo
HDR
AUTO

Blue Flag

2

story and art by
KAITO

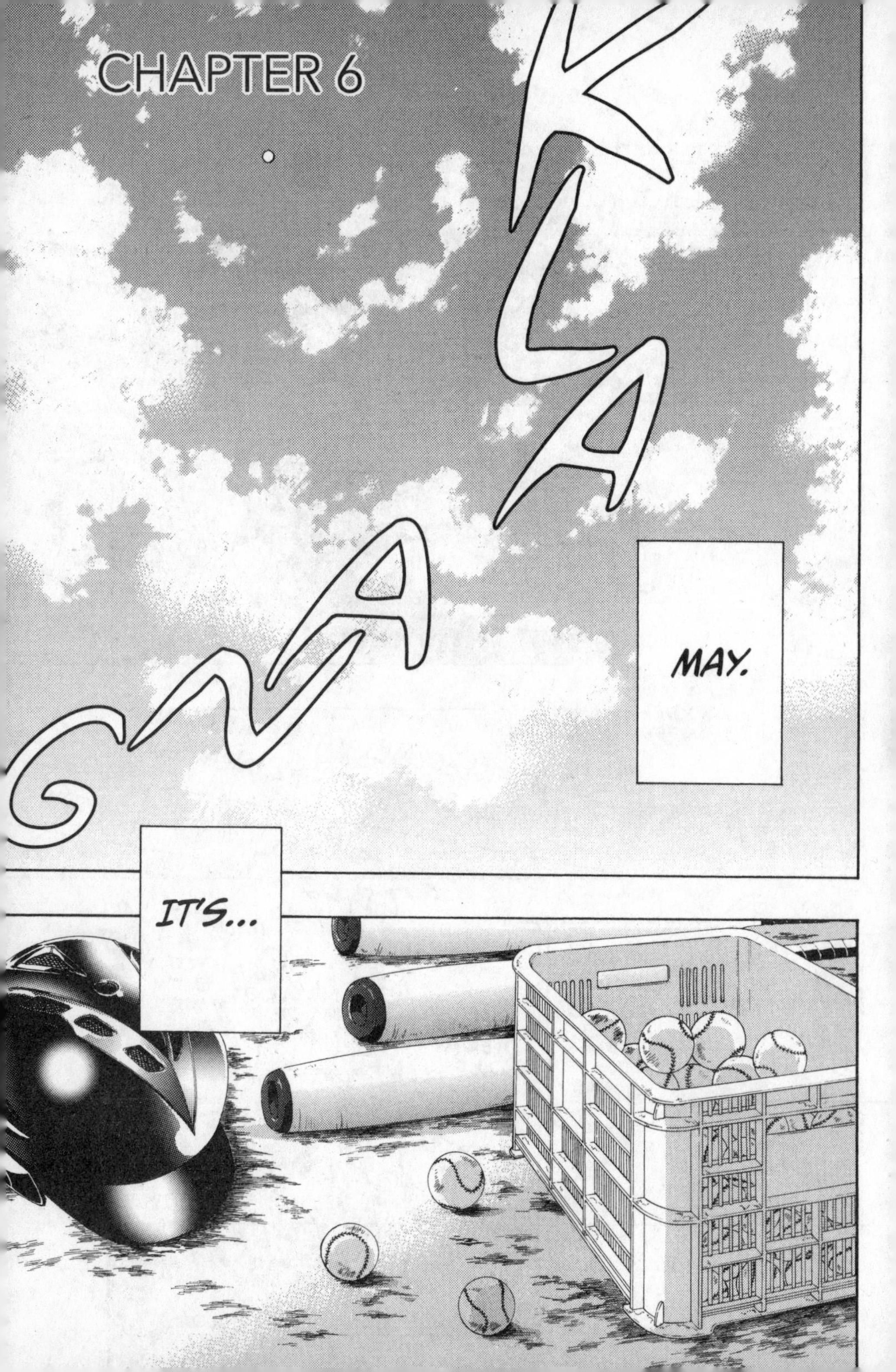
CHAPTER 6
KLAANG
MAY.
IT'S...

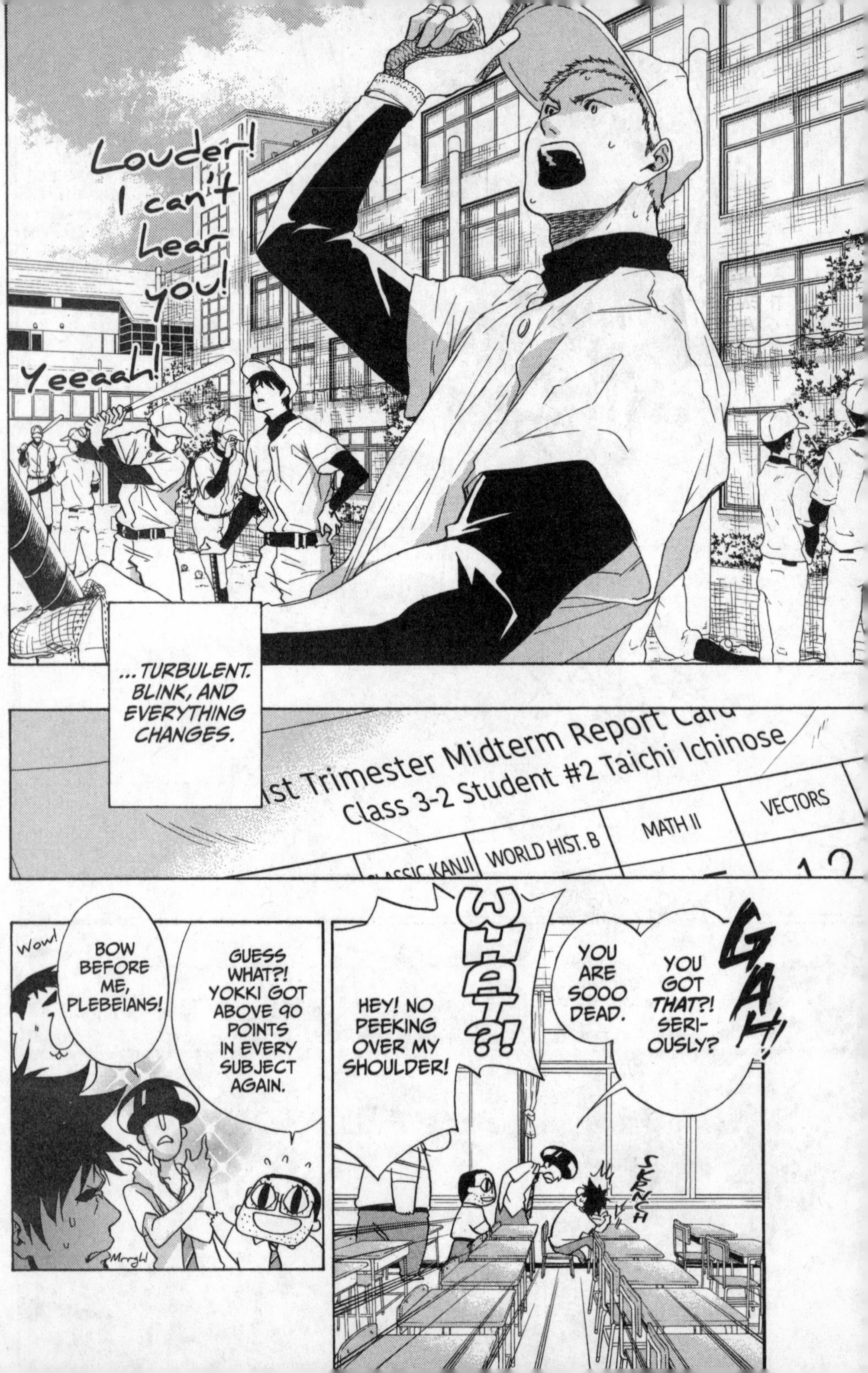
Louder! I can't hear you!
Yeeaah!
...TURBULENT. BLINK, AND EVERYTHING CHANGES.
1st Trimester Midterm Report Card
Class 3-2 Student #2 Taichi Ichinose
CLASSIC KANJI
WORLD HIST. B
MATH II
VECTORS
GAH!
YOU GOT THAT?! SERIOUSLY?
YOU ARE SOOO DEAD.
WHAT?!
HEY! NO PEEKING OVER MY SHOULDER!
SCRNCH
GUESS WHAT?! YOKKI GOT ABOVE 90 POINTS IN EVERY SUBJECT AGAIN.
BOW BEFORE ME, PLEBEIANS!
Wow!
Mrrgh!

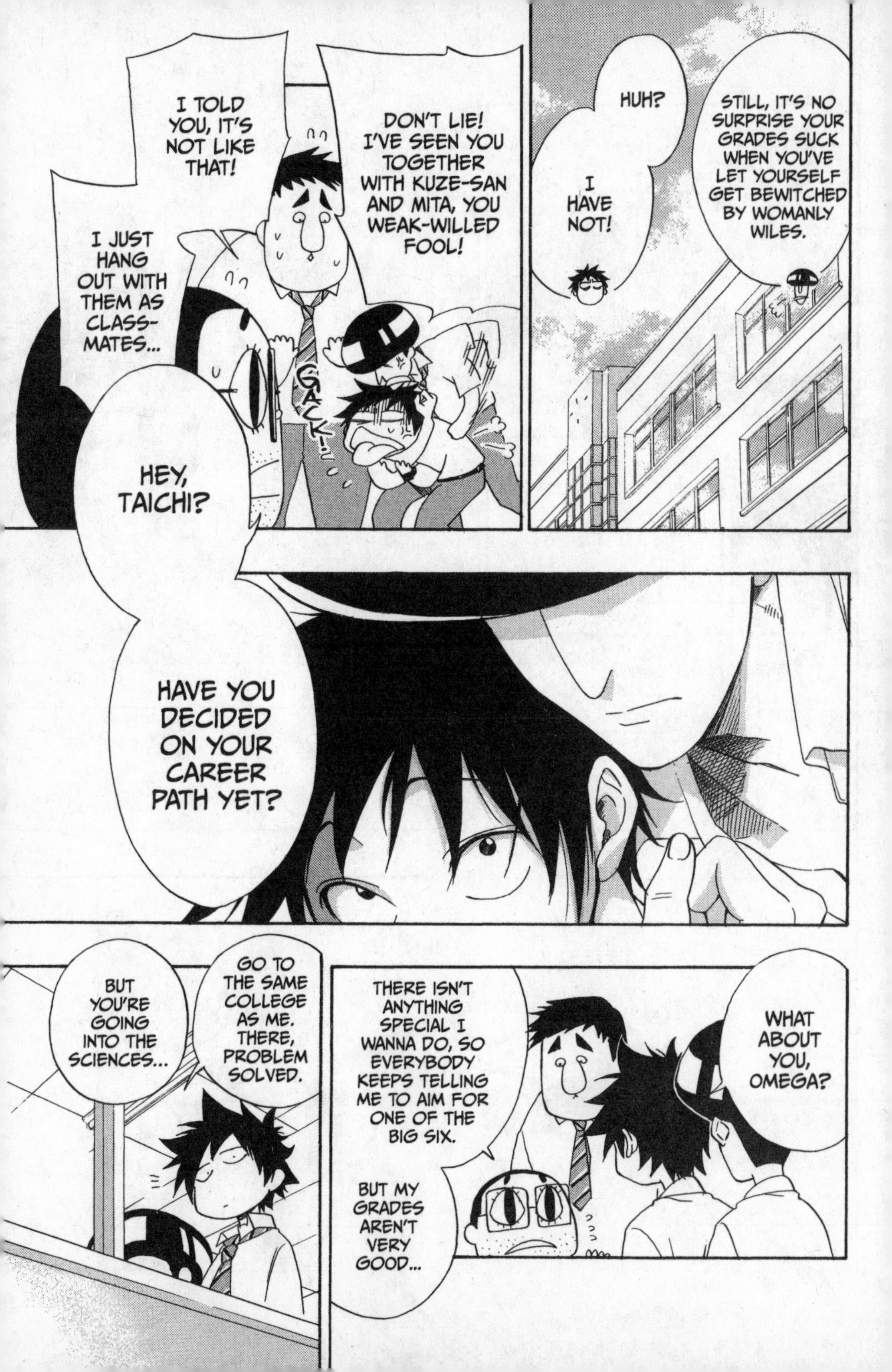
STILL, IT'S NO SURPRISE YOUR GRADES SUCK WHEN YOU'VE LET YOURSELF GET BEWITCHED BY WOMANLY WILES.
HUH?
I HAVE NOT!
DON'T LIE! I'VE SEEN YOU TOGETHER WITH KUZE-SAN AND MITA, YOU WEAK-WILLED FOOL!
I TOLD YOU, IT'S NOT LIKE THAT!
I JUST HANG OUT WITH THEM AS CLASS-MATES...
GACK!
HEY, TAICHI?
HAVE YOU DECIDED ON YOUR CAREER PATH YET?
WHAT ABOUT YOU, OMEGA?
THERE ISN'T ANYTHING SPECIAL I WANNA DO, SO EVERYBODY KEEPS TELLING ME TO AIM FOR ONE OF THE BIG SIX.
BUT MY GRADES AREN'T VERY GOOD...
GO TO THE SAME COLLEGE AS ME. THERE, PROBLEM SOLVED.
BUT YOU'RE GOING INTO THE SCIENCES...

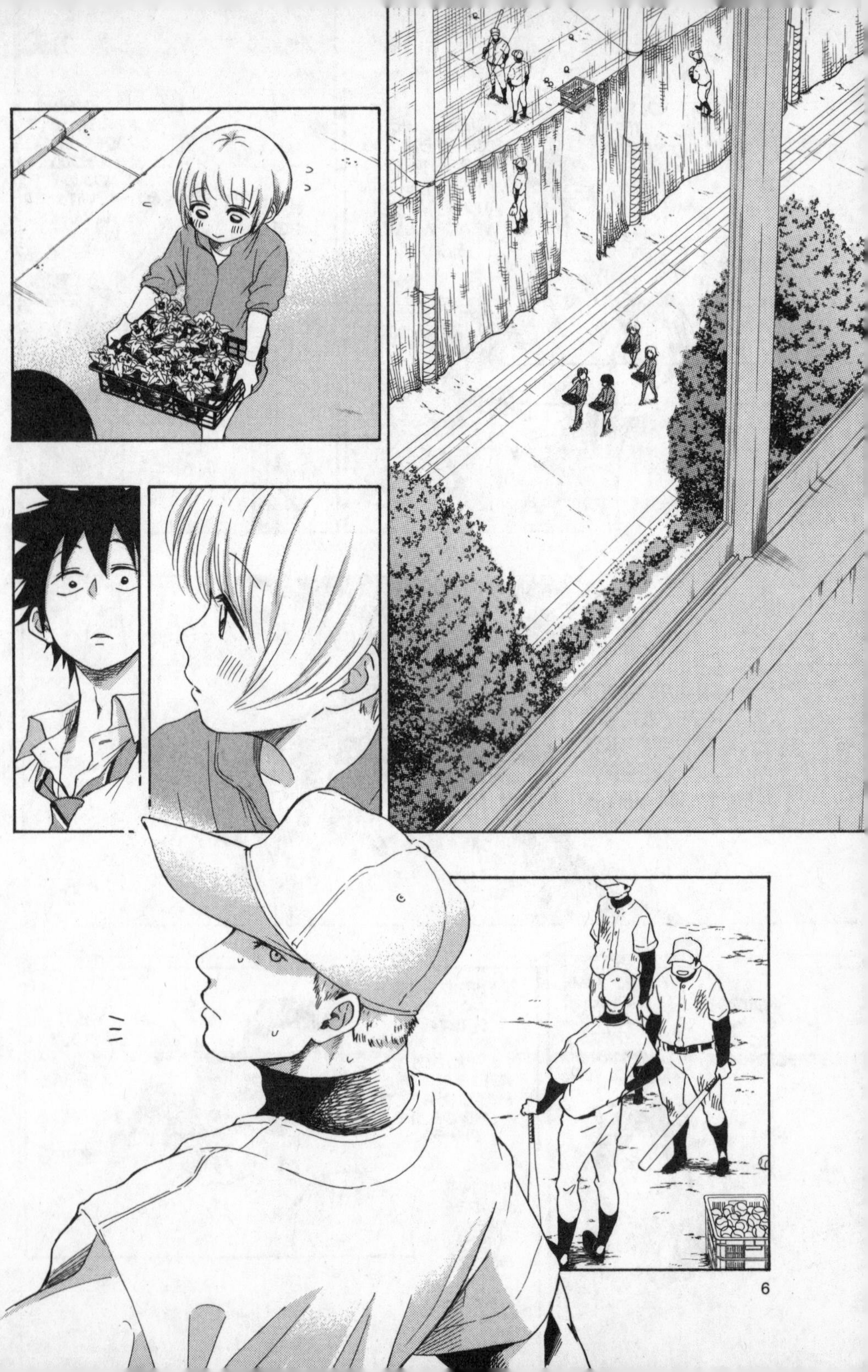

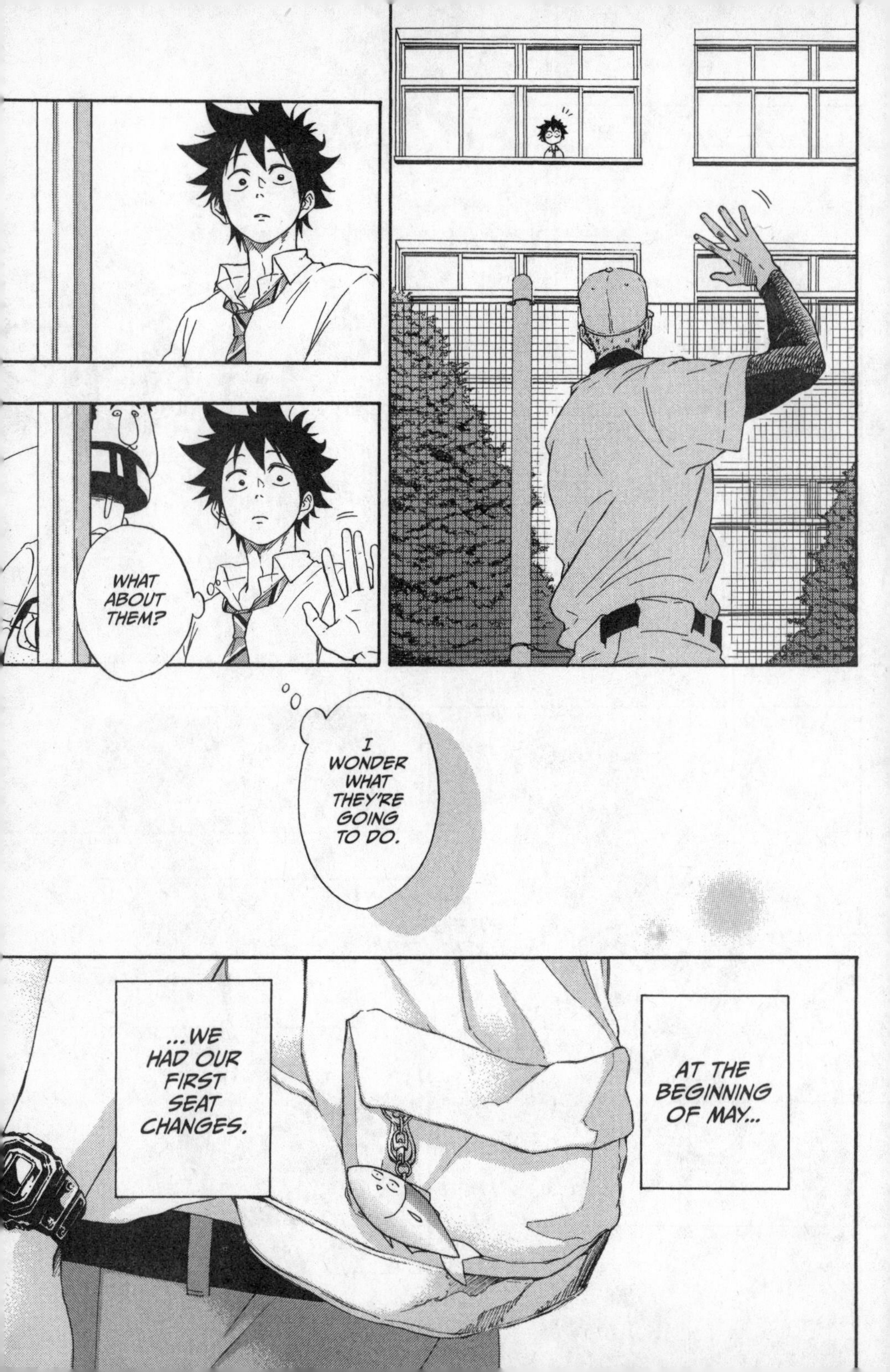
WHAT ABOUT THEM?
I WONDER WHAT THEY'RE GOING TO DO.
AT THE BEGINNING OF MAY...
...WE HAD OUR FIRST SEAT CHANGES.

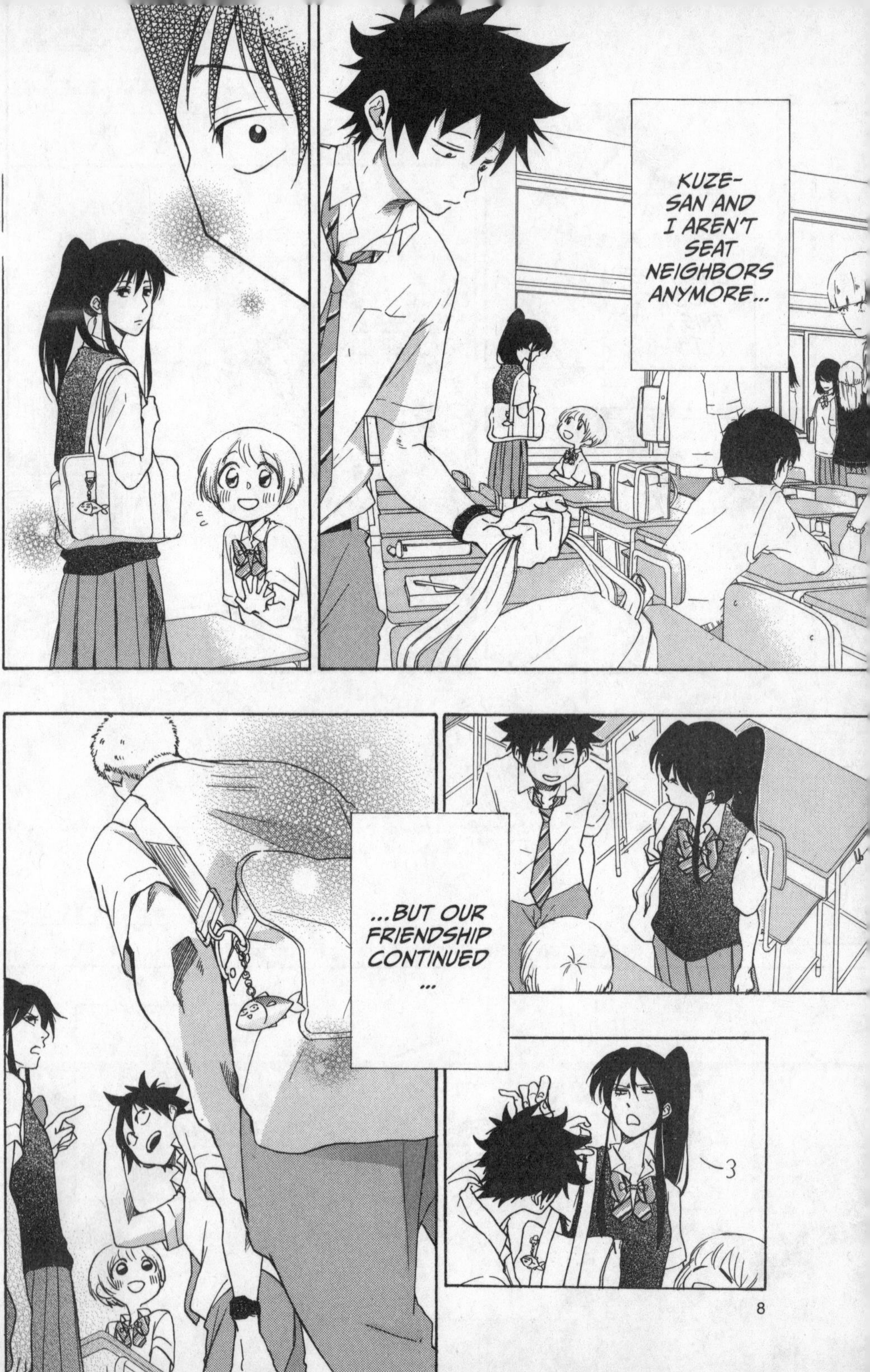
KUZE-SAN AND I AREN'T SEAT NEIGHBORS ANYMORE...
...BUT OUR FRIENDSHIP CONTINUED ...

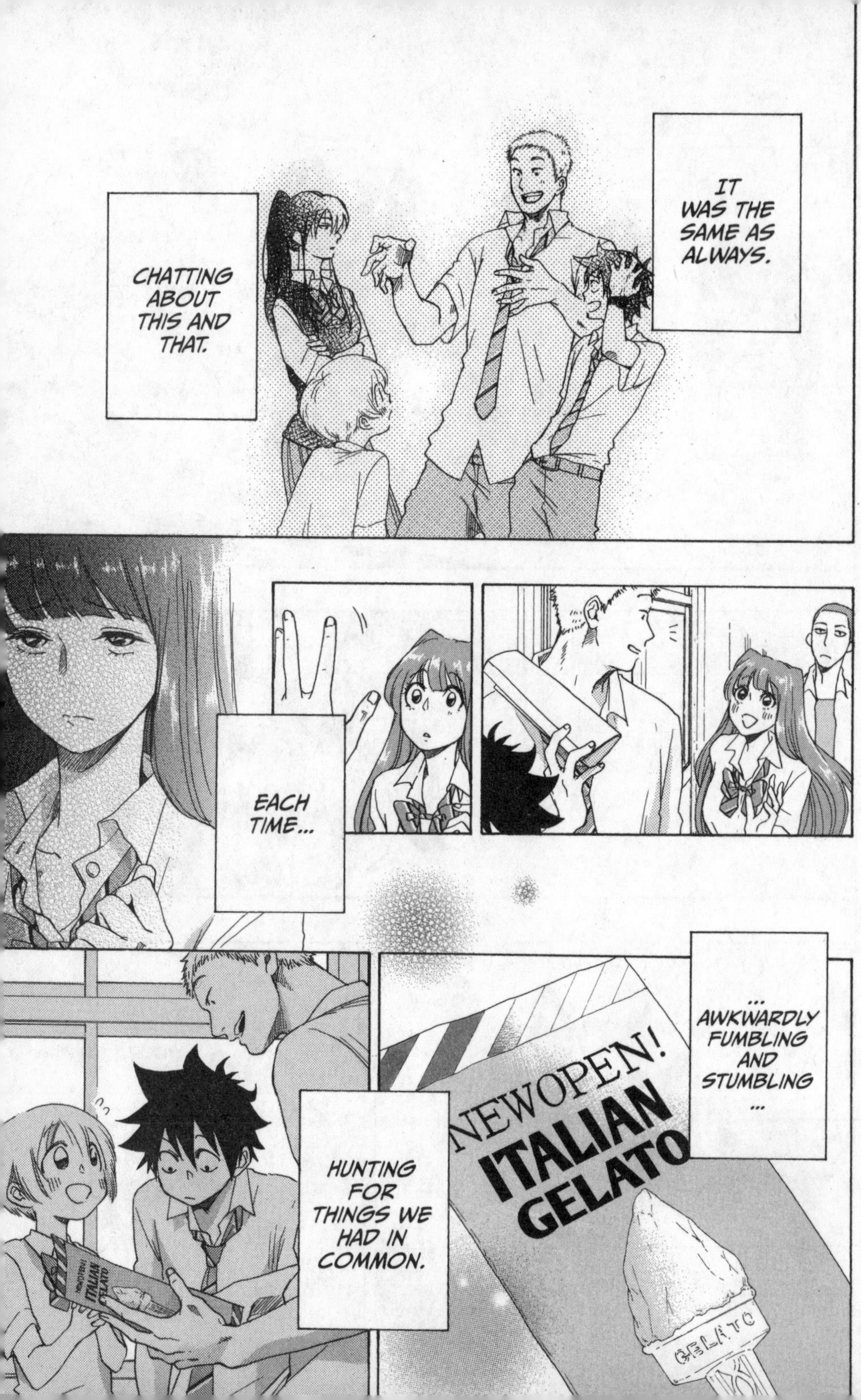
IT WAS THE SAME AS ALWAYS.
CHATTING ABOUT THIS AND THAT.
EACH TIME...
... AWKWARDLY FUMBLING AND STUMBLING ...
NEWOPEN!
ITALIAN GELATO
GELATO
HUNTING FOR THINGS WE HAD IN COMMON.

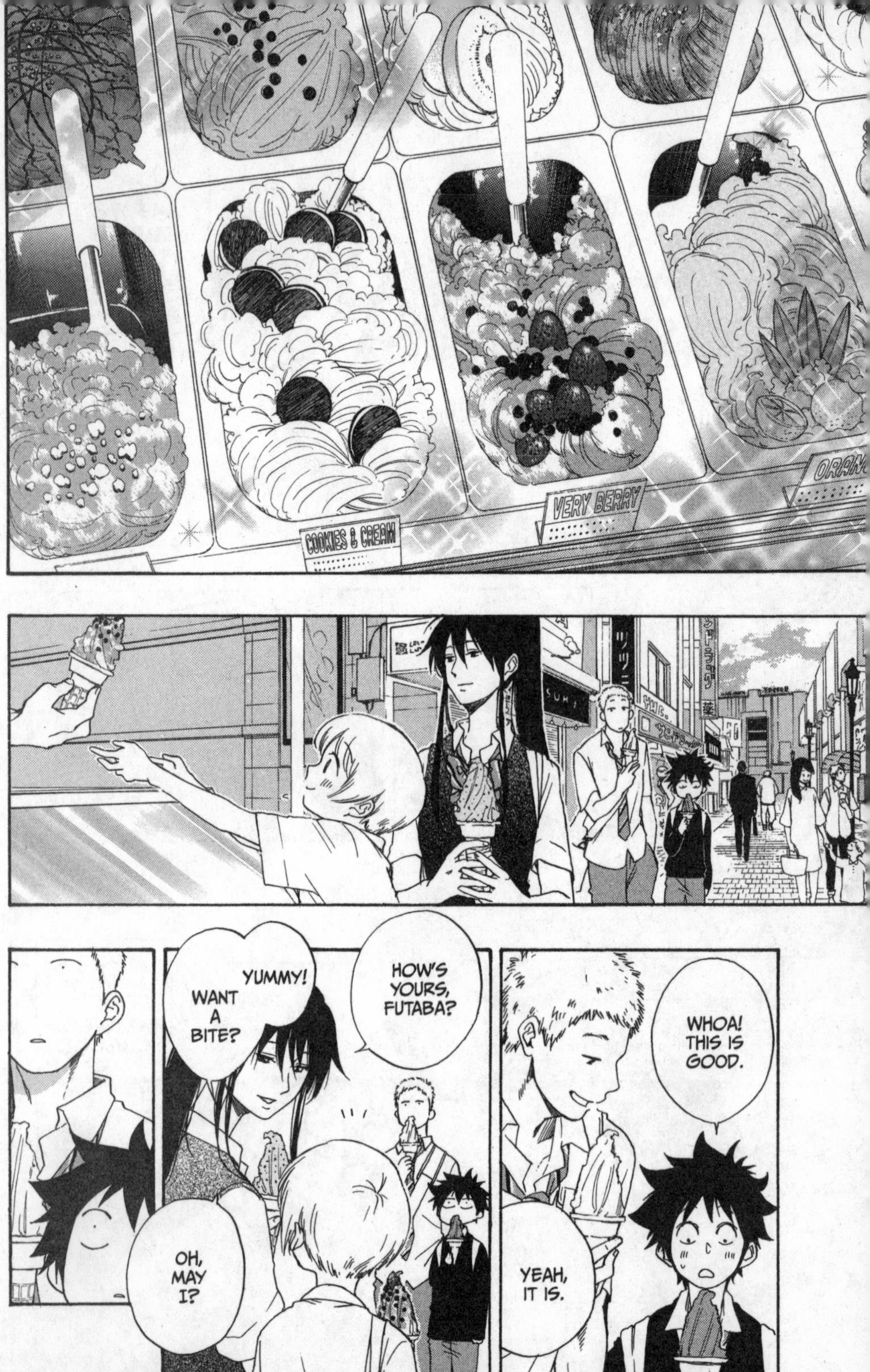
VERY BERRY
COOKIES & CREAM
WHOA! THIS IS GOOD.
YEAH, IT IS.
HOW'S YOURS, FUTABA?
YUMMY! WANT A BITE?
OH, MAY I?

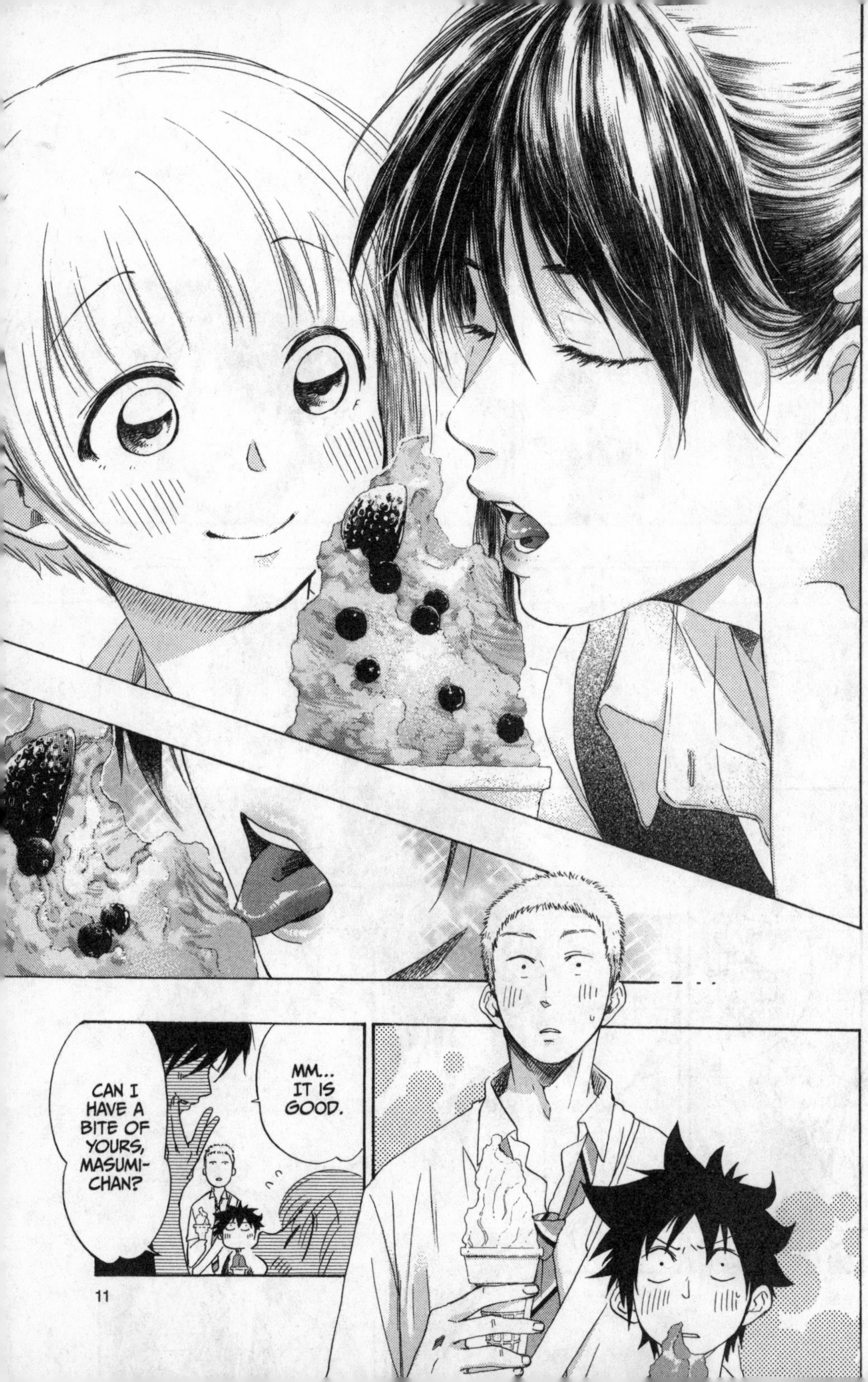
MM... IT IS GOOD.
CAN I HAVE A BITE OF YOURS, MASUMI-CHAN?

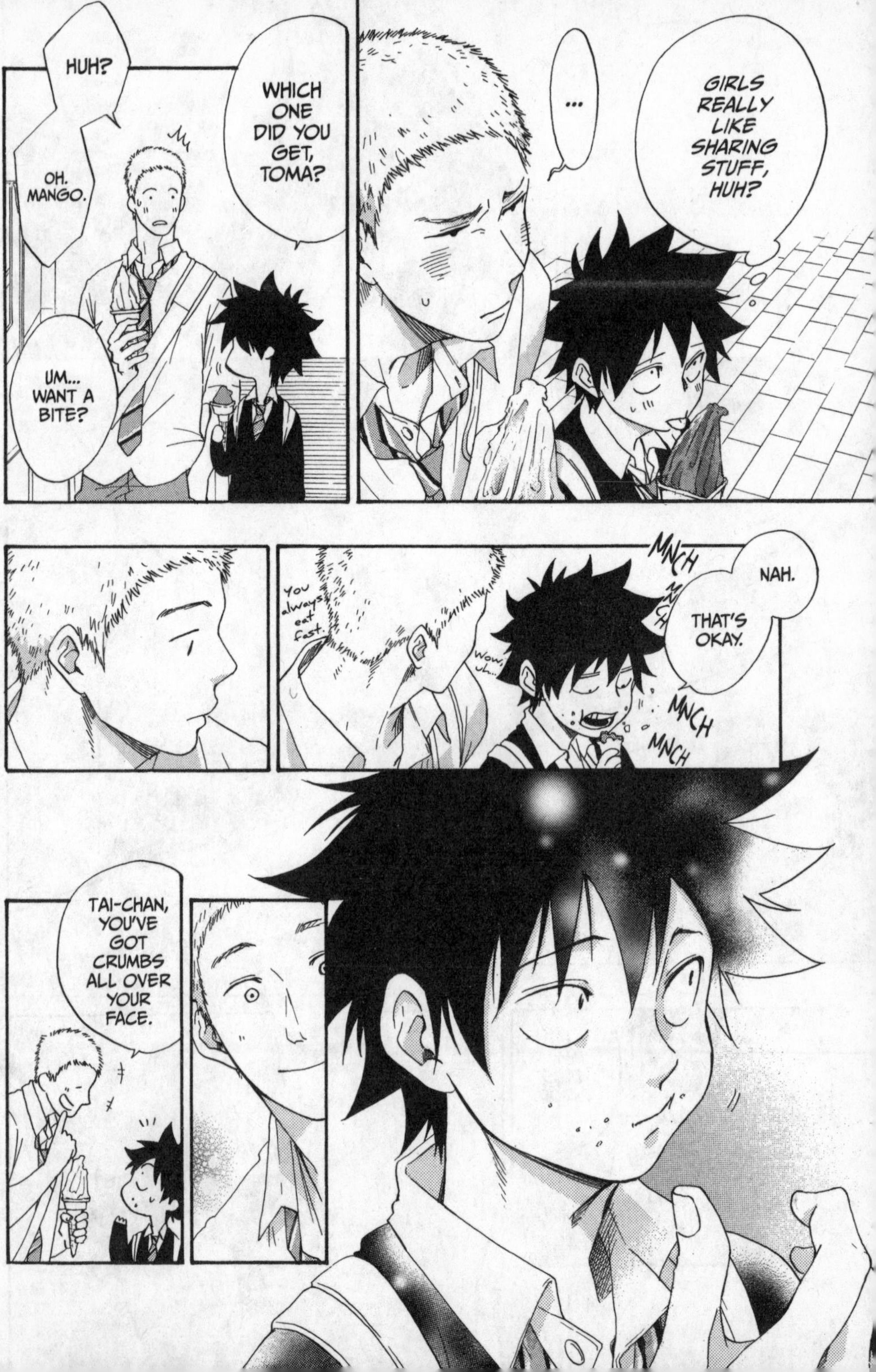
GIRLS REALLY LIKE SHARING STUFF, HUH?
...
WHICH ONE DID YOU GET, TOMA?
HUH?
OH. MANGO.
UM... WANT A BITE?
MNCH MNCH
NAH.
THAT'S OKAY.
MNCH MNCH
Wow, uh...
You always eat fast.
TAI-CHAN, YOU'VE GOT CRUMBS ALL OVER YOUR FACE.

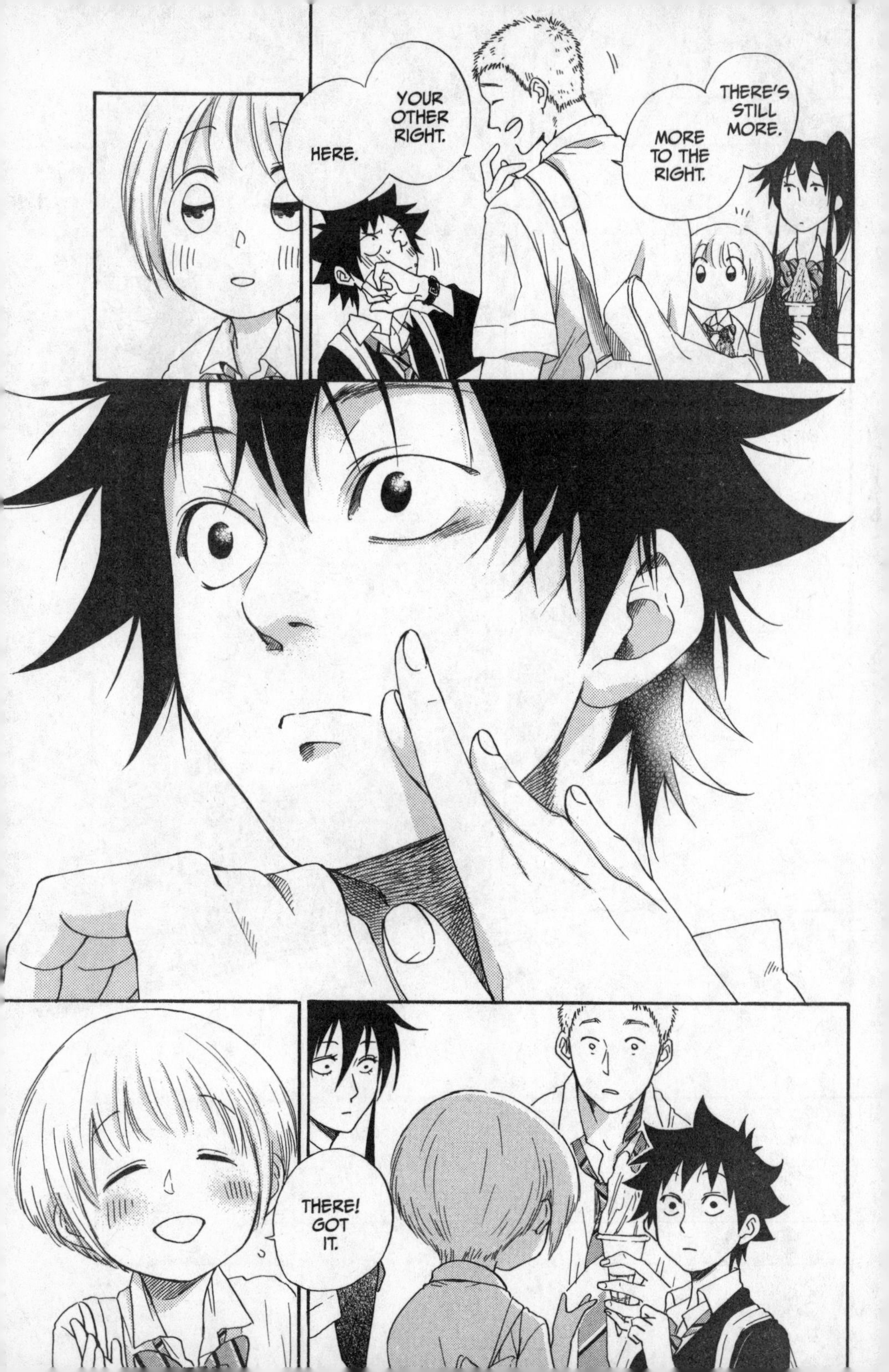
THERE'S STILL MORE.
MORE TO THE RIGHT.
YOUR OTHER RIGHT.
HERE.
THERE! GOT IT.

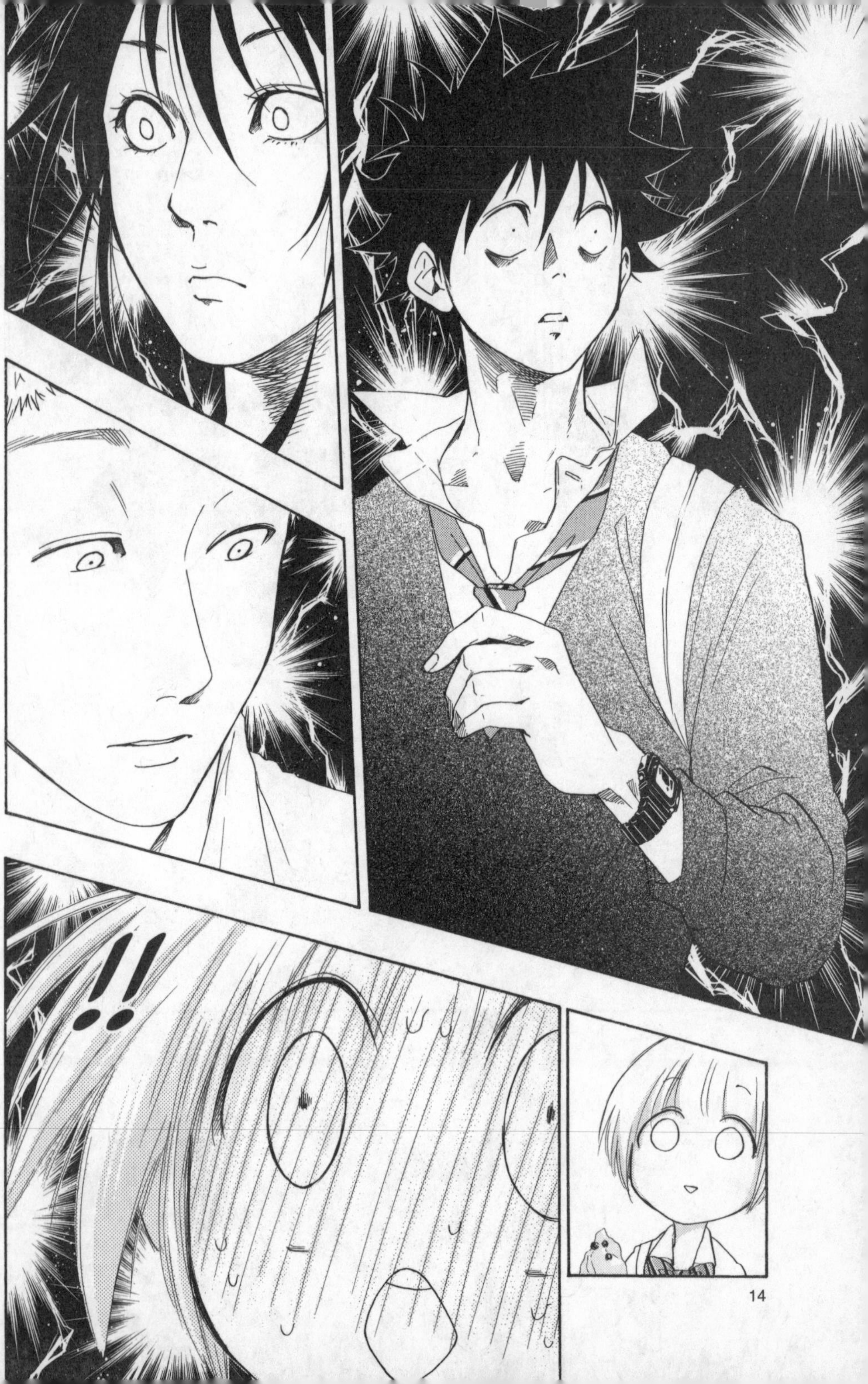
!!

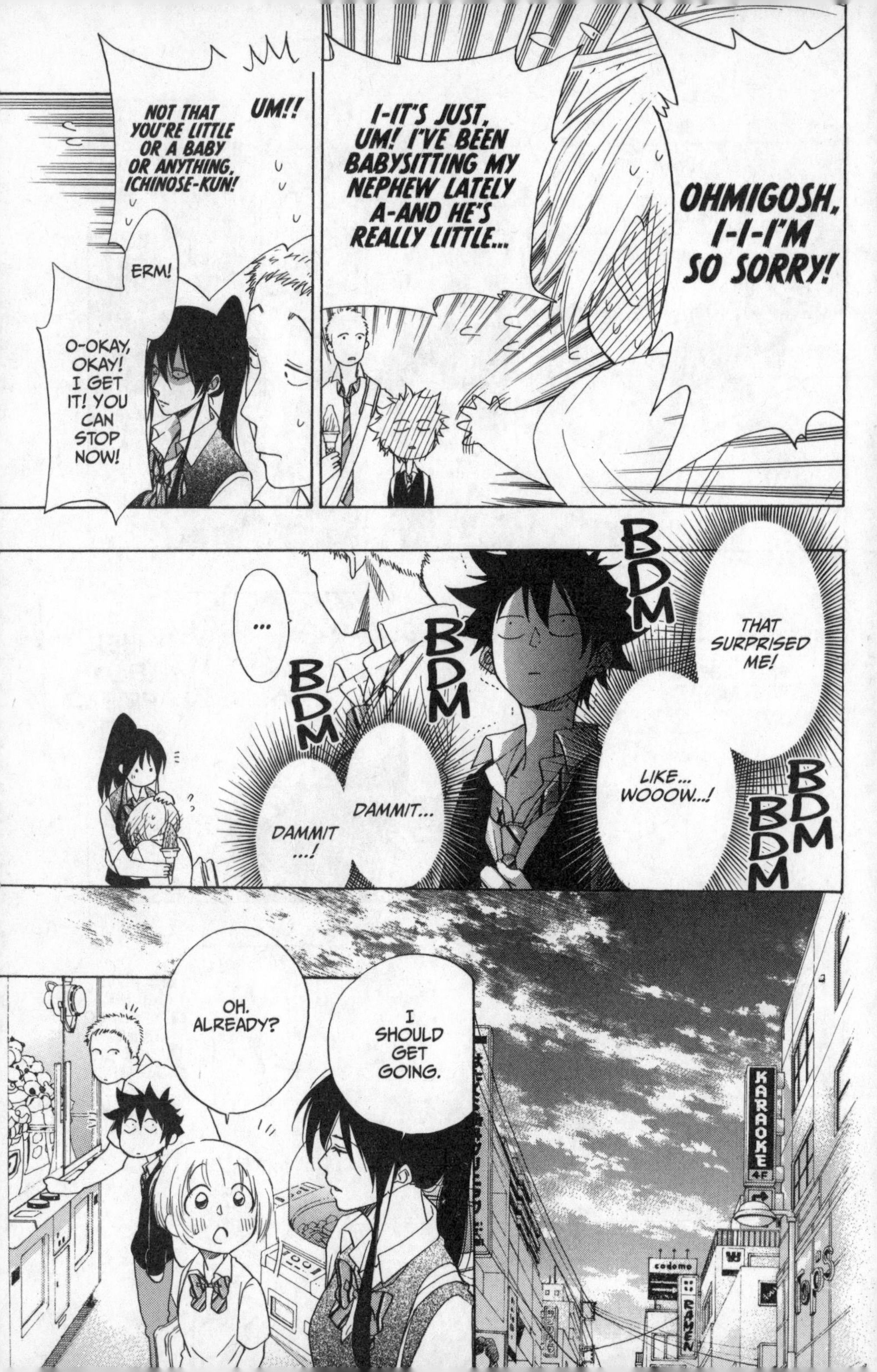
OHMIGOSH, I-I-I'M SO SORRY!
I-IT'S JUST, UM! I'VE BEEN BABYSITTING MY NEPHEW LATELY A-AND HE'S REALLY LITTLE...
UM!!
NOT THAT YOU'RE LITTLE OR A BABY OR ANYTHING, ICHINOSE-KUN!
ERM!
O-OKAY, OKAY! I GET IT! YOU CAN STOP NOW!
BDM
THAT SURPRISED ME!
BDM BDM
LIKE... WOOOW...!
BDM
DAMMIT...
BDM
DAMMIT ...!
...
I SHOULD GET GOING.
OH. ALREADY?
KARAOKE
4F
codomo
RAMEN

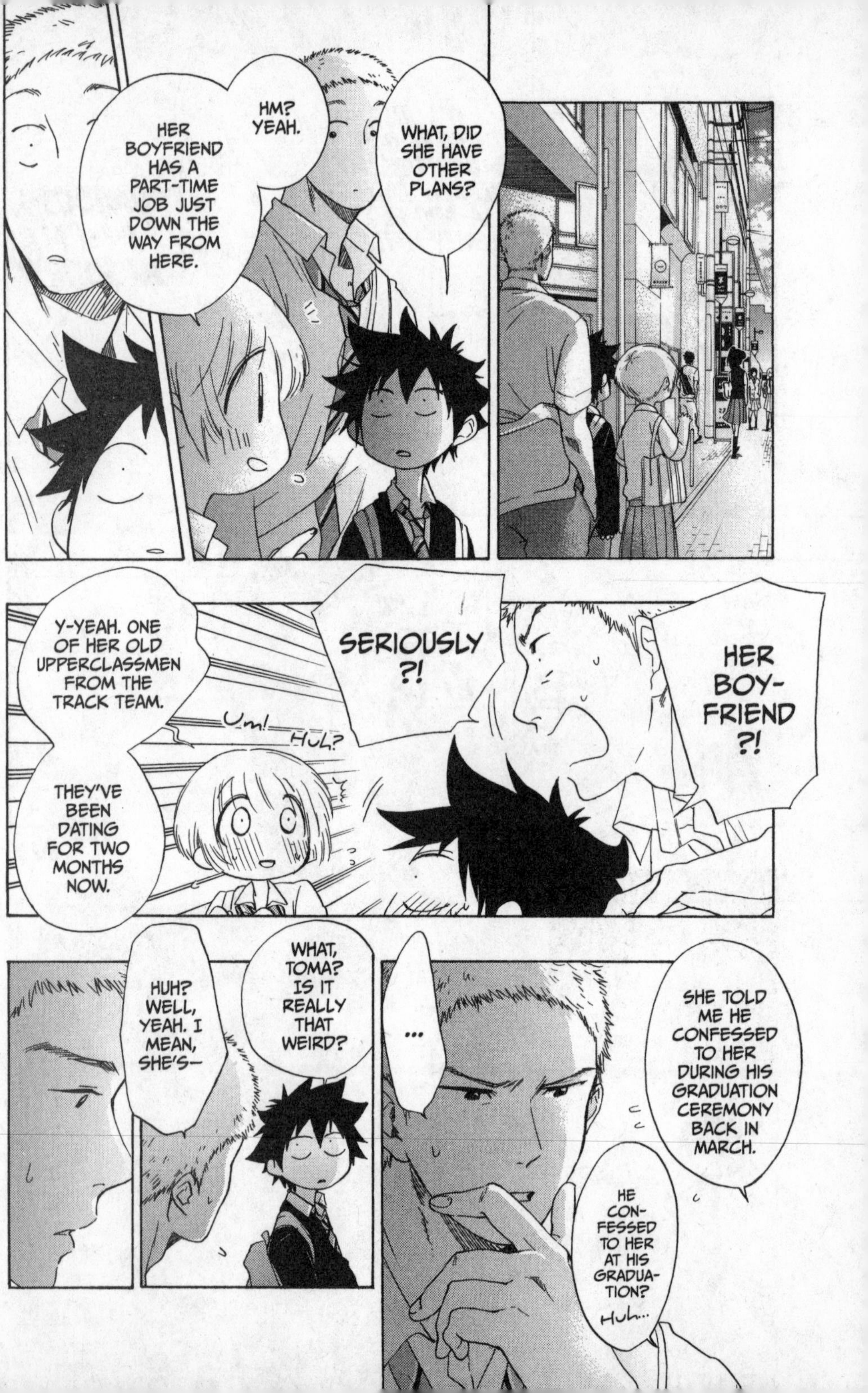
WHAT, DID SHE HAVE OTHER PLANS?
HM? YEAH.
HER BOYFRIEND HAS A PART-TIME JOB JUST DOWN THE WAY FROM HERE.
HER BOY-FRIEND?!
SERIOUSLY?!
Huh?
Um!
Y-YEAH. ONE OF HER OLD UPPERCLASSMEN FROM THE TRACK TEAM.
THEY'VE BEEN DATING FOR TWO MONTHS NOW.
SHE TOLD ME HE CONFESSED TO HER DURING HIS GRADUATION CEREMONY BACK IN MARCH.
...
HE CON-FESSED TO HER AT HIS GRADUA-TION?
Huh...
WHAT, TOMA? IS IT REALLY THAT WEIRD?
HUH? WELL, YEAH. I MEAN, SHE'S—

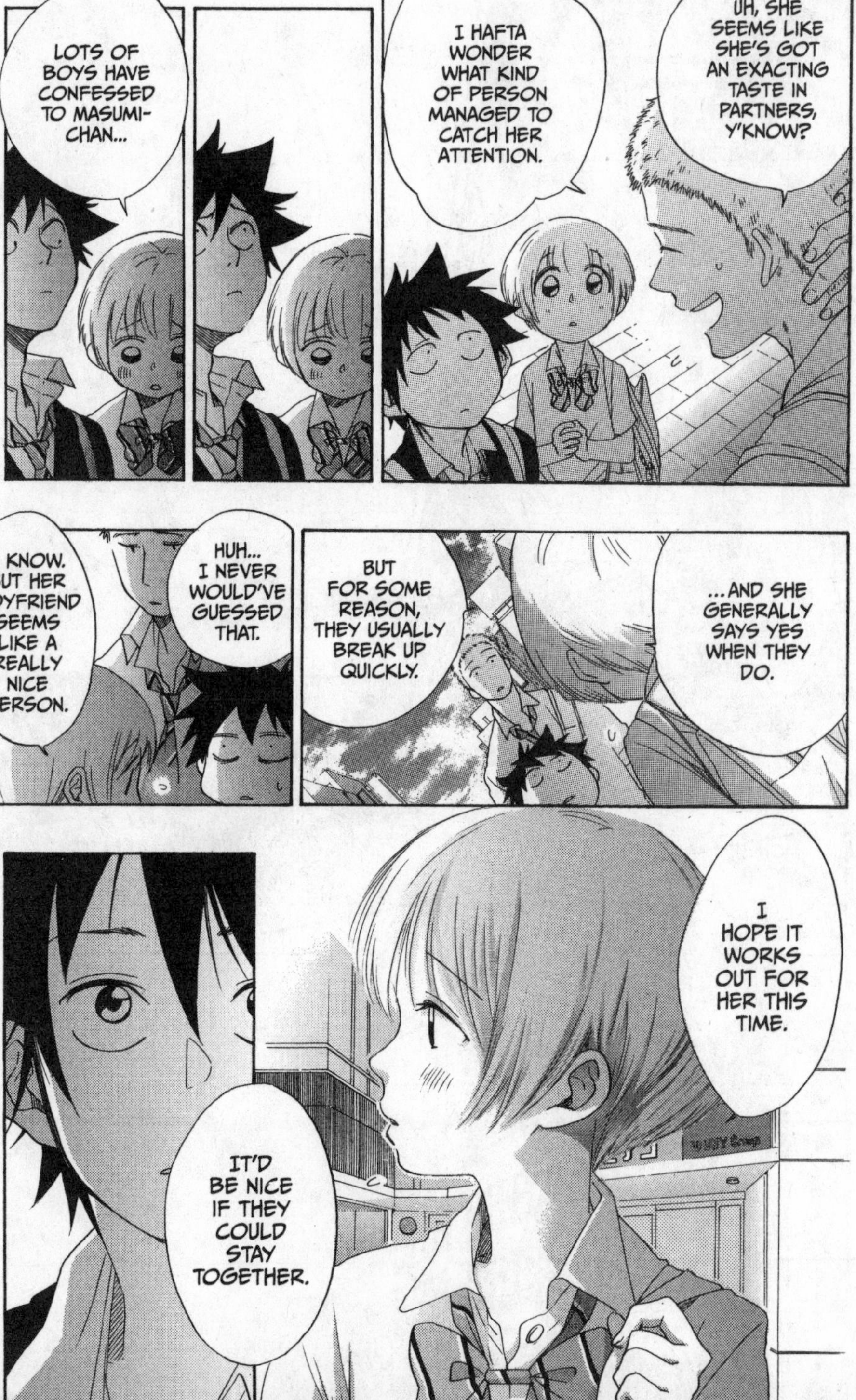
UH, SHE SEEMS LIKE SHE'S GOT AN EXACTING TASTE IN PARTNERS, Y'KNOW?
I HAFTA WONDER WHAT KIND OF PERSON MANAGED TO CATCH HER ATTENTION.
LOTS OF BOYS HAVE CONFESSED TO MASUMI-CHAN...
...AND SHE GENERALLY SAYS YES WHEN THEY DO.
BUT FOR SOME REASON, THEY USUALLY BREAK UP QUICKLY.
HUH... I NEVER WOULD'VE GUESSED THAT.
I KNOW. BUT HER BOYFRIEND SEEMS LIKE A REALLY NICE PERSON.
I HOPE IT WORKS OUT FOR HER THIS TIME.
IT'D BE NICE IF THEY COULD STAY TOGETHER.

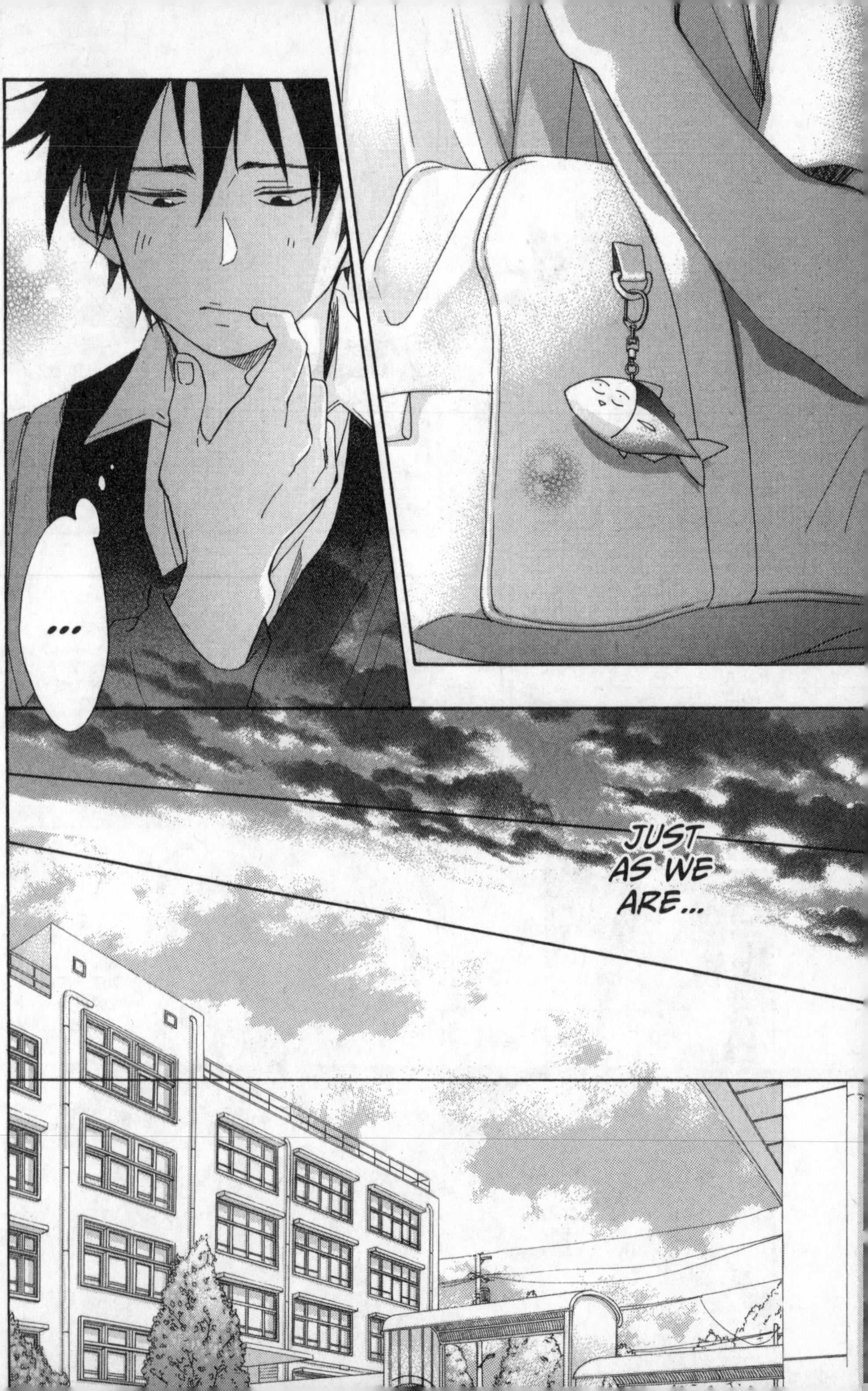
...
JUST AS WE ARE...

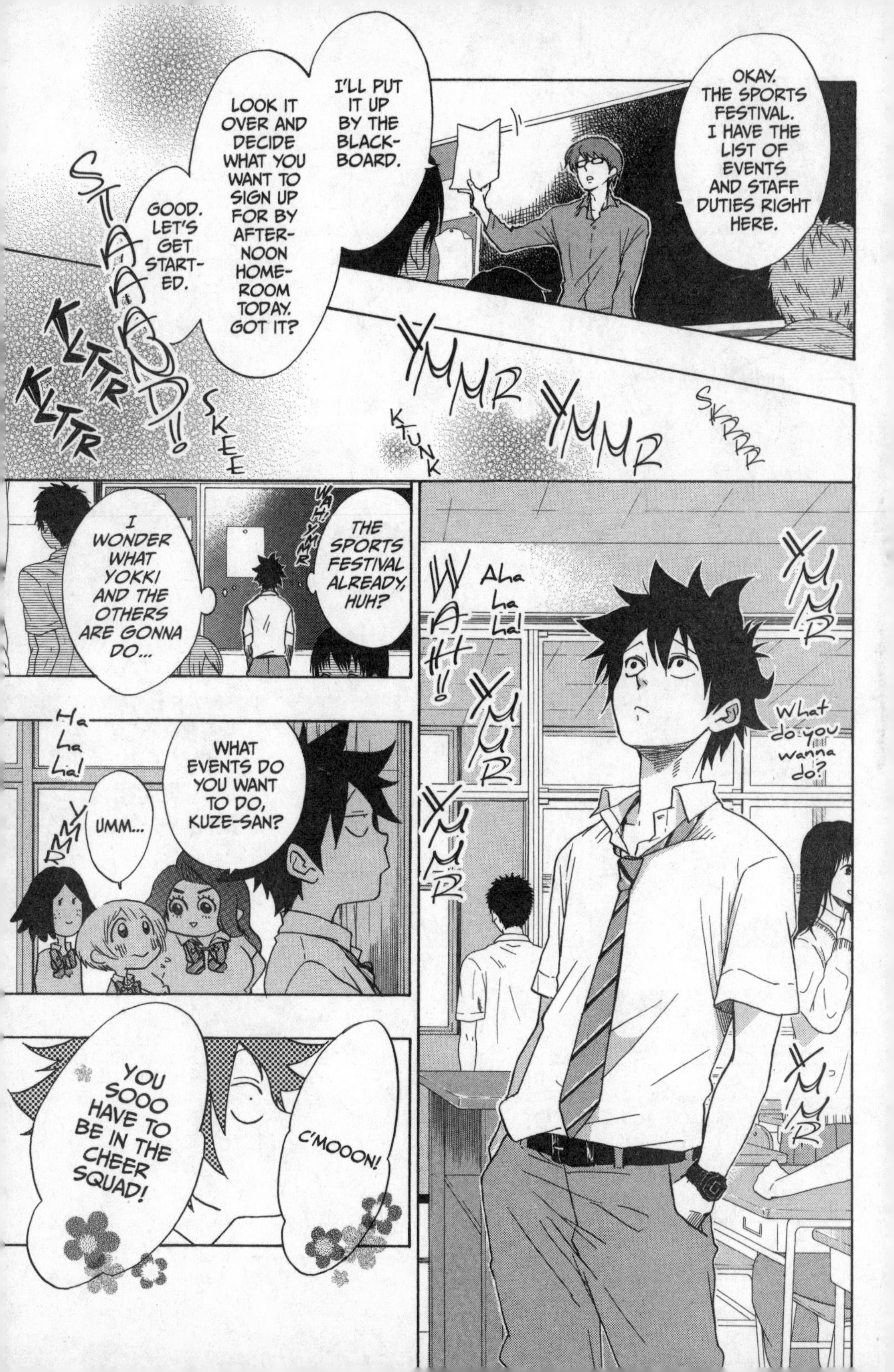
OKAY. THE SPORTS FESTIVAL. I HAVE THE LIST OF EVENTS AND STAFF DUTIES RIGHT HERE.
I'LL PUT IT UP BY THE BLACKBOARD.
LOOK IT OVER AND DECIDE WHAT YOU WANT TO SIGN UP FOR BY AFTERNOON HOMEROOM TODAY. GOT IT?
GOOD. LET'S GET STARTED.
STAAAND!!
KLTTR KLTTR
SKEE
YMMR YMMR
KTUNK
SKRRR
YMMR
WAH!!
Aha ha ha!
YMMR
YMMR
What do you wanna do?
YMMR
THE SPORTS FESTIVAL ALREADY, HUH?
WAH YMMR
I WONDER WHAT YOKKI AND THE OTHERS ARE GONNA DO...
WHAT EVENTS DO YOU WANT TO DO, KUZE-SAN?
UMM...
Ha ha ha!
YMMR
C'MOOON!
YOU SOOO HAVE TO BE IN THE CHEER SQUAD!

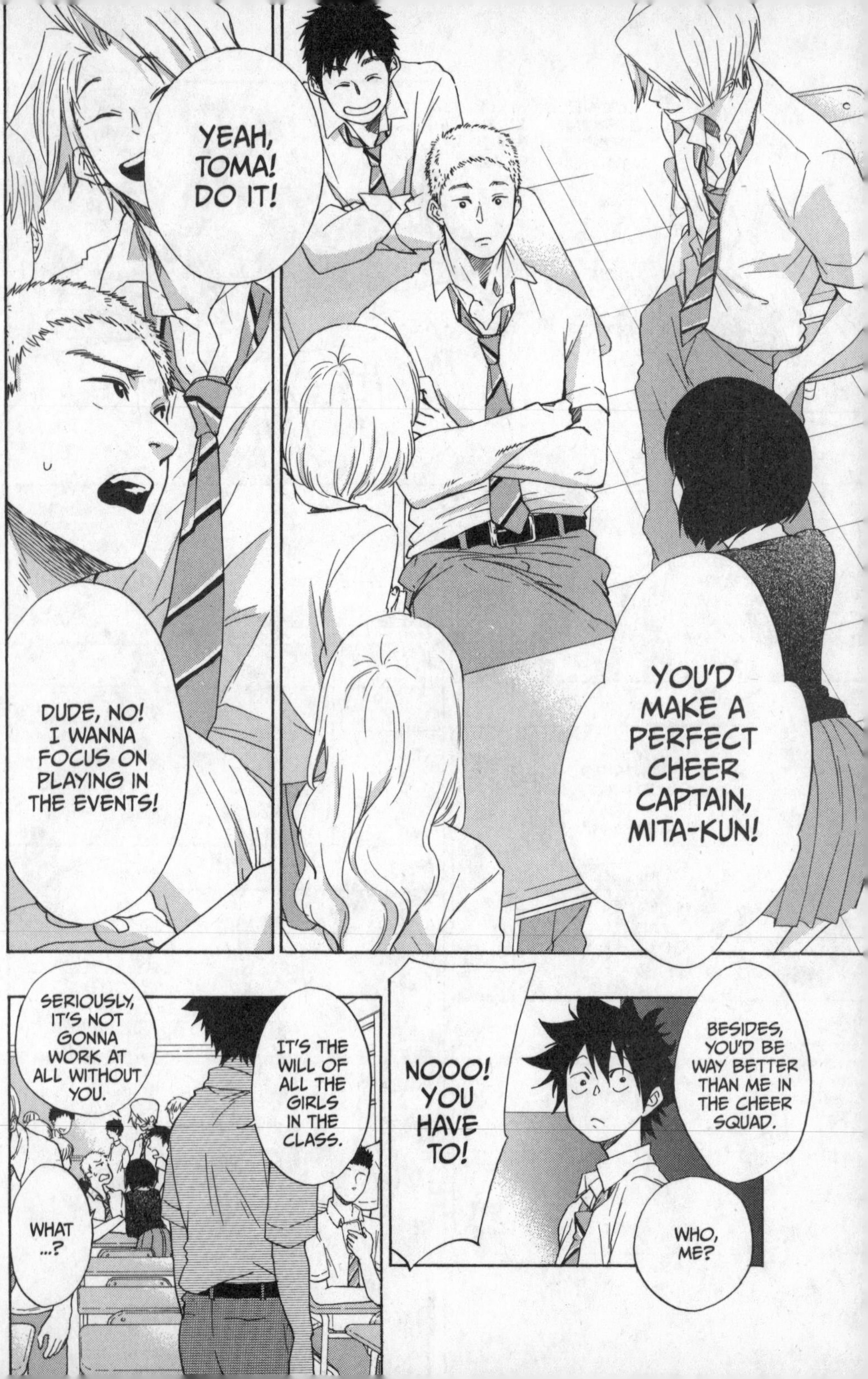
YOU'D MAKE A PERFECT CHEER CAPTAIN, MITA-KUN!
YEAH, TOMA! DO IT!
DUDE, NO! I WANNA FOCUS ON PLAYING IN THE EVENTS!
BESIDES, YOU'D BE WAY BETTER THAN ME IN THE CHEER SQUAD.
WHO, ME?
NOOO! YOU HAVE TO!
IT'S THE WILL OF ALL THE GIRLS IN THE CLASS.
SERIOUSLY, IT'S NOT GONNA WORK AT ALL WITHOUT YOU.
WHAT ...?

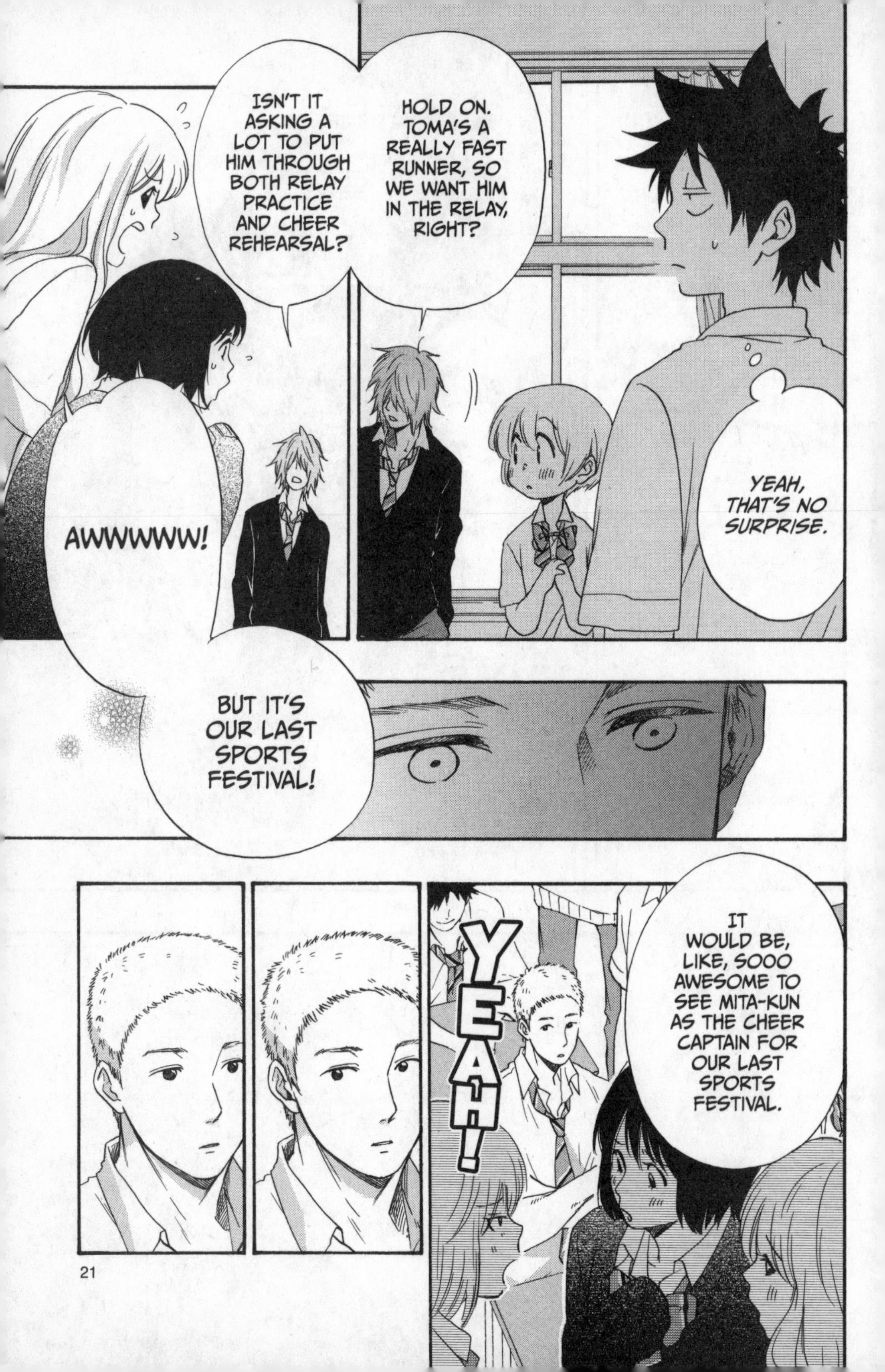
HOLD ON. TOMA'S A REALLY FAST RUNNER, SO WE WANT HIM IN THE RELAY, RIGHT?
YEAH, THAT'S NO SURPRISE.
ISN'T IT ASKING A LOT TO PUT HIM THROUGH BOTH RELAY PRACTICE AND CHEER REHEARSAL?
AWWWWW!
BUT IT'S OUR LAST SPORTS FESTIVAL!
IT WOULD BE, LIKE, SOOO AWESOME TO SEE MITA-KUN AS THE CHEER CAPTAIN FOR OUR LAST SPORTS FESTIVAL.
YEAH!

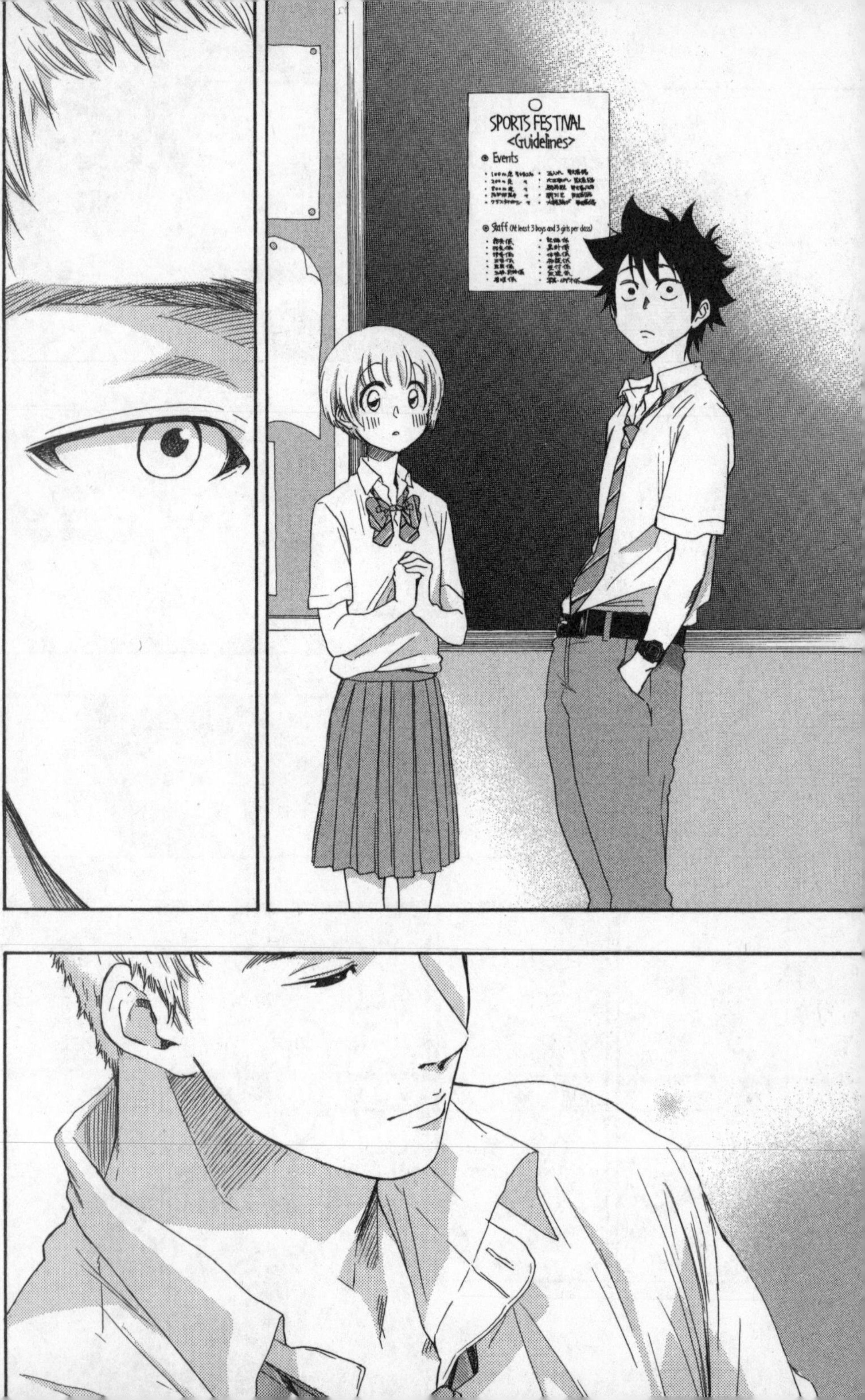
SPORTS FESTIVAL
<Guidelines>
Events
Staff (At least 3 boys and 3 girls per class)

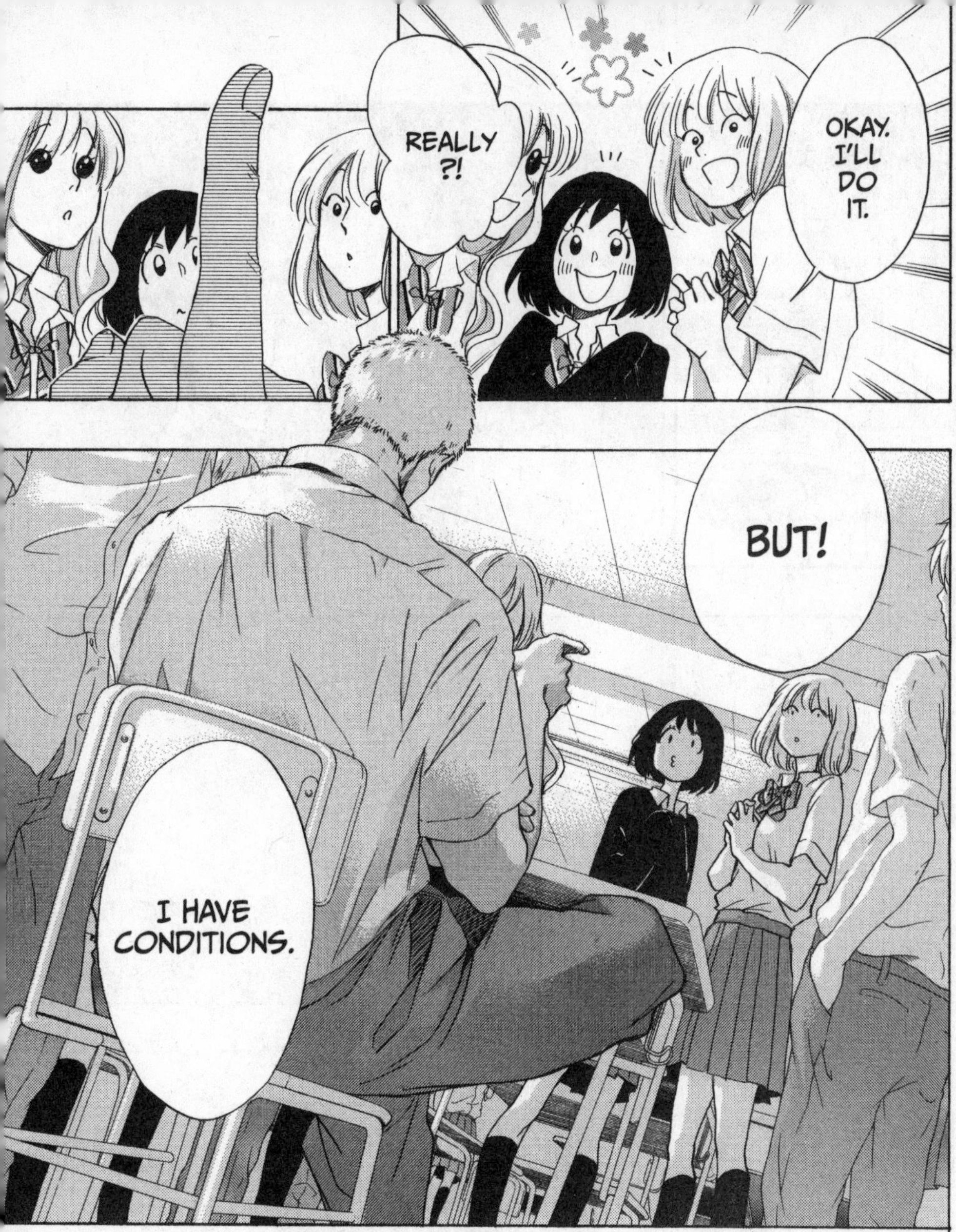
OKAY. I'LL DO IT.
REALLY?!
BUT!
I HAVE CONDITIONS.

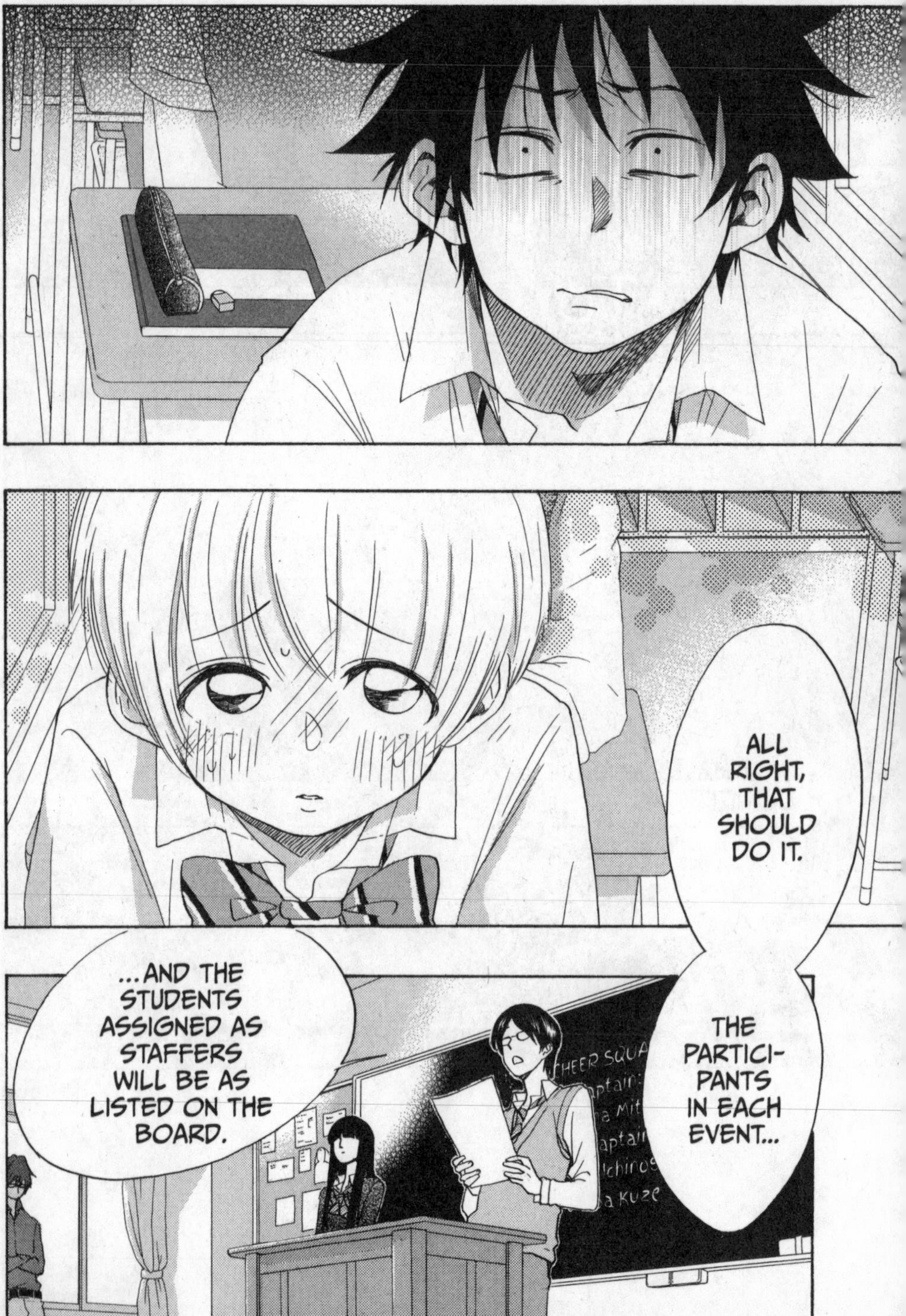
ALL RIGHT, THAT SHOULD DO IT.
THE PARTICI-PANTS IN EACH EVENT...
...AND THE STUDENTS ASSIGNED AS STAFFERS WILL BE AS LISTED ON THE BOARD.

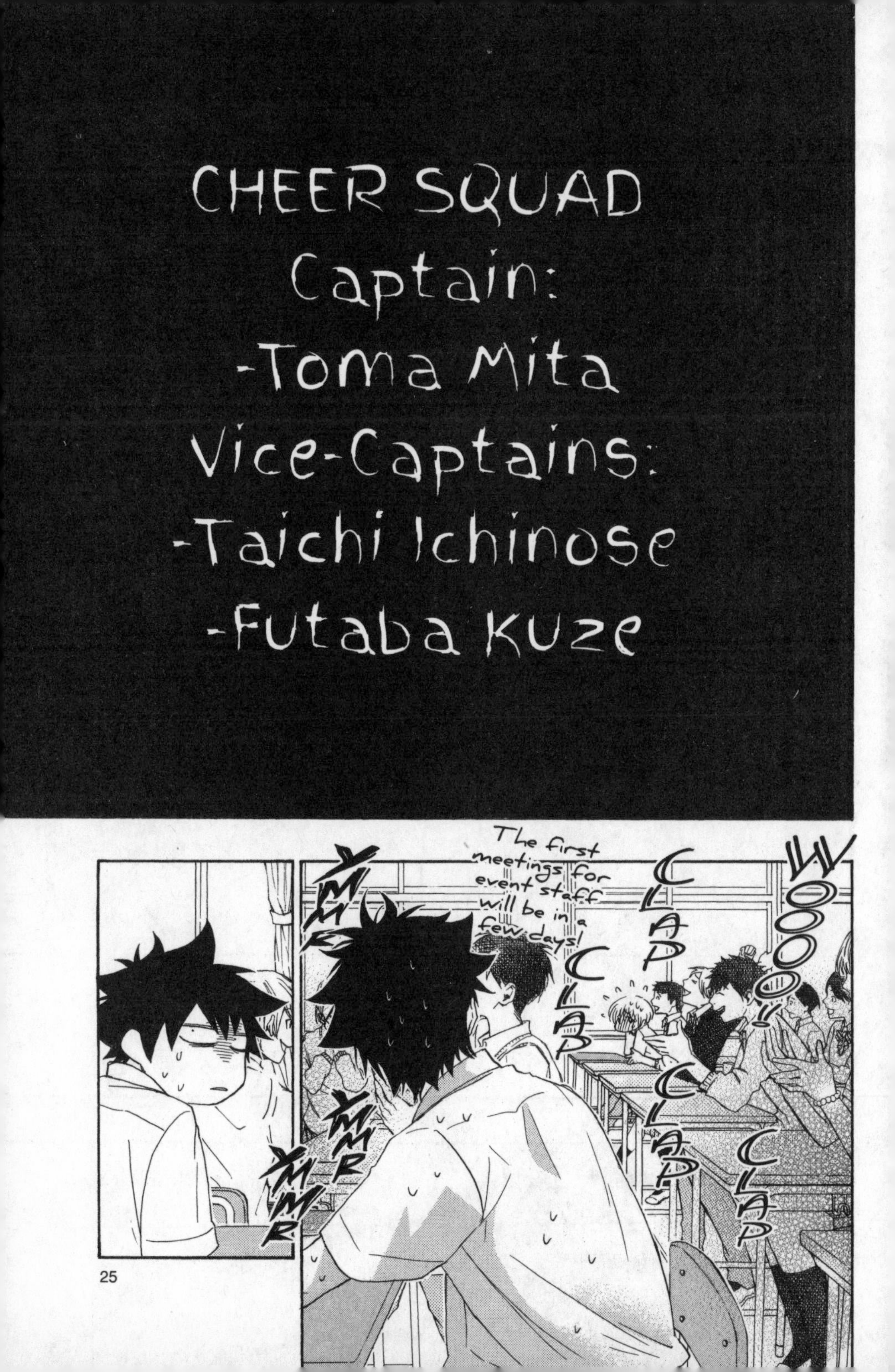
CHEER SQUAD
Captain:
-Toma Mita
Vice-Captains:
-Taichi Ichinose
-Futaba Kuze
WOOOO!
CLAP
CLAP
CLAP
The first meetings for event staff will be in a few days!
CLAP
CLAP
CLAP
YMMR
YMMR
YMMR

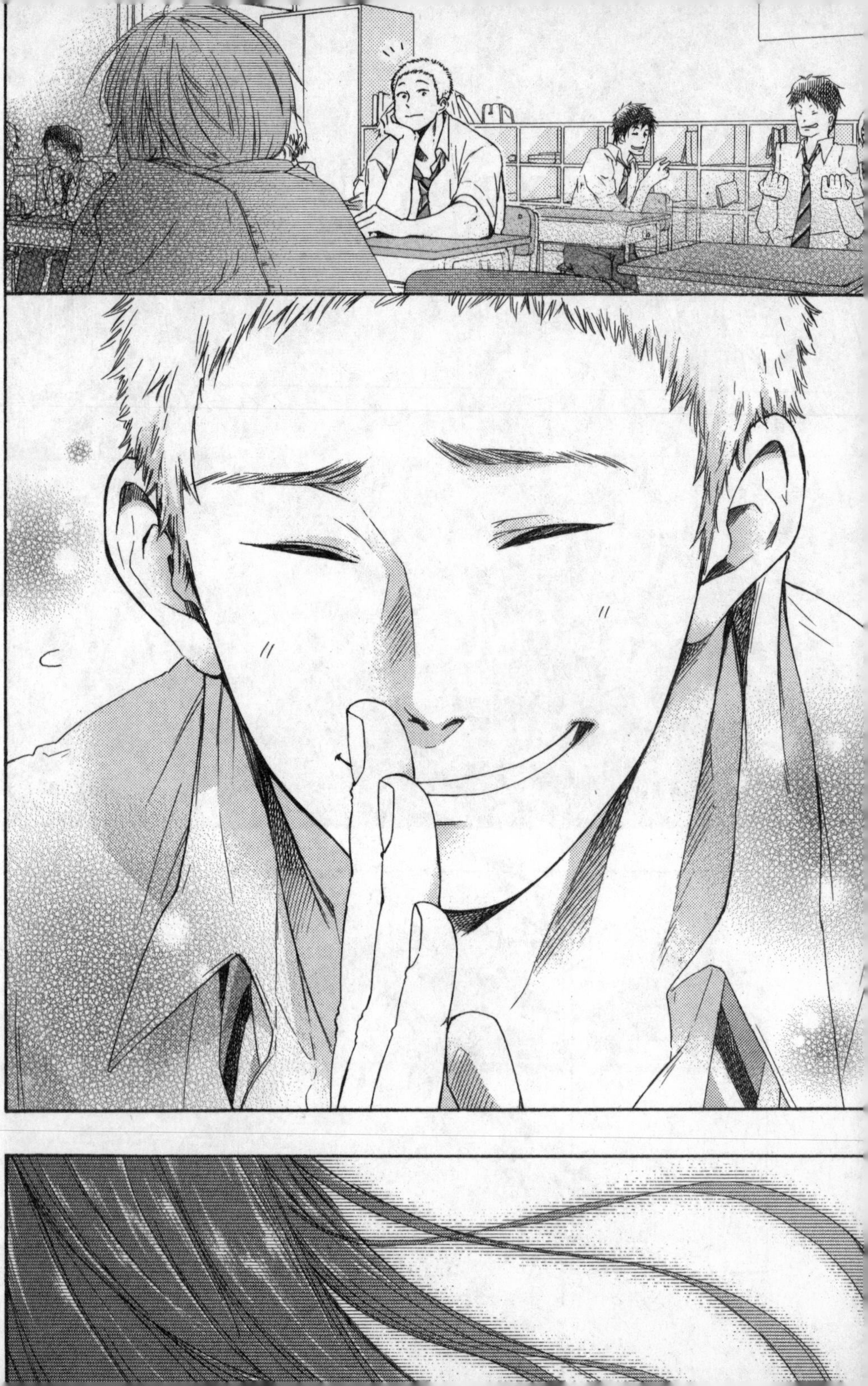

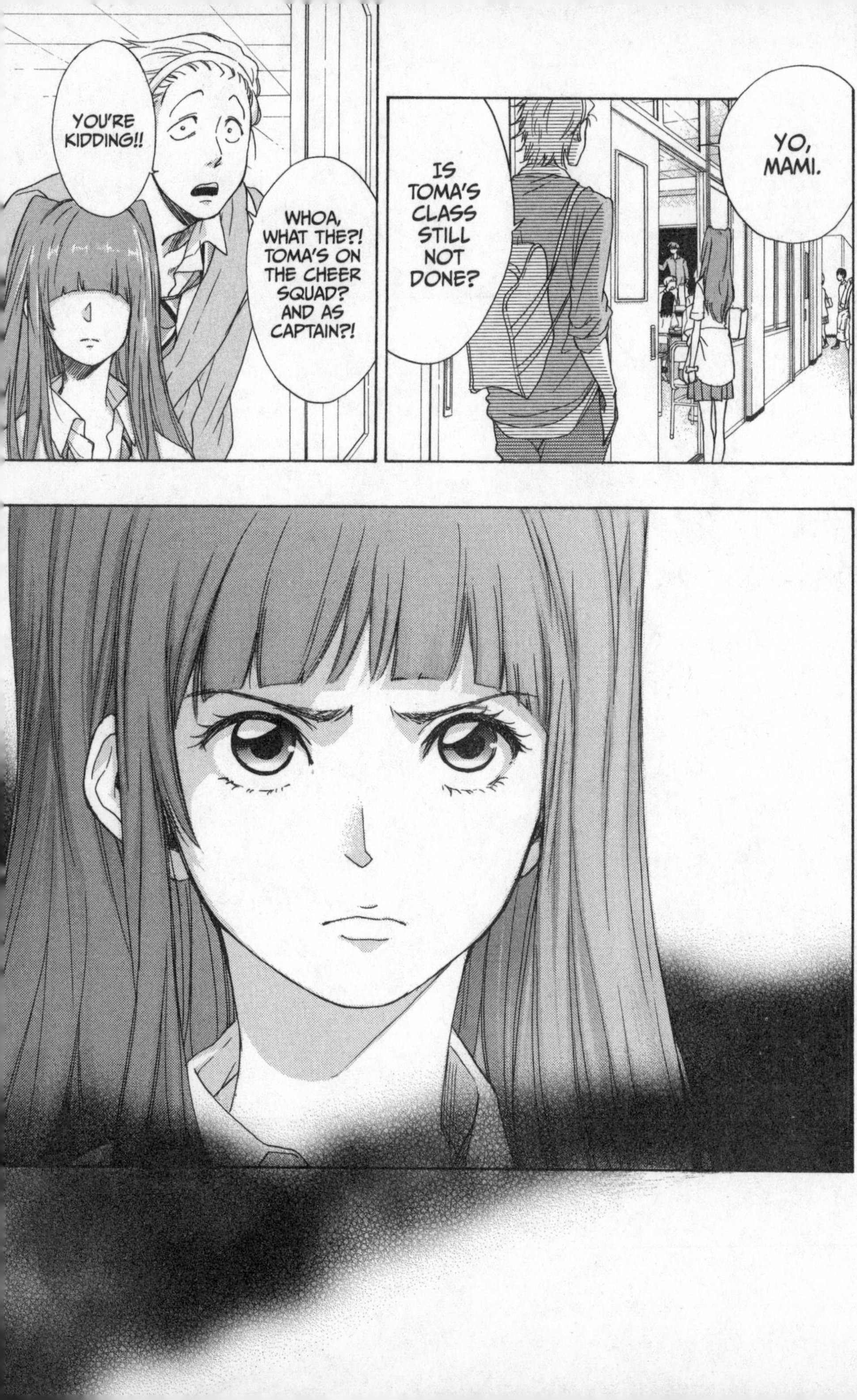
YO, MAMI.
IS TOMA'S CLASS STILL NOT DONE?
WHOA, WHAT THE?! TOMA'S ON THE CHEER SQUAD? AND AS CAPTAIN?!
YOU'RE KIDDING!!

Toma
Mango

Taichi
Matcha

Masumi
Mint Chocolate

Futaba
Very Berry

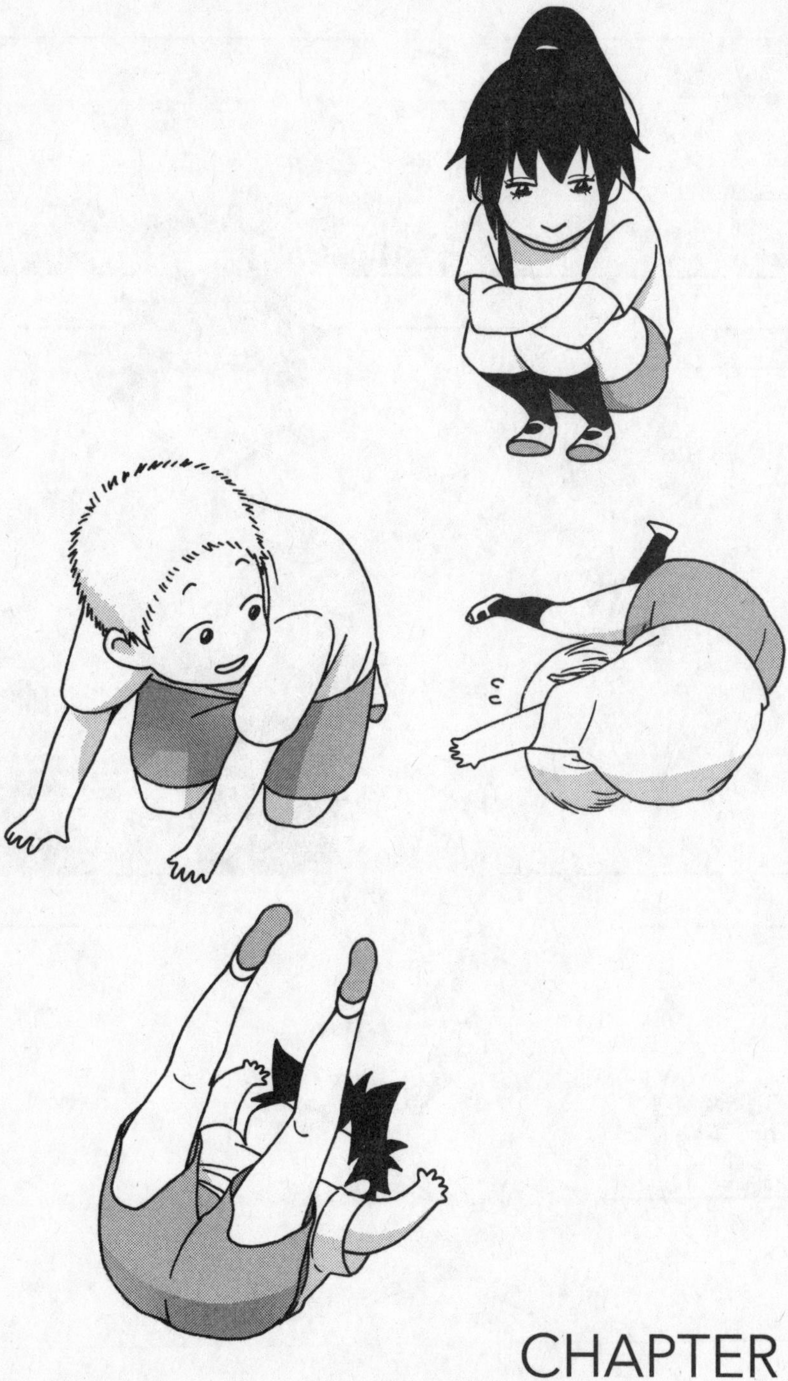

CHAPTER 7

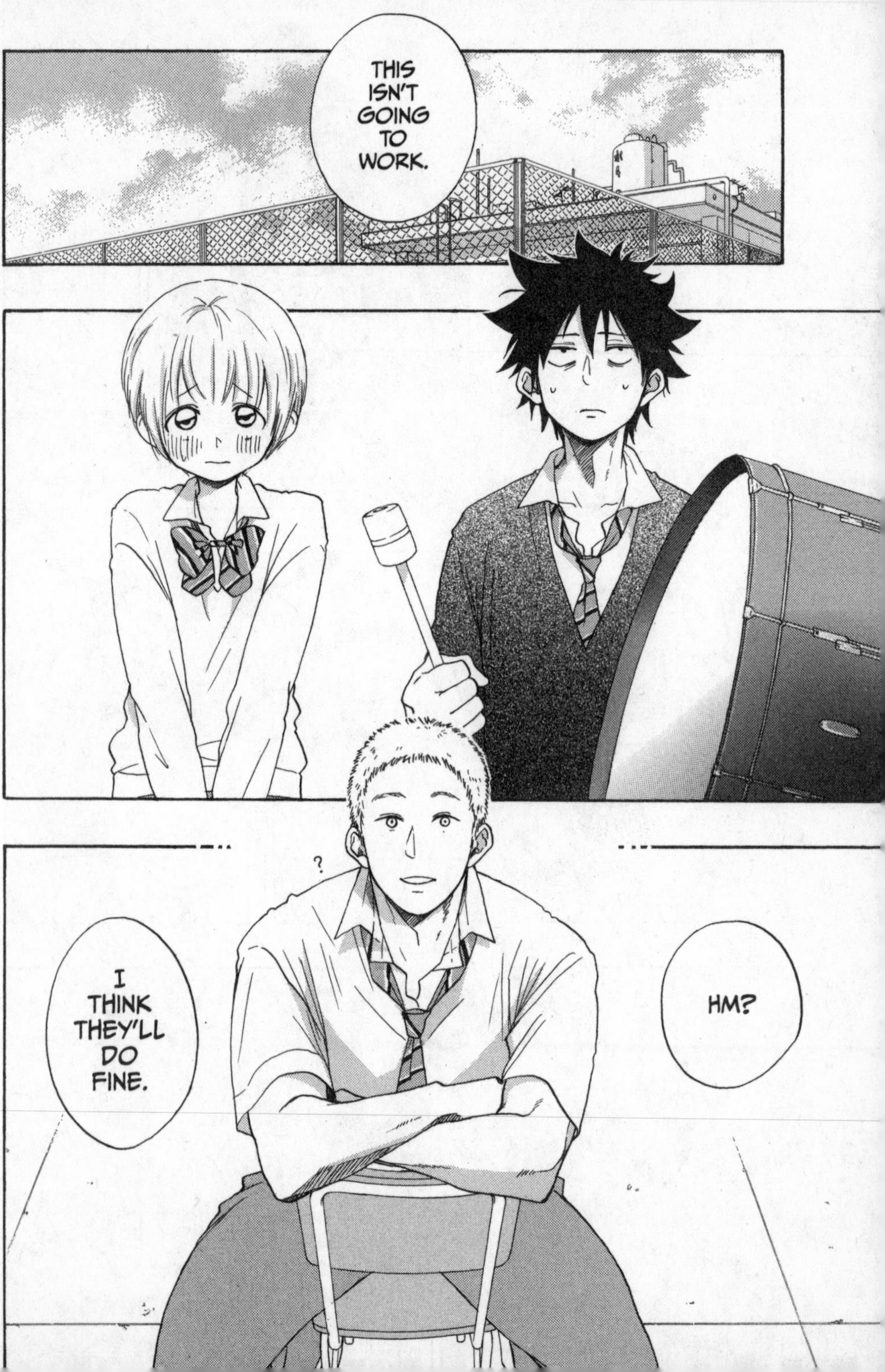
THIS ISN'T GOING TO WORK.
?
HM?
I THINK THEY'LL DO FINE.

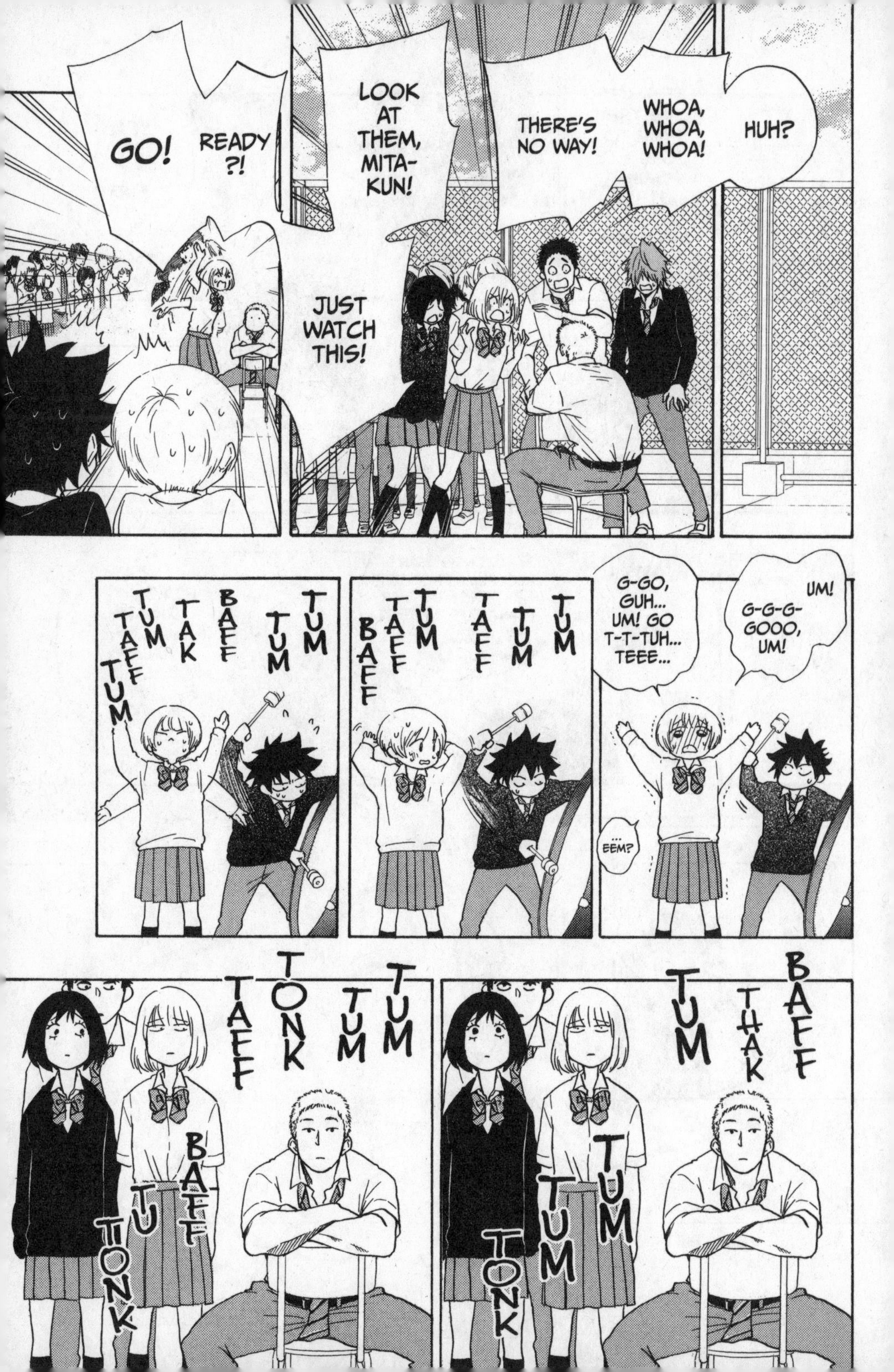
HUH?
WHOA, WHOA, WHOA!
THERE'S NO WAY!
LOOK AT THEM, MITA-KUN!
JUST WATCH THIS!
READY?!
GO!
UM!
G-G-G-GOOO, UM!
G-GO, GUH... UM! GO T-T-TUH... TEEE...
...EEM?
TUM
TUM
TAFF
TUM
TAFF
BAFF
TUM
TUM
BAFF
TAK
TUM
TAFF
TUM
BAFF
THAK
TUM
TUM
TUM
TONK
TUM
TUM
TONK
TAFF
BAFF
TU
TONK

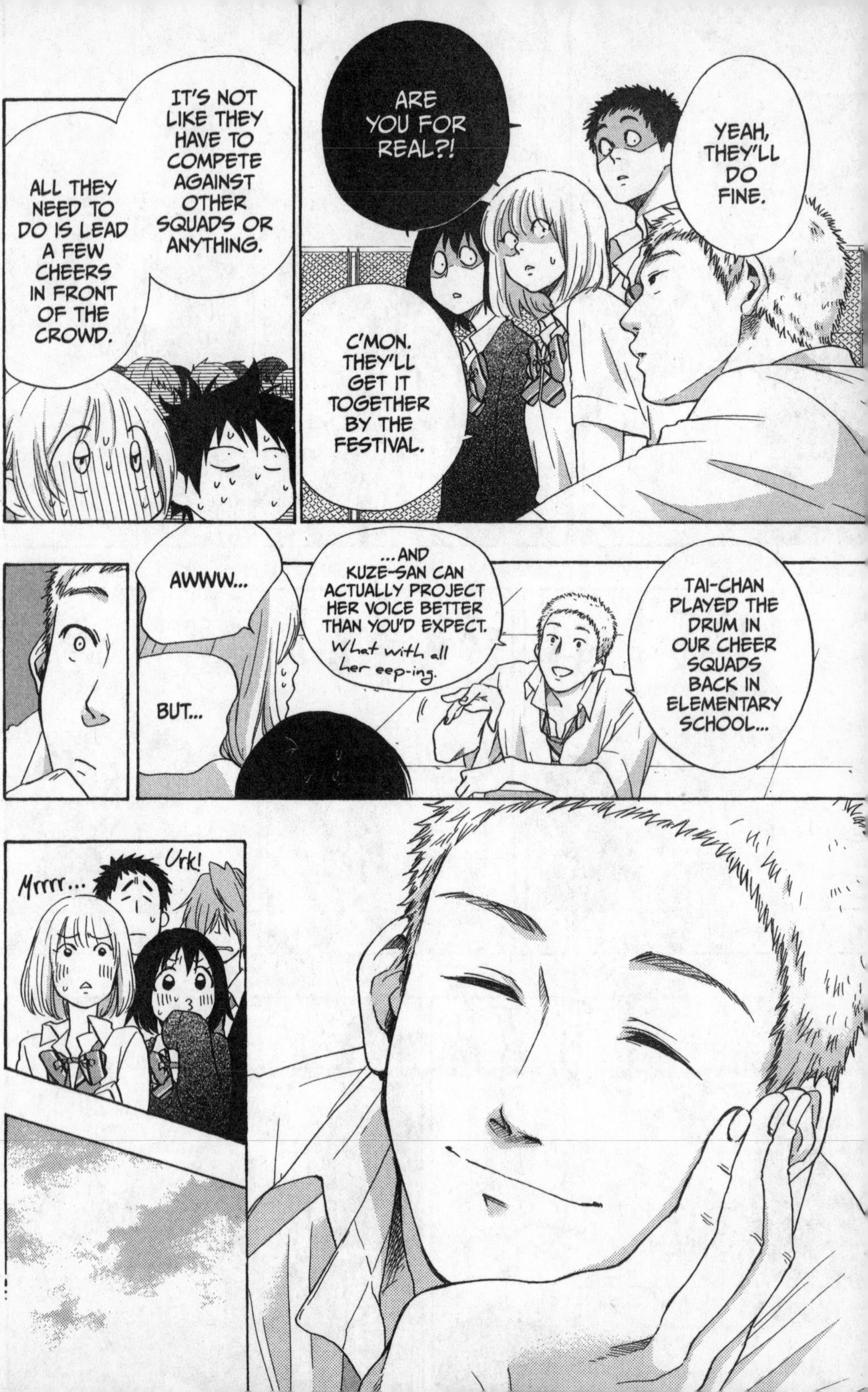
YEAH, THEY'LL DO FINE.
ARE YOU FOR REAL?!
C'MON. THEY'LL GET IT TOGETHER BY THE FESTIVAL.
IT'S NOT LIKE THEY HAVE TO COMPETE AGAINST OTHER SQUADS OR ANYTHING.
ALL THEY NEED TO DO IS LEAD A FEW CHEERS IN FRONT OF THE CROWD.
TAI-CHAN PLAYED THE DRUM IN OUR CHEER SQUADS BACK IN ELEMENTARY SCHOOL...
...AND KUZE-SAN CAN ACTUALLY PROJECT HER VOICE BETTER THAN YOU'D EXPECT.
What with all her eep-ing.
AWWW...
BUT...
Urk!
Mrrrr...

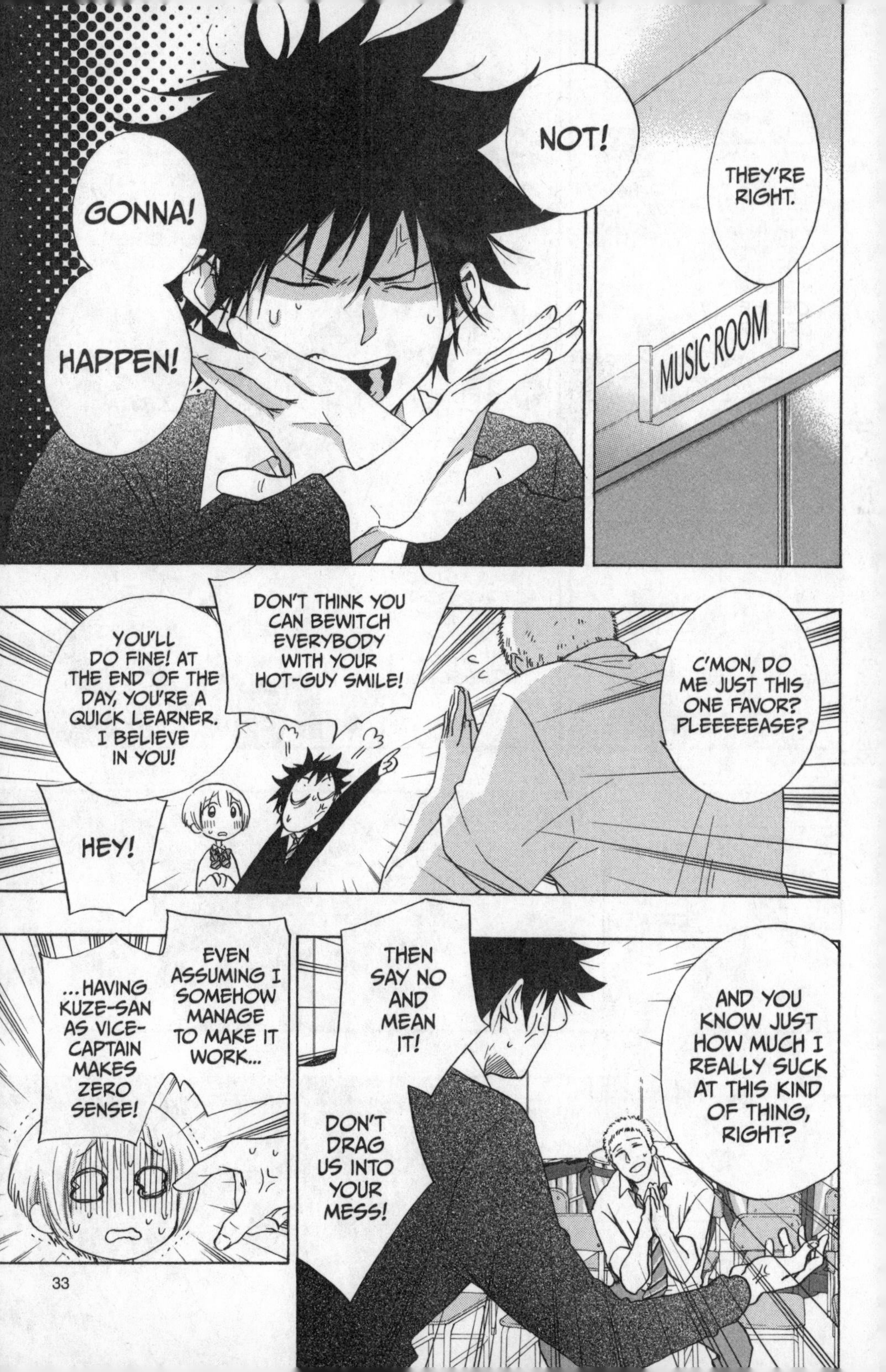
THEY'RE RIGHT.
MUSIC ROOM
NOT!
GONNA!
HAPPEN!
C'MON, DO ME JUST THIS ONE FAVOR? PLEEEEEASE?
DON'T THINK YOU CAN BEWITCH EVERYBODY WITH YOUR HOT-GUY SMILE!
YOU'LL DO FINE! AT THE END OF THE DAY, YOU'RE A QUICK LEARNER. I BELIEVE IN YOU!
HEY!
AND YOU KNOW JUST HOW MUCH I REALLY SUCK AT THIS KIND OF THING, RIGHT?
THEN SAY NO AND MEAN IT!
DON'T DRAG US INTO YOUR MESS!
EVEN ASSUMING I SOMEHOW MANAGE TO MAKE IT WORK...
...HAVING KUZE-SAN AS VICE-CAPTAIN MAKES ZERO SENSE!

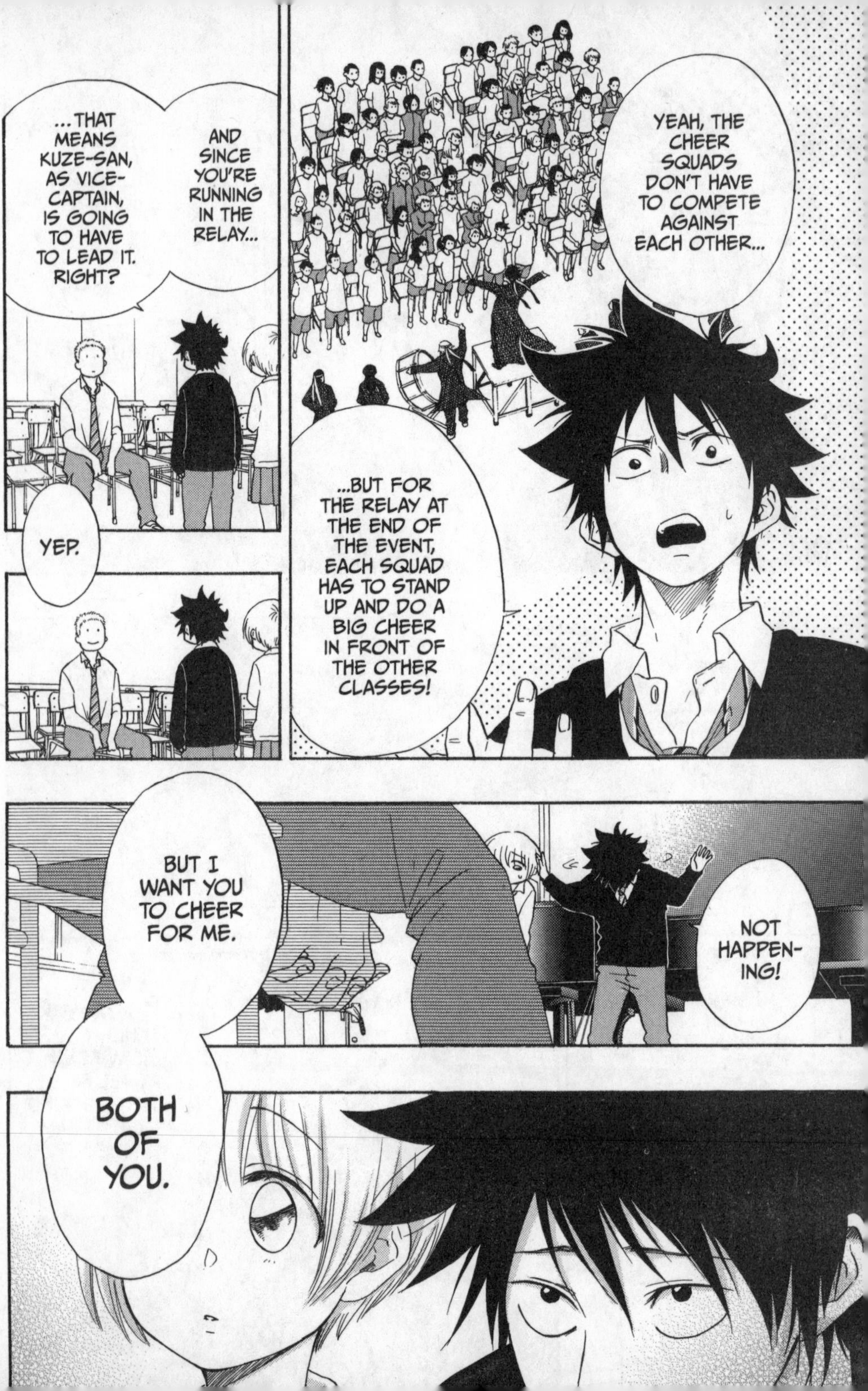
YEAH, THE CHEER SQUADS DON'T HAVE TO COMPETE AGAINST EACH OTHER...
...BUT FOR THE RELAY AT THE END OF THE EVENT, EACH SQUAD HAS TO STAND UP AND DO A BIG CHEER IN FRONT OF THE OTHER CLASSES!
AND SINCE YOU'RE RUNNING IN THE RELAY...
...THAT MEANS KUZE-SAN, AS VICE-CAPTAIN, IS GOING TO HAVE TO LEAD IT. RIGHT?
YEP.
NOT HAPPEN-ING!
BUT I WANT YOU TO CHEER FOR ME.
BOTH OF YOU.

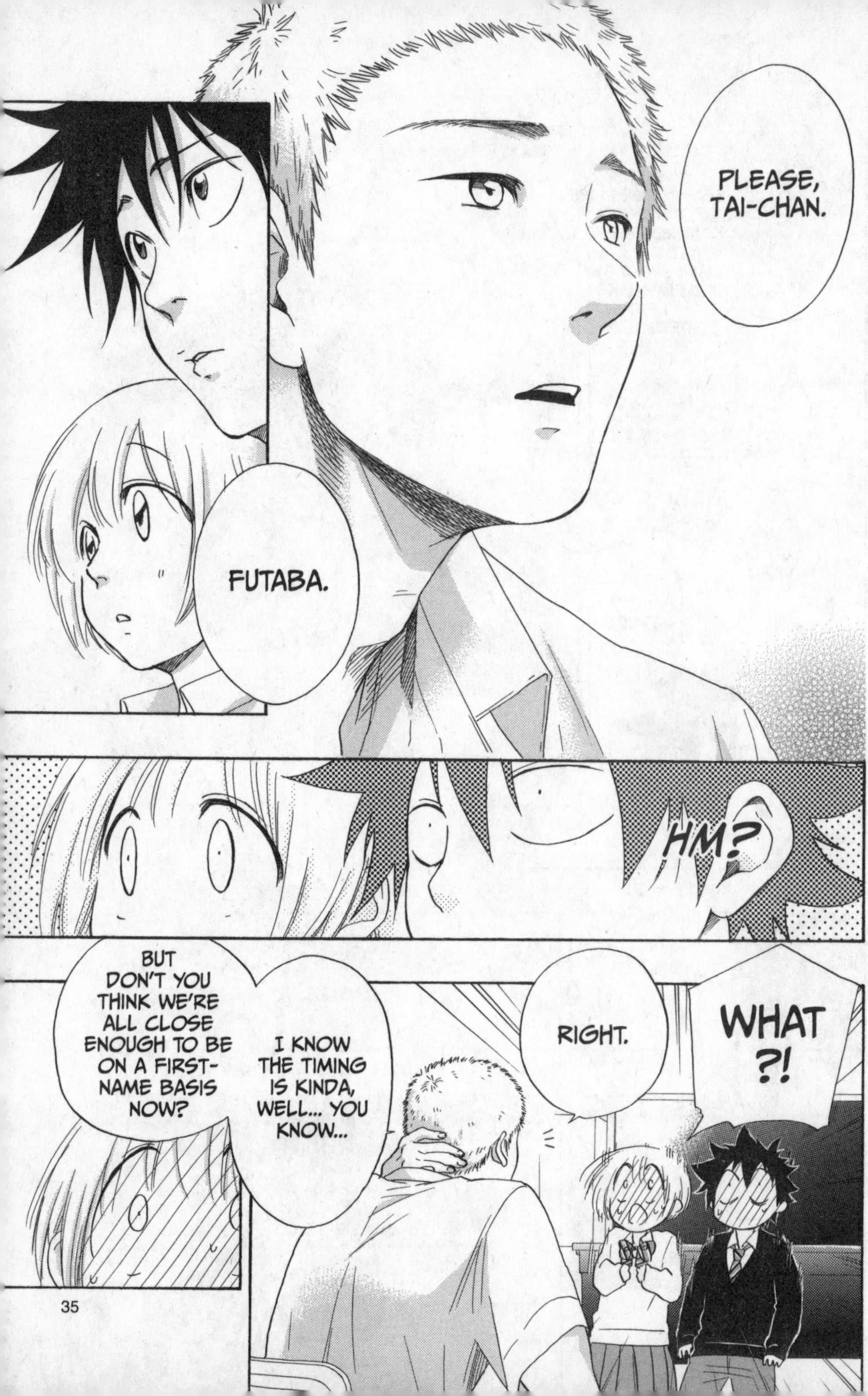
PLEASE, TAI-CHAN.
FUTABA.
HM?
WHAT ?!
RIGHT.
I KNOW THE TIMING IS KINDA, WELL... YOU KNOW...
BUT DON'T YOU THINK WE'RE ALL CLOSE ENOUGH TO BE ON A FIRST-NAME BASIS NOW?

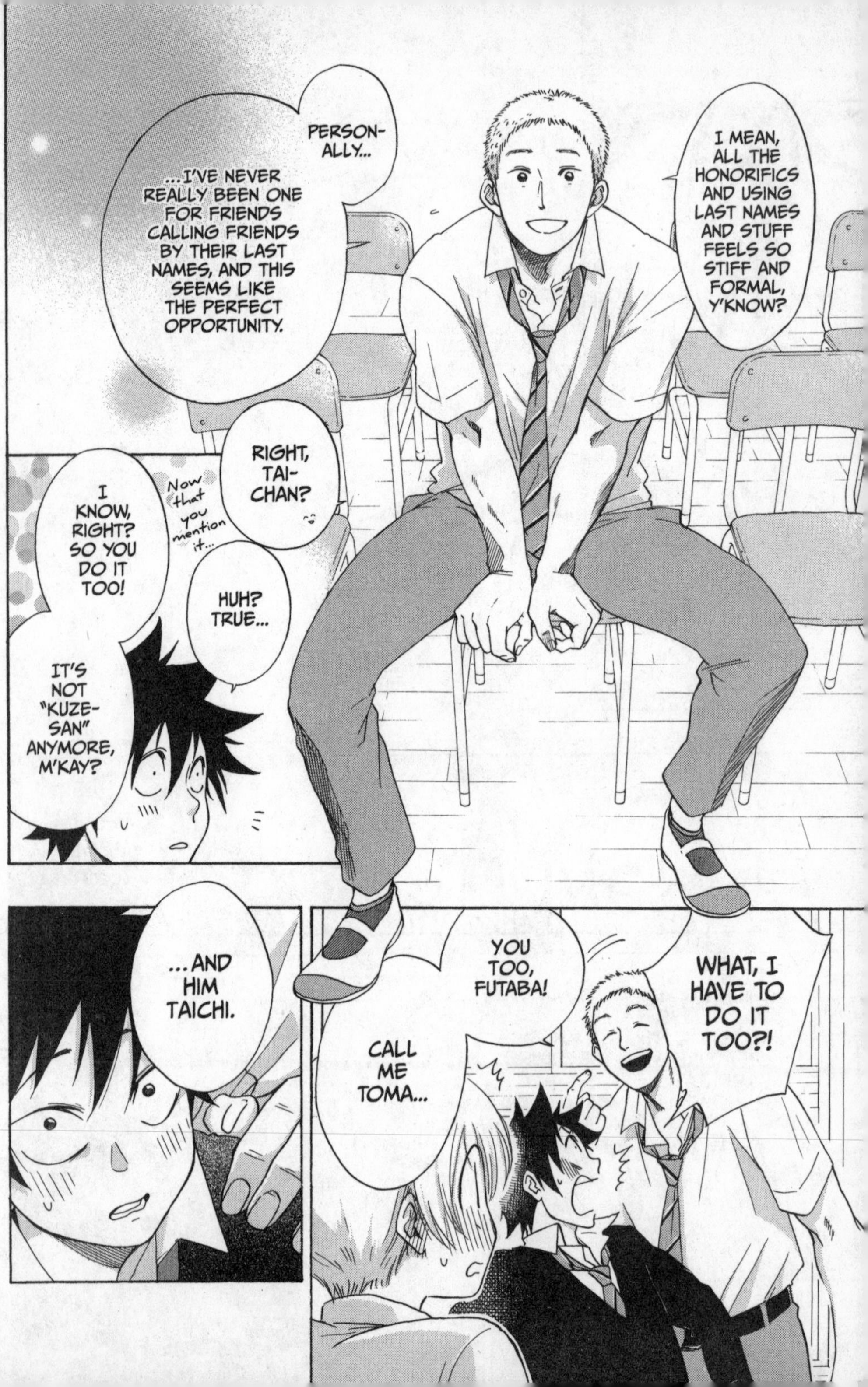
PERSON-ALLY...
...I'VE NEVER REALLY BEEN ONE FOR FRIENDS CALLING FRIENDS BY THEIR LAST NAMES, AND THIS SEEMS LIKE THE PERFECT OPPORTUNITY.
I MEAN, ALL THE HONORIFICS AND USING LAST NAMES AND STUFF FEELS SO STIFF AND FORMAL, Y'KNOW?
RIGHT, TAI-CHAN?
Now that you mention it...
HUH? TRUE...
I KNOW, RIGHT? SO YOU DO IT TOO!
IT'S NOT "KUZE-SAN" ANYMORE, M'KAY?
WHAT, I HAVE TO DO IT TOO?!
YOU TOO, FUTABA!
CALL ME TOMA...
...AND HIM TAICHI.

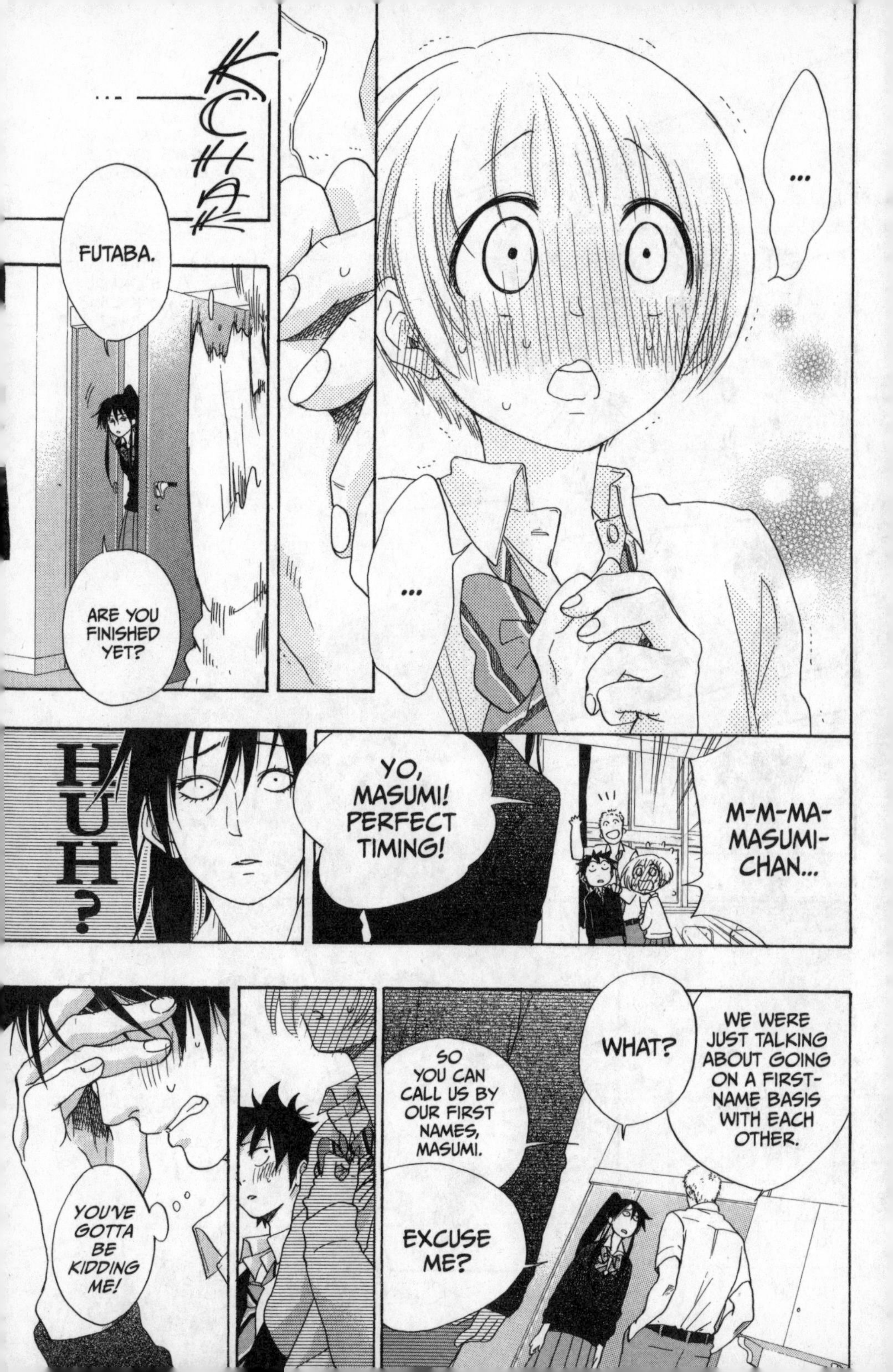
...
...
... —
KCHAK
FUTABA.
ARE YOU FINISHED YET?
M-M-MA-MASUMI-CHAN...
YO, MASUMI! PERFECT TIMING!
HUH?
WE WERE JUST TALKING ABOUT GOING ON A FIRST-NAME BASIS WITH EACH OTHER.
WHAT?
SO YOU CAN CALL US BY OUR FIRST NAMES, MASUMI.
EXCUSE ME?
YOU'VE GOTTA BE KIDDING ME!

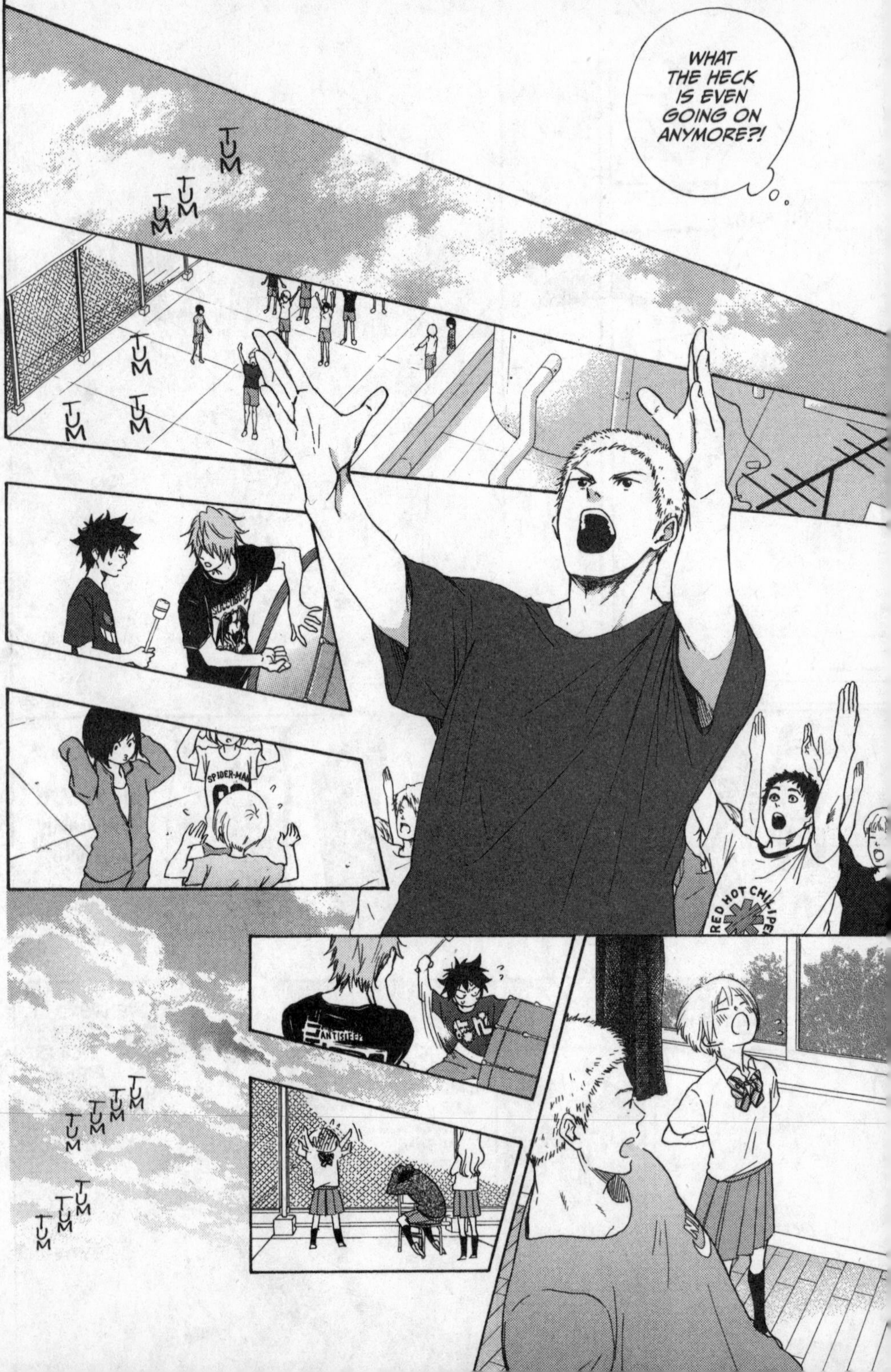
WHAT THE HECK IS EVEN GOING ON ANYMORE?!
TUM
TUM
TUM
TUM
TUM
TUM
TUM
TUM
TUM
TUM
TUM
TUM
TUM

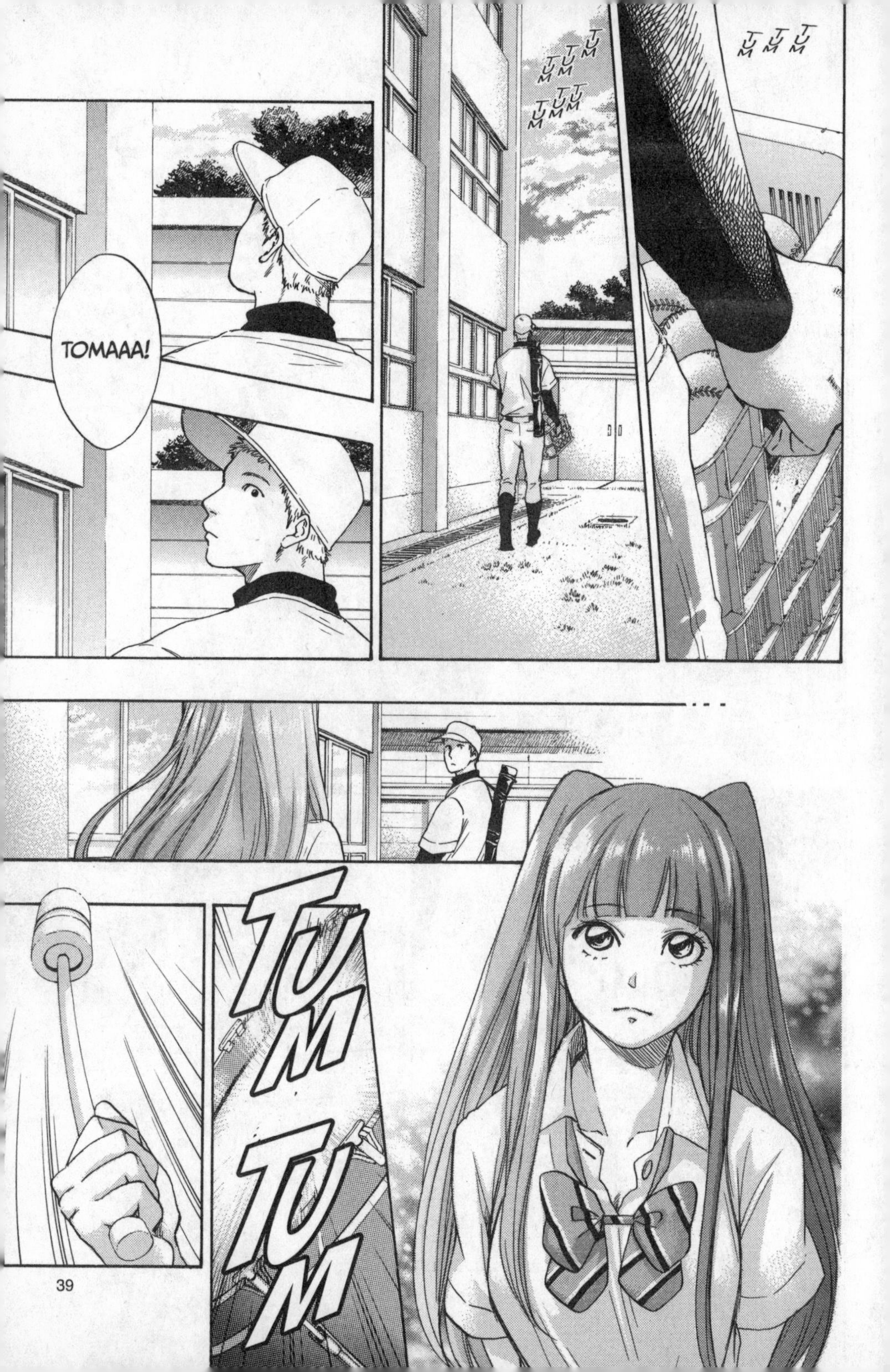
TUM TUM TUM
TUM TUM
TUM TUM
TOMAAA!
TUM TUM TUM

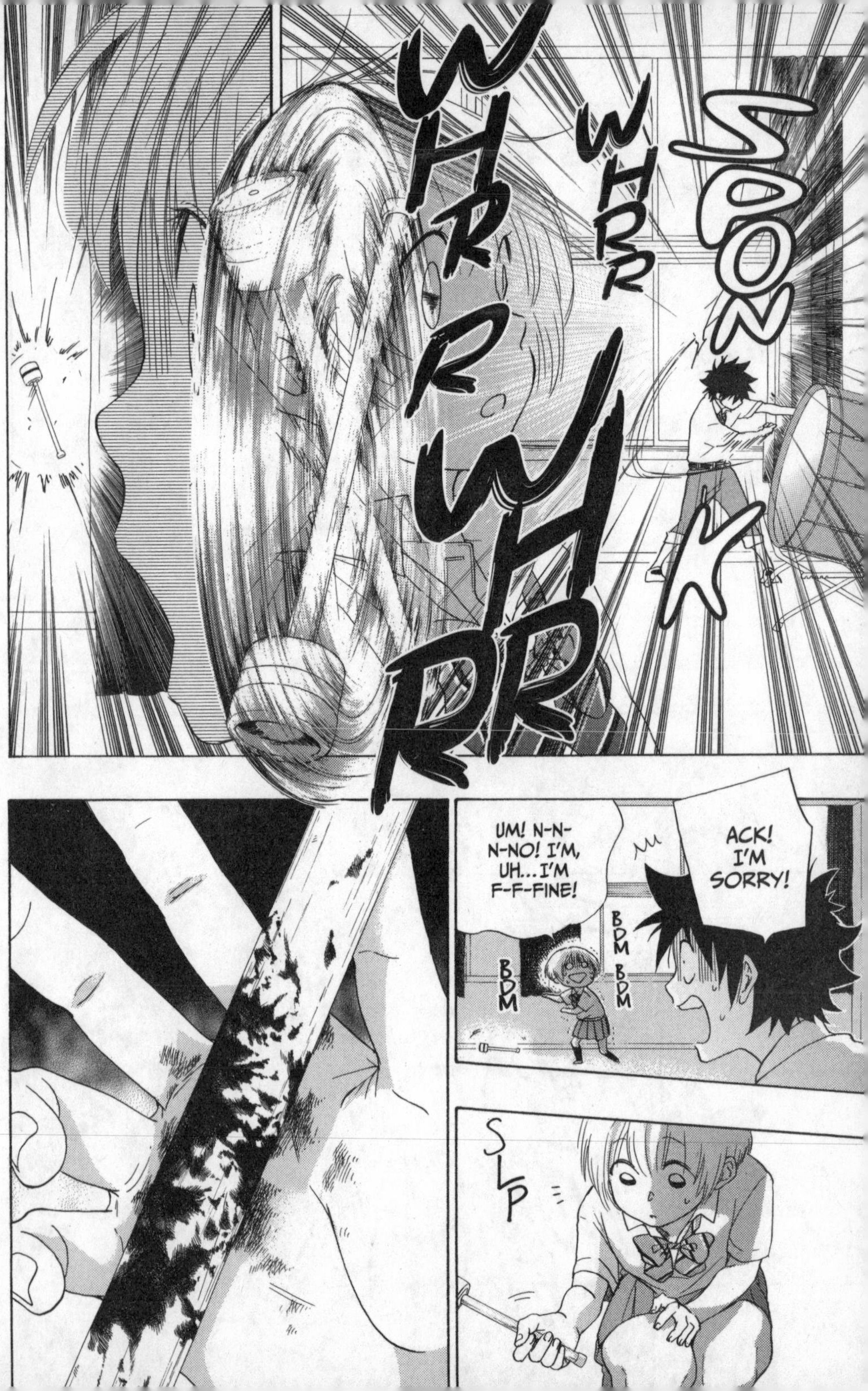
SPOON
WHRR
WHRR WHRR
K
ACK! I'M SORRY!
UM! N-N-N-NO! I'M, UH...I'M F-F-FINE!
BDM BDM
BDM BDM
SLP

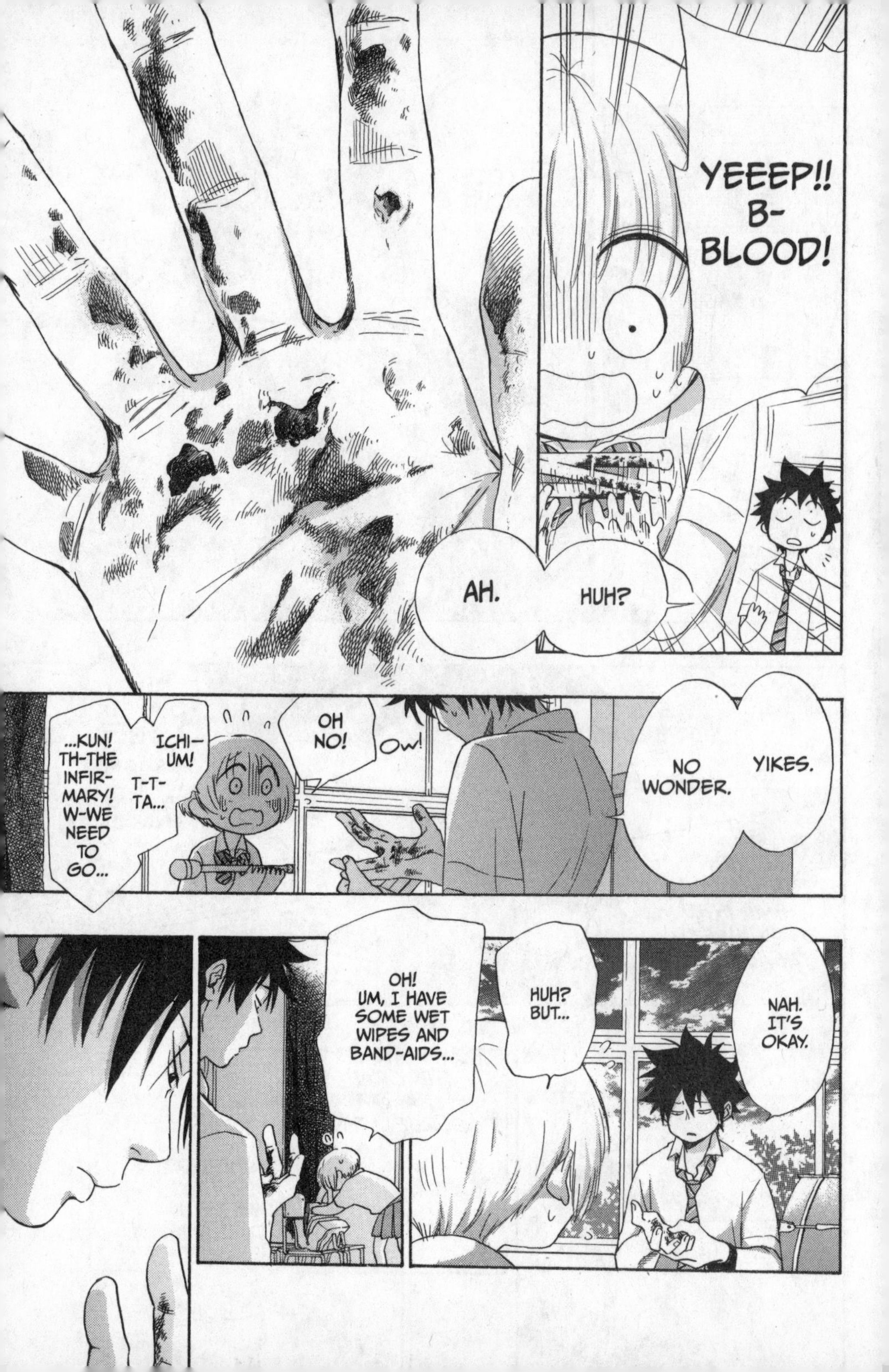
YEEEP!! B-BLOOD!
HUH?
AH.
YIKES.
NO WONDER.
OW!
OH NO!
ICHI- UM! T-T-TA...
...KUN! TH-THE INFIRMARY! W-WE NEED TO GO...
NAH. IT'S OKAY.
HUH? BUT...
OH! UM, I HAVE SOME WET WIPES AND BAND-AIDS...

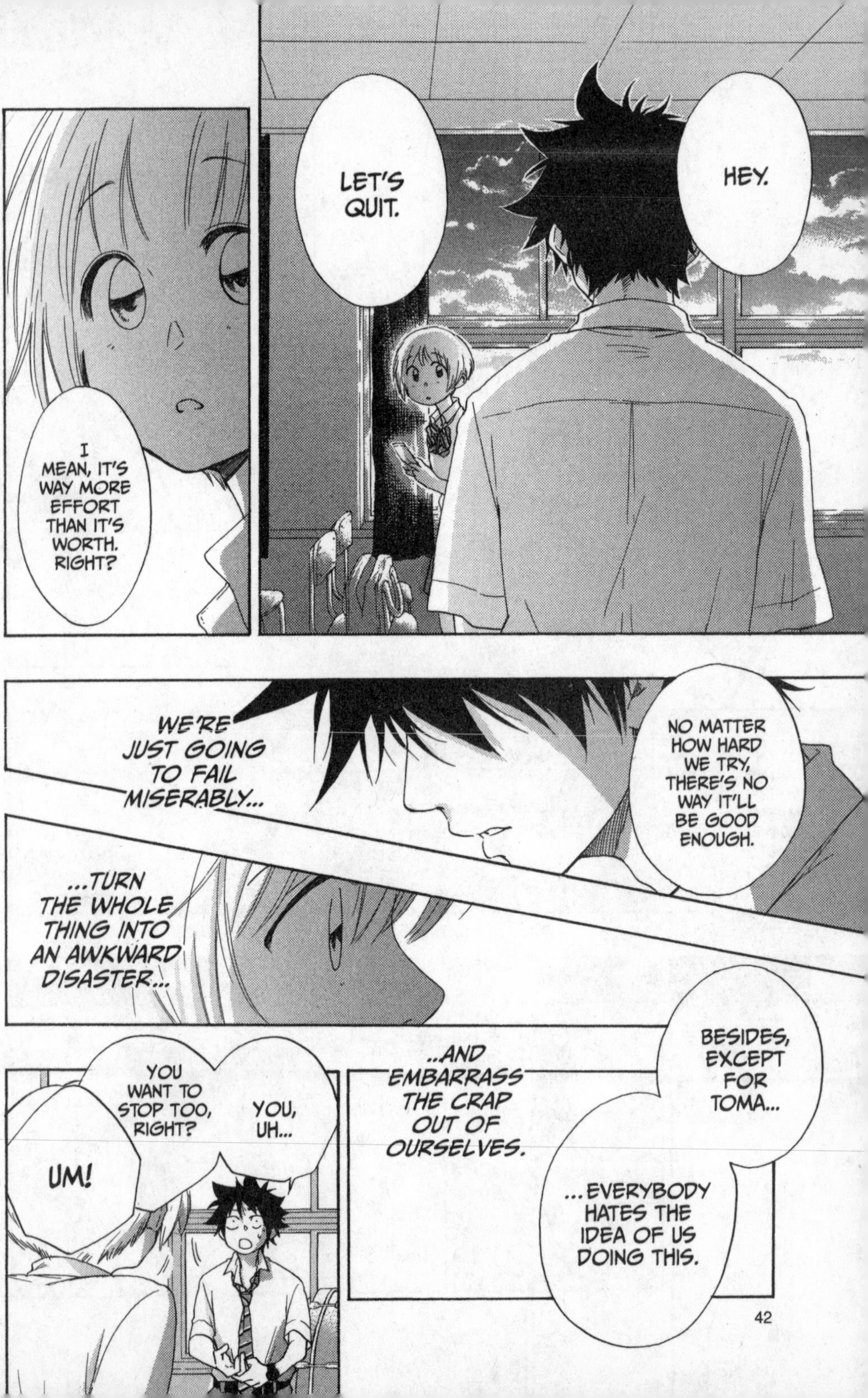
HEY.
LET'S QUIT.
I MEAN, IT'S WAY MORE EFFORT THAN IT'S WORTH. RIGHT?
NO MATTER HOW HARD WE TRY, THERE'S NO WAY IT'LL BE GOOD ENOUGH.
WE'RE JUST GOING TO FAIL MISERABLY...
...TURN THE WHOLE THING INTO AN AWKWARD DISASTER...
...AND EMBARRASS THE CRAP OUT OF OURSELVES.
BESIDES, EXCEPT FOR TOMA...
...EVERYBODY HATES THE IDEA OF US DOING THIS.
YOU, UH...
YOU WANT TO STOP TOO, RIGHT?
UM!

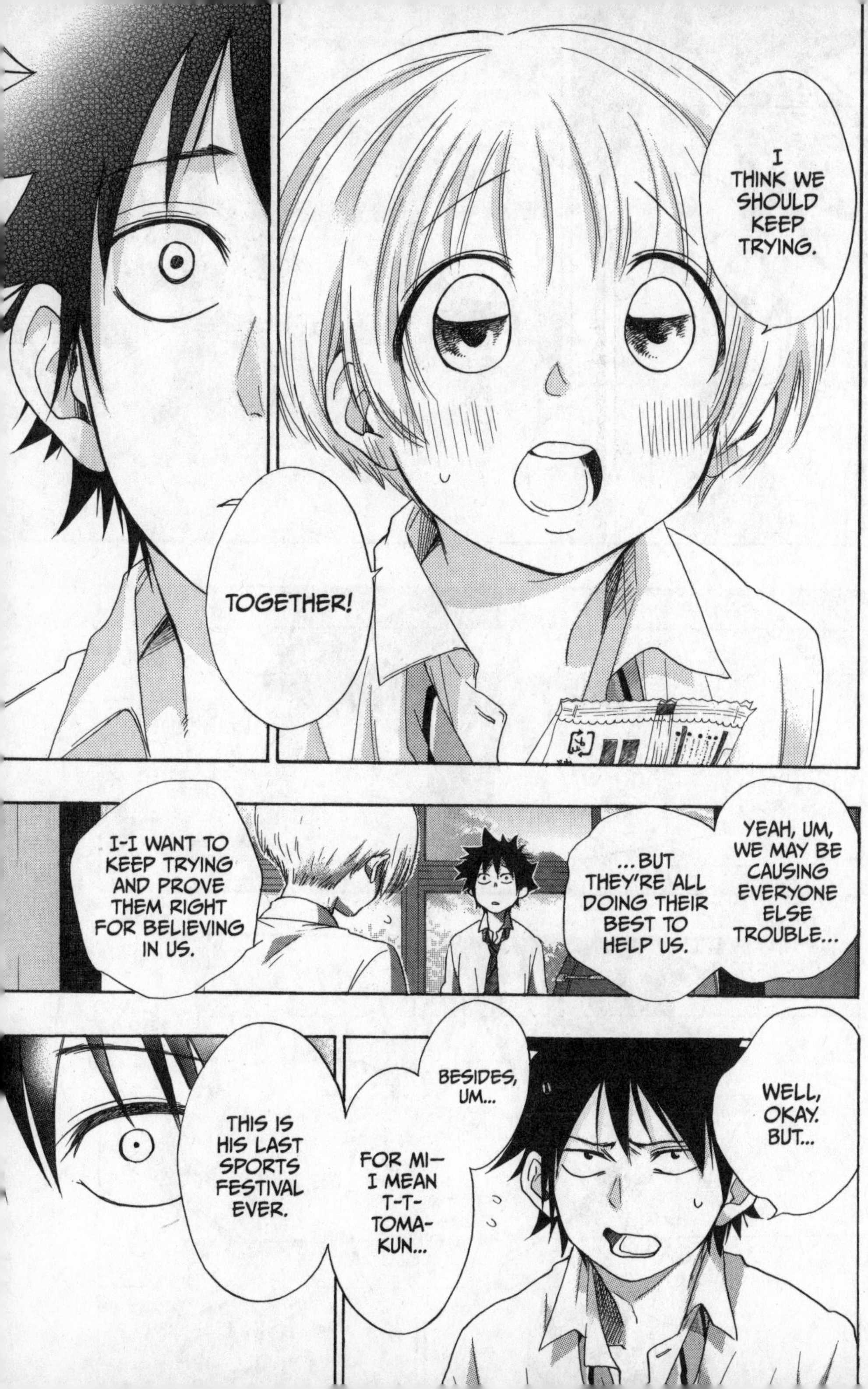
I THINK WE SHOULD KEEP TRYING.
TOGETHER!
YEAH, UM, WE MAY BE CAUSING EVERYONE ELSE TROUBLE...
...BUT THEY'RE ALL DOING THEIR BEST TO HELP US.
I-I WANT TO KEEP TRYING AND PROVE THEM RIGHT FOR BELIEVING IN US.
WELL, OKAY. BUT...
BESIDES, UM...
FOR MI— I MEAN T-T-TOMA-KUN...
THIS IS HIS LAST SPORTS FESTIVAL EVER.

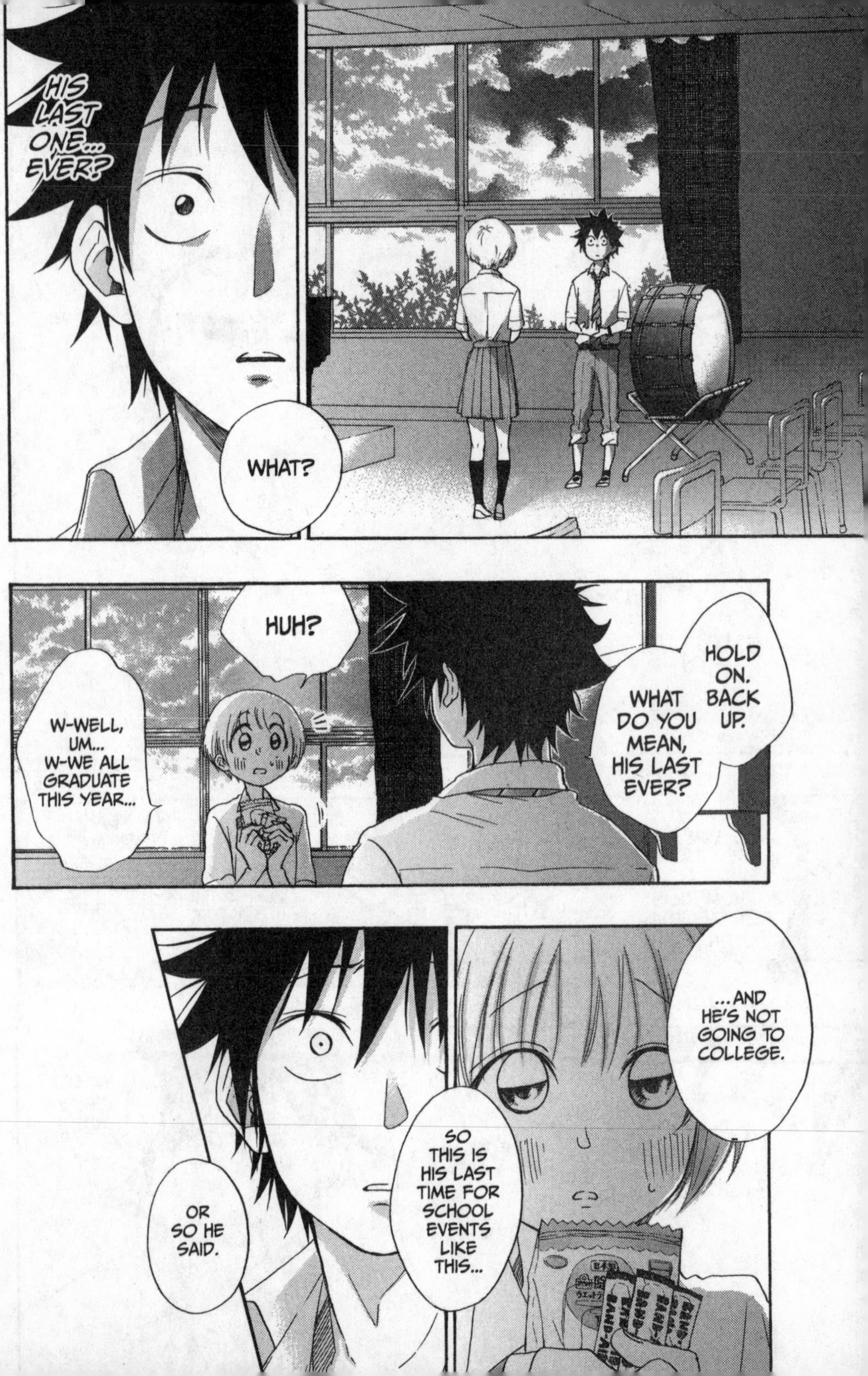
HIS LAST ONE... EVER?
WHAT?
HOLD ON. BACK UP.
WHAT DO YOU MEAN, HIS LAST EVER?
HUH?
W-WELL, UM... W-WE ALL GRADUATE THIS YEAR...
...AND HE'S NOT GOING TO COLLEGE.
SO THIS IS HIS LAST TIME FOR SCHOOL EVENTS LIKE THIS...
OR SO HE SAID.

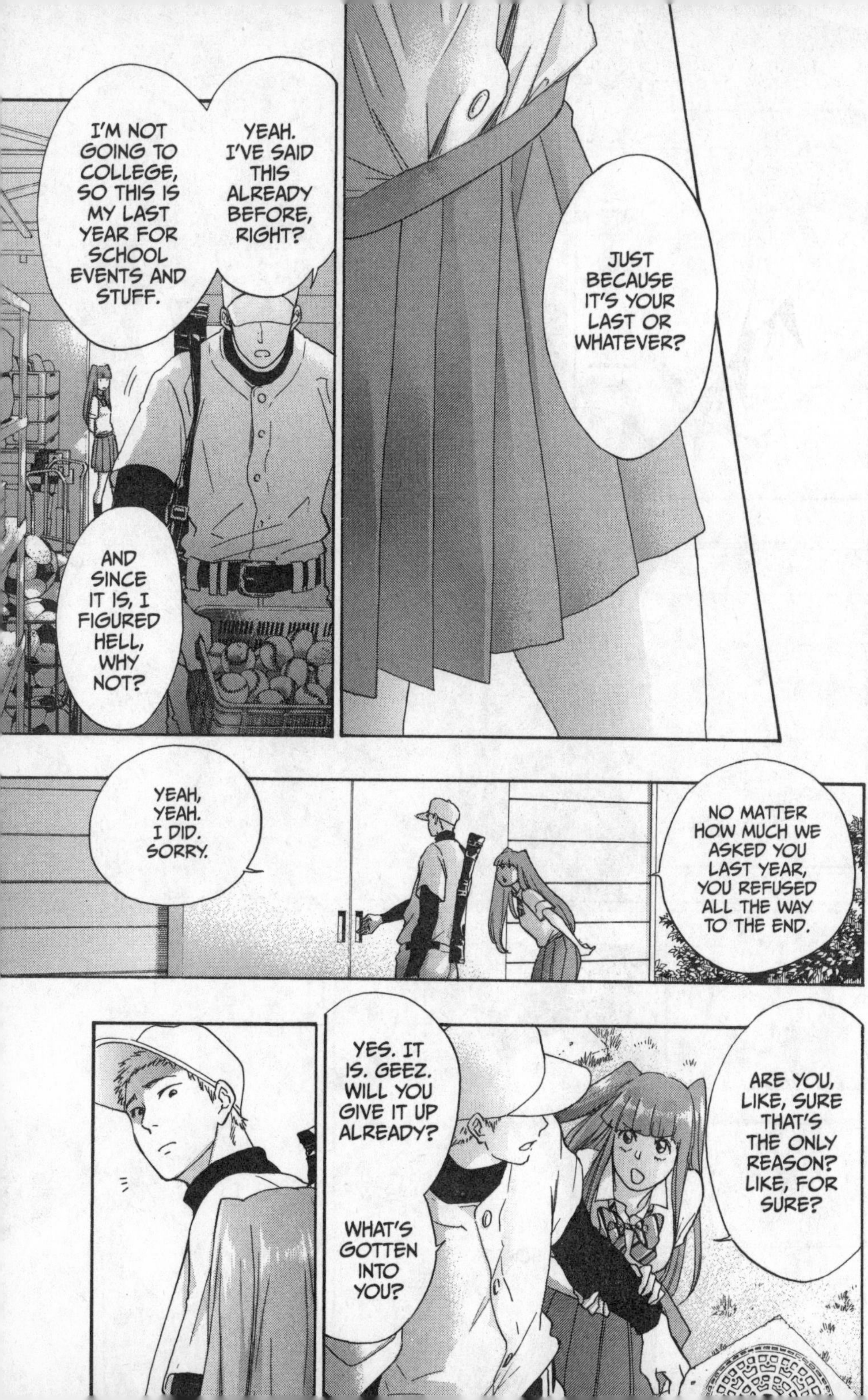
JUST BECAUSE IT'S YOUR LAST OR WHATEVER?
YEAH. I'VE SAID THIS ALREADY BEFORE, RIGHT?
I'M NOT GOING TO COLLEGE, SO THIS IS MY LAST YEAR FOR SCHOOL EVENTS AND STUFF.
AND SINCE IT IS, I FIGURED HELL, WHY NOT?
NO MATTER HOW MUCH WE ASKED YOU LAST YEAR, YOU REFUSED ALL THE WAY TO THE END.
YEAH, YEAH. I DID. SORRY.
ARE YOU, LIKE, SURE THAT'S THE ONLY REASON? LIKE, FOR SURE?
YES. IT IS. GEEZ. WILL YOU GIVE IT UP ALREADY?
WHAT'S GOTTEN INTO YOU?

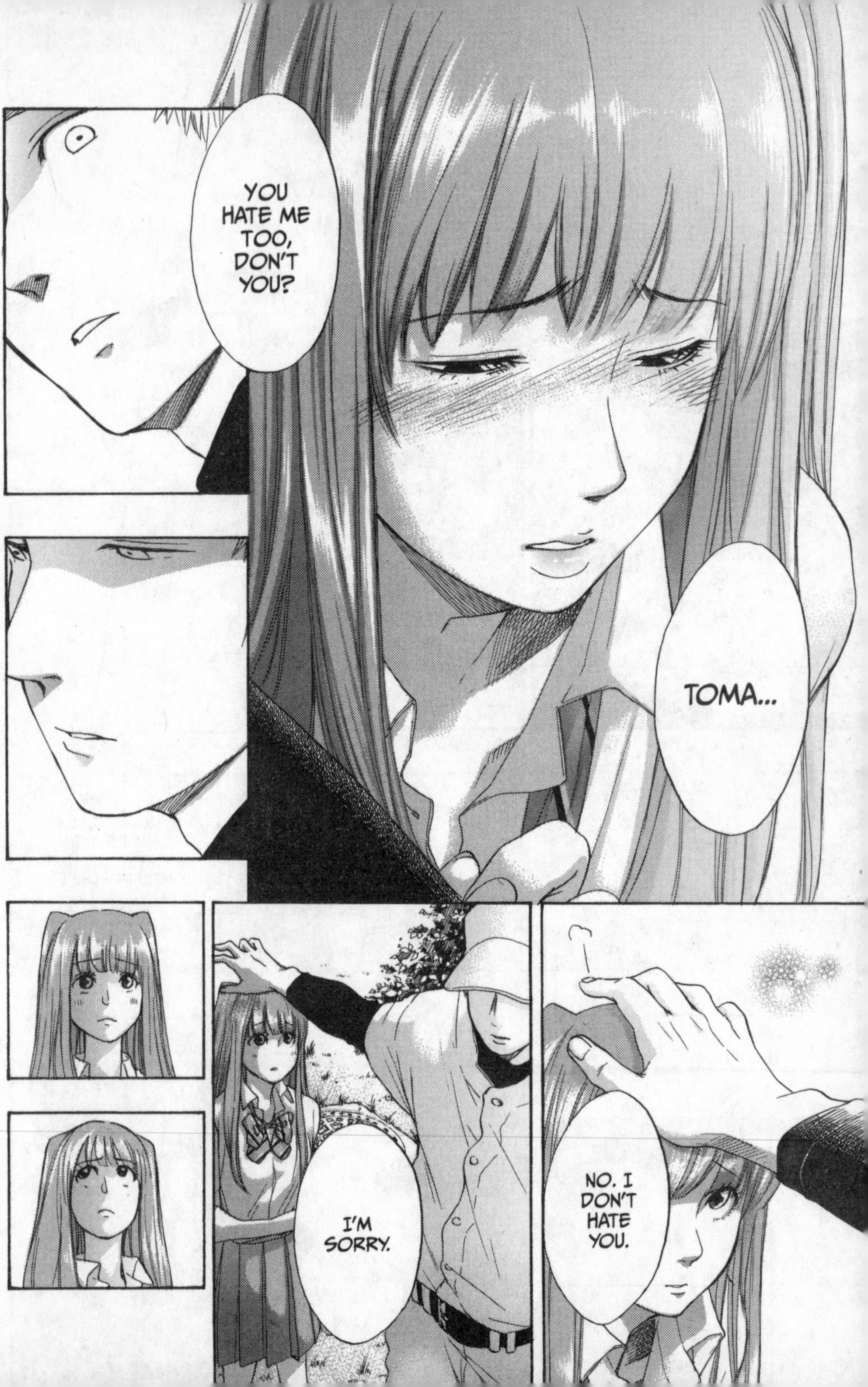
YOU HATE ME TOO, DON'T YOU?
TOMA...
NO. I DON'T HATE YOU.
I'M SORRY.

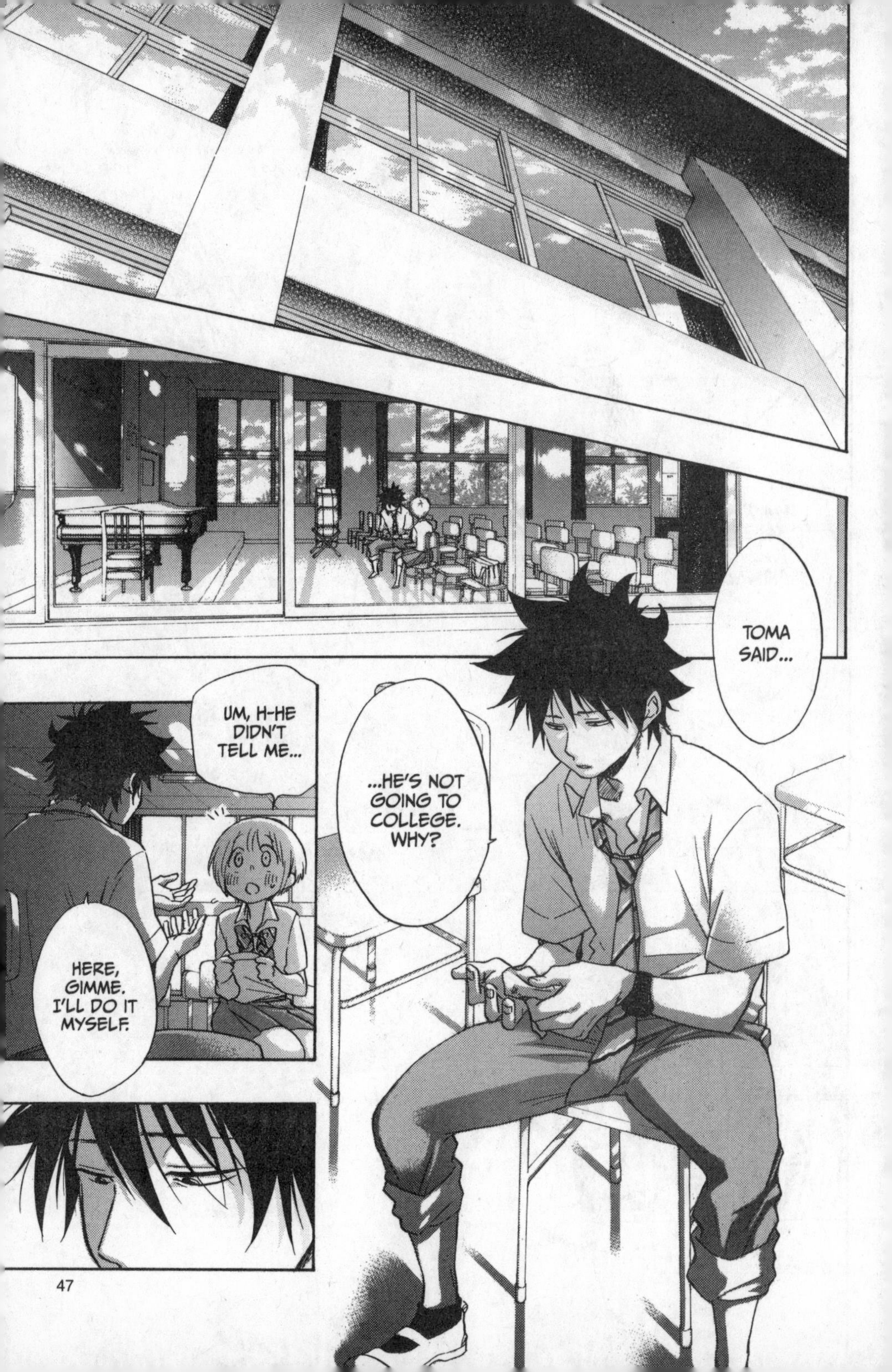
TOMA SAID...
...HE'S NOT GOING TO COLLEGE. WHY?
UM, H-HE DIDN'T TELL ME...
HERE, GIMME. I'LL DO IT MYSELF.

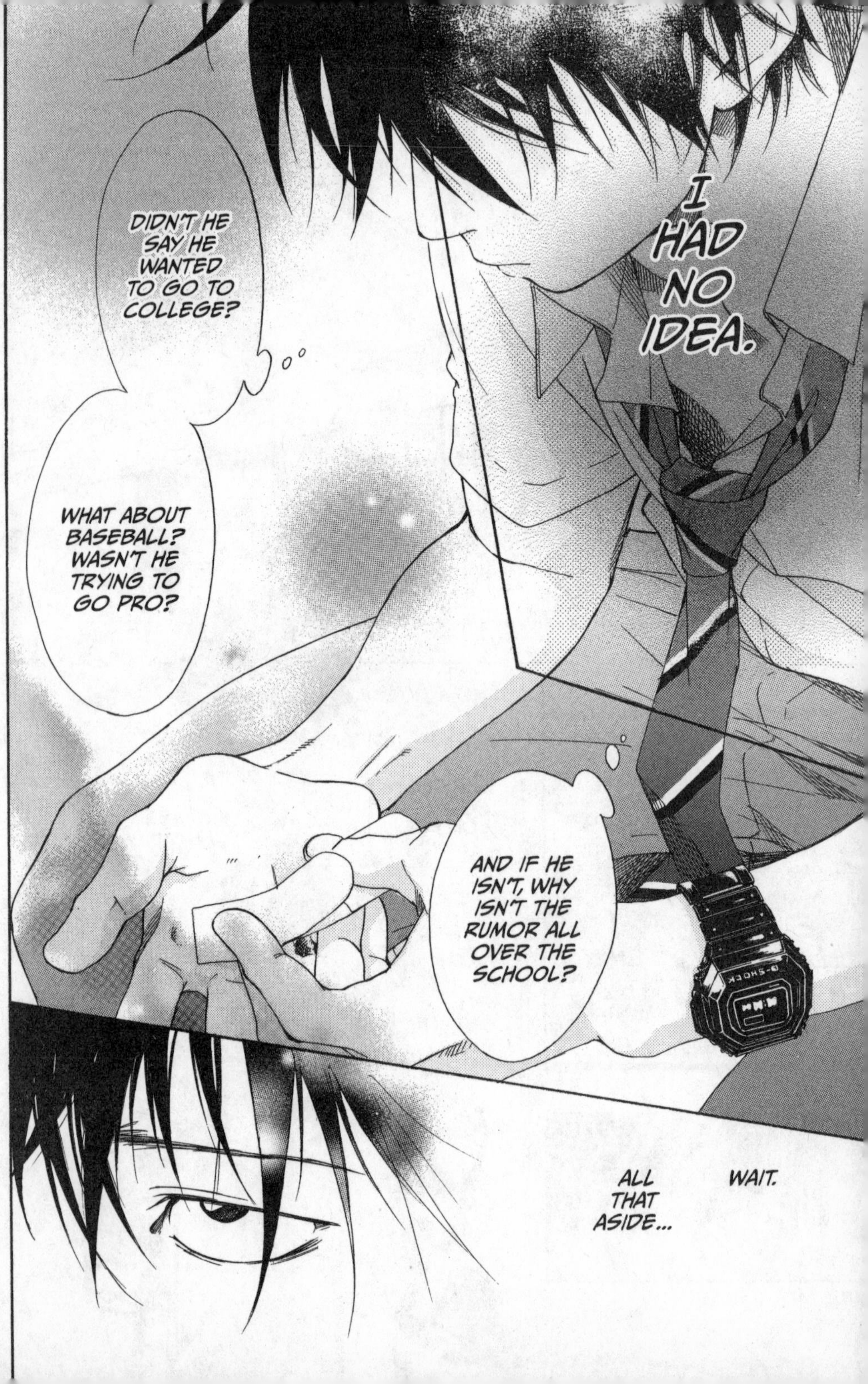
I HAD NO IDEA.
DIDN'T HE SAY HE WANTED TO GO TO COLLEGE?
WHAT ABOUT BASEBALL? WASN'T HE TRYING TO GO PRO?
AND IF HE ISN'T, WHY ISN'T THE RUMOR ALL OVER THE SCHOOL?
...
WAIT.
ALL THAT ASIDE...

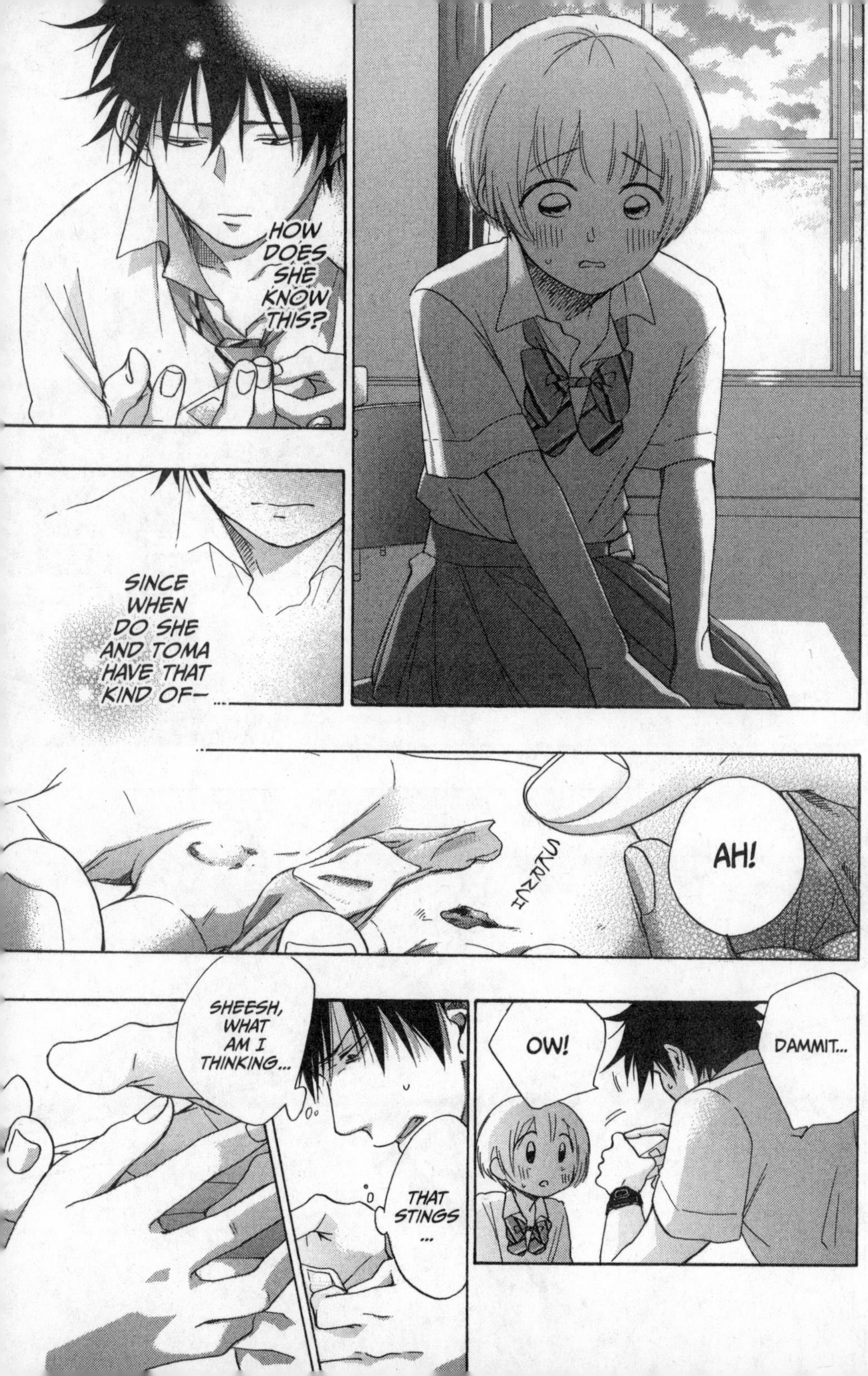
HOW DOES SHE KNOW THIS?
SINCE WHEN DO SHE AND TOMA HAVE THAT KIND OF—...
...
AH!
SURUZUI
DAMMIT...
OW!
SHEESH, WHAT AM I THINKING...
THAT STINGS...

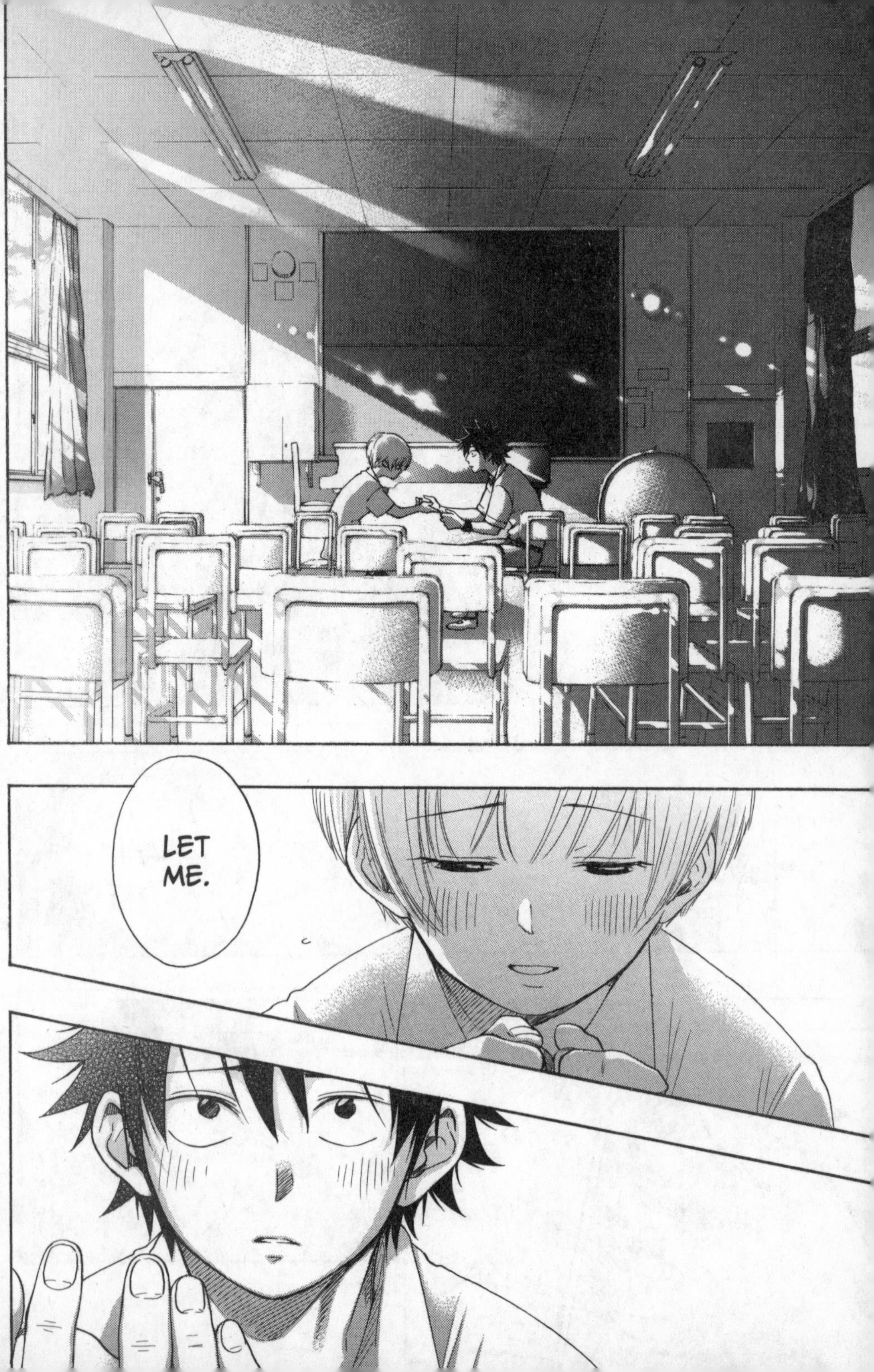
LET ME.

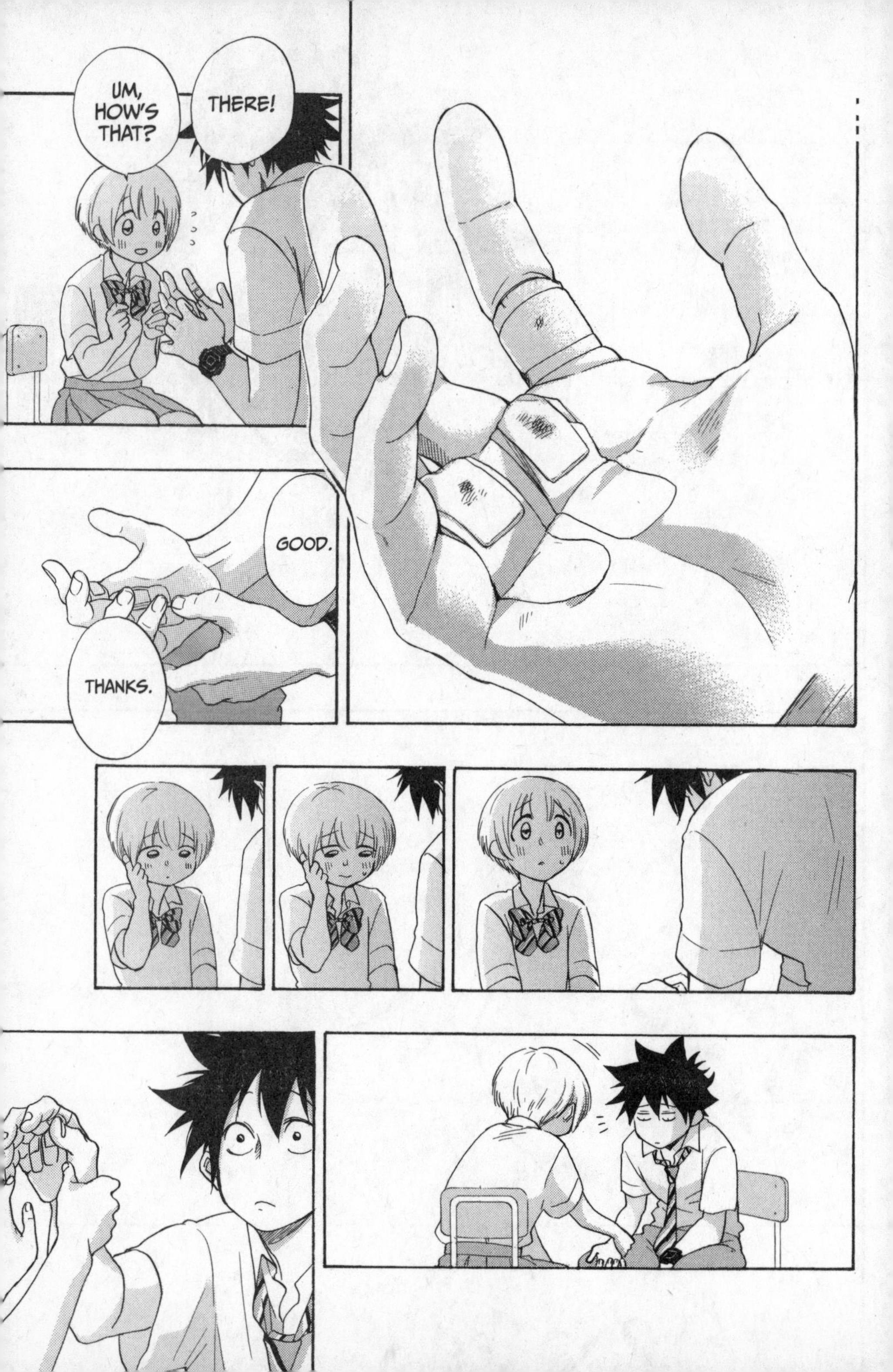
THERE!
UM, HOW'S THAT?
GOOD.
THANKS.

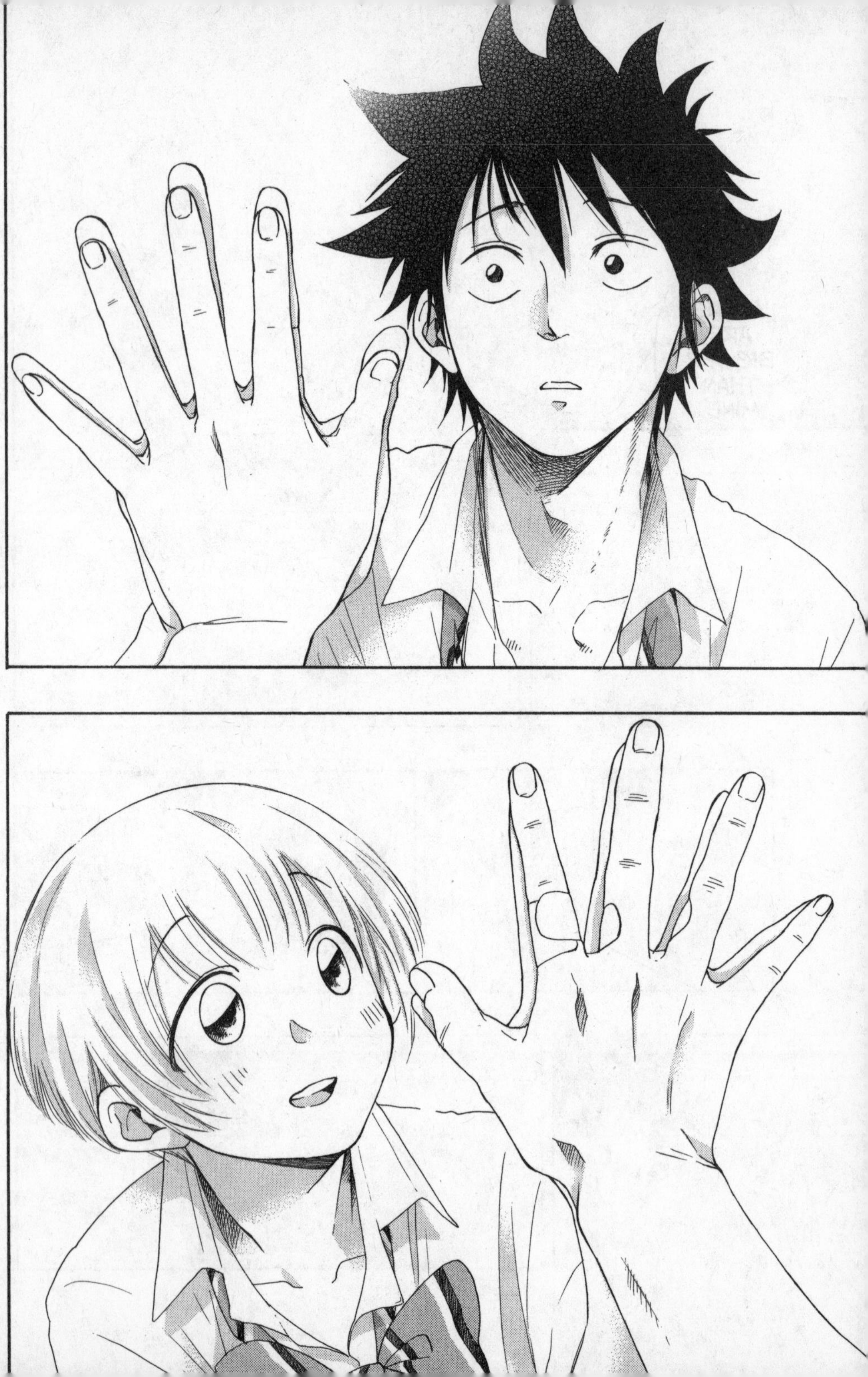

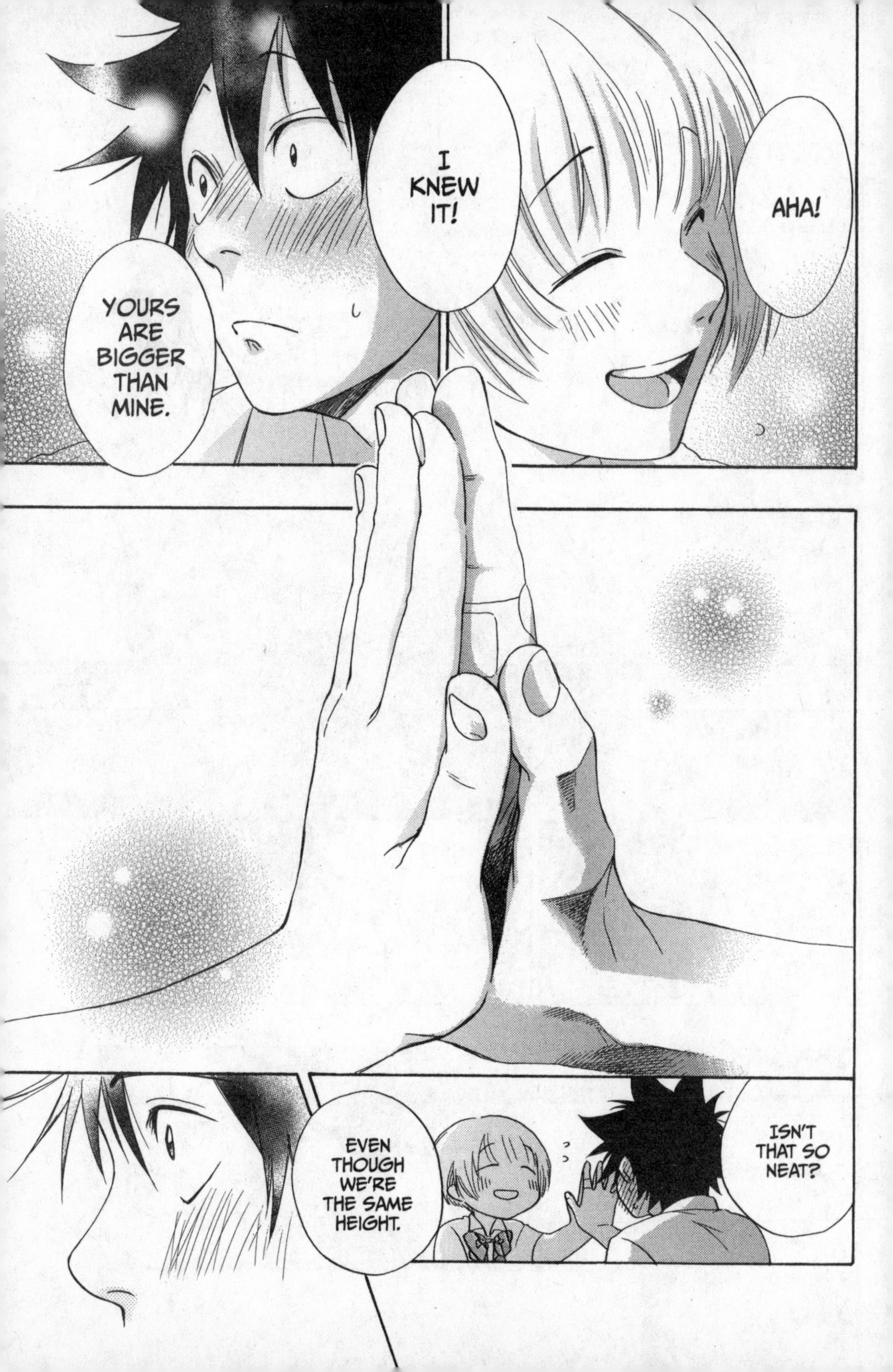
AHA!
I KNEW IT!
YOURS ARE BIGGER THAN MINE.
ISN'T THAT SO NEAT?
EVEN THOUGH WE'RE THE SAME HEIGHT.

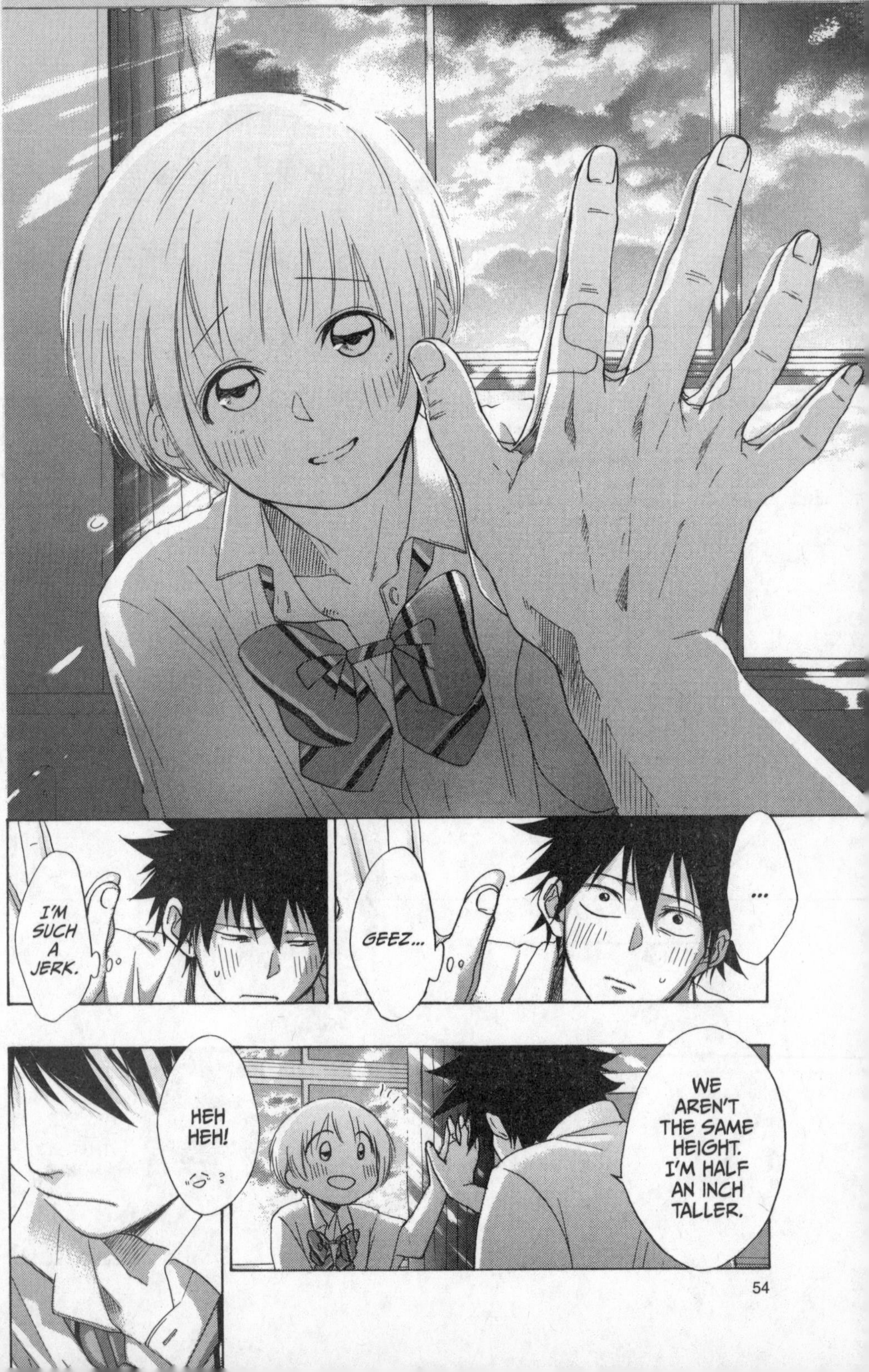
...
GEEZ...
I'M SUCH A JERK.
WE AREN'T THE SAME HEIGHT. I'M HALF AN INCH TALLER.
HEH HEH!

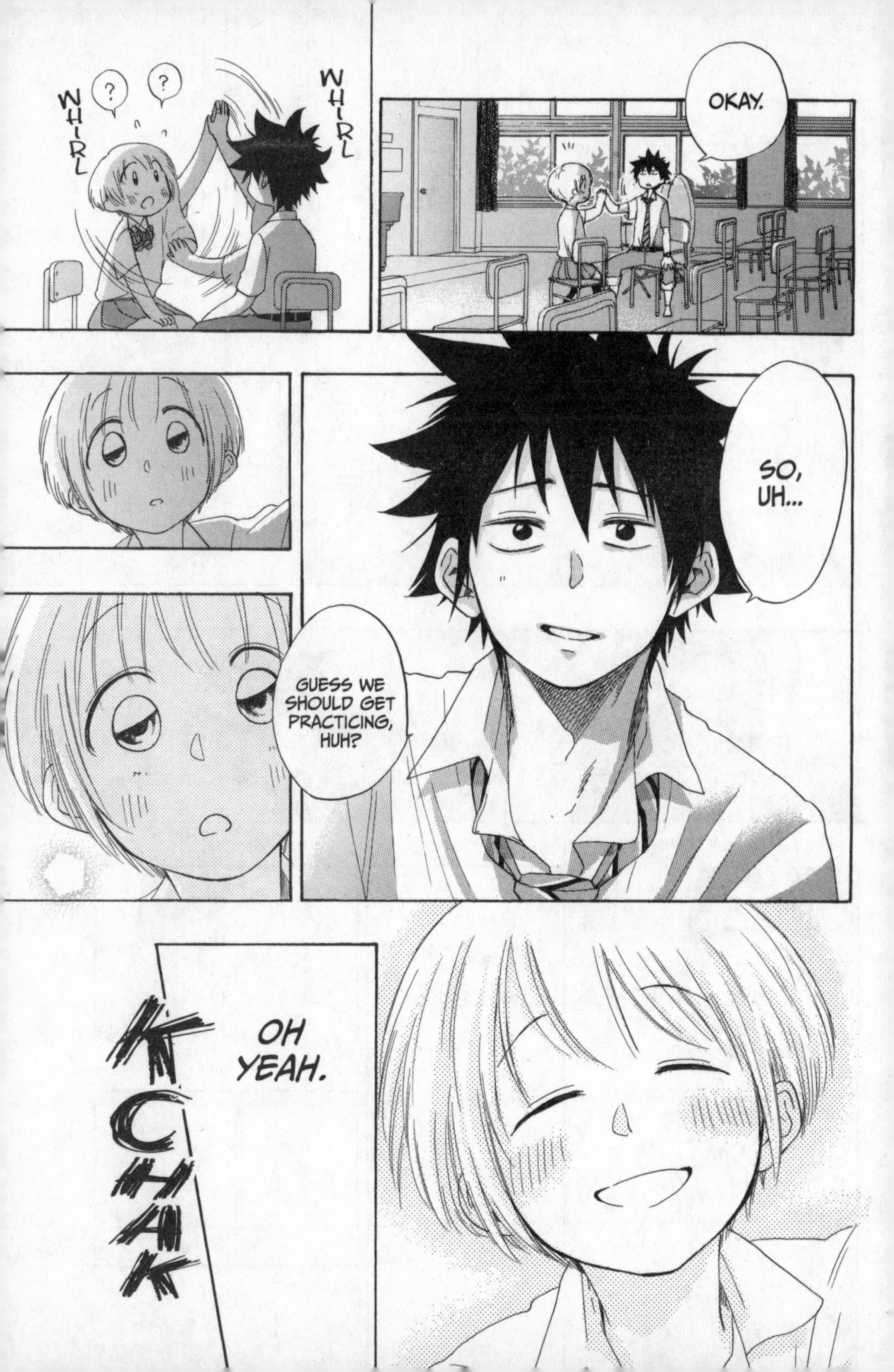
OKAY.
WHIRL
?
?
WHIRL
SO, UH...
GUESS WE SHOULD GET PRACTICING, HUH?
OH YEAH.
KCHAK

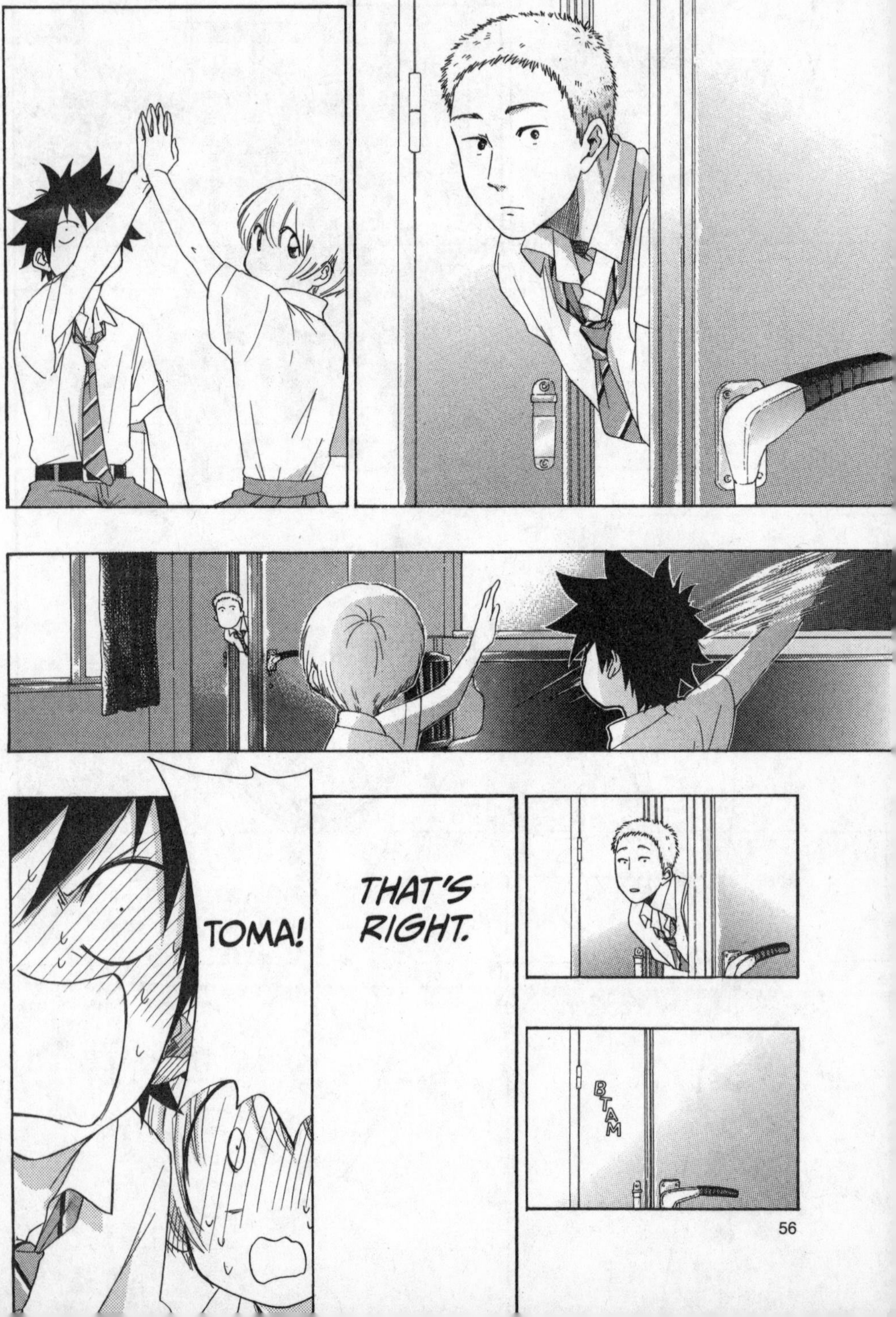
BTAM
THAT'S RIGHT.
TOMA!

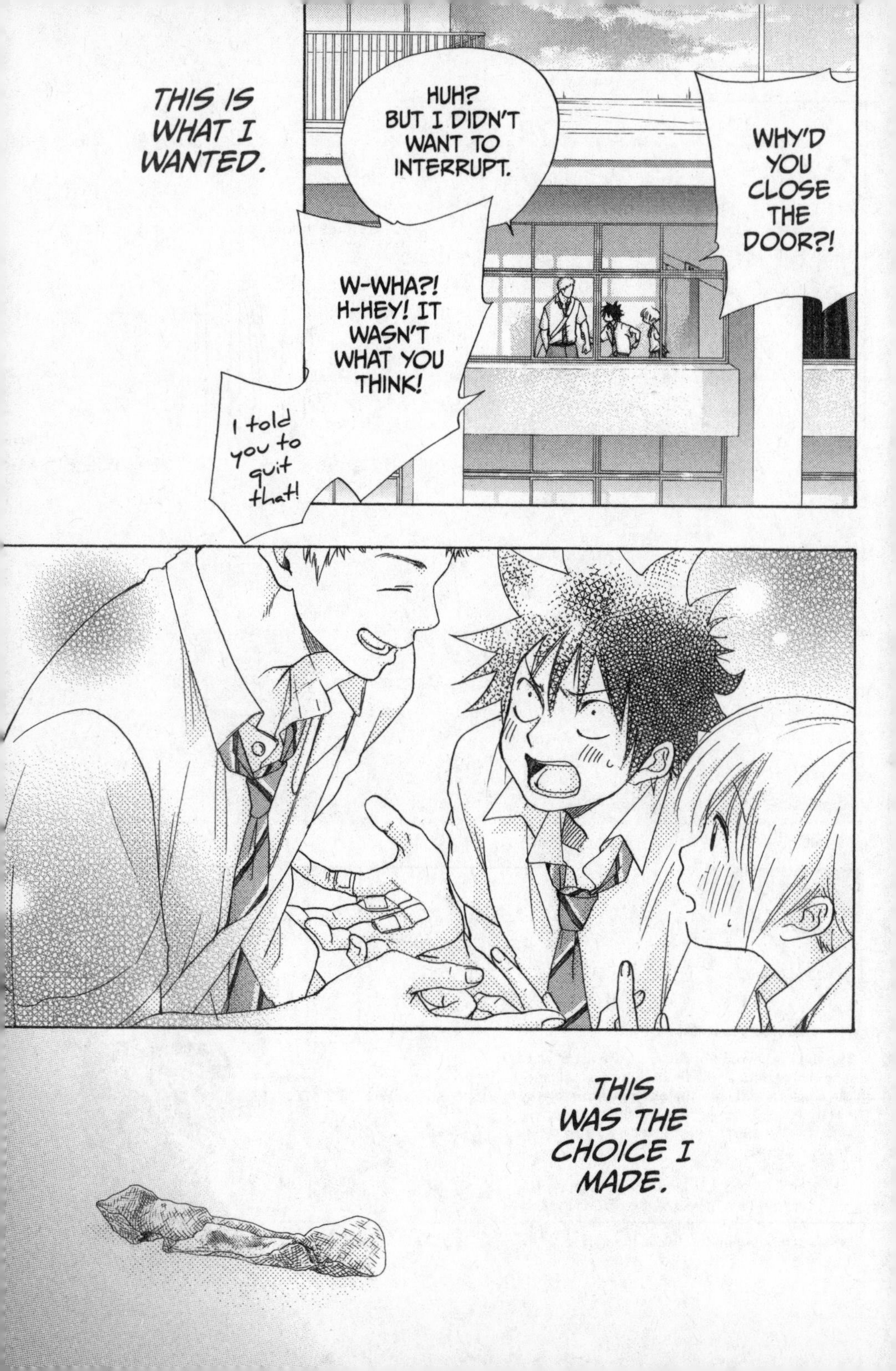
WHY'D YOU CLOSE THE DOOR?!
HUH? BUT I DIDN'T WANT TO INTERRUPT.
W-WHA?! H-HEY! IT WASN'T WHAT YOU THINK!
I told you to quit that!
THIS IS WHAT I WANTED.
THIS WAS THE CHOICE I MADE.

The Characters as Animals, Part 3

Mami & Co. weren't officially on the list of char-
acters my editor and I decided on animals for,
but since we did it for the others, I figured why
not them too? The three are at the top of their
class's social hierarchy, so I decided they'd be a
trio of raptors.

I thought Kensuke was kinda eagle-like, and
Shingo could be a hawk maybe. Then I looked
both birds up... Turns out the only really major
difference between the two is their size.

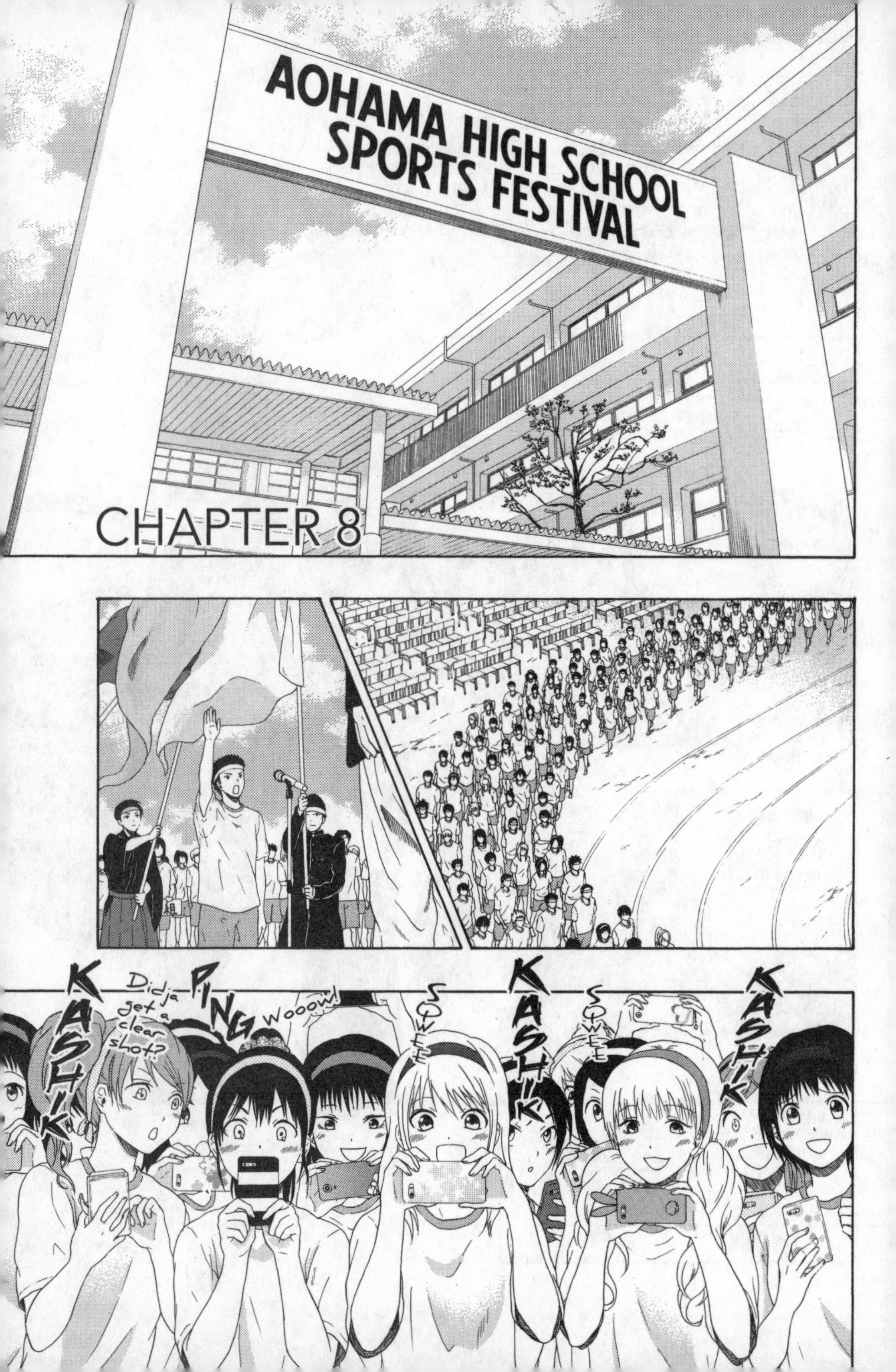
AOHAMA HIGH SCHOOL SPORTS FESTIVAL
CHAPTER 8
KASHIK
SWEE
KASHIK
SWEE
Wooow!
PING
Didja get a clear shot?
KASHIK

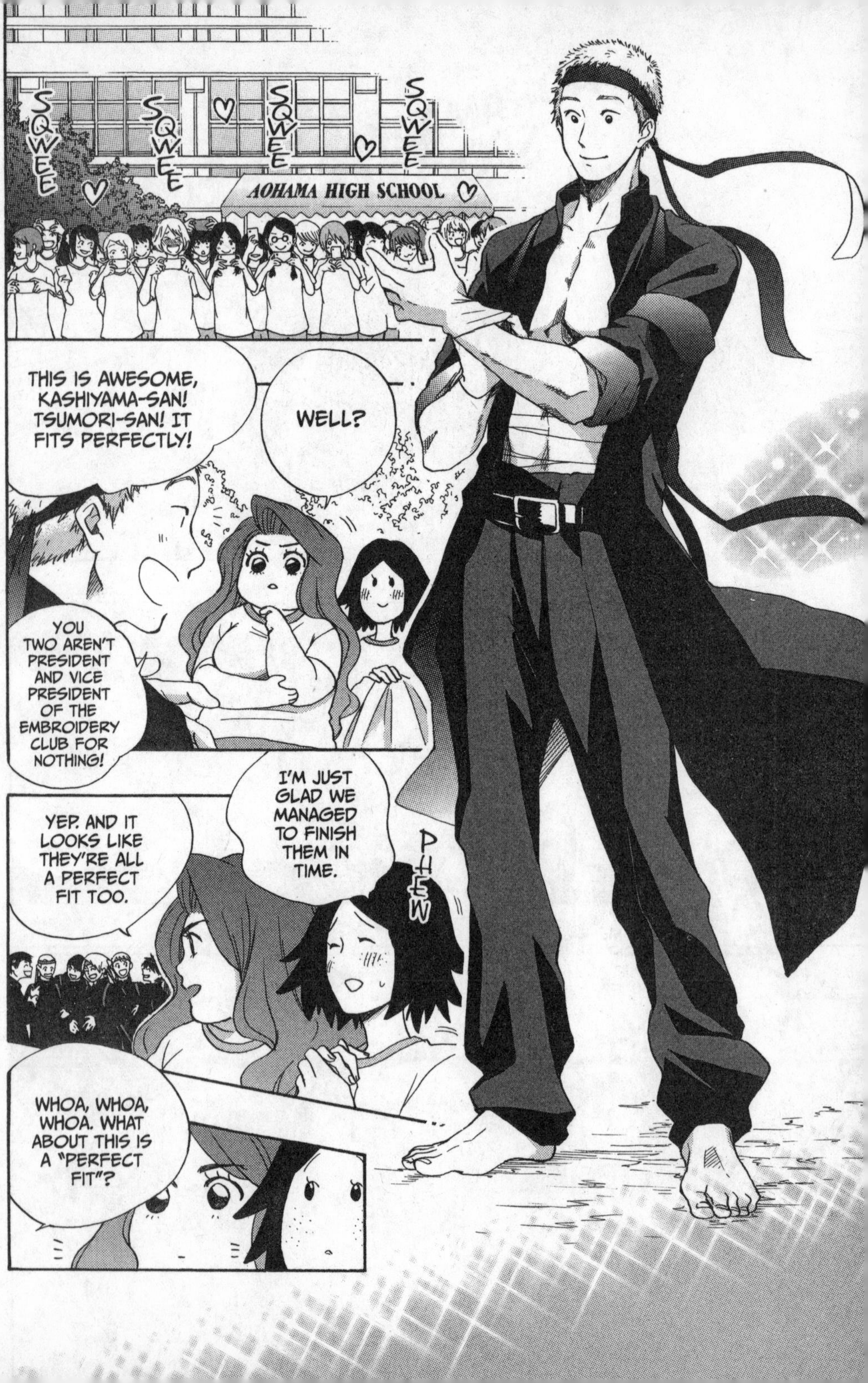
SQWEE
SQWEE
SQWEE
SQWEE
AOHAMA HIGH SCHOOL
WELL?
THIS IS AWESOME, KASHIYAMA-SAN! TSUMORI-SAN! IT FITS PERFECTLY!
YOU TWO AREN'T PRESIDENT AND VICE PRESIDENT OF THE EMBROIDERY CLUB FOR NOTHING!
I'M JUST GLAD WE MANAGED TO FINISH THEM IN TIME.
PHEW
YEP. AND IT LOOKS LIKE THEY'RE ALL A PERFECT FIT TOO.
WHOA, WHOA, WHOA. WHAT ABOUT THIS IS A "PERFECT FIT"?

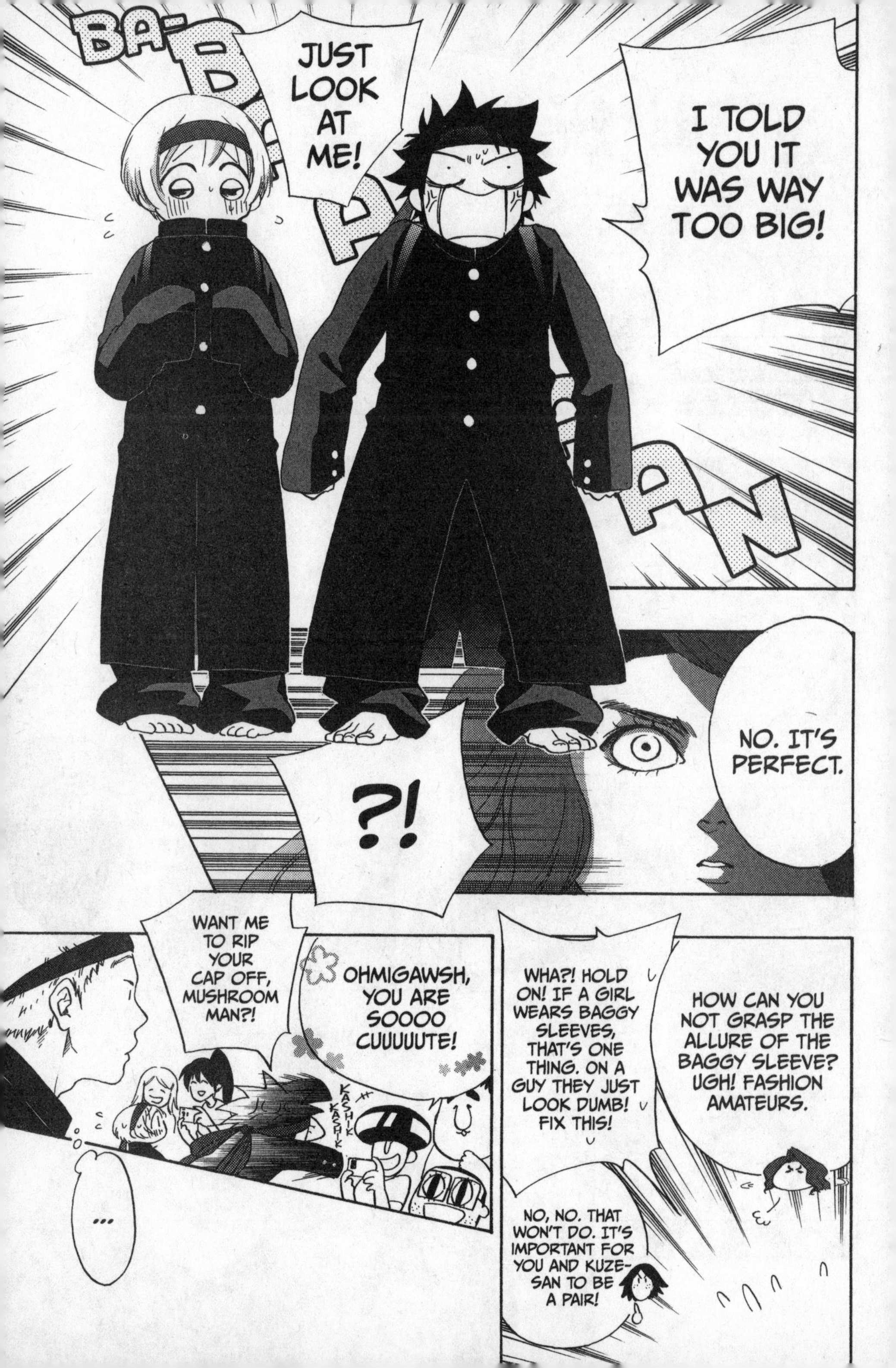
I TOLD YOU IT WAS WAY TOO BIG!
JUST LOOK AT ME!
BA-
NO. IT'S PERFECT.
?!
HOW CAN YOU NOT GRASP THE ALLURE OF THE BAGGY SLEEVE? UGH! FASHION AMATEURS.
WHA?! HOLD ON! IF A GIRL WEARS BAGGY SLEEVES, THAT'S ONE THING. ON A GUY THEY JUST LOOK DUMB! FIX THIS!
NO, NO. THAT WON'T DO. IT'S IMPORTANT FOR YOU AND KUZE-SAN TO BE A PAIR!
OHMIGAWSH, YOU ARE SOOOO CUUUUUTE!
KASHIK KASHIK
WANT ME TO RIP YOUR CAP OFF, MUSHROOM MAN?!
...

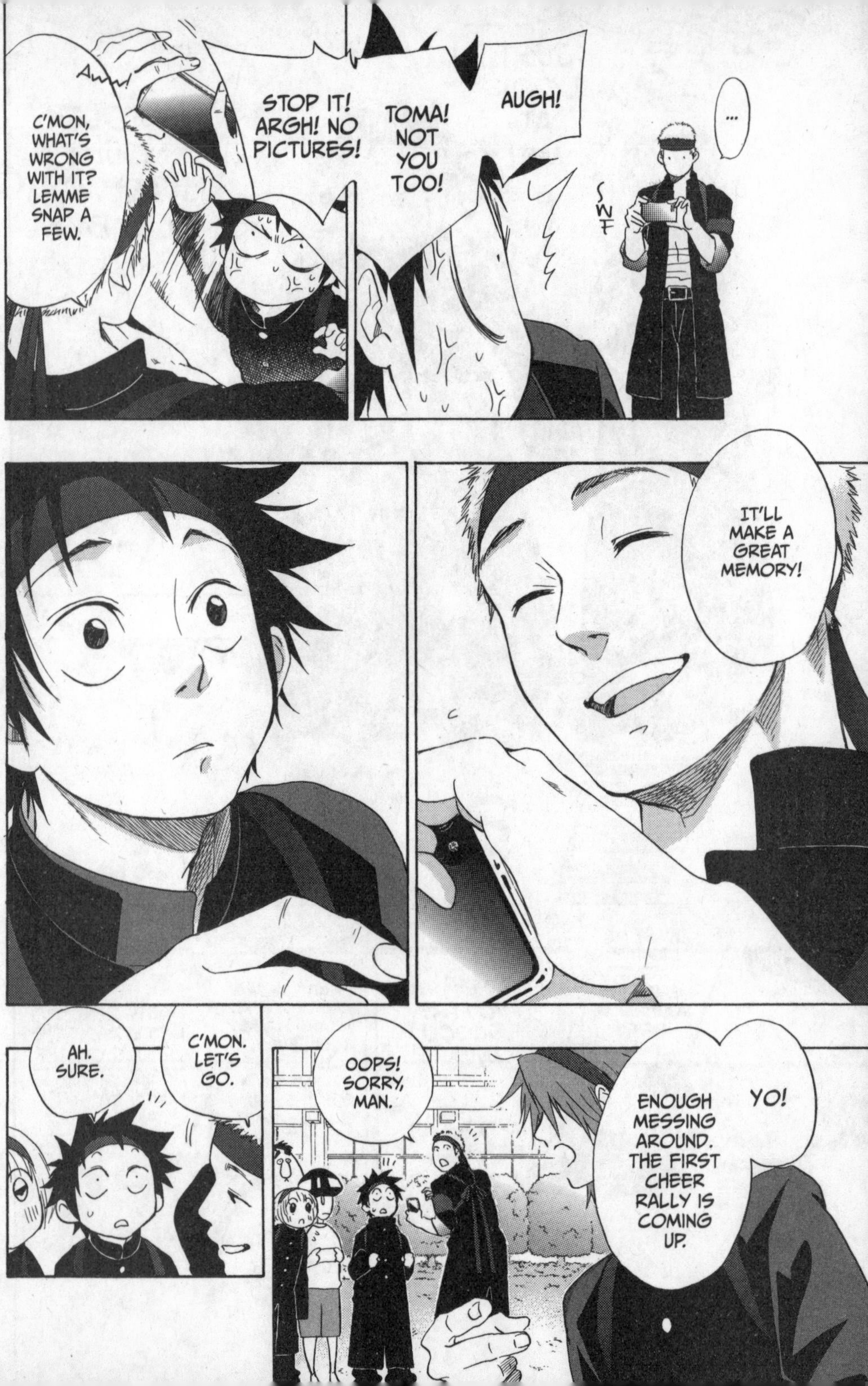
...
AUGH!
TOMA! NOT YOU TOO!
SWF
STOP IT! ARGH! NO PICTURES!
Aww!
C'MON, WHAT'S WRONG WITH IT? LEMME SNAP A FEW.
IT'LL MAKE A GREAT MEMORY!
YO!
ENOUGH MESSING AROUND. THE FIRST CHEER RALLY IS COMING UP.
OOPS! SORRY, MAN.
C'MON. LET'S GO.
AH. SURE.

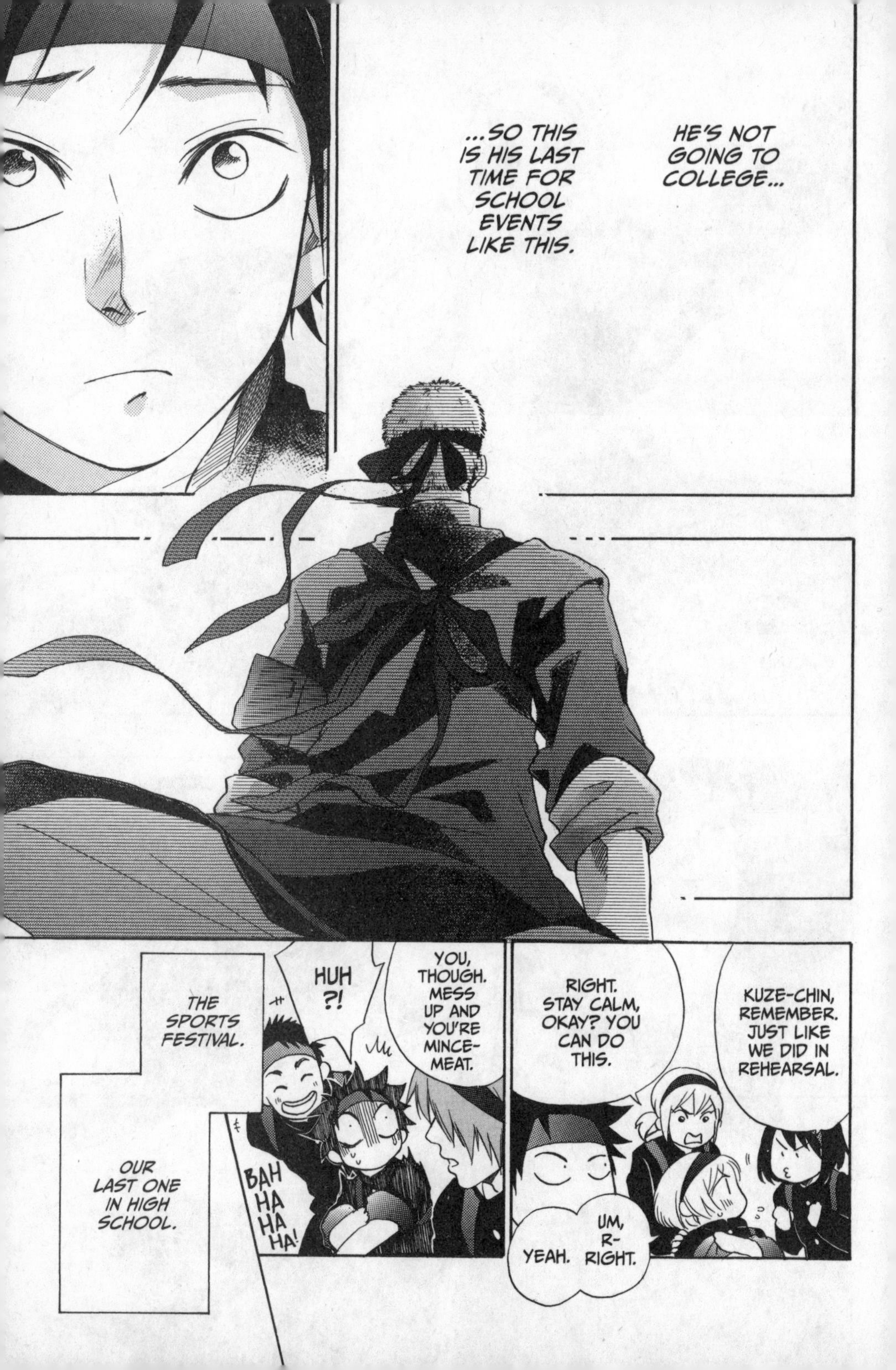
HE'S NOT GOING TO COLLEGE...
...SO THIS IS HIS LAST TIME FOR SCHOOL EVENTS LIKE THIS.
KUZE-CHIN, REMEMBER. JUST LIKE WE DID IN REHEARSAL.
RIGHT. STAY CALM, OKAY? YOU CAN DO THIS.
UM, R-RIGHT.
YEAH.
YOU, THOUGH. MESS UP AND YOU'RE MINCE-MEAT.
HUH ?!
THE SPORTS FESTIVAL.
BAH HA HA HA!
OUR LAST ONE IN HIGH SCHOOL.

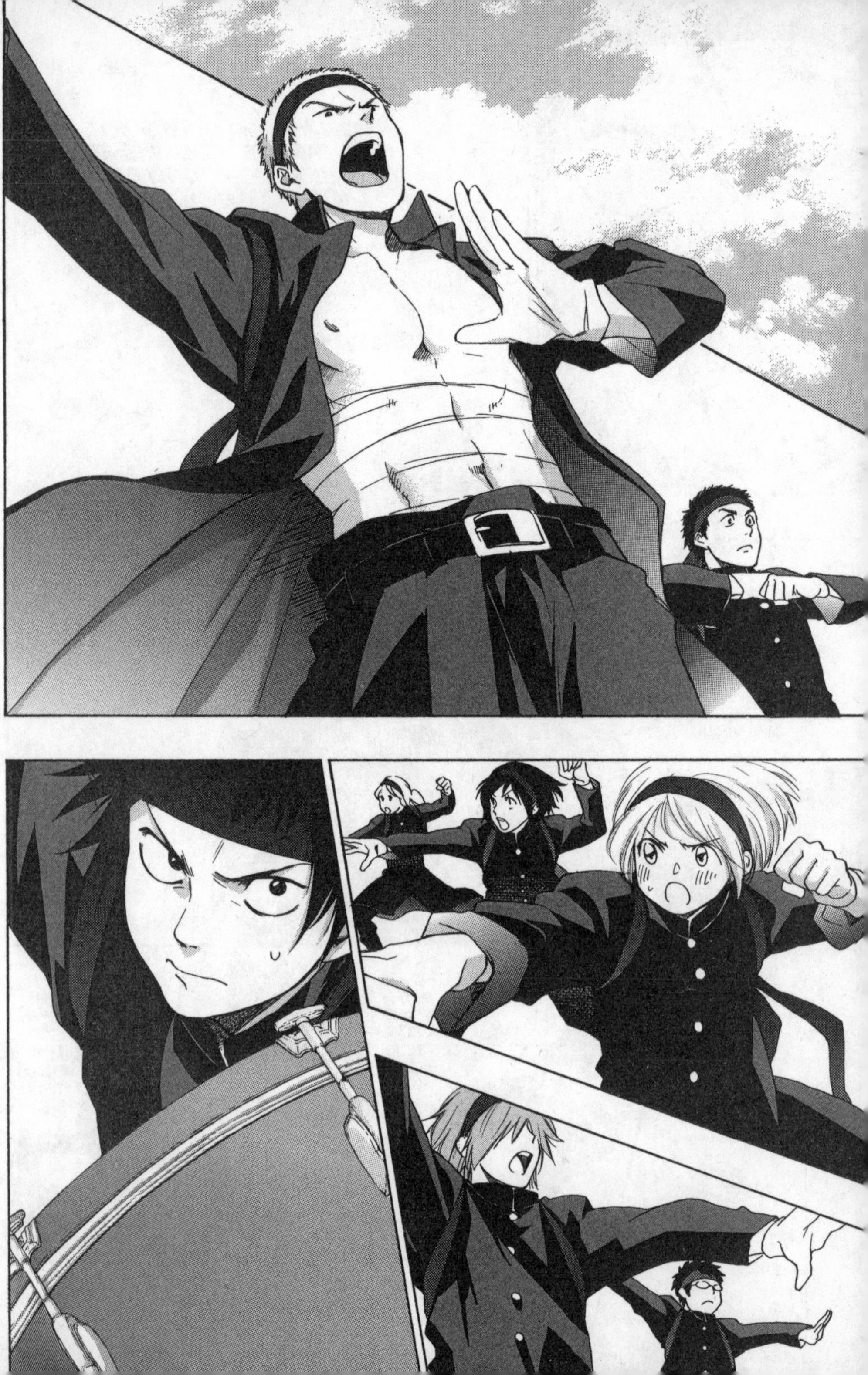

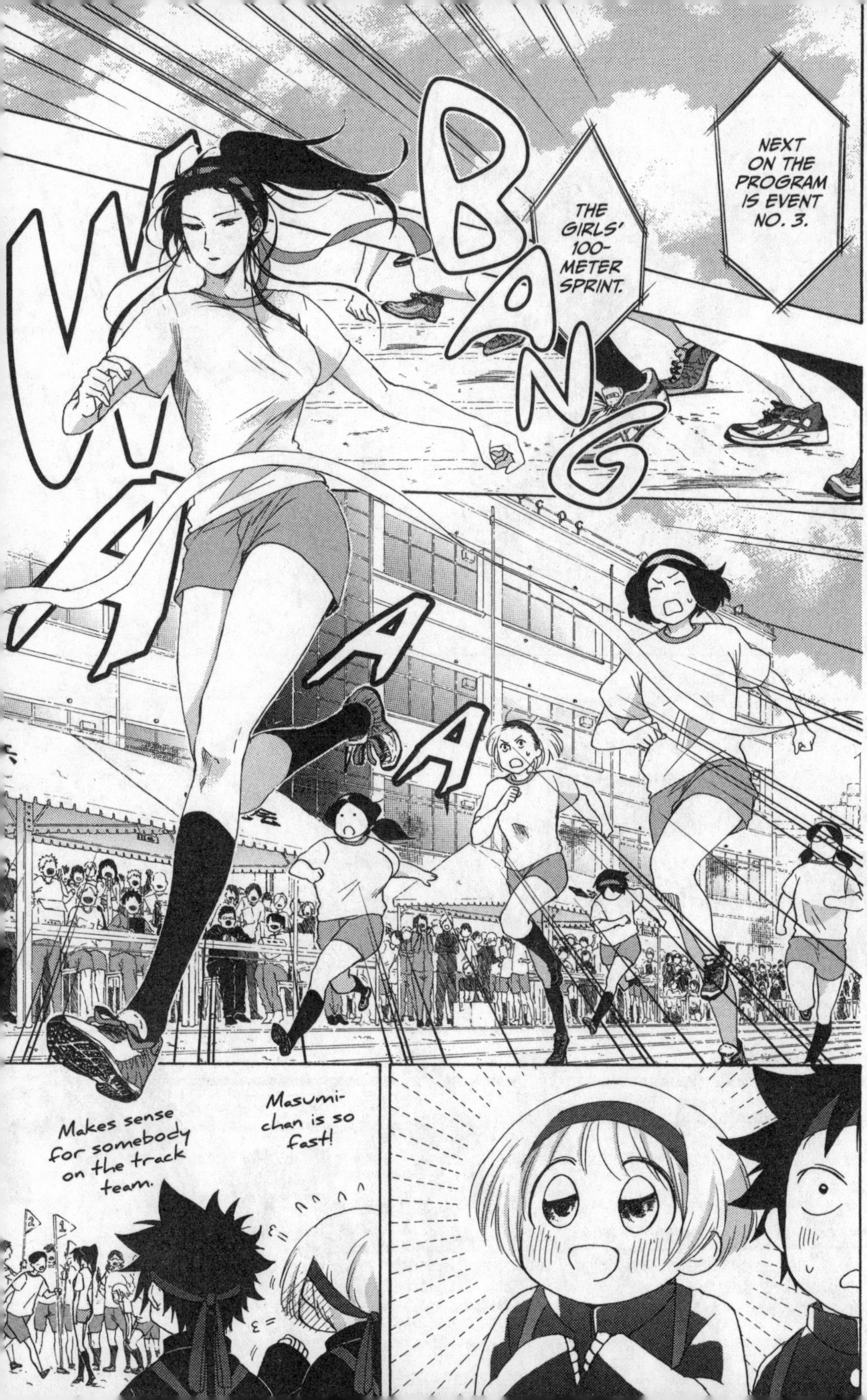
NEXT ON THE PROGRAM IS EVENT NO. 3.
THE GIRLS' 100-METER SPRINT.
BANG
WAAAA
Masumi-chan is so fast!
Makes sense for somebody on the track team.

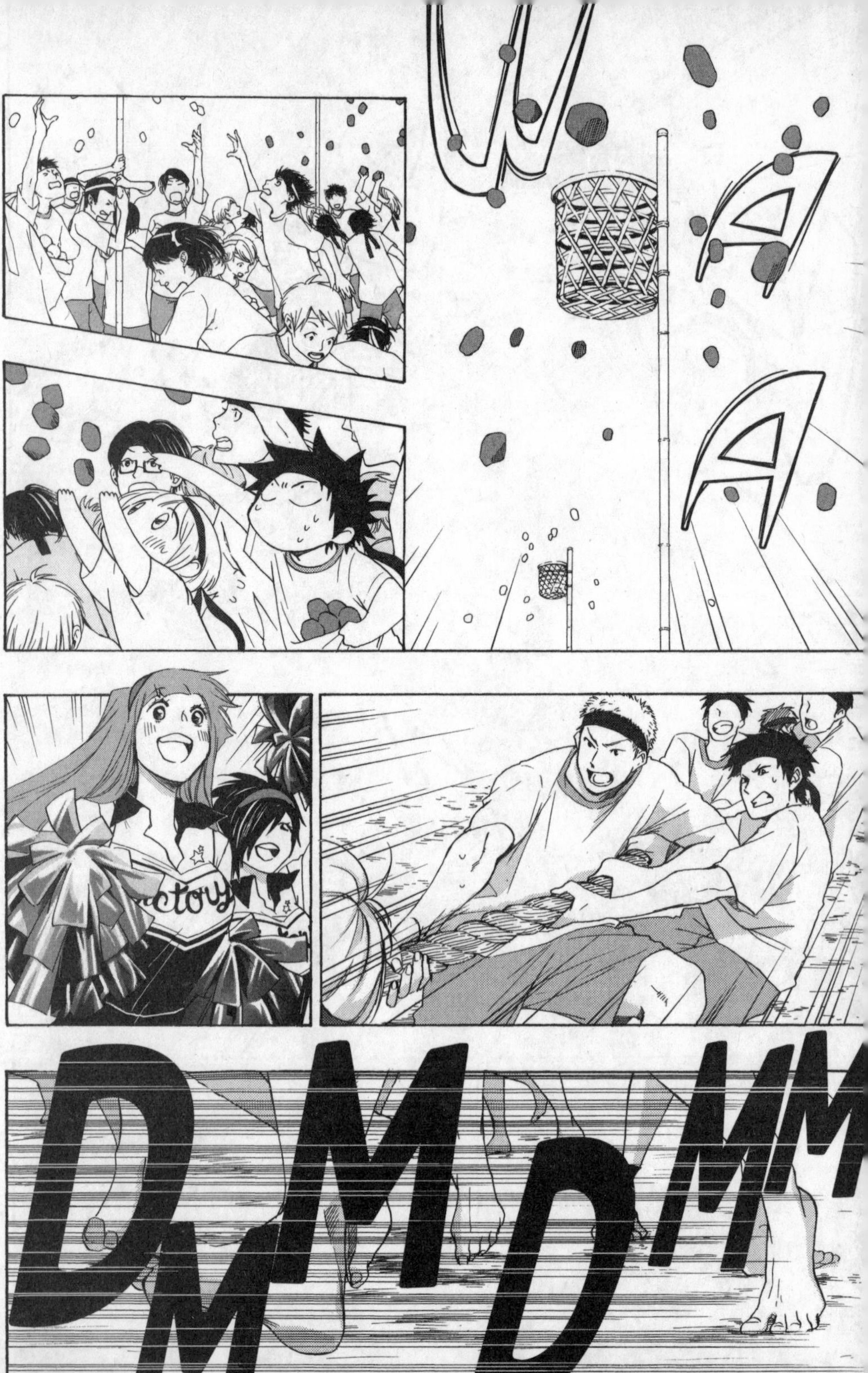
WAA
ctory
DMM DMMM

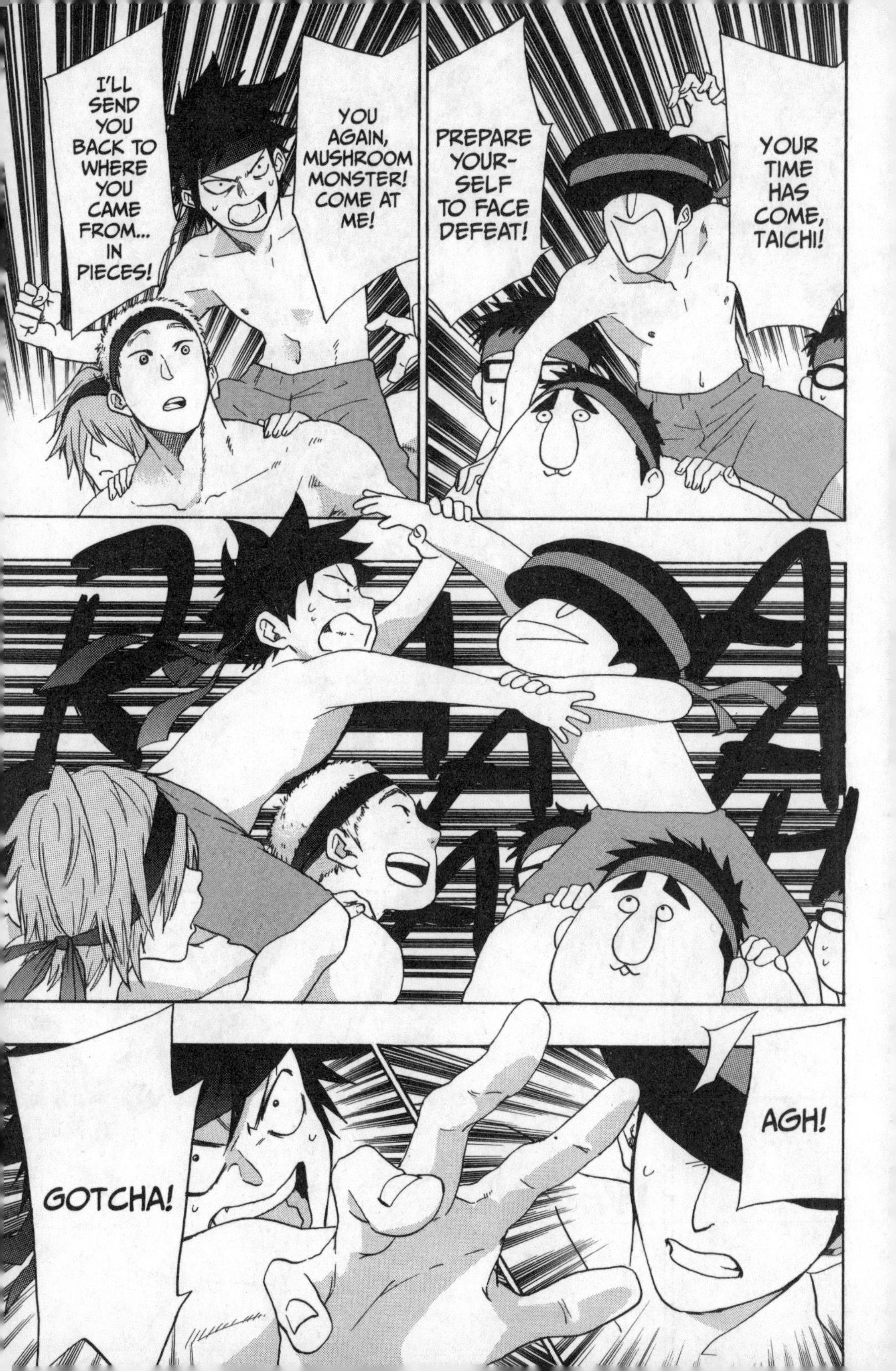
YOUR TIME HAS COME, TAICHI!
PREPARE YOUR-SELF TO FACE DEFEAT!
YOU AGAIN, MUSHROOM MONSTER! COME AT ME!
I'LL SEND YOU BACK TO WHERE YOU CAME FROM... IN PIECES!
AGH!
GOTCHA!

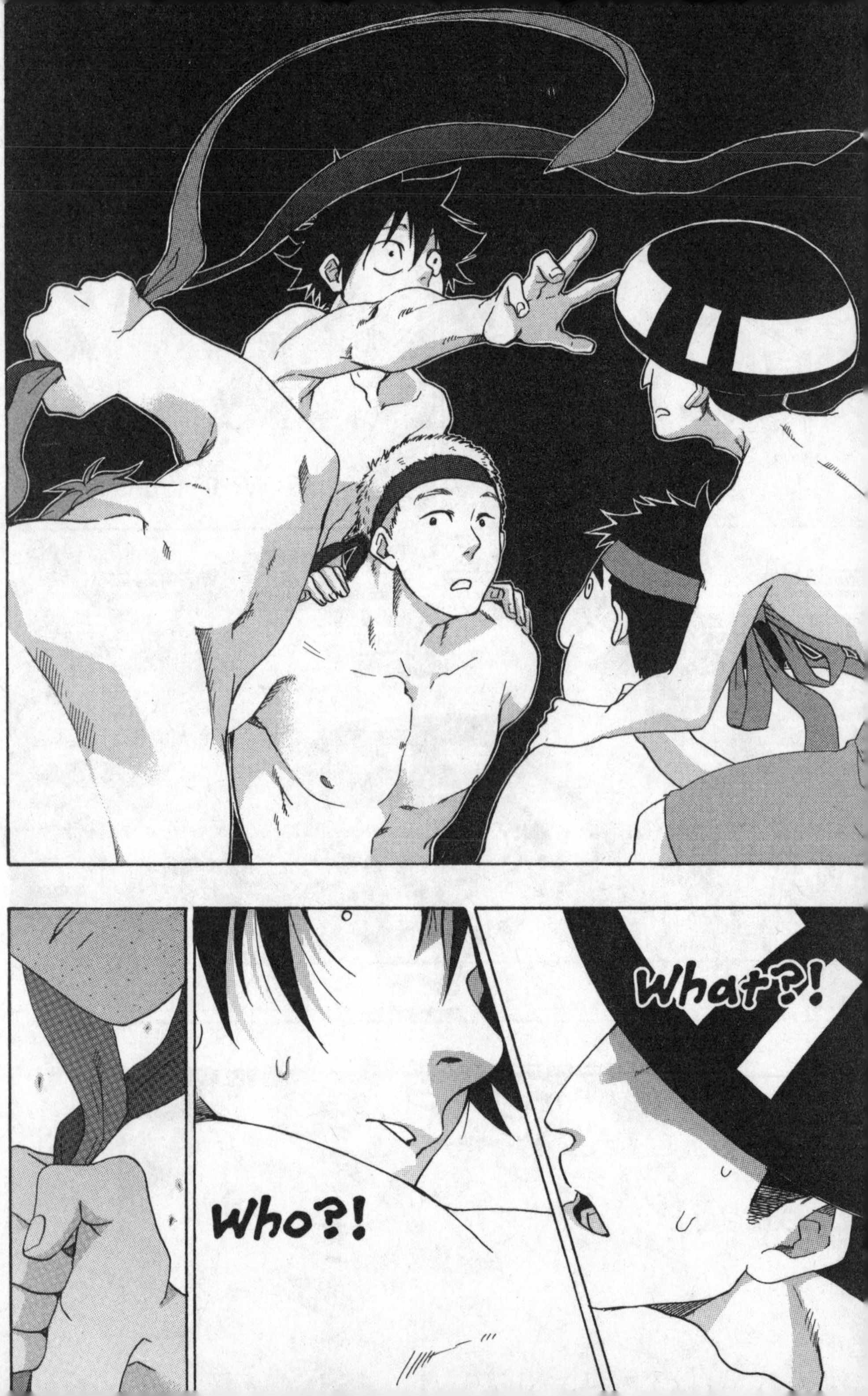
What?!
Who?!

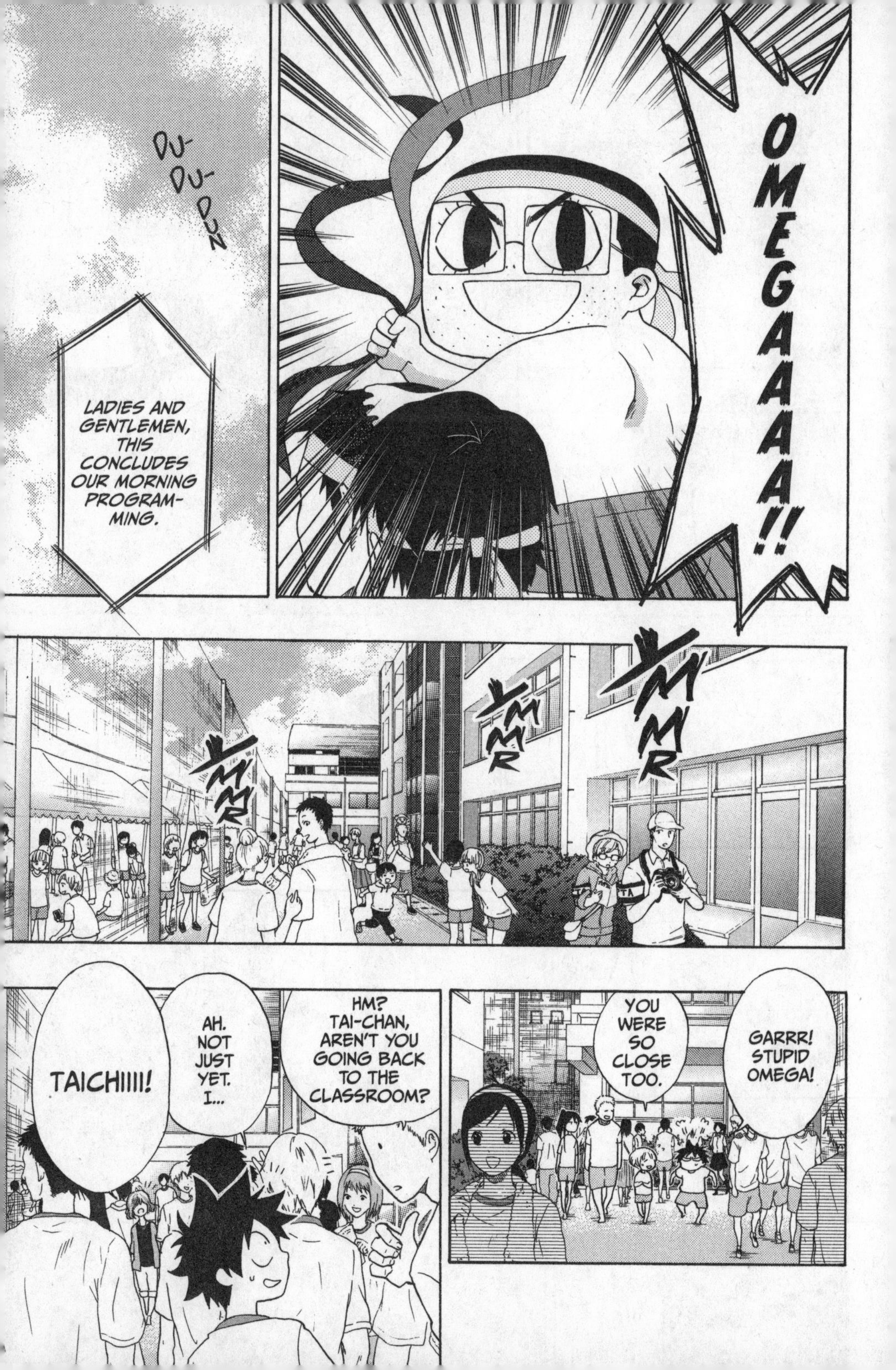
OMEGAAAAA!!
DU-DU-DUN
LADIES AND GENTLEMEN, THIS CONCLUDES OUR MORNING PROGRAM-MING.
MMR
MMR
MMR
GARRR! STUPID OMEGA!
YOU WERE SO CLOSE TOO.
HM? TAI-CHAN, AREN'T YOU GOING BACK TO THE CLASSROOM?
AH. NOT JUST YET. I...
TAICHIIIII!

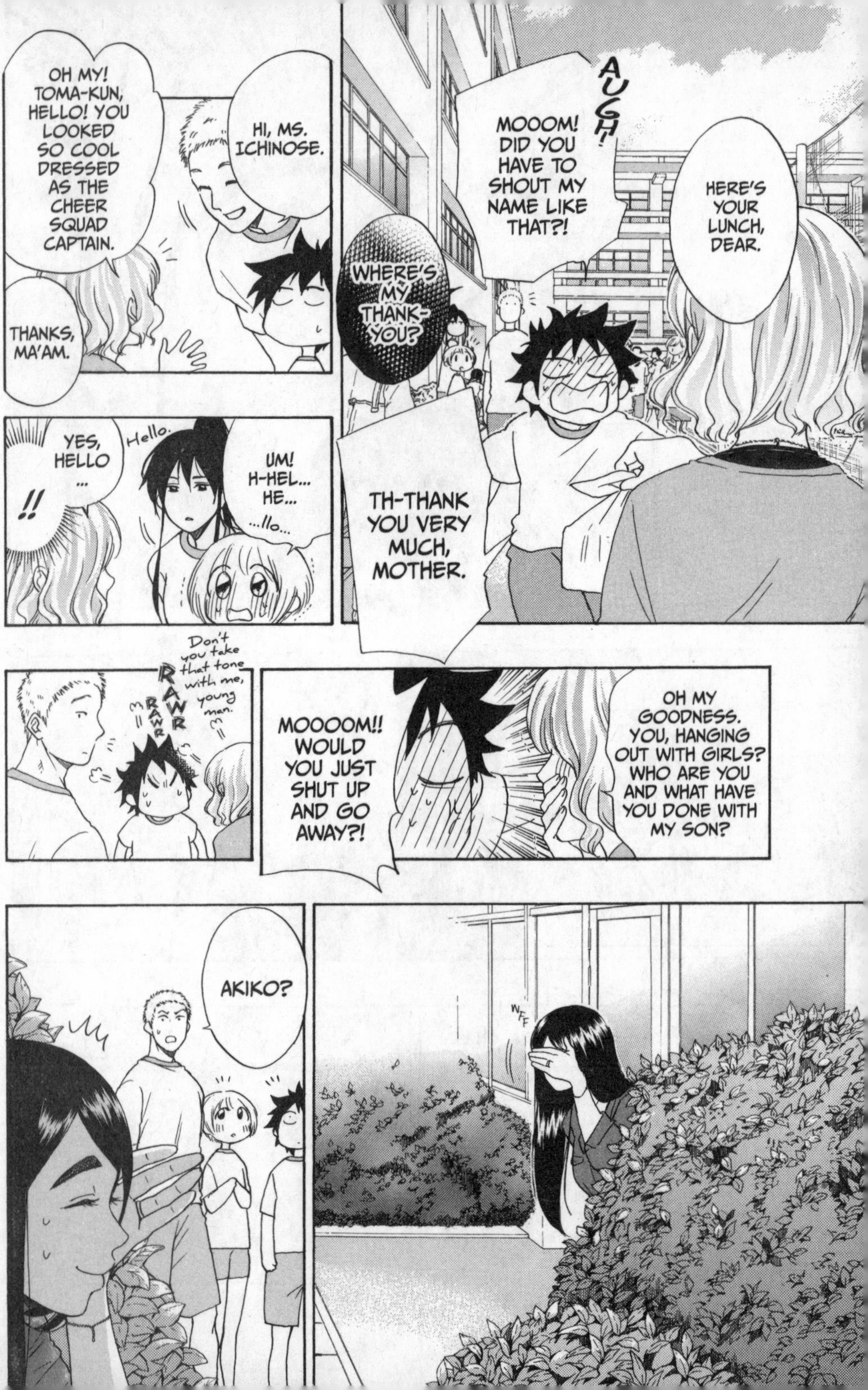
HERE'S YOUR LUNCH, DEAR.
AUGH!
MOOOM! DID YOU HAVE TO SHOUT MY NAME LIKE THAT?!
WHERE'S MY THANK-YOU?
TH-THANK YOU VERY MUCH, MOTHER.
HI, MS. ICHINOSE.
OH MY! TOMA-KUN, HELLO! YOU LOOKED SO COOL DRESSED AS THE CHEER SQUAD CAPTAIN.
THANKS, MA'AM.
Hello.
YES, HELLO ...
!!
UM! H-HEL... HE... ...llo...
OH MY GOODNESS. YOU, HANGING OUT WITH GIRLS? WHO ARE YOU AND WHAT HAVE YOU DONE WITH MY SON?
MOOOOM!! WOULD YOU JUST SHUT UP AND GO AWAY?!
Don't you take that tone with me, young man.
RAWR
RAWR
WFF
AKIKO?

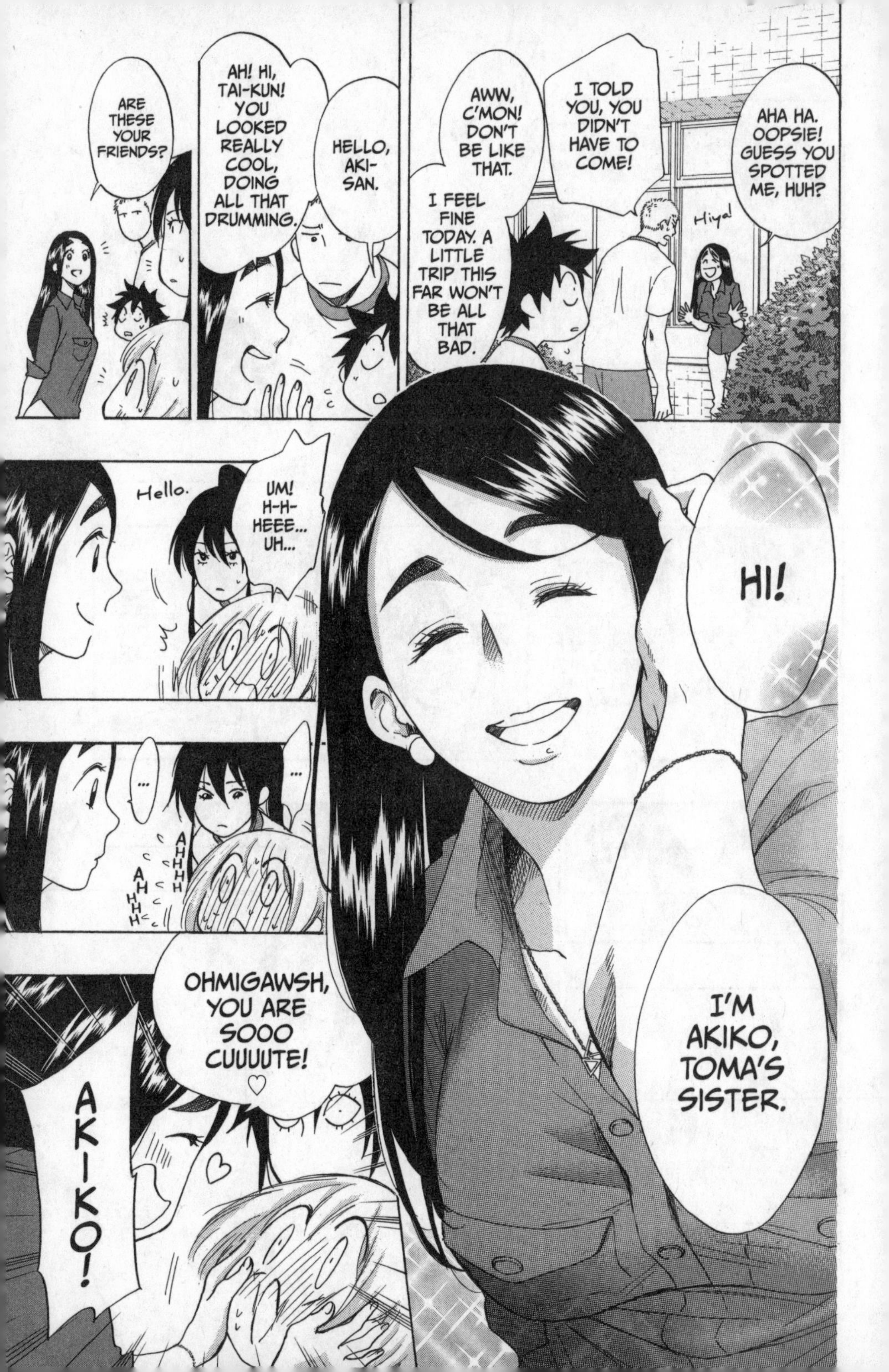
AHA HA. OOPSIE! GUESS YOU SPOTTED ME, HUH?
Hiya!
I TOLD YOU, YOU DIDN'T HAVE TO COME!
AWW, C'MON! DON'T BE LIKE THAT.
I FEEL FINE TODAY. A LITTLE TRIP THIS FAR WON'T BE ALL THAT BAD.
HELLO, AKI-SAN.
AH! HI, TAI-KUN! YOU LOOKED REALLY COOL, DOING ALL THAT DRUMMING.
ARE THESE YOUR FRIENDS?
HI!
I'M AKIKO, TOMA'S SISTER.
UM! H-H-HEEE... UH...
Hello.
...
...
AHHHH
AHHHH
OHMIGAWSH, YOU ARE SOOO CUUUUTE! ♡
AKIKO!

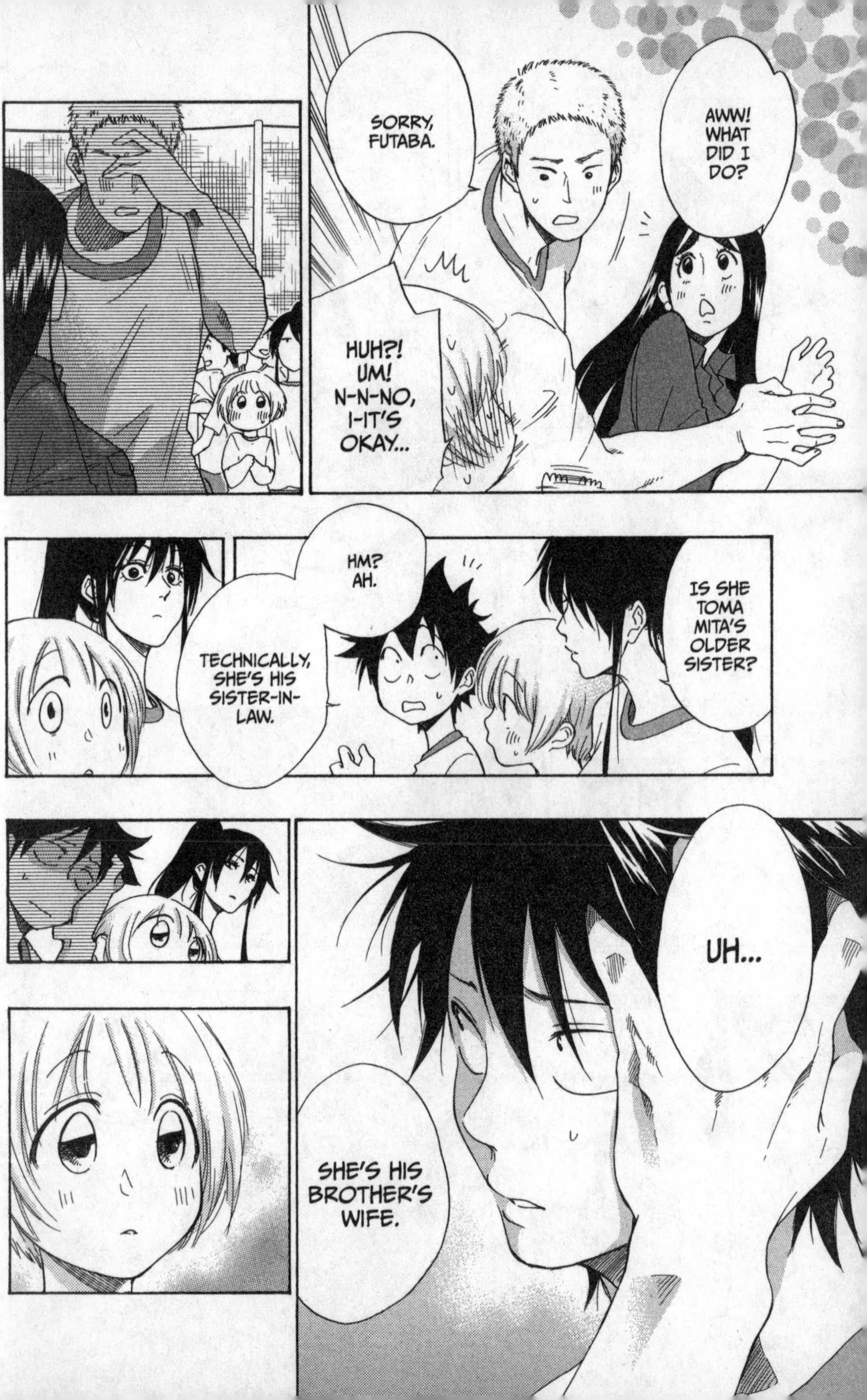
AWW! WHAT DID I DO?
SORRY, FUTABA.
HUH?! UM! N-N-NO, I-IT'S OKAY...
IS SHE TOMA MITA'S OLDER SISTER?
HM? AH.
TECHNICALLY, SHE'S HIS SISTER-IN-LAW.
UH...
SHE'S HIS BROTHER'S WIFE.

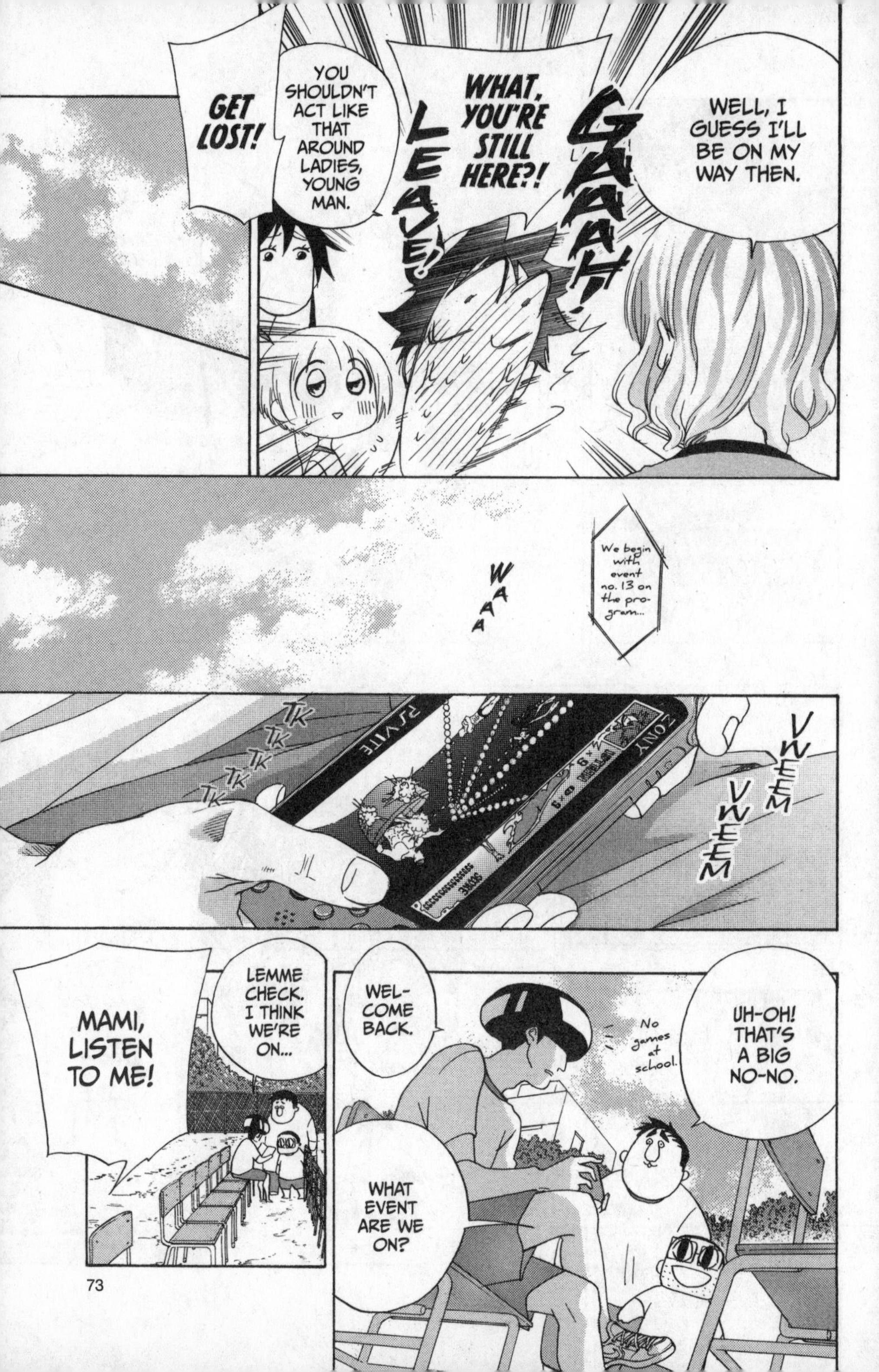
WELL, I GUESS I'LL BE ON MY WAY THEN.
GAAAH!
WHAT, YOU'RE STILL HERE?!
LEAVE!
YOU SHOULDN'T ACT LIKE THAT AROUND LADIES, YOUNG MAN.
GET LOST!
We begin with event no. 13 on the program...
WAAA
VWEEM
VWEEM
TK TK TK TK TK
UH-OH! THAT'S A BIG NO-NO.
No games at school.
WEL-COME BACK.
WHAT EVENT ARE WE ON?
LEMME CHECK. I THINK WE'RE ON...
MAMI, LISTEN TO ME!

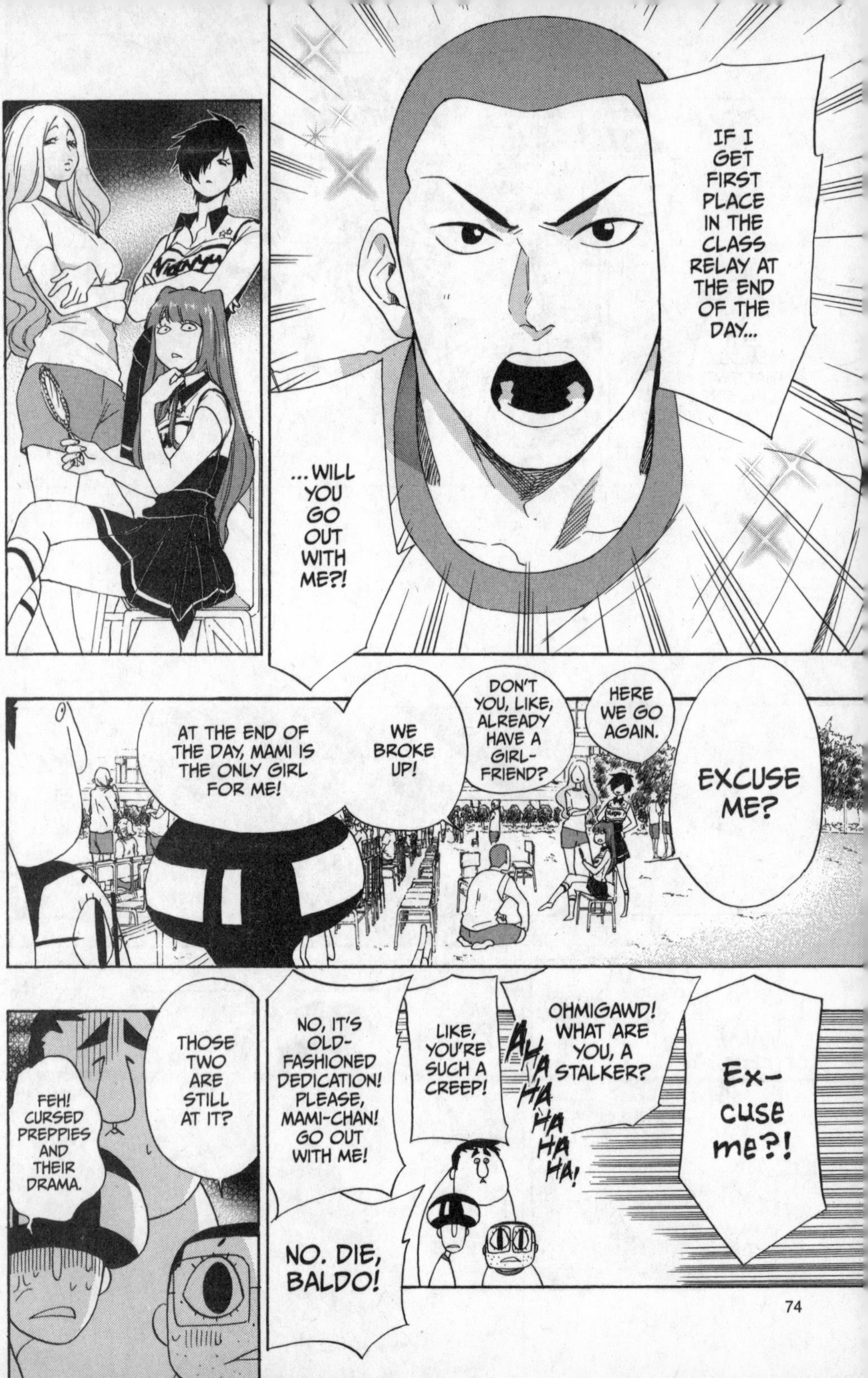
IF I GET FIRST PLACE IN THE CLASS RELAY AT THE END OF THE DAY...
...WILL YOU GO OUT WITH ME?!
EXCUSE ME?
HERE WE GO AGAIN.
DON'T YOU, LIKE, ALREADY HAVE A GIRL-FRIEND?
WE BROKE UP!
AT THE END OF THE DAY, MAMI IS THE ONLY GIRL FOR ME!
Ex-cuse me?!
OHMIGAWD! WHAT ARE YOU, A STALKER?
AHA HA HA HA HA!
LIKE, YOU'RE SUCH A CREEP!
NO, IT'S OLD-FASHIONED DEDICATION! PLEASE, MAMI-CHAN! GO OUT WITH ME!
NO. DIE, BALDO!
THOSE TWO ARE STILL AT IT?
FEH! CURSED PREPPIES AND THEIR DRAMA.

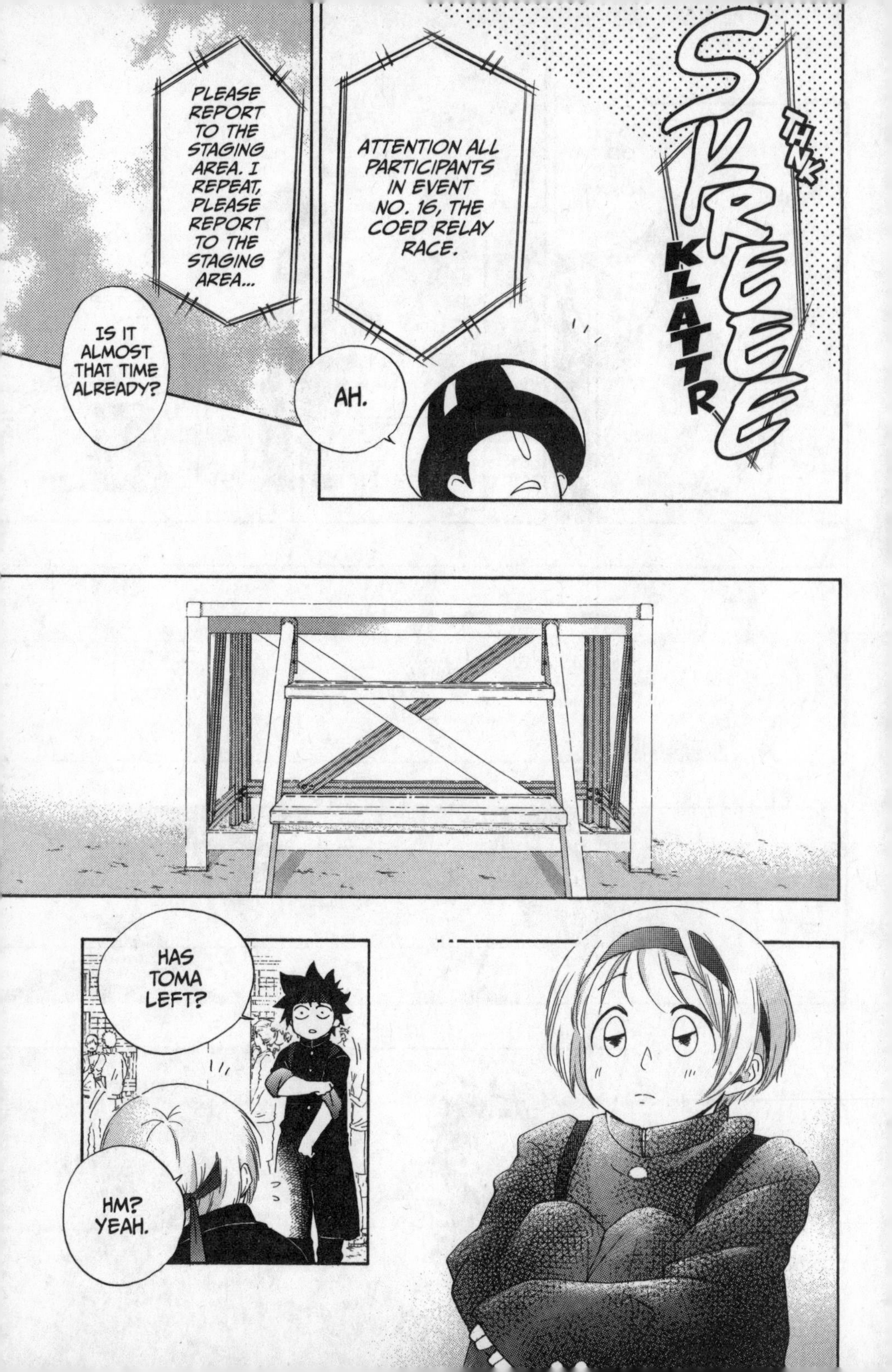

SKREEEE
THNK
KLATTR
ATTENTION ALL PARTICIPANTS IN EVENT NO. 16, THE COED RELAY RACE.
PLEASE REPORT TO THE STAGING AREA. I REPEAT, PLEASE REPORT TO THE STAGING AREA...
AH.
IS IT ALMOST THAT TIME ALREADY?
HAS TOMA LEFT?
HM? YEAH.

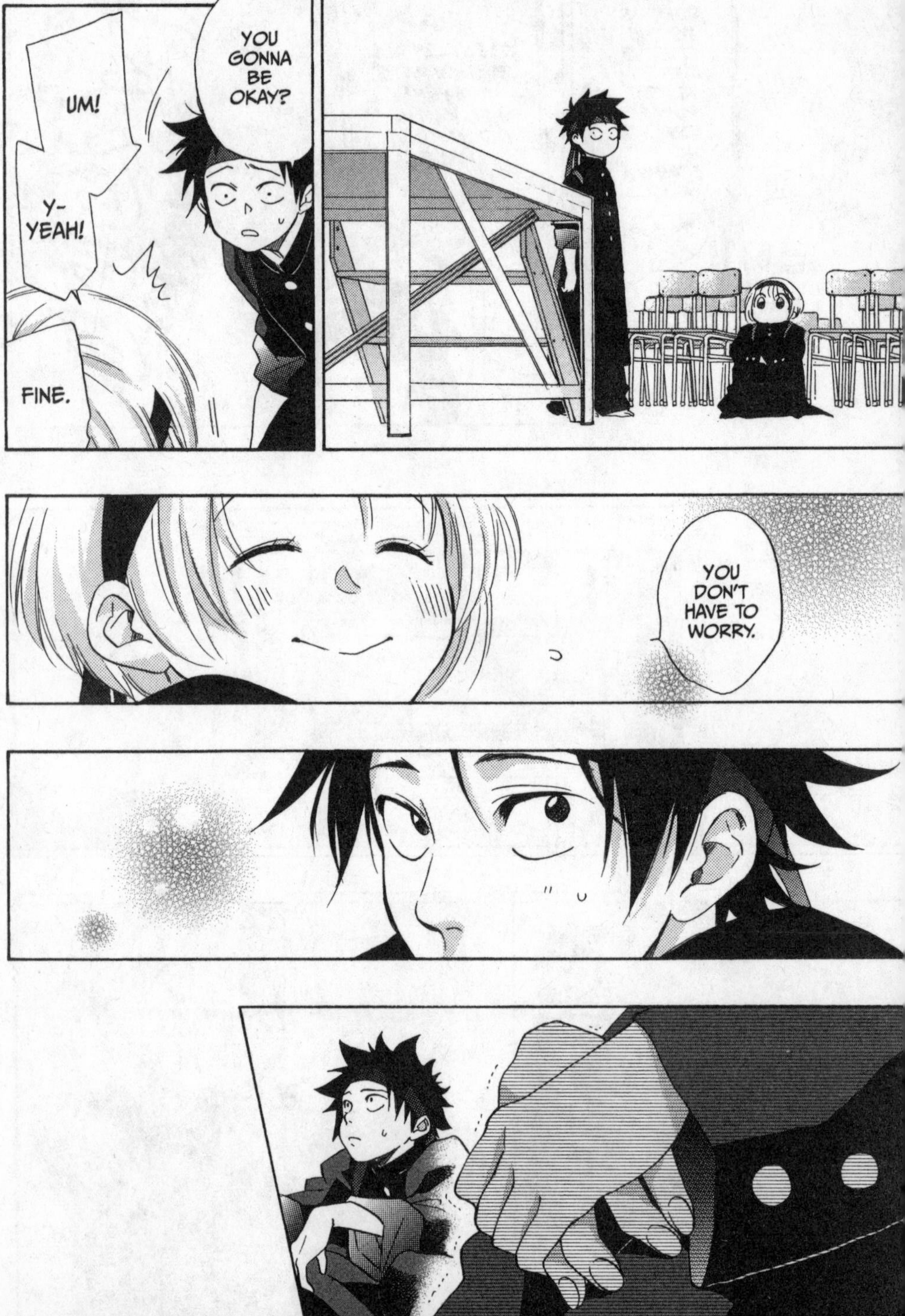
YOU GONNA BE OKAY?
UM!
Y-YEAH!
FINE.
YOU DON'T HAVE TO WORRY.

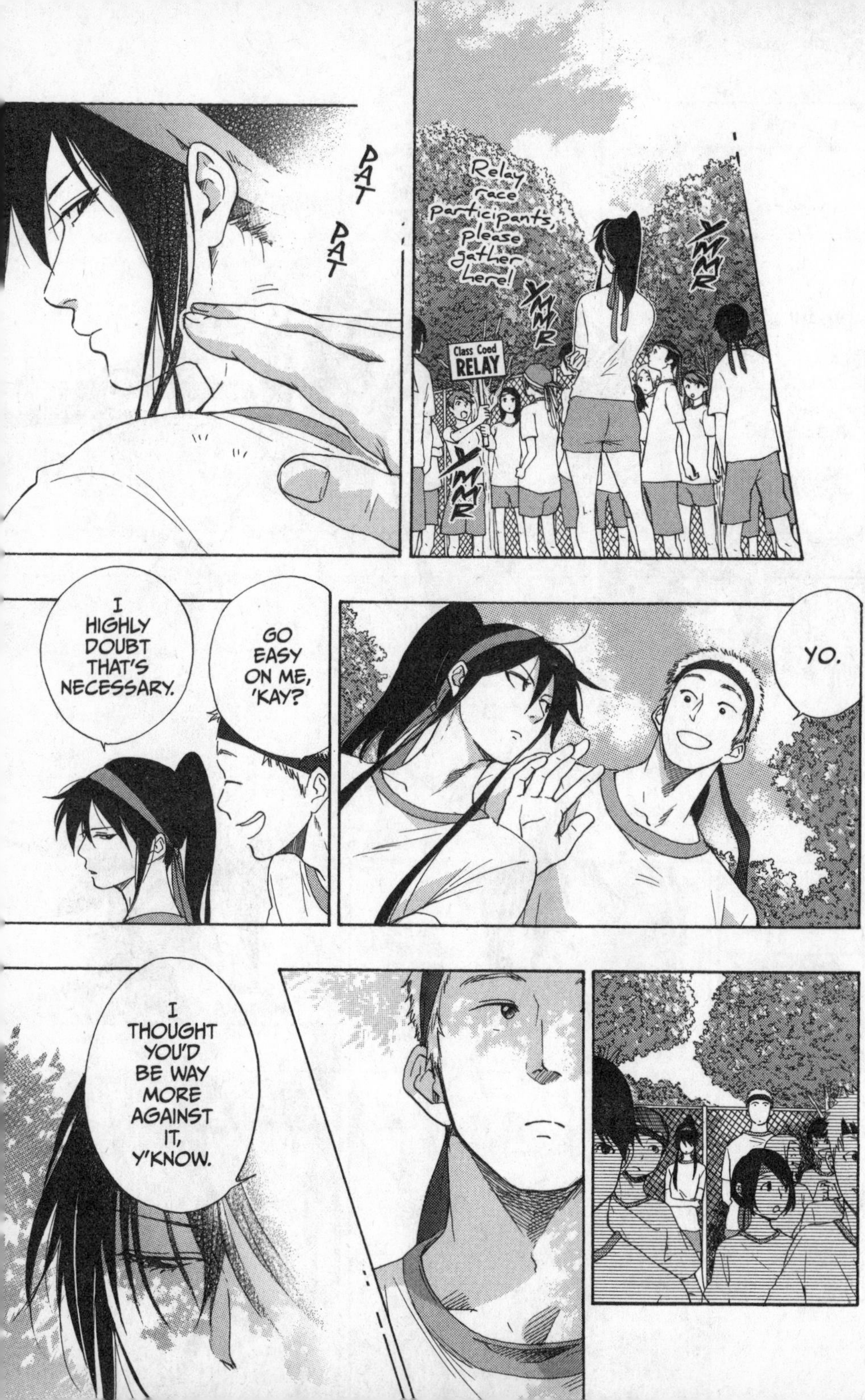
Relay race participants, please gather here!
YMMR
YMMR
Class Coed RELAY
YMMR
PAT
PAT
PAT
YO.
GO EASY ON ME, 'KAY?
I HIGHLY DOUBT THAT'S NECESSARY.
I THOUGHT YOU'D BE WAY MORE AGAINST IT, Y'KNOW.

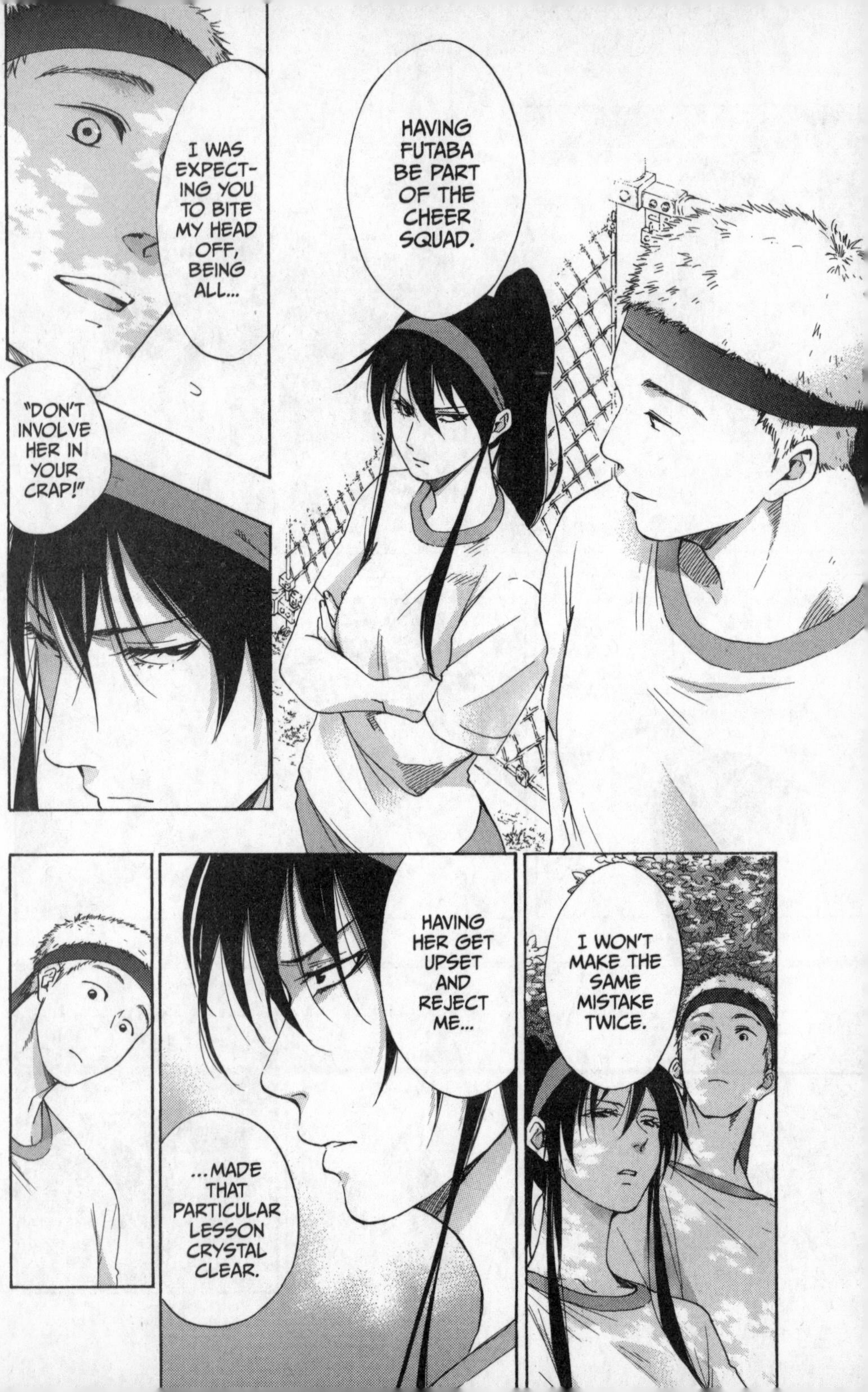
HAVING FUTABA BE PART OF THE CHEER SQUAD.
I WAS EXPECTING YOU TO BITE MY HEAD OFF, BEING ALL...
"DON'T INVOLVE HER IN YOUR CRAP!"
I WON'T MAKE THE SAME MISTAKE TWICE.
HAVING HER GET UPSET AND REJECT ME...
...MADE THAT PARTICULAR LESSON CRYSTAL CLEAR.

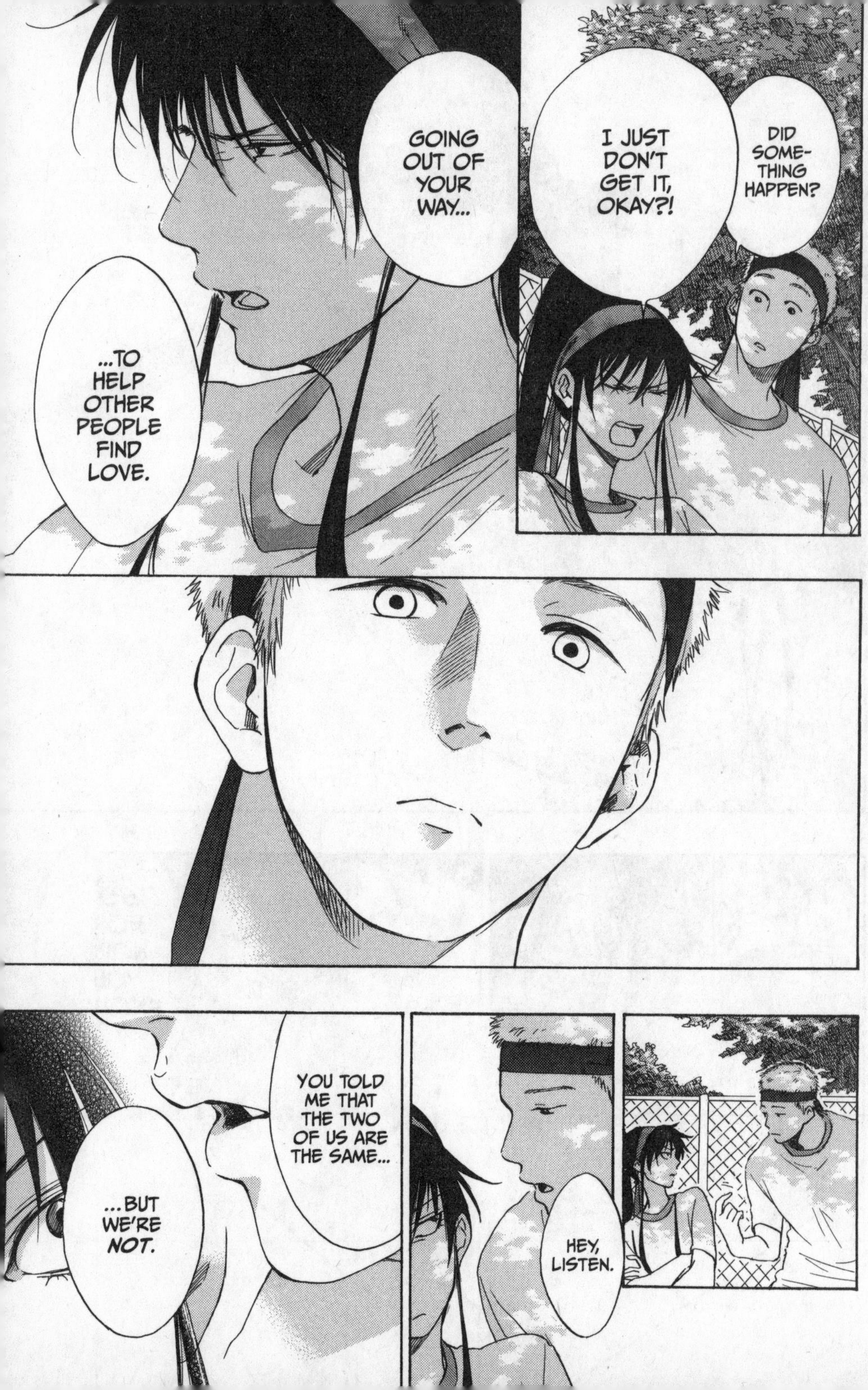
DID SOMETHING HAPPEN?
I JUST DON'T GET IT, OKAY?!
GOING OUT OF YOUR WAY...
...TO HELP OTHER PEOPLE FIND LOVE.
HEY, LISTEN.
YOU TOLD ME THAT THE TWO OF US ARE THE SAME...
...BUT WE'RE *NOT*.

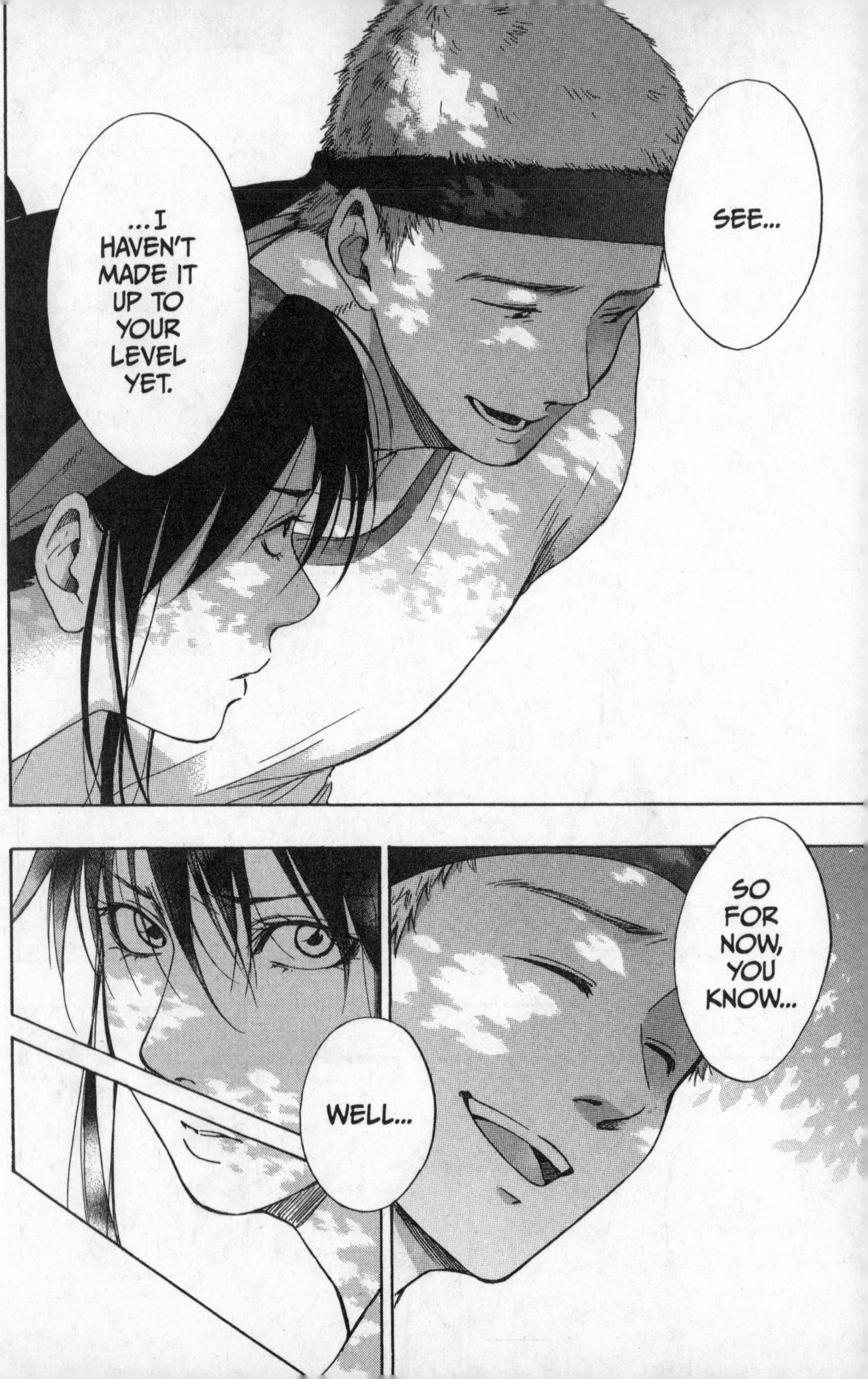
SEE...
...I HAVEN'T MADE IT UP TO YOUR LEVEL YET.
SO FOR NOW, YOU KNOW...
WELL...

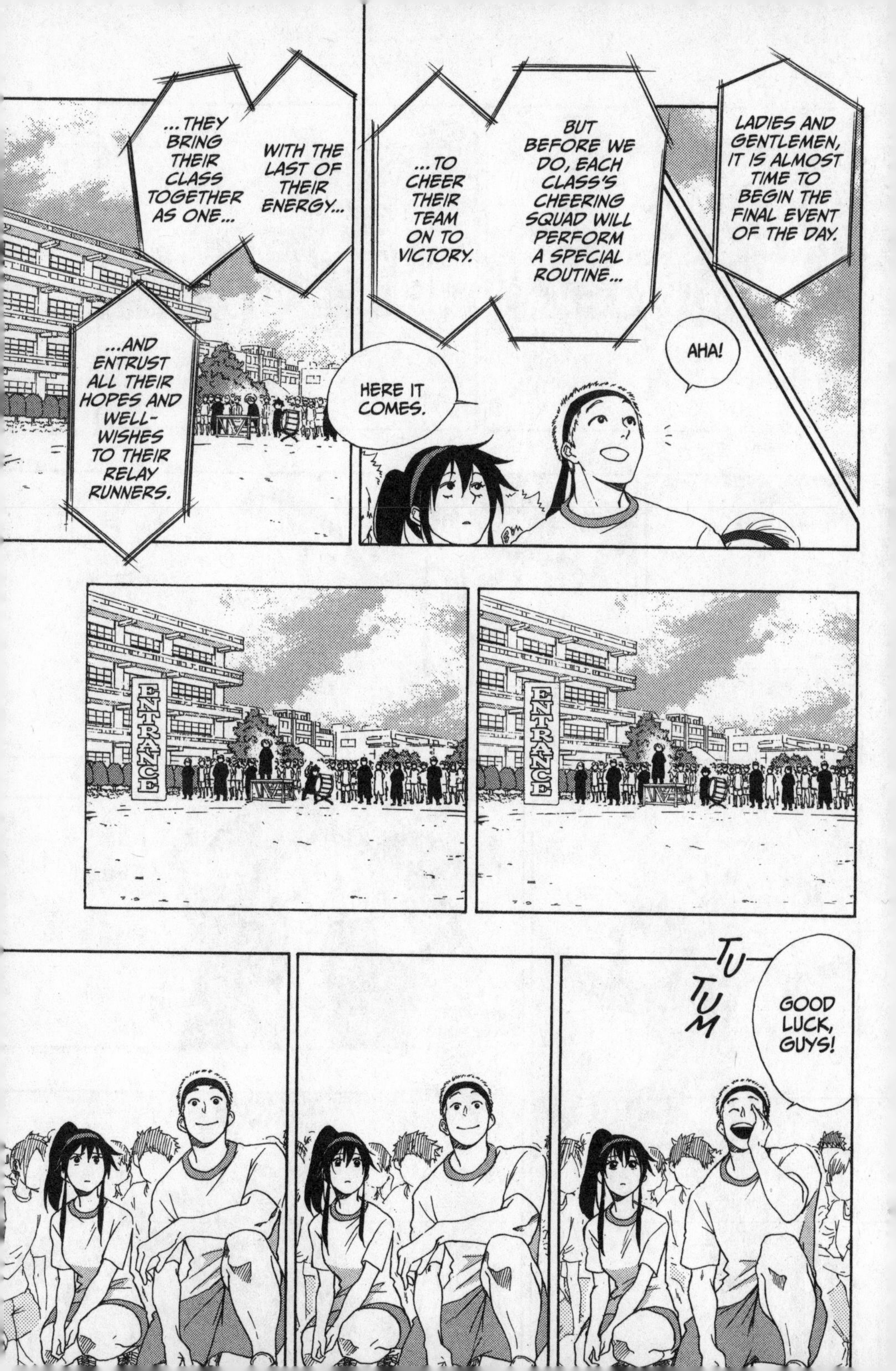
LADIES AND GENTLEMEN, IT IS ALMOST TIME TO BEGIN THE FINAL EVENT OF THE DAY.
BUT BEFORE WE DO, EACH CLASS'S CHEERING SQUAD WILL PERFORM A SPECIAL ROUTINE...
...TO CHEER THEIR TEAM ON TO VICTORY.
AHA!
HERE IT COMES.
WITH THE LAST OF THEIR ENERGY...
...THEY BRING THEIR CLASS TOGETHER AS ONE...
...AND ENTRUST ALL THEIR HOPES AND WELL-WISHES TO THEIR RELAY RUNNERS.
ENTRANCE
ENTRANCE
TU TUM
GOOD LUCK, GUYS!

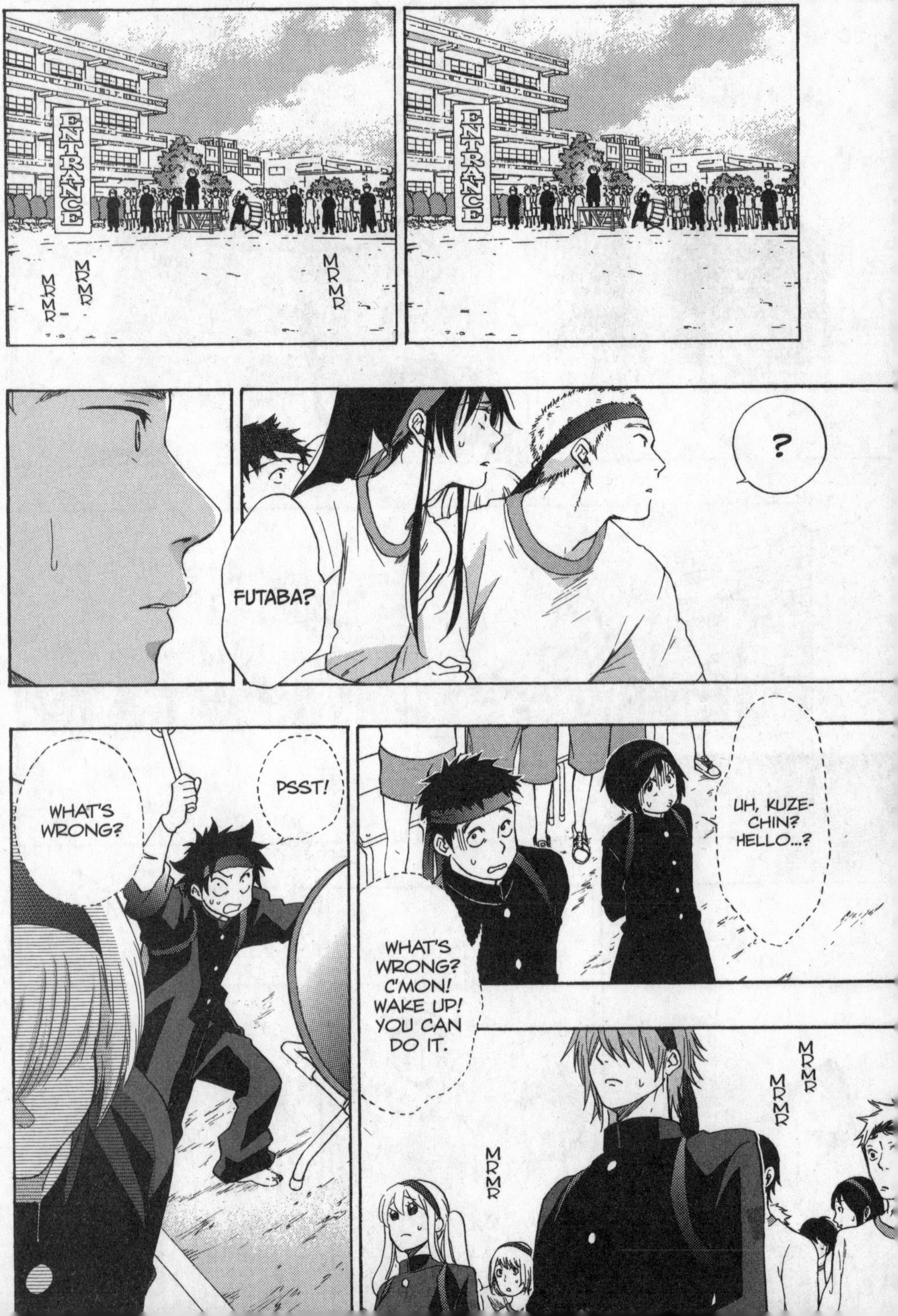
ENTRANCE
ENTRANCE
MRMR
MRMR
MRMR
?
FUTABA?
UH, KUZE-CHIN? HELLO...?
WHAT'S WRONG? C'MON! WAKE UP! YOU CAN DO IT.
MRMR
MRMR
MRMR
PSST!
WHAT'S WRONG?

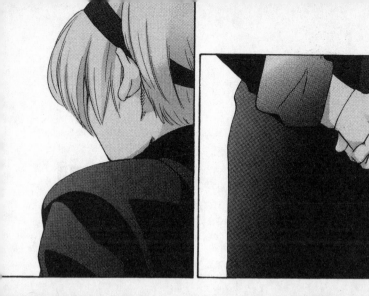

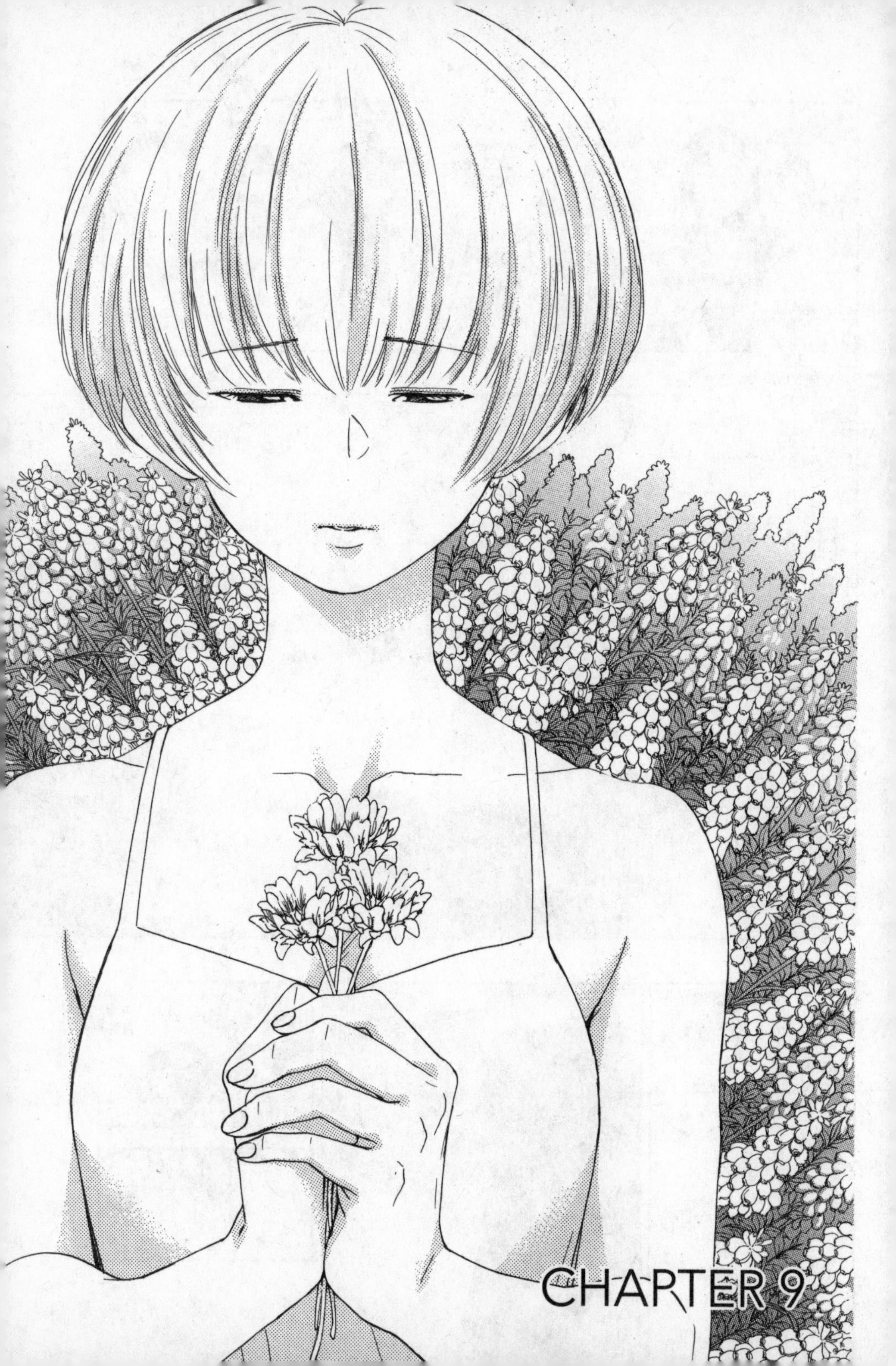
CHAPTER 9

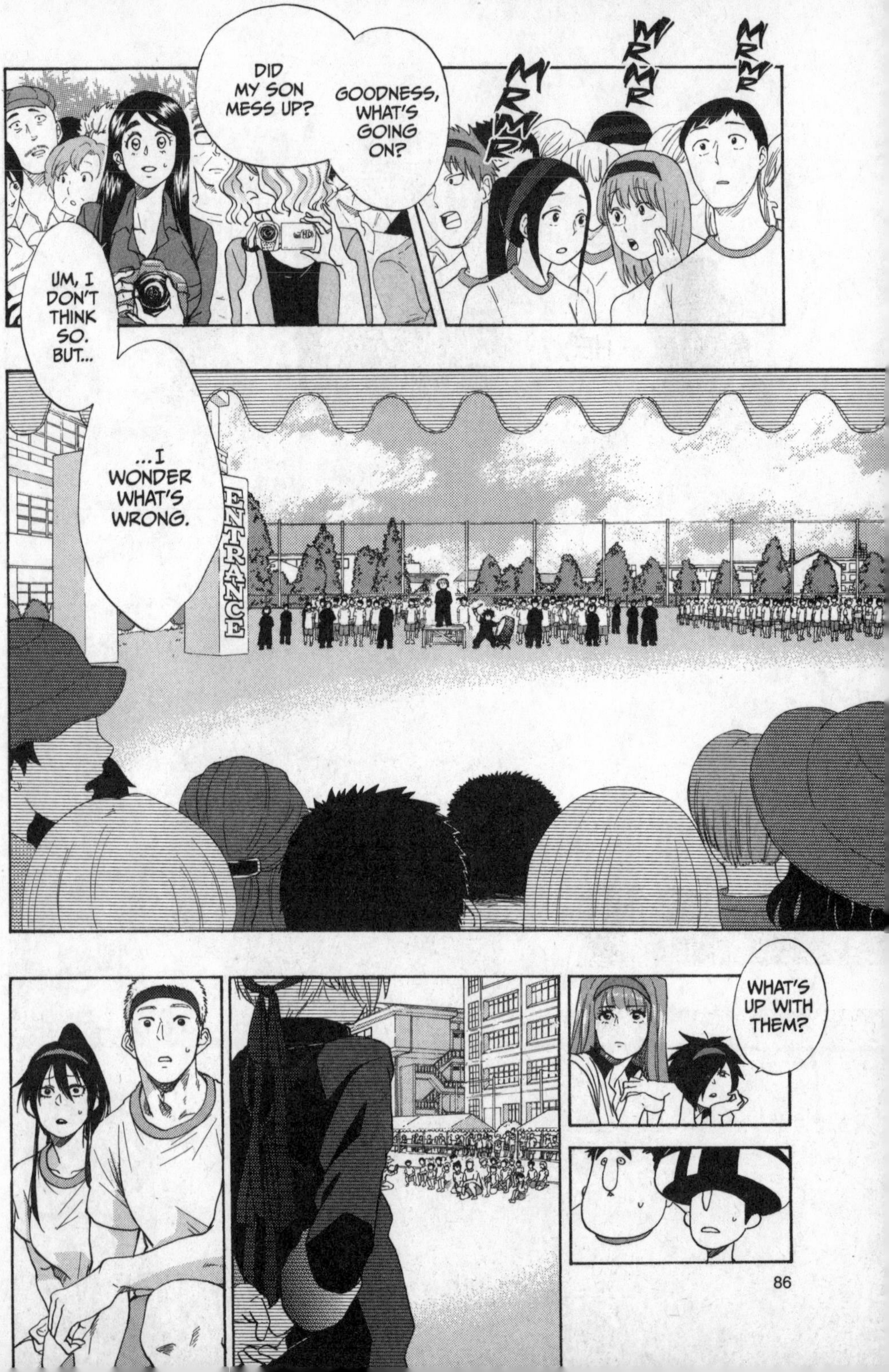
MRMR
MRMR
MRMR
GOODNESS, WHAT'S GOING ON?
DID MY SON MESS UP?
UM, I DON'T THINK SO. BUT...
...I WONDER WHAT'S WRONG.
ENTRANCE
WHAT'S UP WITH THEM?

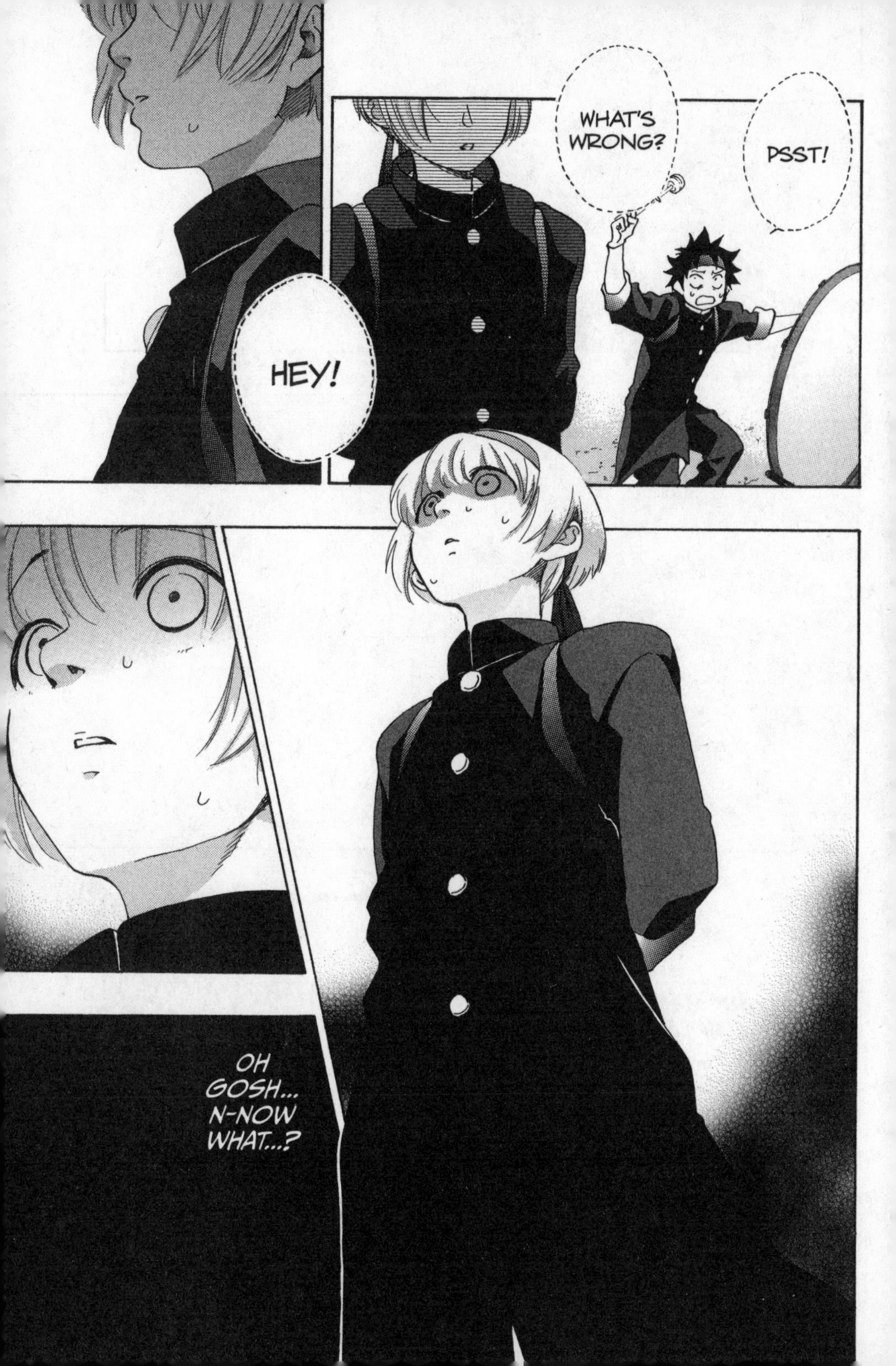
PSST!
WHAT'S WRONG?
HEY!
OH GOSH... N-NOW WHAT...?

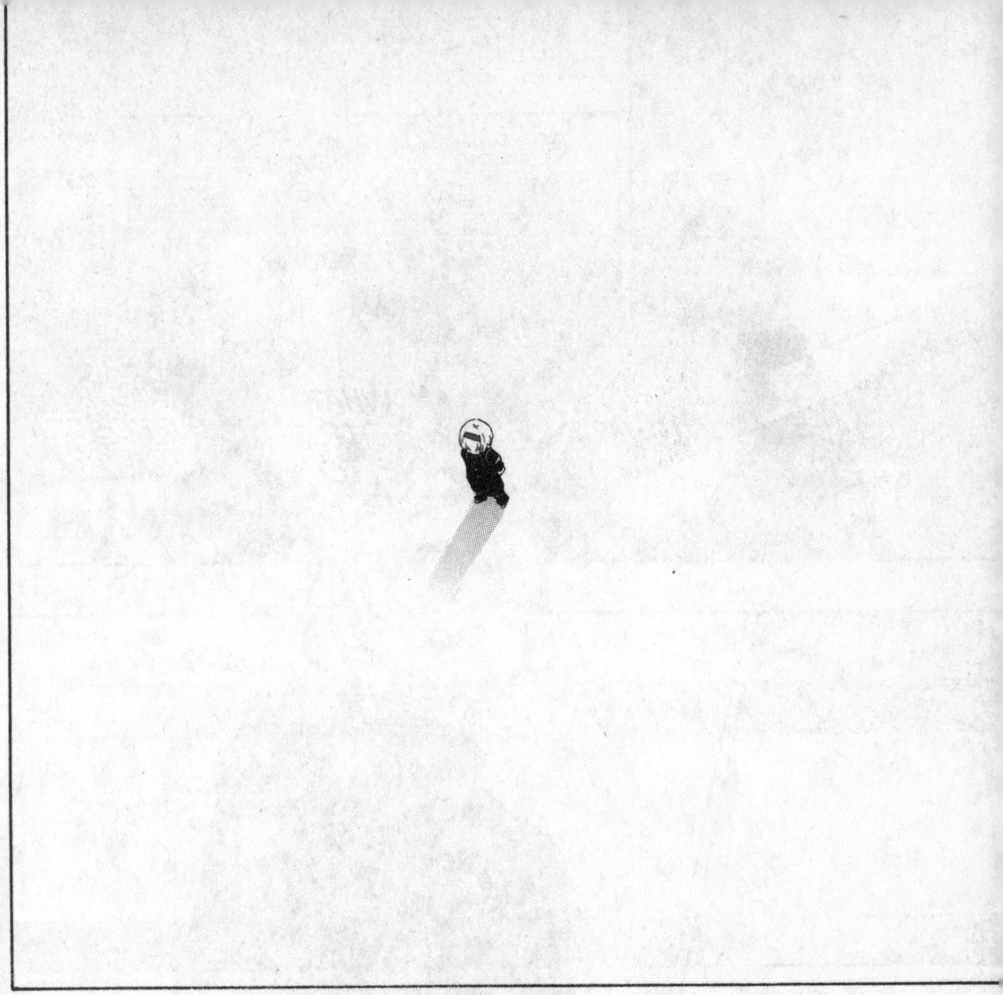

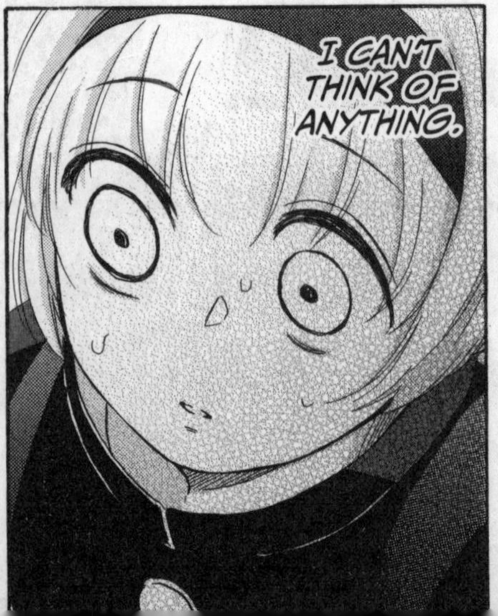
I CAN'T THINK OF ANYTHING.

MY MIND'S COMPLETELY BLANK.

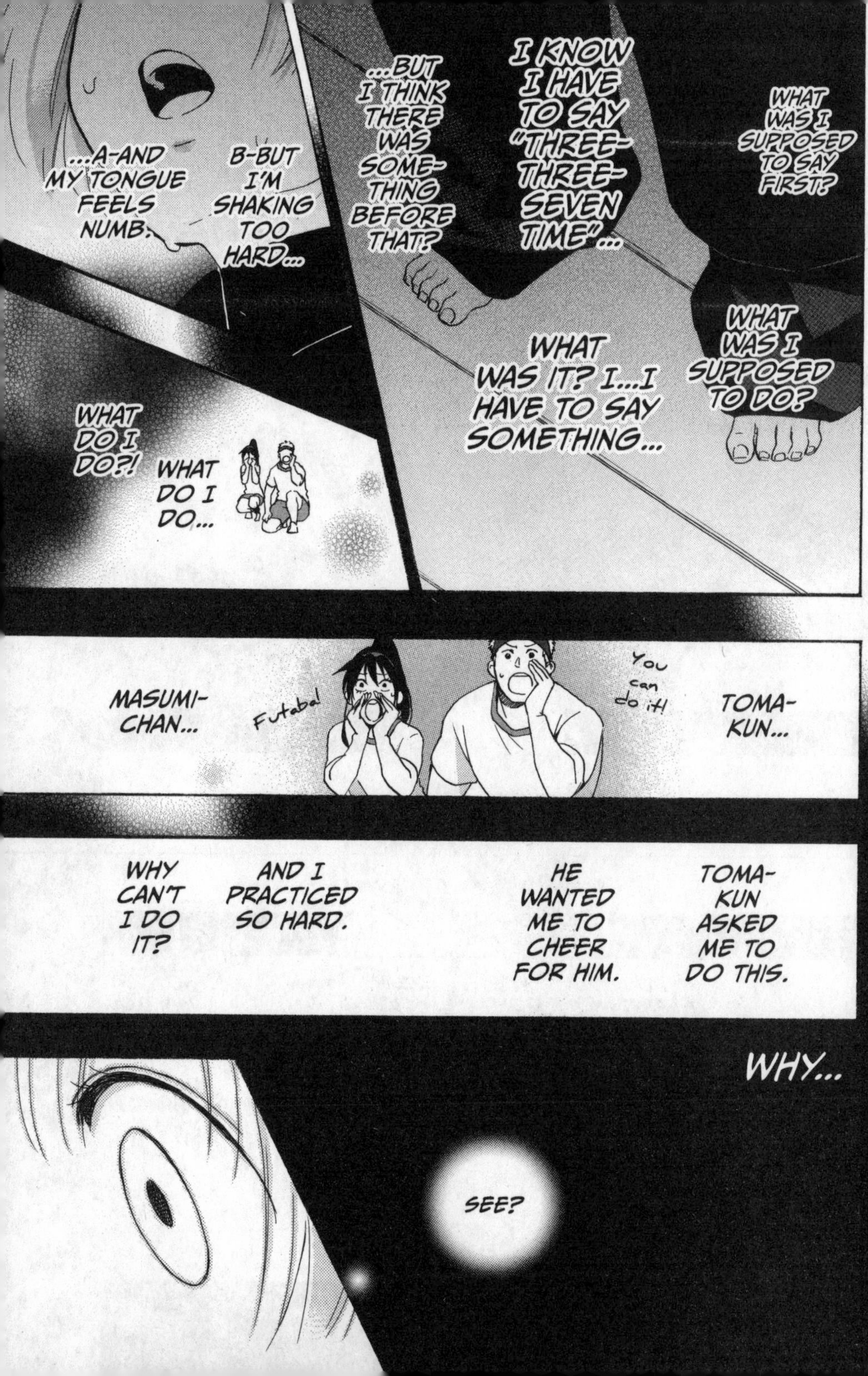
WHAT WAS I SUPPOSED TO SAY FIRST?
I KNOW I HAVE TO SAY "THREE-THREE-SEVEN TIME"...
...BUT I THINK THERE WAS SOMETHING BEFORE THAT?
B-BUT I'M SHAKING TOO HARD...
...A-AND MY TONGUE FEELS NUMB.
WHAT WAS I SUPPOSED TO DO?
WHAT WAS IT? I...I HAVE TO SAY SOMETHING...
WHAT DO I DO...
WHAT DO I DO?!
TOMA-KUN...
You can do it!
Futaba!
MASUMI-CHAN...
TOMA-KUN ASKED ME TO DO THIS.
HE WANTED ME TO CHEER FOR HIM.
AND I PRACTICED SO HARD.
WHY CAN'T I DO IT?
WHY...
SEE?

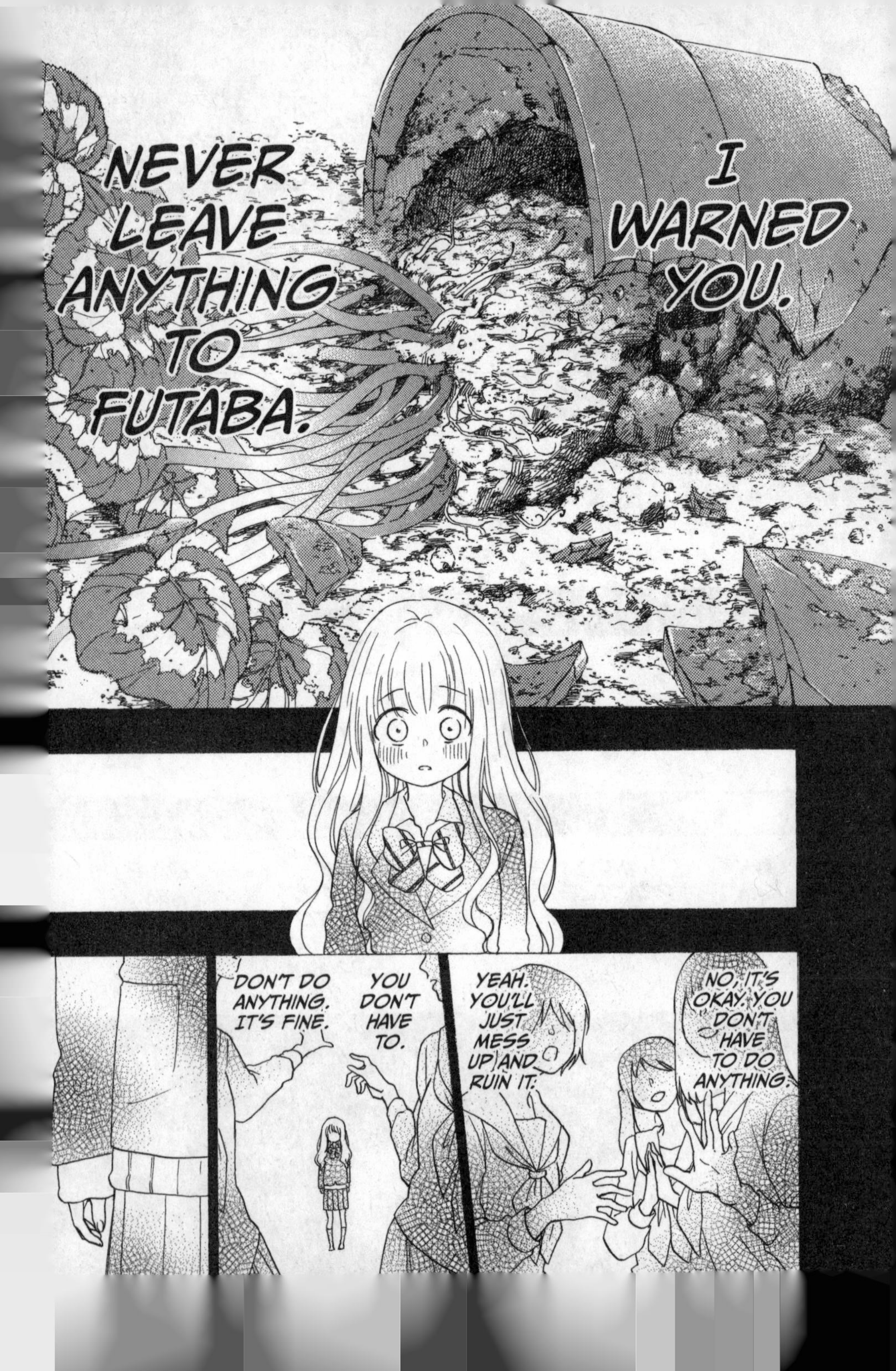
I WARNED YOU.
NEVER LEAVE ANYTHING TO FUTABA.
NO, IT'S OKAY. YOU DON'T HAVE TO DO ANYTHING.
YEAH. YOU'LL JUST MESS UP AND RUIN IT.
YOU DON'T HAVE TO.
DON'T DO ANYTHING. IT'S FINE.

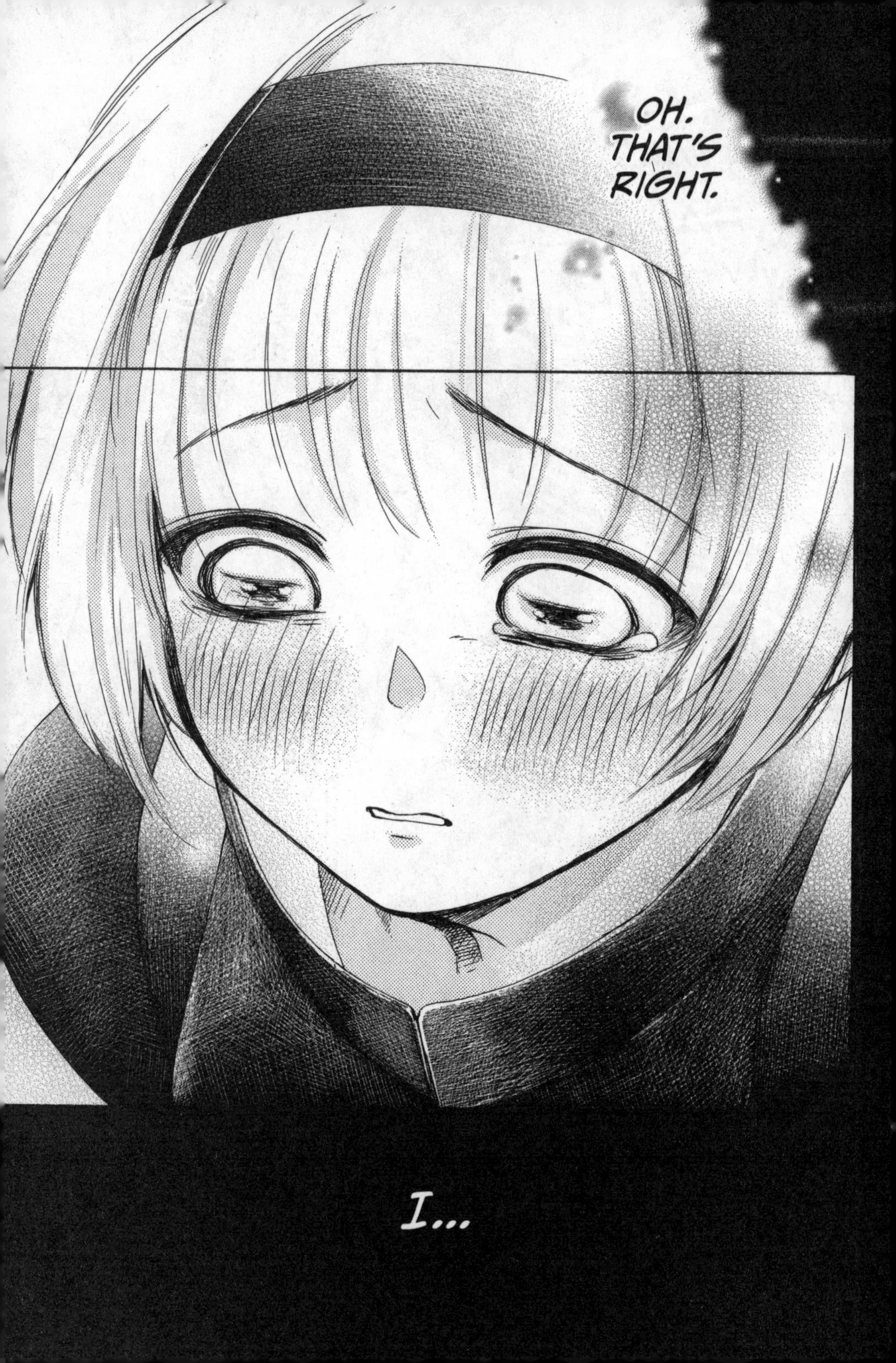
OH. THAT'S RIGHT.
I...

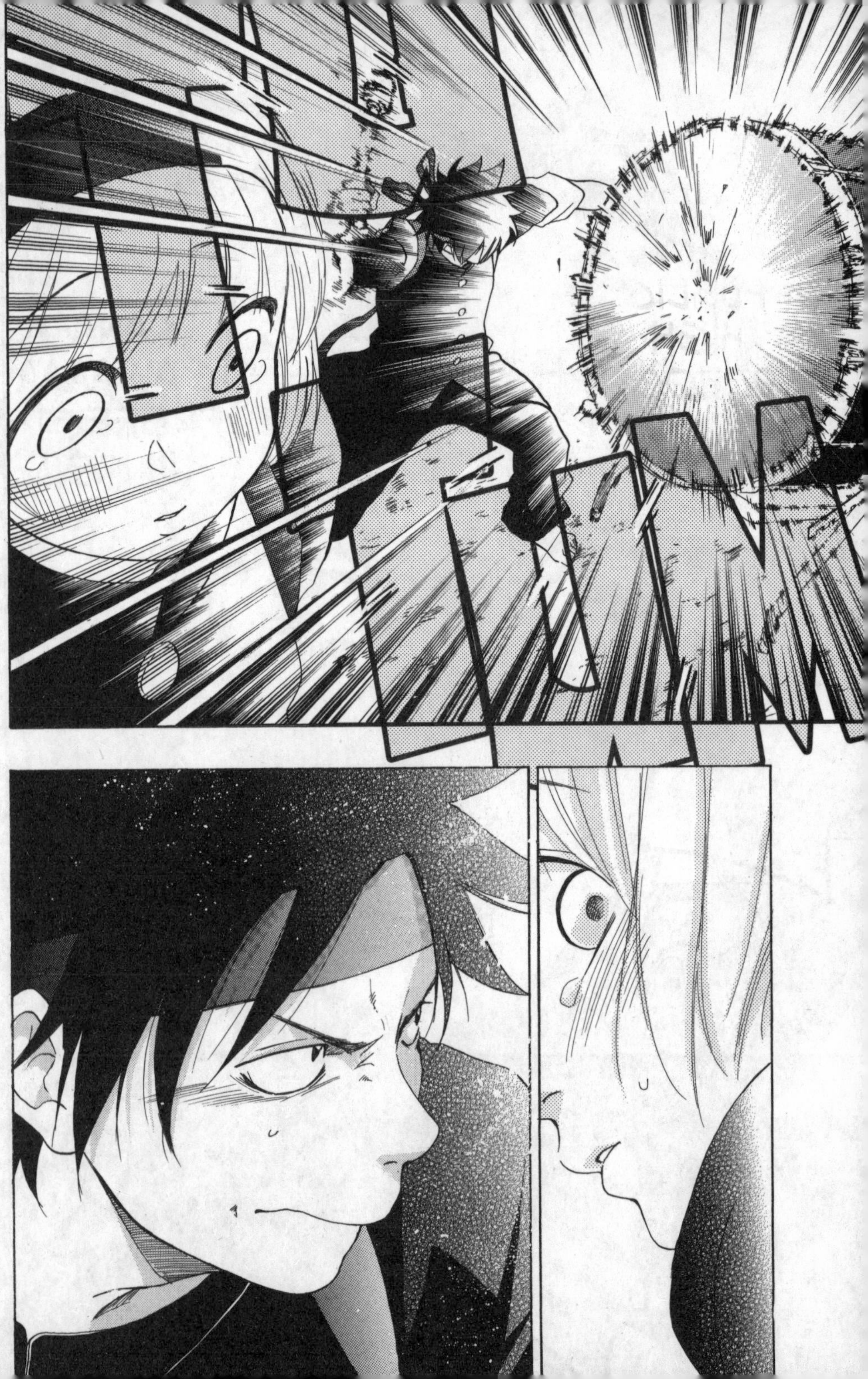

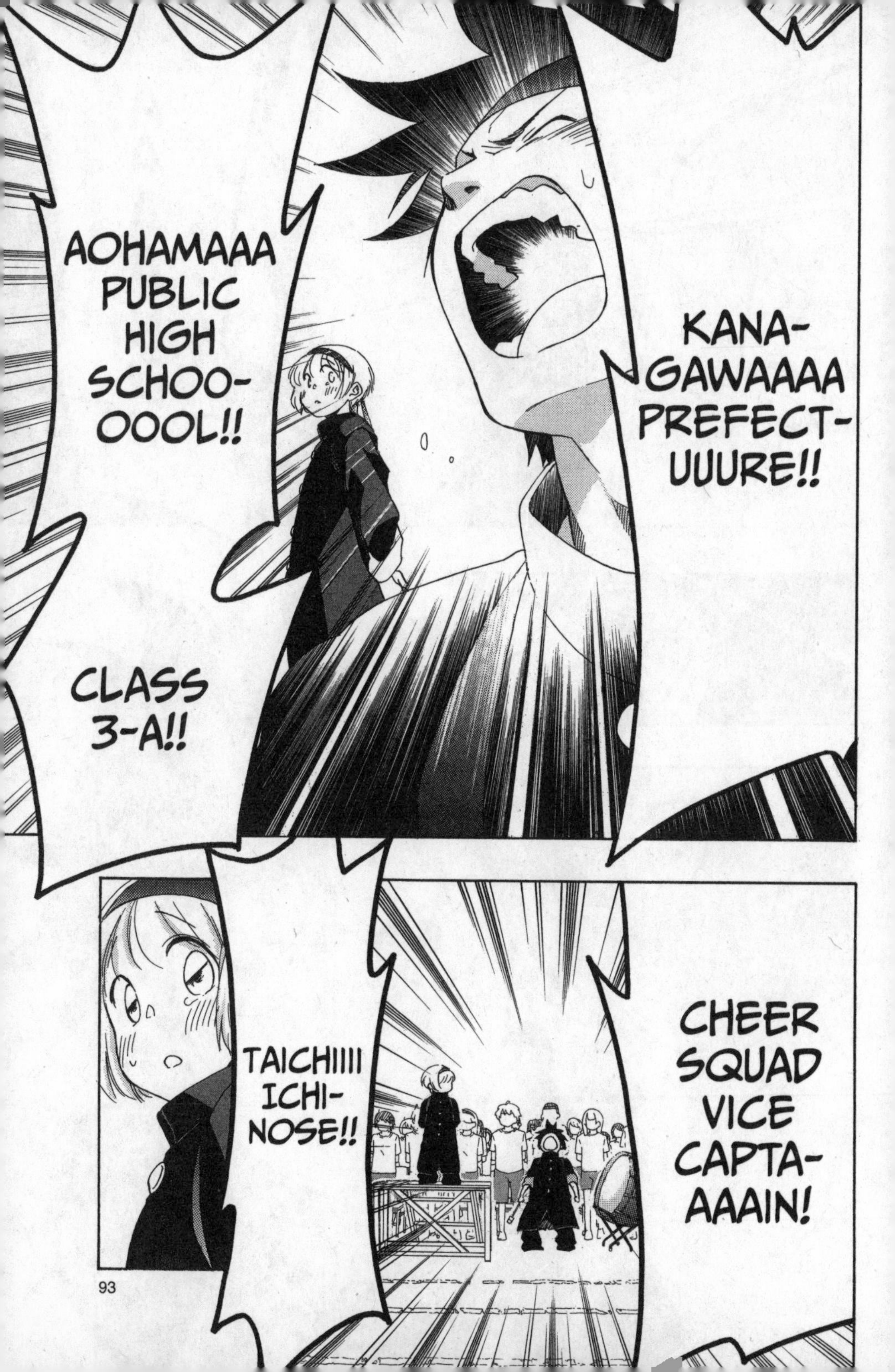
KANA-GAWAAAA PREFECT-UUURE!!
AOHAMAAA PUBLIC HIGH SCHOO-OOOL!!
CLASS 3-A!!
CHEER SQUAD VICE CAPTA-AAAIN!
TAICHIIIII ICHI-NOSE!!

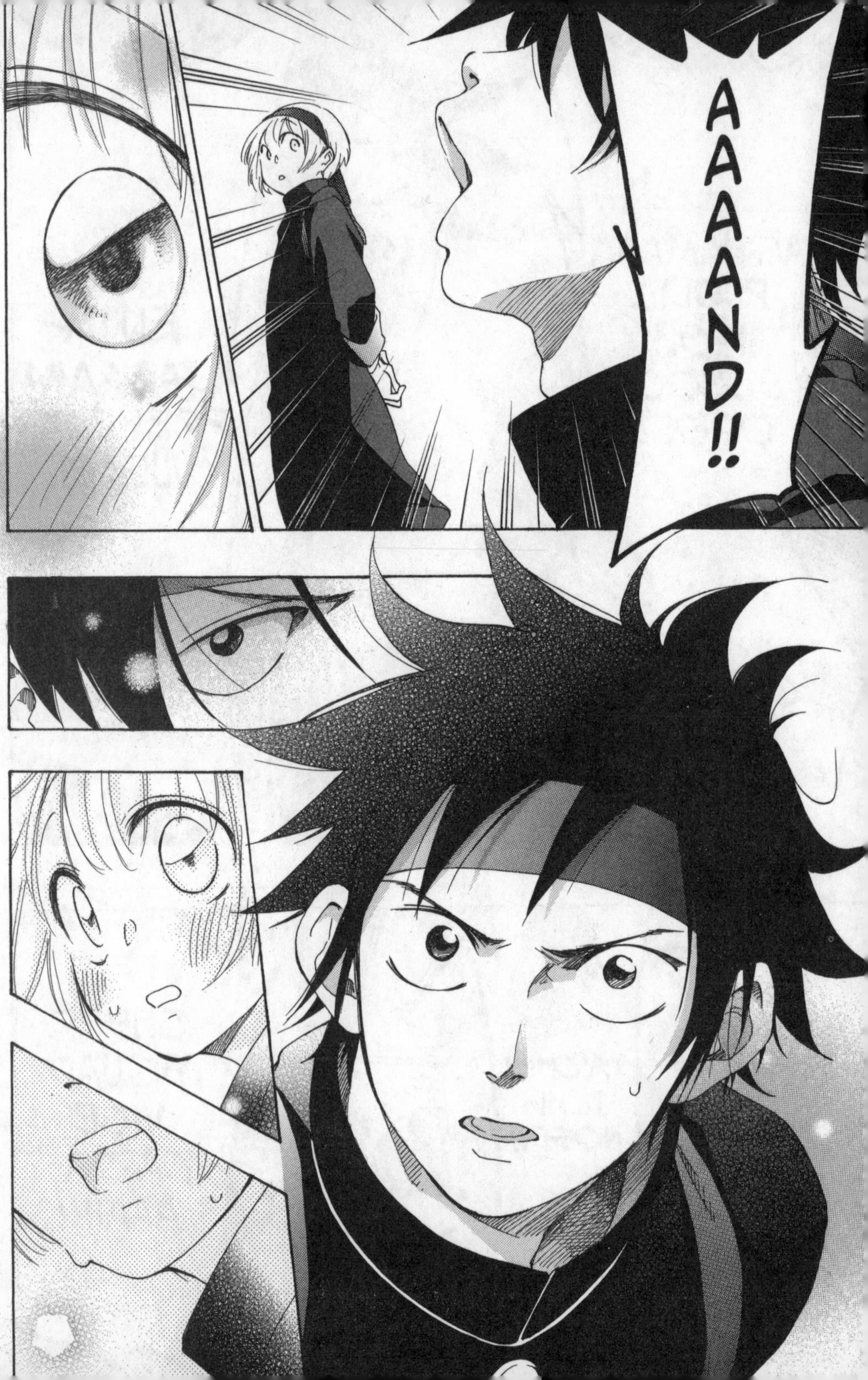
AAAAND!!

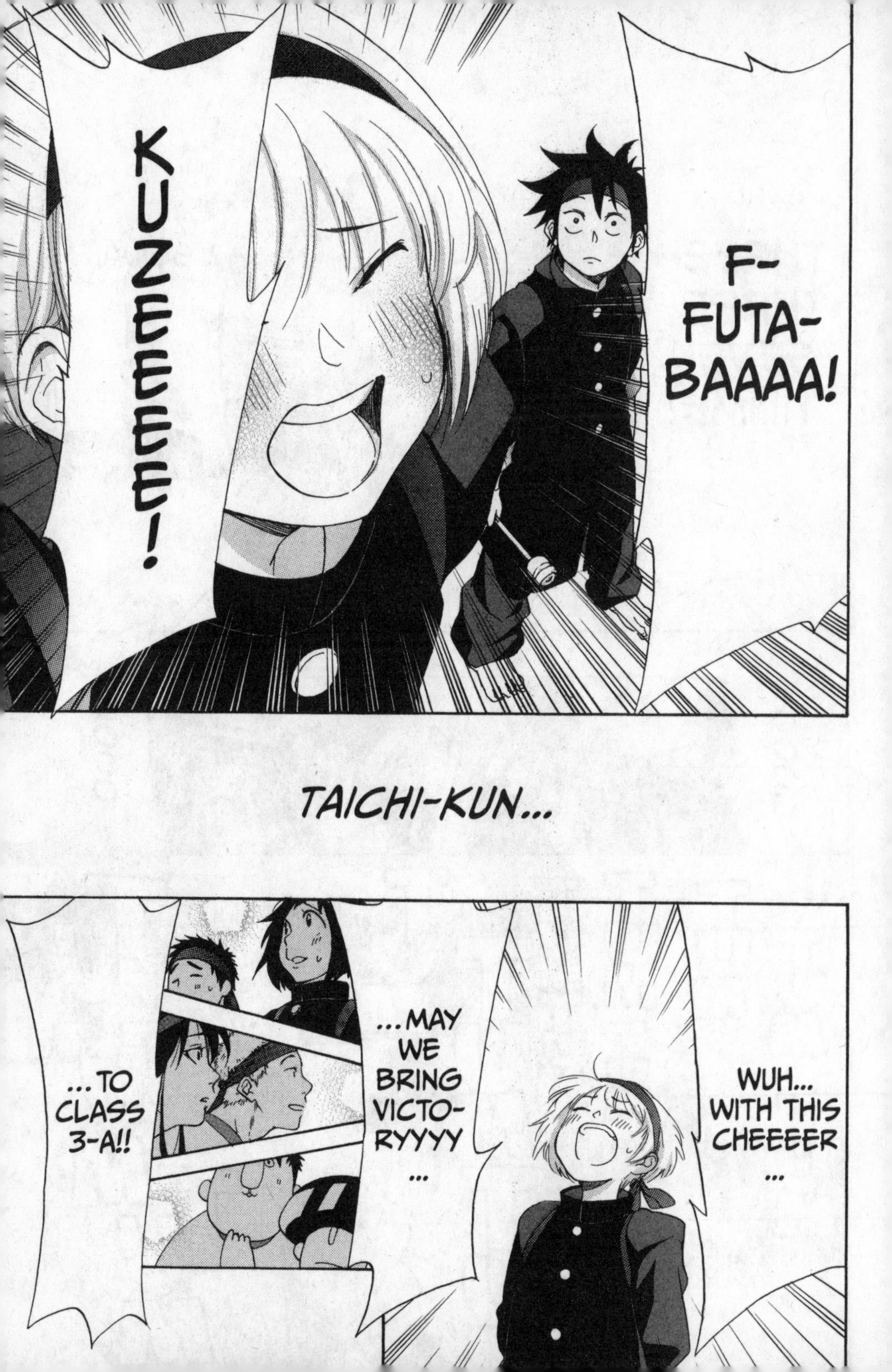
F-FUTA-BAAAA!
KUZEEEEEE!
TAICHI-KUN...
WUH... WITH THIS CHEEEER ...
...MAY WE BRING VICTO-RYYYY ...
...TO CLASS 3-A!!

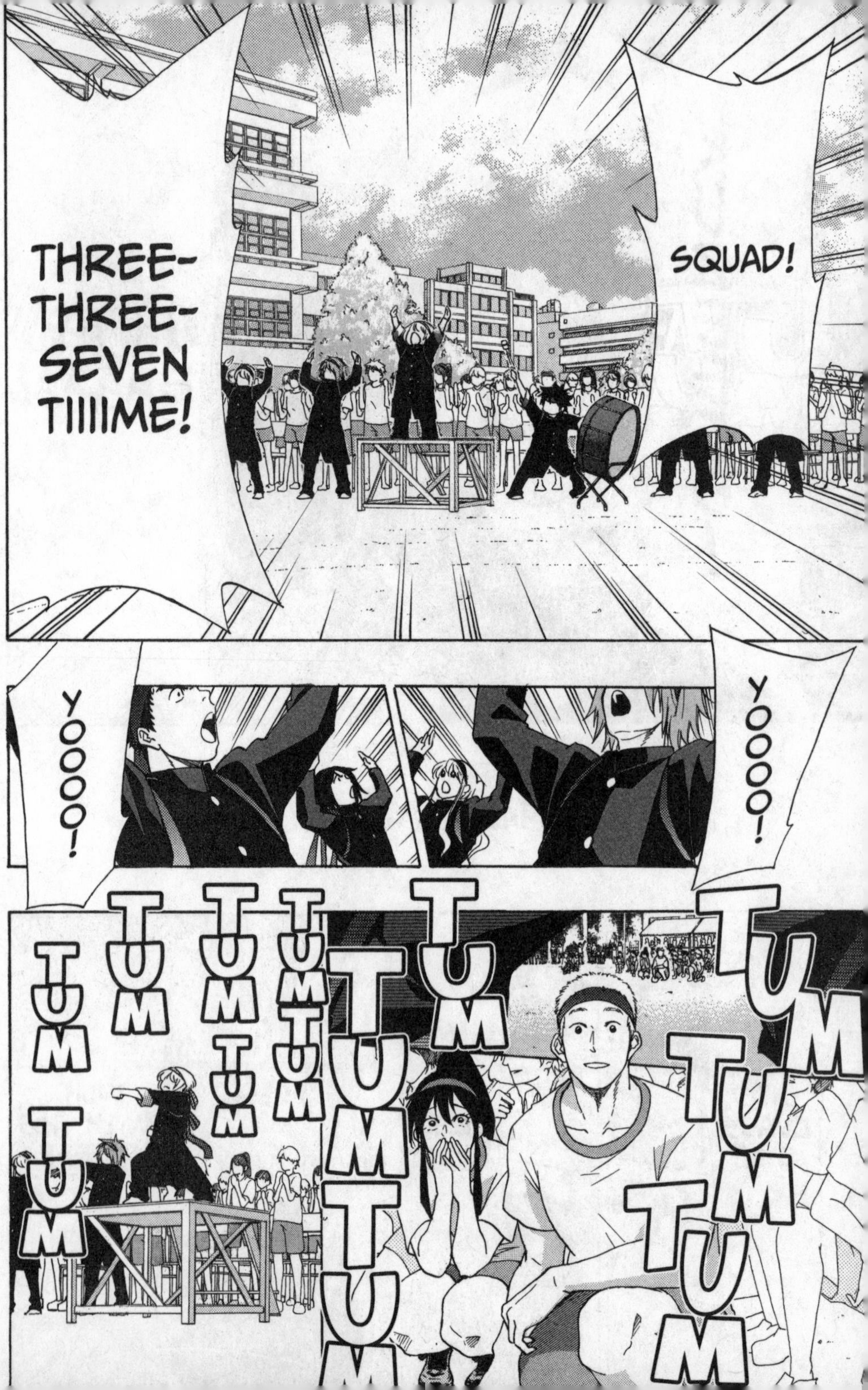
SQUAD!
THREE-THREE-SEVEN TIIIIME!
YOOOO!
YOOOO!
TUM TUM TUM TUM
TUM
TUM TUM TUM TUM
TUM TUM TUM
TUM TUM TUM
TUM
TUM TUM

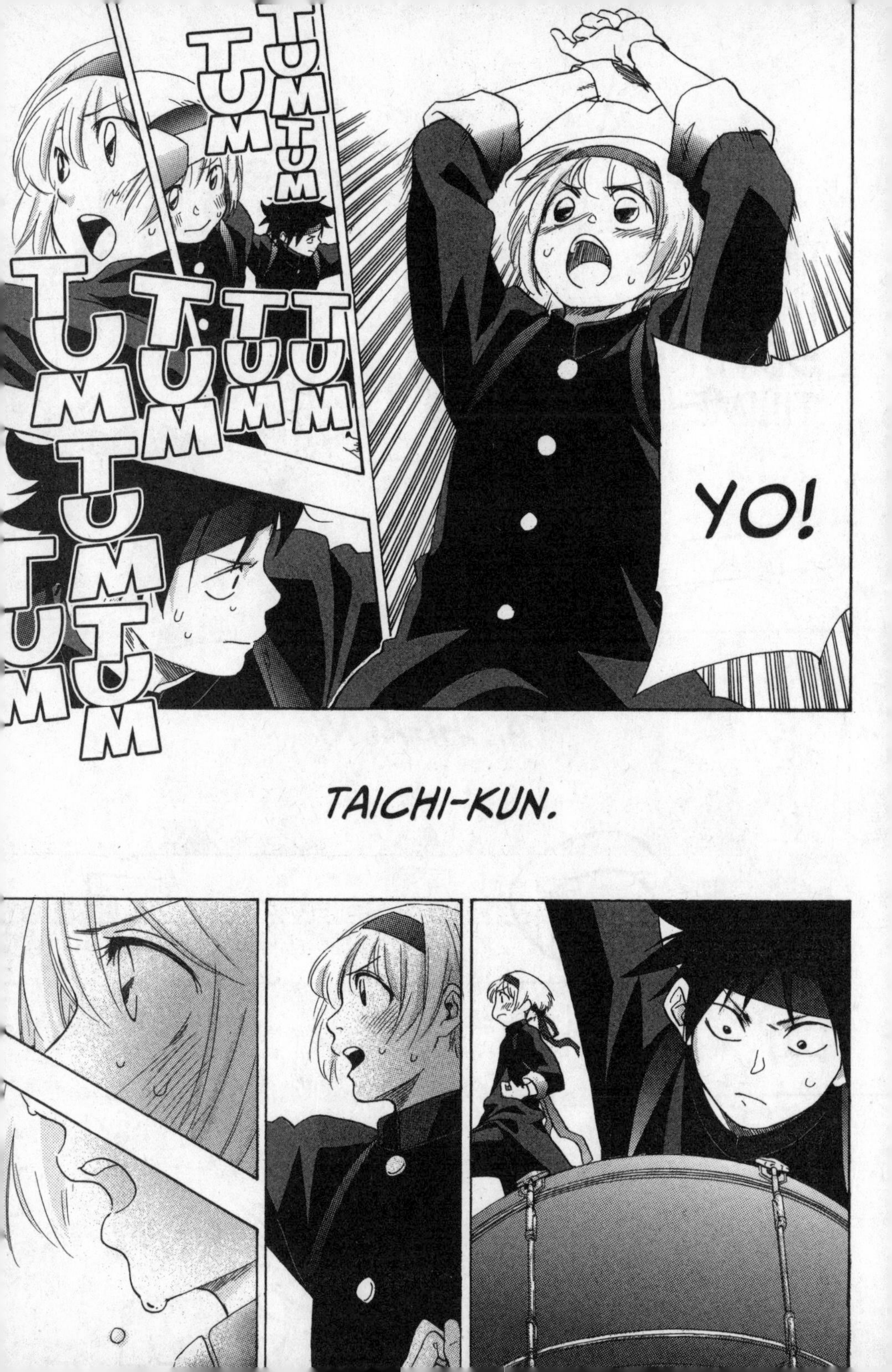
YO!
TUM TUM TUM
TUM TUM
TUM TUM TUM TUM
TUM TUM
TUM
TAICHI-KUN.

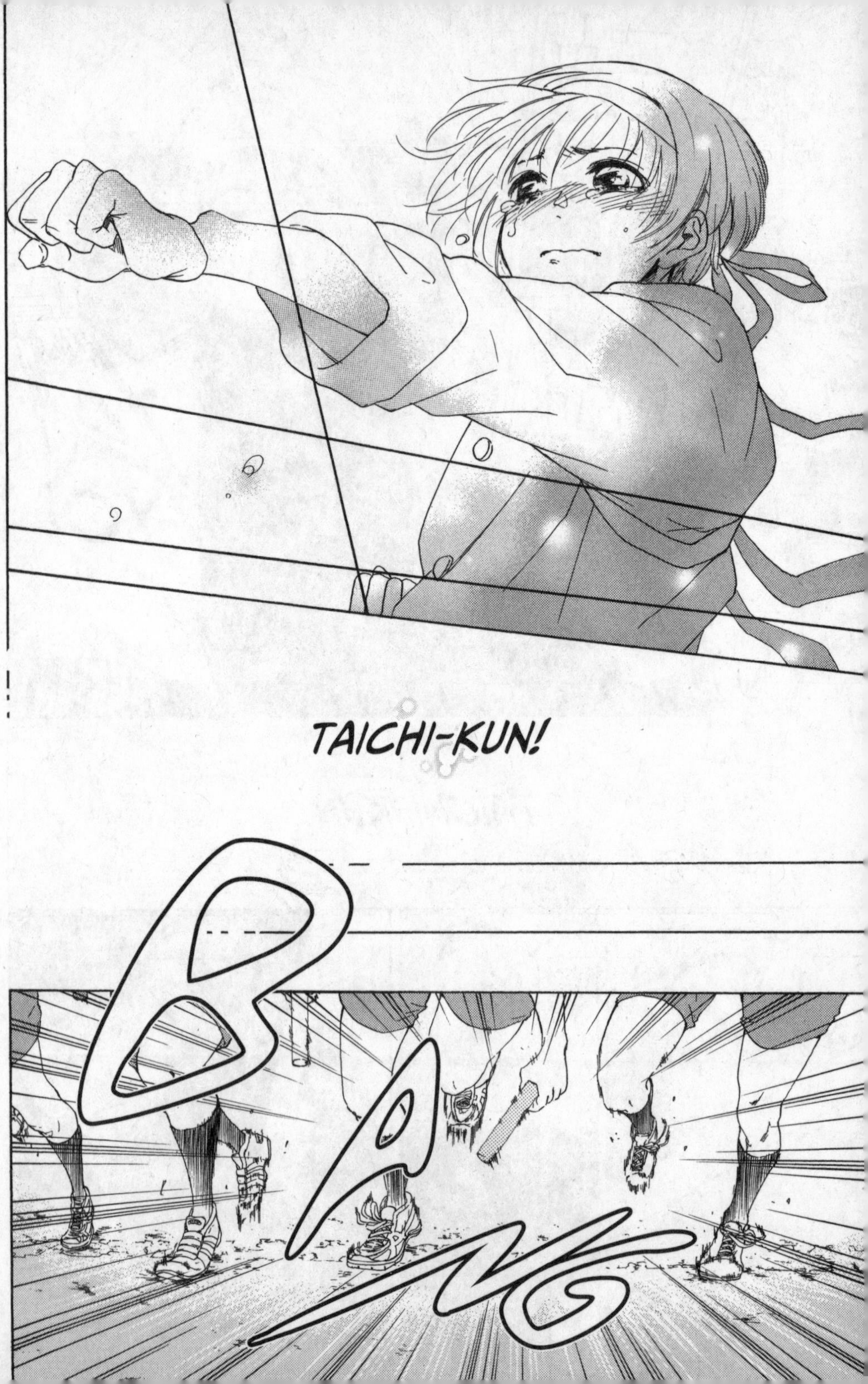
TAICHI-KUN!
BANG

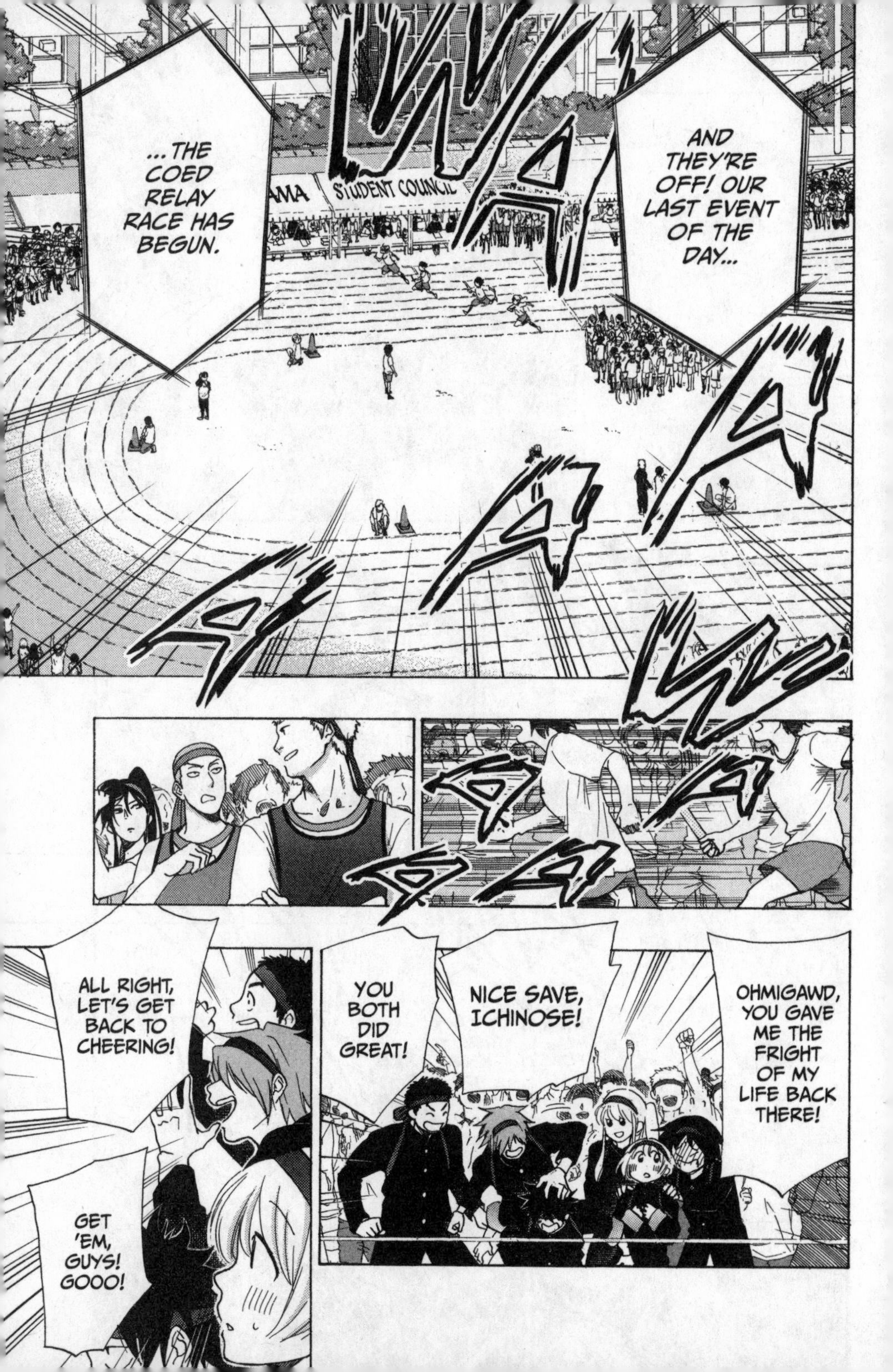
AND THEY'RE OFF! OUR LAST EVENT OF THE DAY...
...THE COED RELAY RACE HAS BEGUN.
STUDENT COUNCIL
OHMIGAWD, YOU GAVE ME THE FRIGHT OF MY LIFE BACK THERE!
NICE SAVE, ICHINOSE!
YOU BOTH DID GREAT!
ALL RIGHT, LET'S GET BACK TO CHEERING!
GET 'EM, GUYS! GOOO!

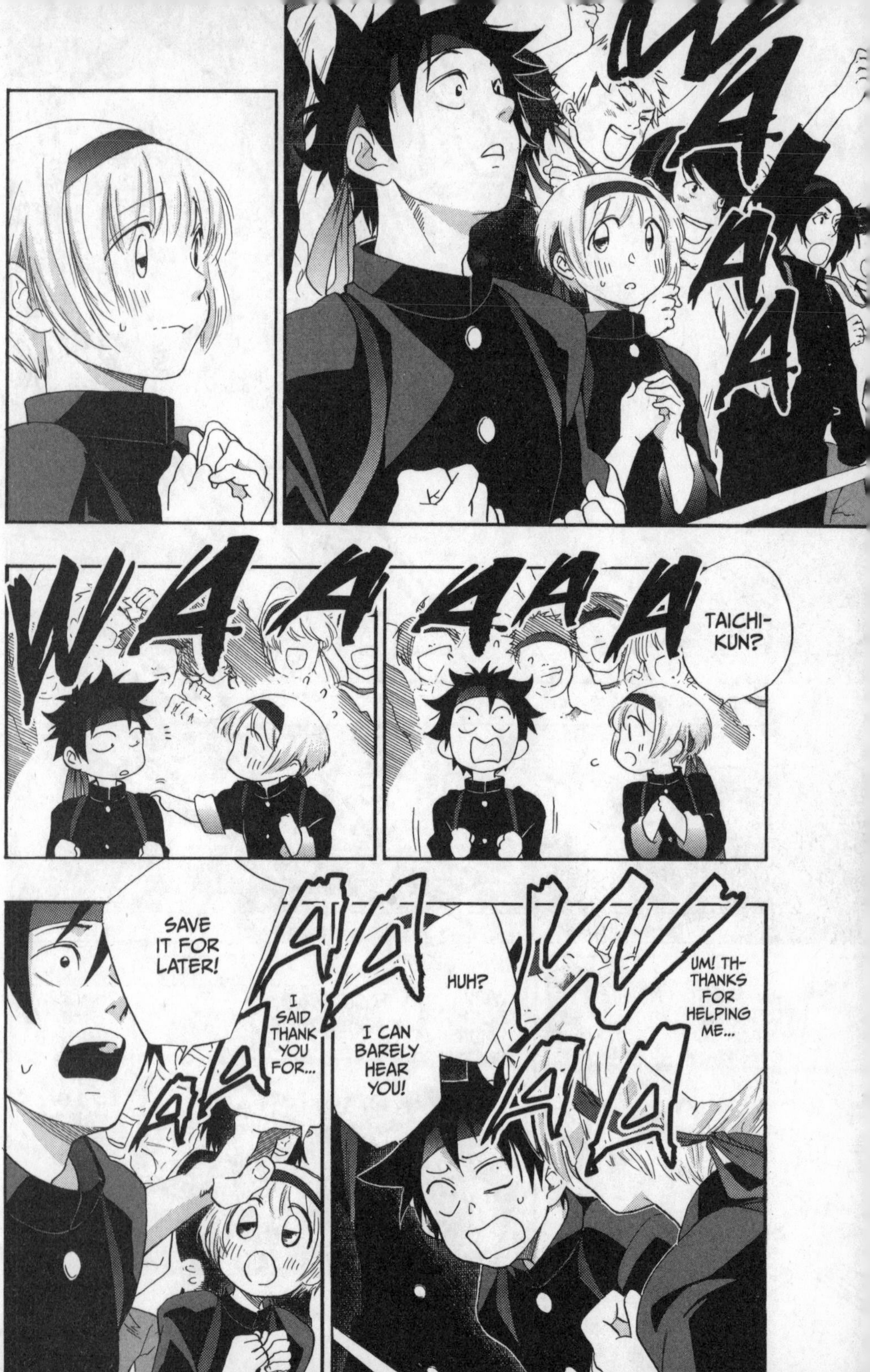

WAAA
WAAAAAA
TAICHI-KUN?
UM! TH-THANKS FOR HELPING ME...
HUH?
I CAN BARELY HEAR YOU!
I SAID THANK YOU FOR...
SAVE IT FOR LATER!

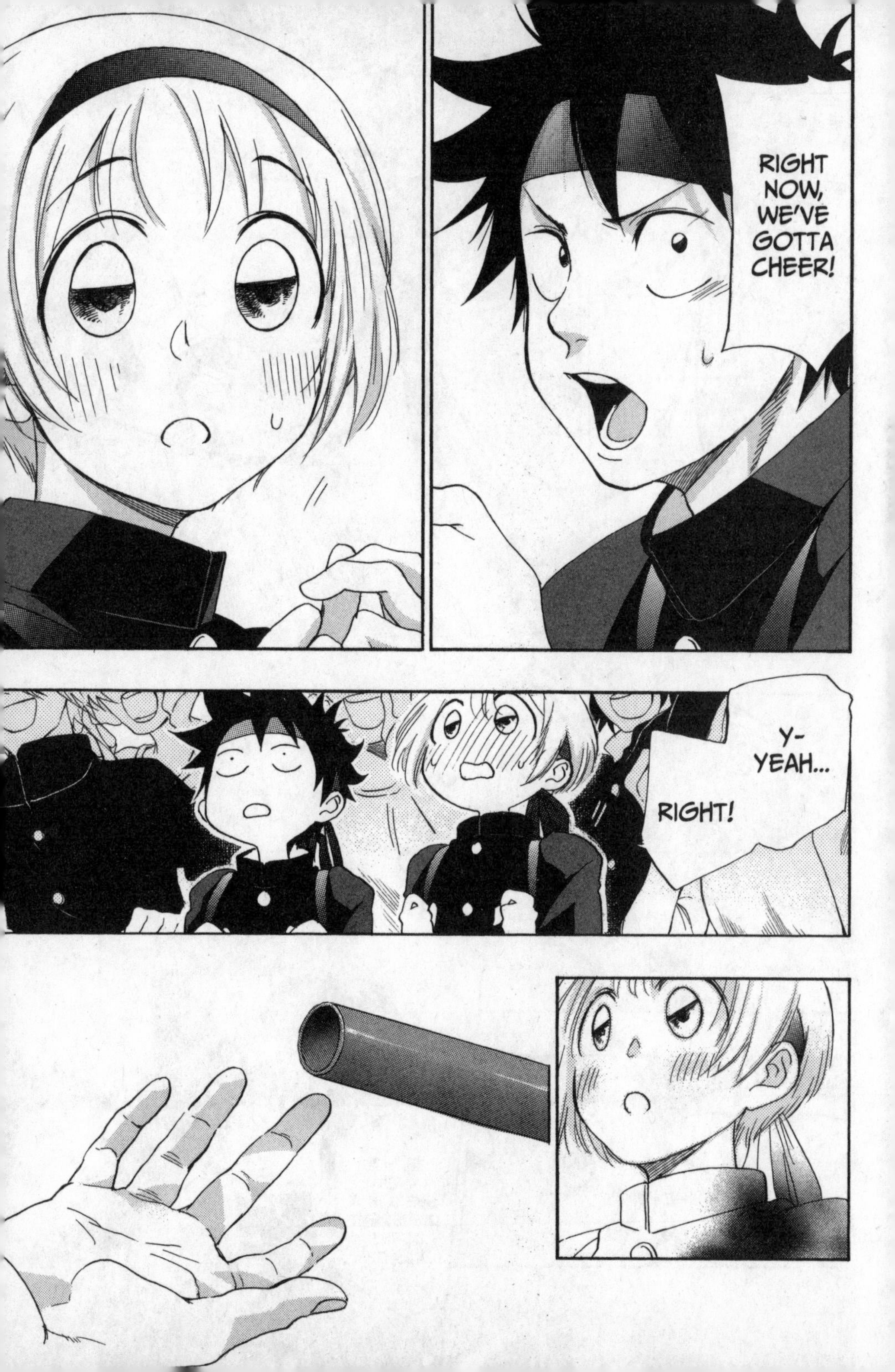
RIGHT NOW, WE'VE GOTTA CHEER!
Y- YEAH...
RIGHT!

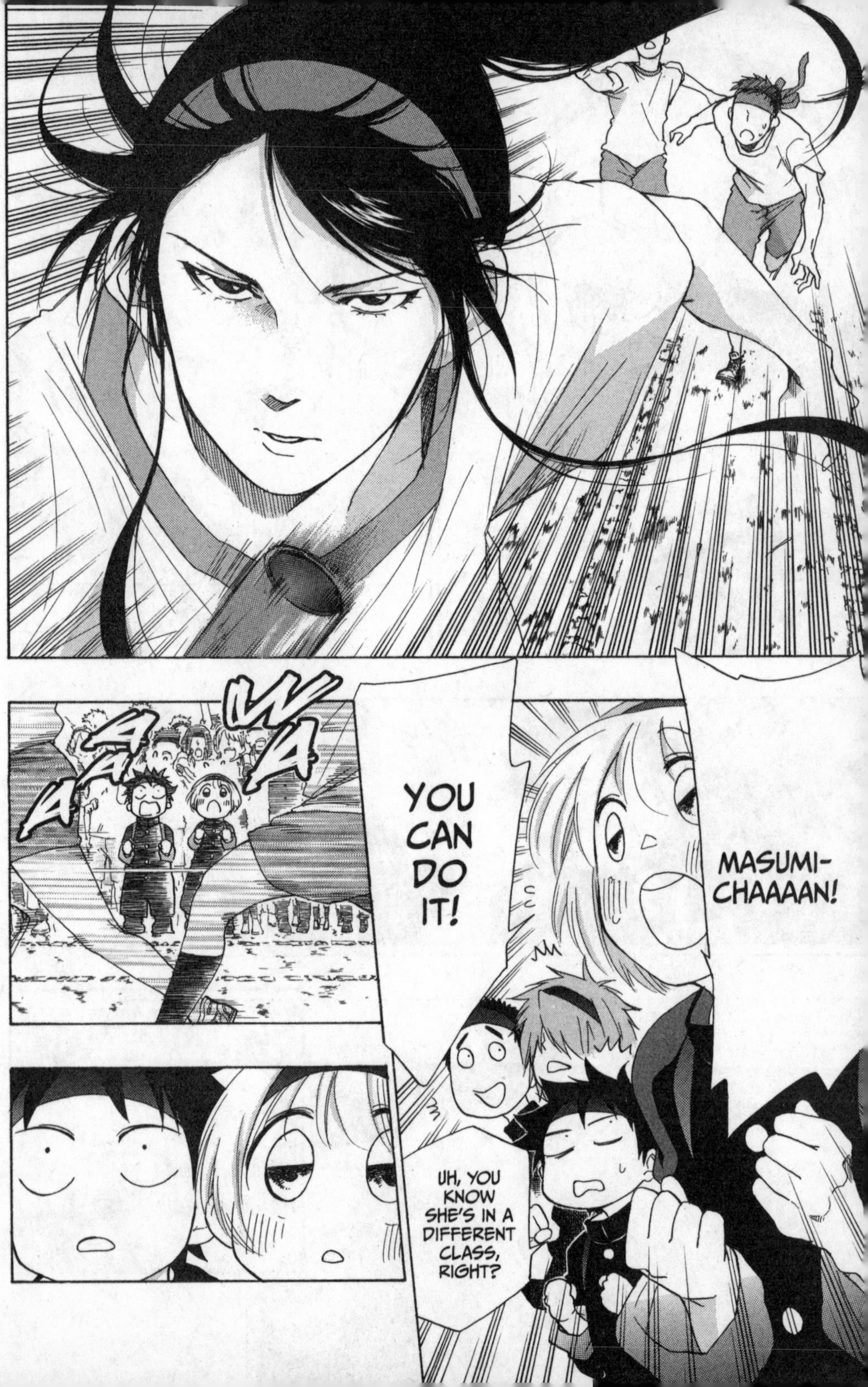
MASUMI-CHAAAAN!
YOU CAN DO IT!
UH, YOU KNOW SHE'S IN A DIFFERENT CLASS, RIGHT?
WAAAA

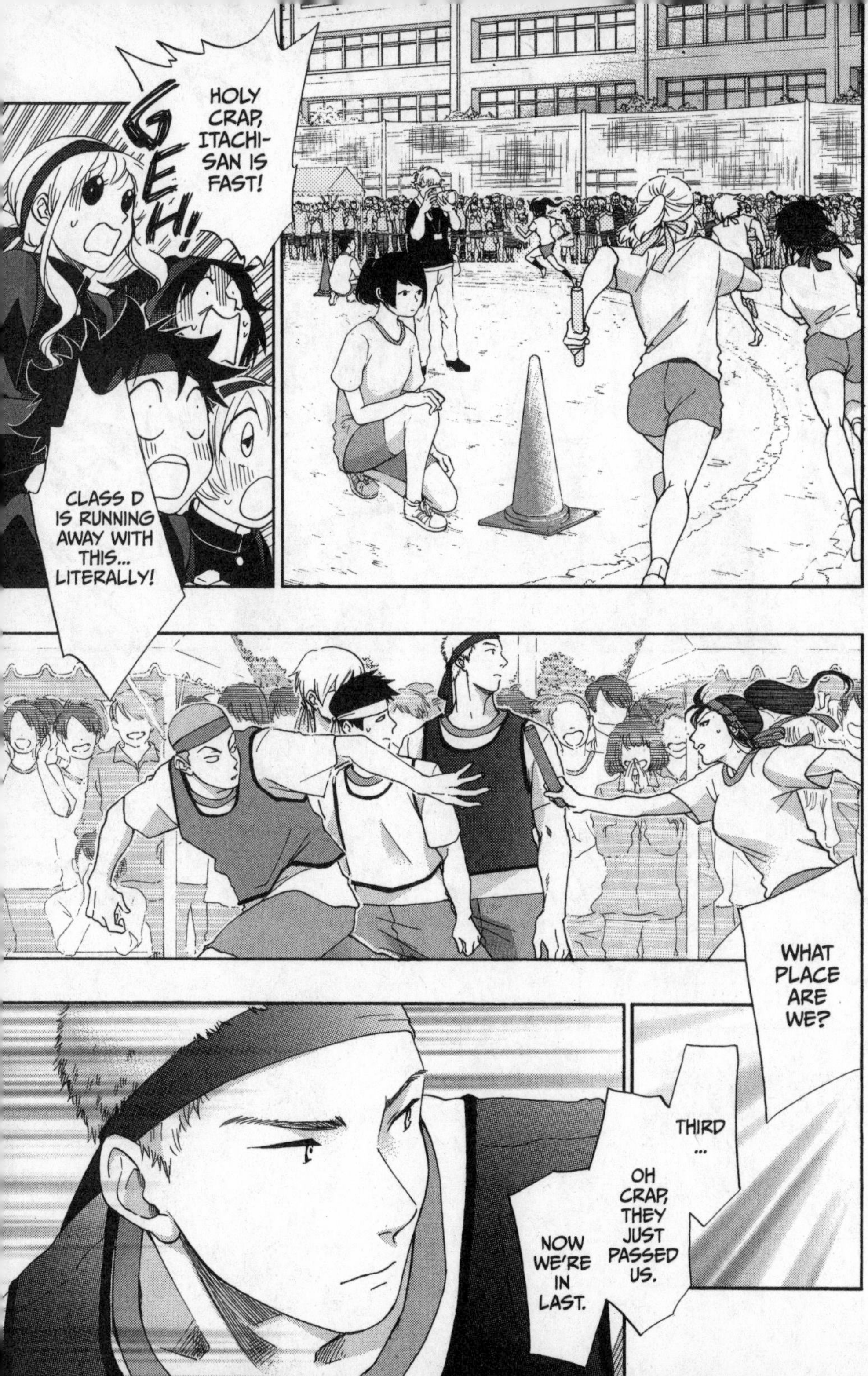
GEH!
HOLY CRAP, ITACHI-SAN IS FAST!
CLASS D IS RUNNING AWAY WITH THIS... LITERALLY!
WHAT PLACE ARE WE?
THIRD ...
OH CRAP, THEY JUST PASSED US.
NOW WE'RE IN LAST.

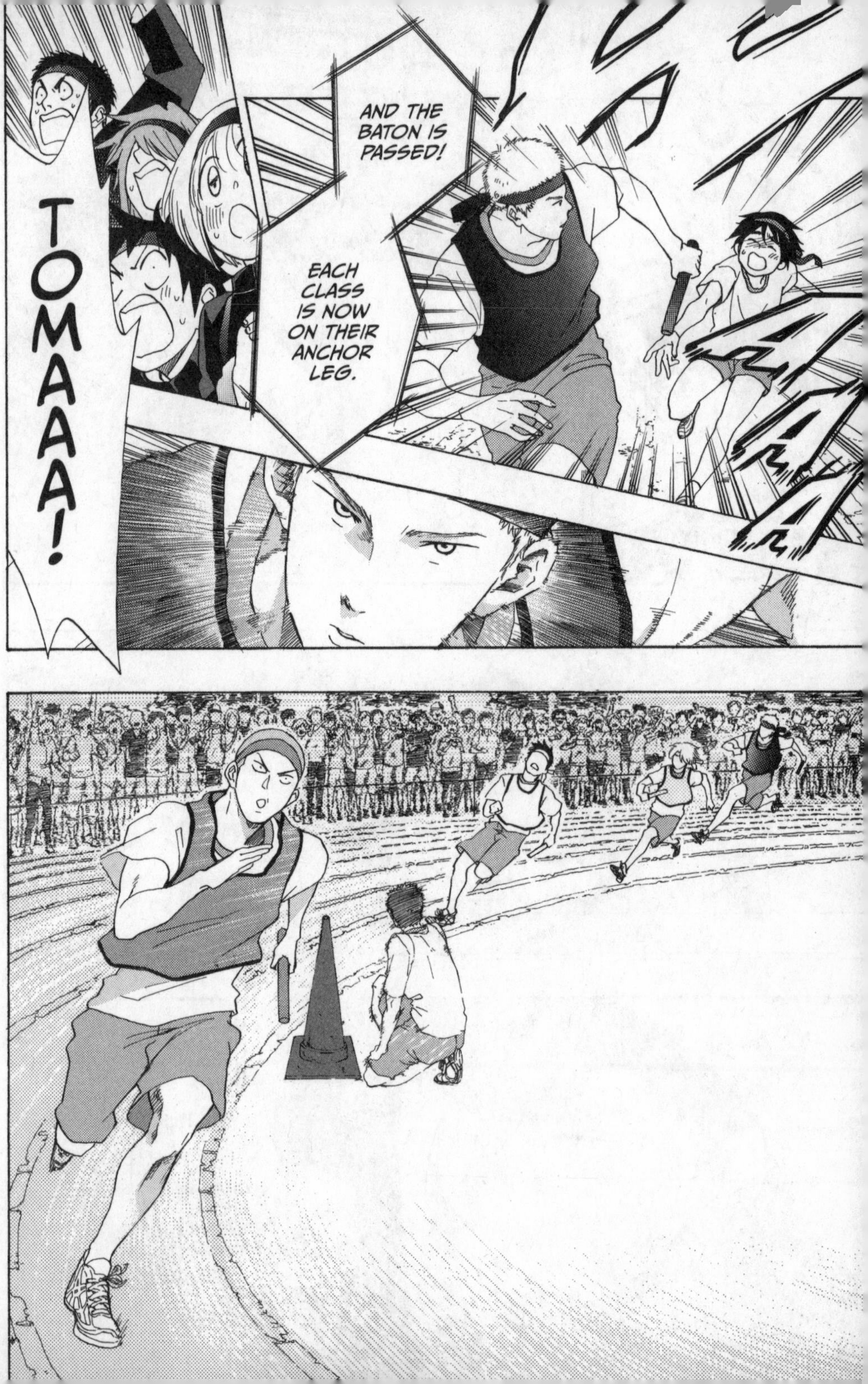
AND THE BATON IS PASSED!
EACH CLASS IS NOW ON THEIR ANCHOR LEG.
TOMAAA!

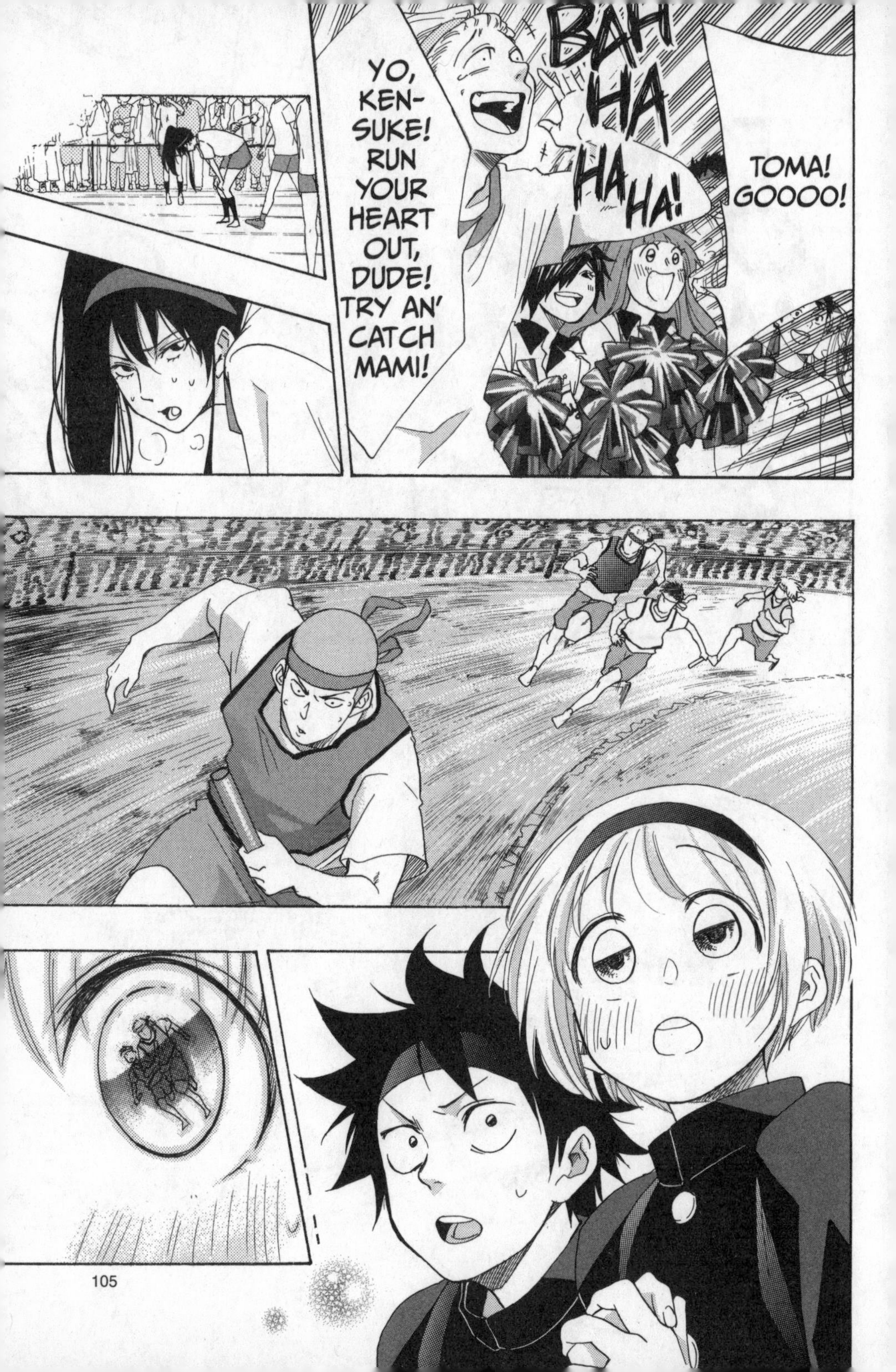
TOMA! GOOOO!
BAH HA HA HA HA!
YO, KEN-SUKE! RUN YOUR HEART OUT, DUDE! TRY AN' CATCH MAMI!

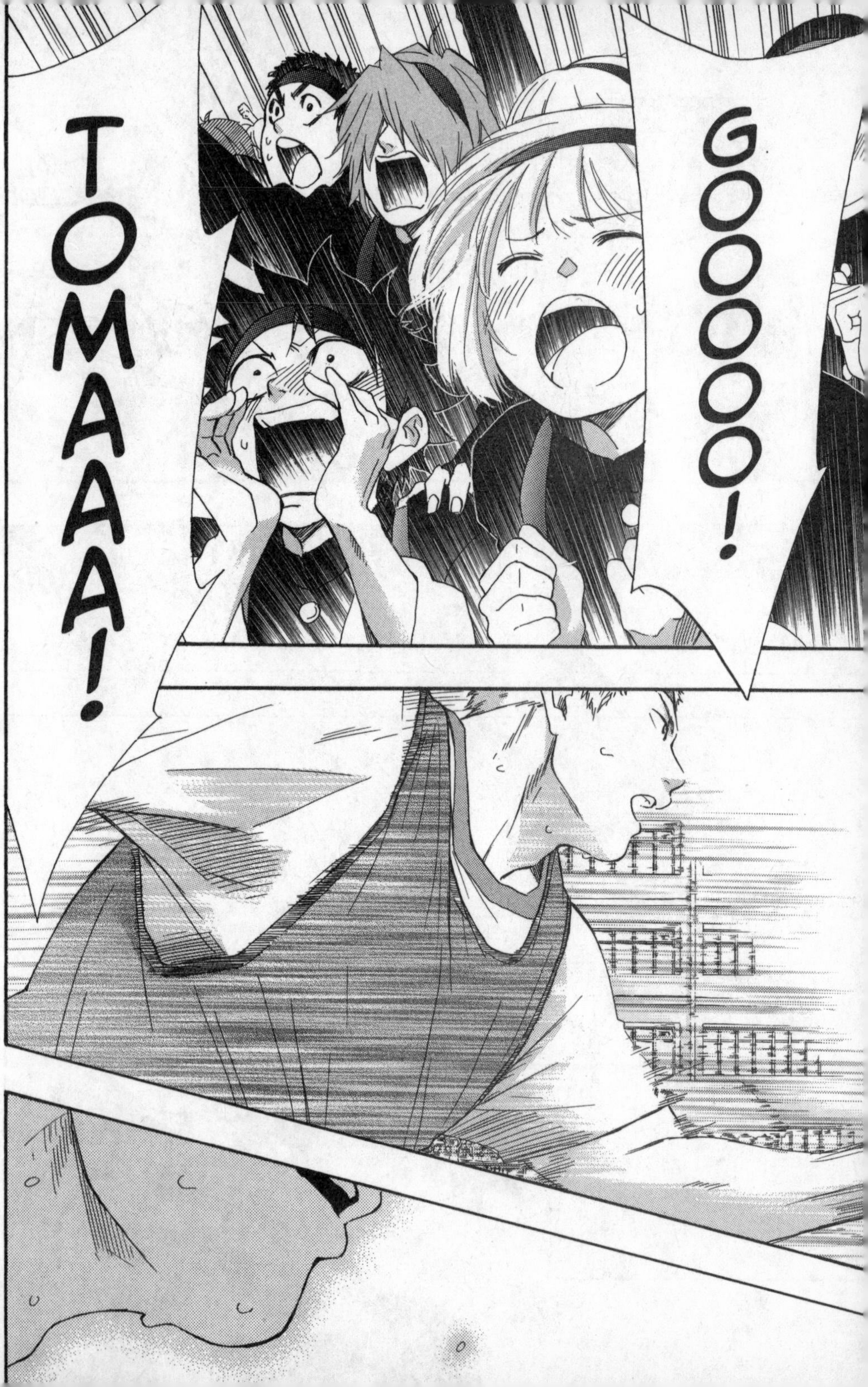
GOOOOO!
TOMAAA!

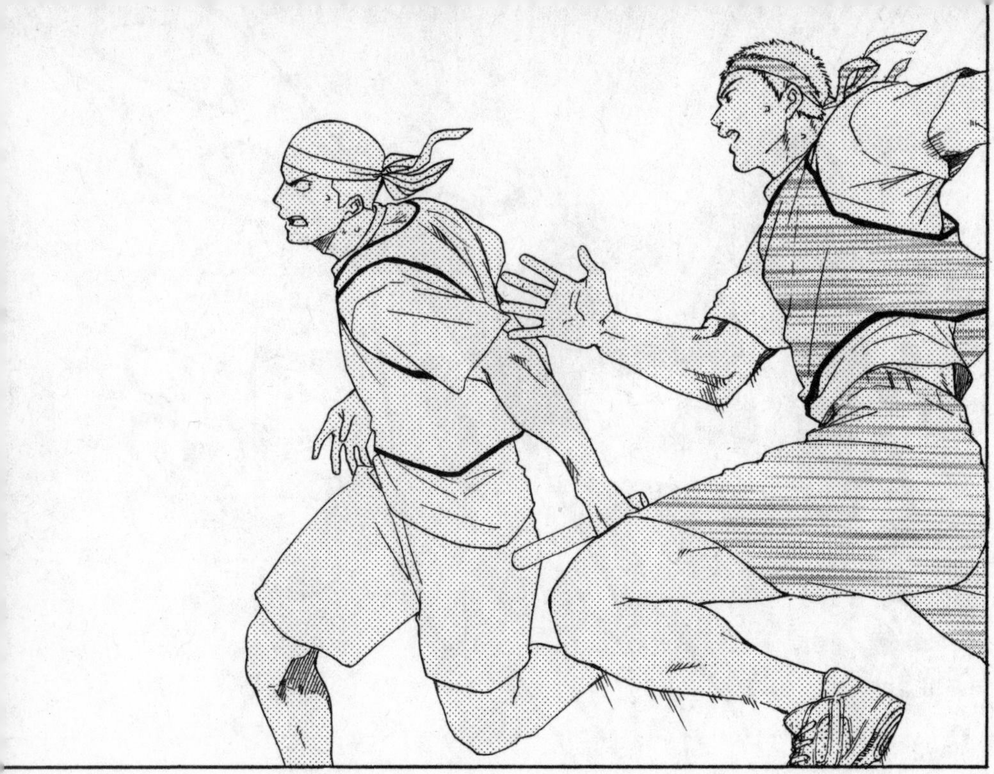
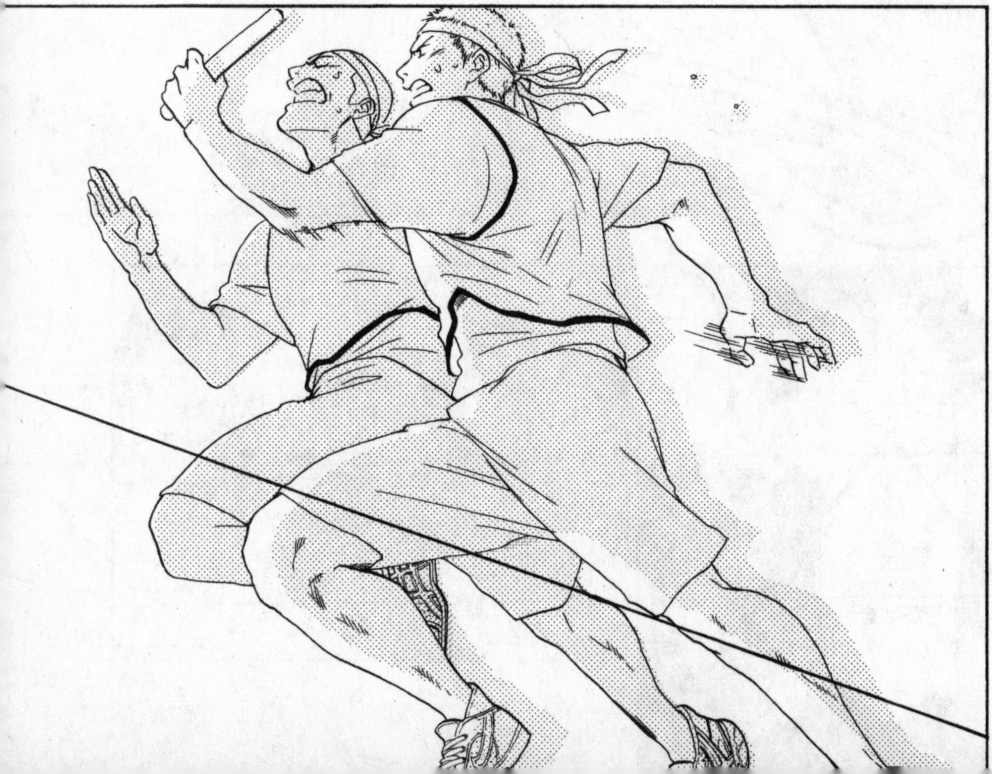

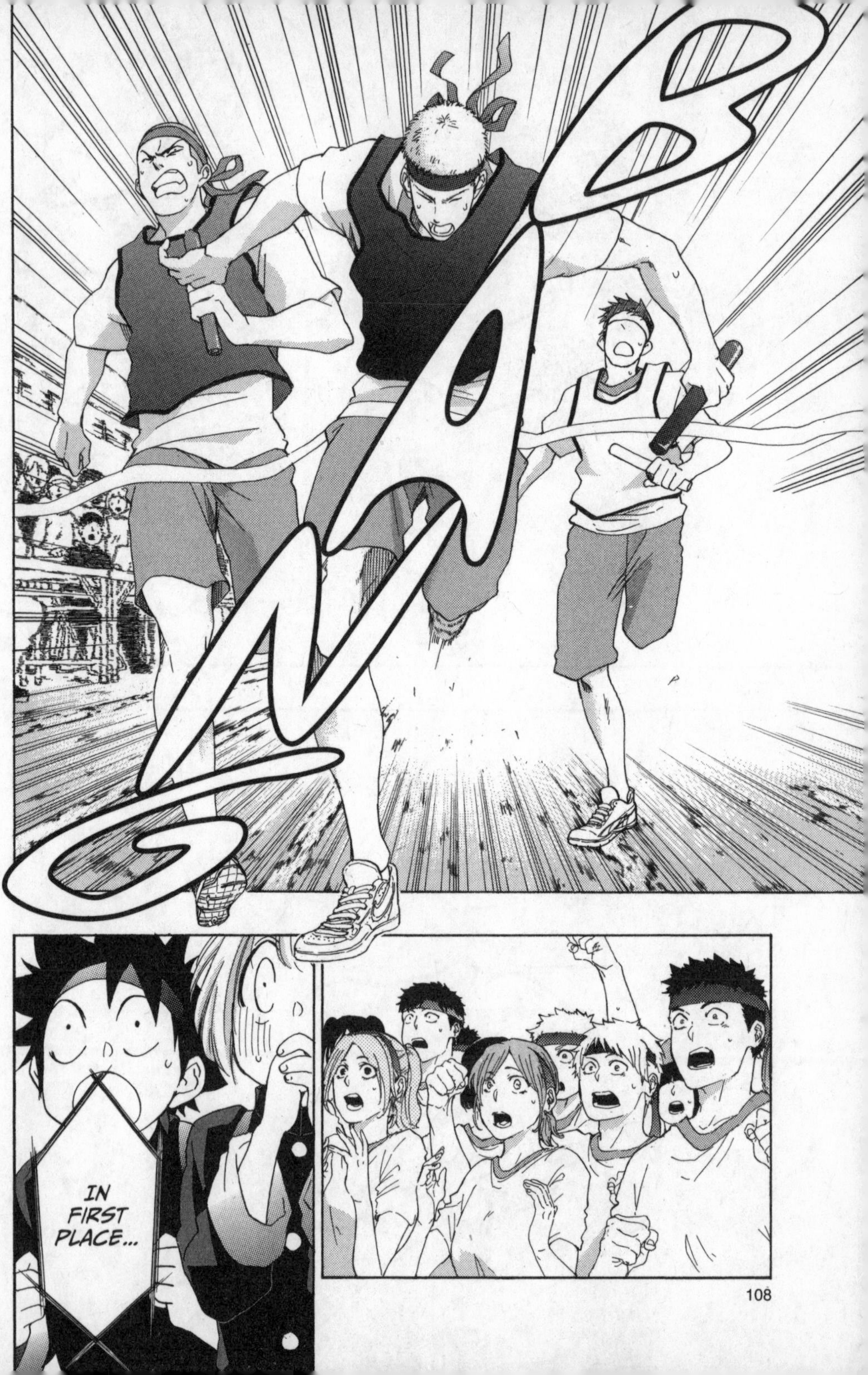
IN FIRST PLACE...

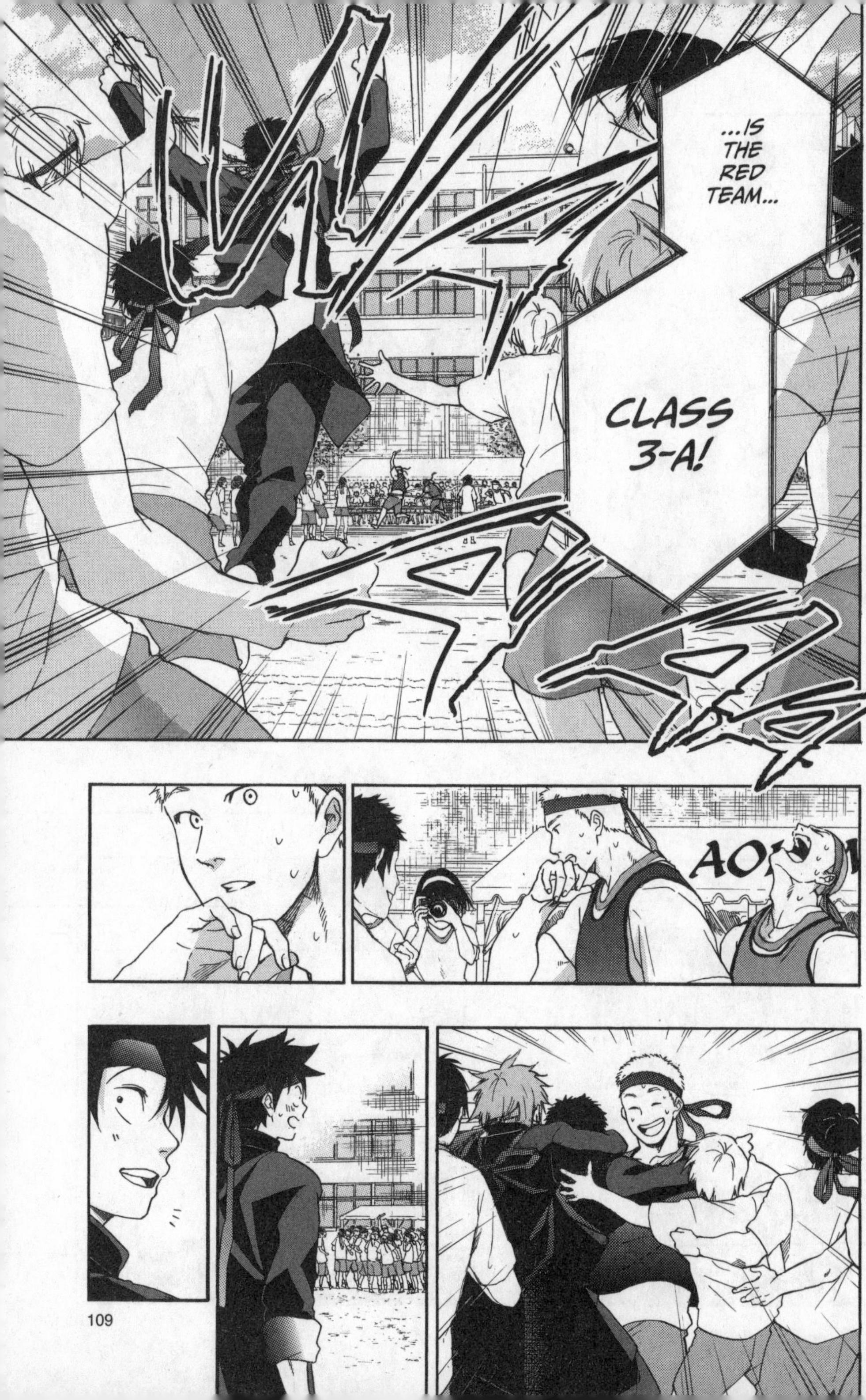
...IS THE RED TEAM...
CLASS 3-A!
AO

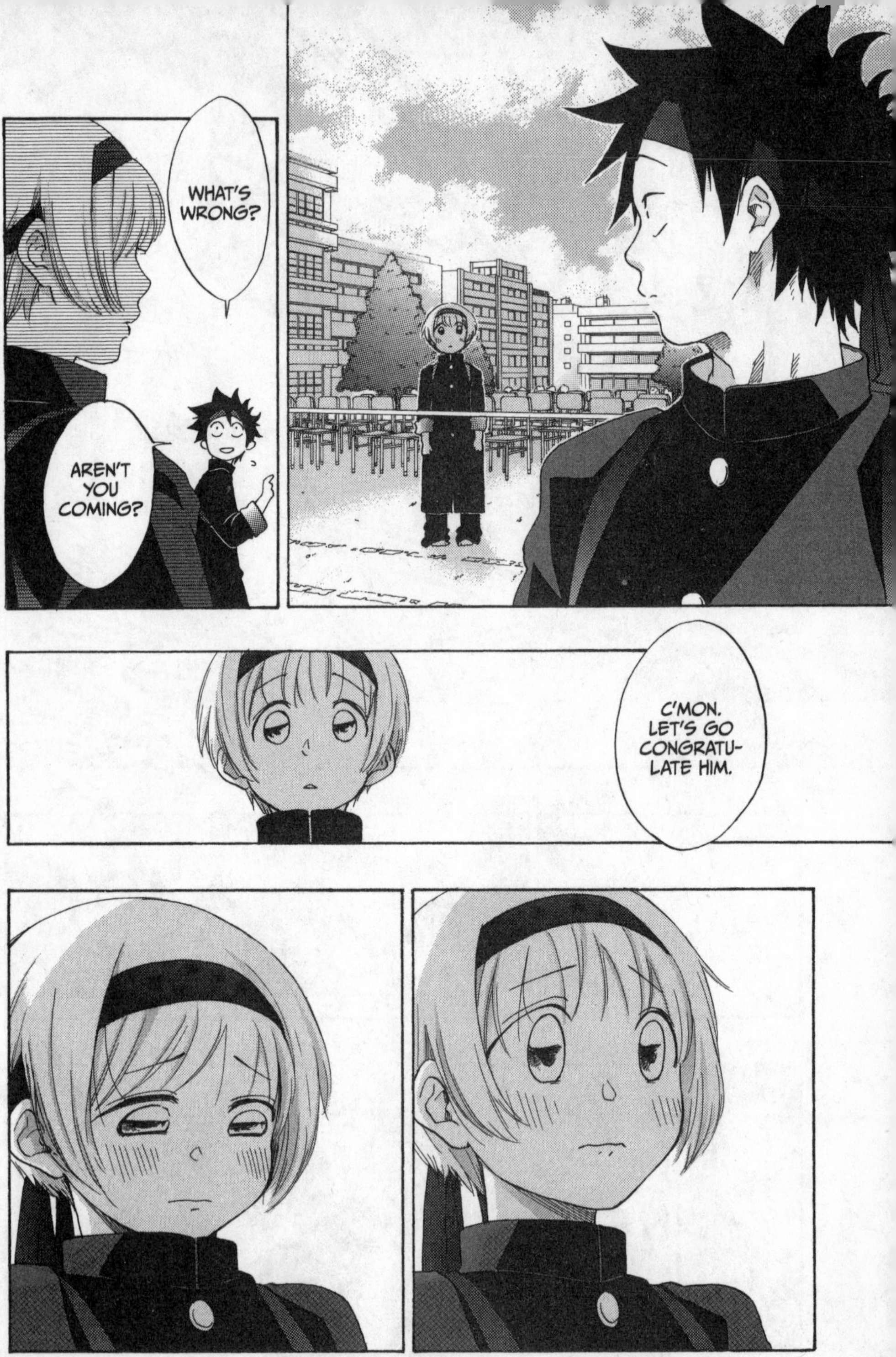
WHAT'S WRONG?
AREN'T YOU COMING?
C'MON. LET'S GO CONGRATU-LATE HIM.

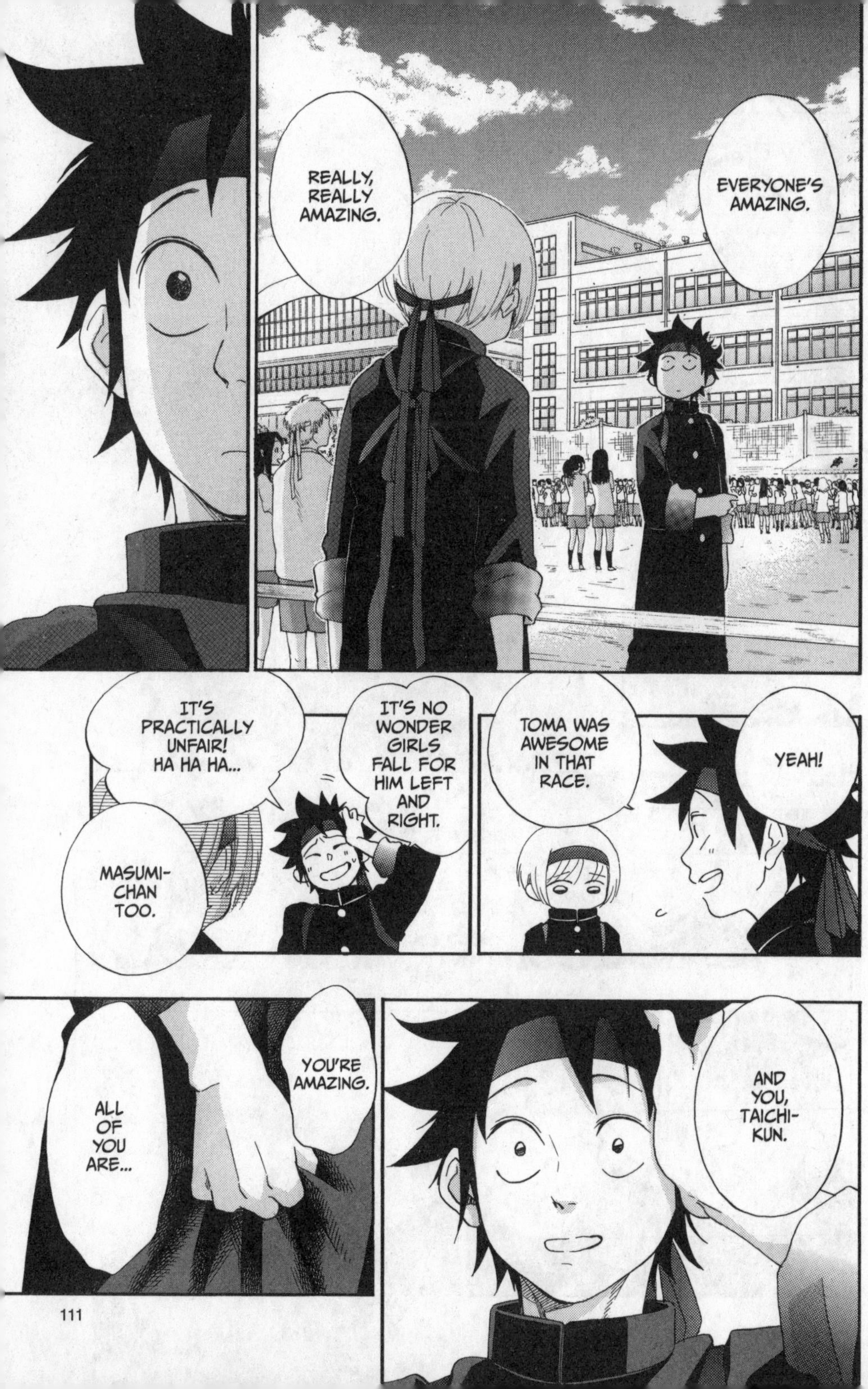
EVERYONE'S AMAZING.
REALLY, REALLY AMAZING.
YEAH!
TOMA WAS AWESOME IN THAT RACE.
IT'S NO WONDER GIRLS FALL FOR HIM LEFT AND RIGHT.
IT'S PRACTICALLY UNFAIR! HA HA HA...
MASUMI-CHAN TOO.
AND YOU, TAICHI-KUN.
YOU'RE AMAZING.
ALL OF YOU ARE...

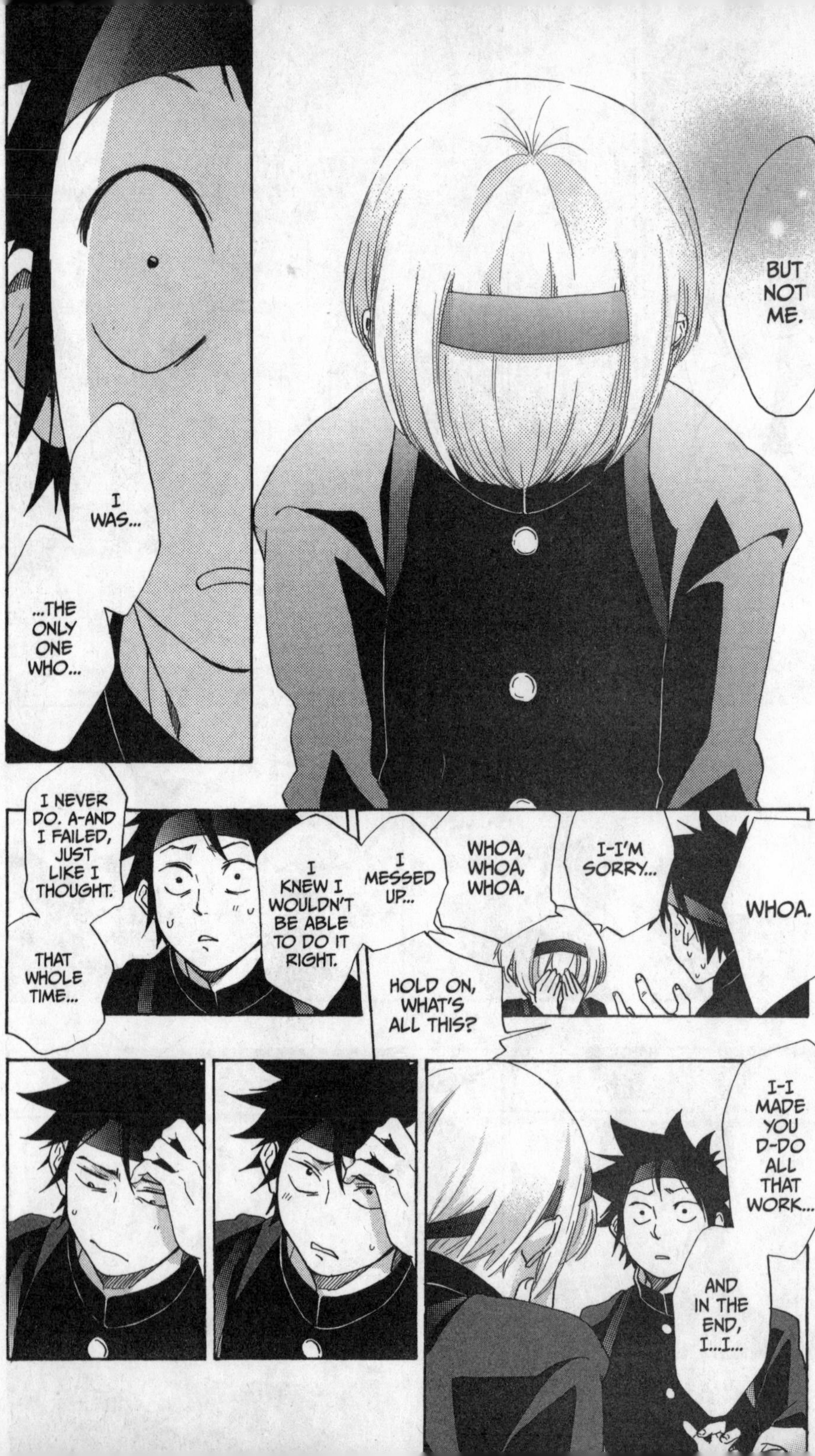
BUT NOT ME.
I WAS...
...THE ONLY ONE WHO...
WHOA.
I-I'M SORRY...
WHOA, WHOA, WHOA.
HOLD ON, WHAT'S ALL THIS?
I MESSED UP...
I KNEW I WOULDN'T BE ABLE TO DO IT RIGHT.
I NEVER DO. A-AND I FAILED, JUST LIKE I THOUGHT.
THAT WHOLE TIME...
I-I MADE YOU D-DO ALL THAT WORK...
AND IN THE END, I...I...

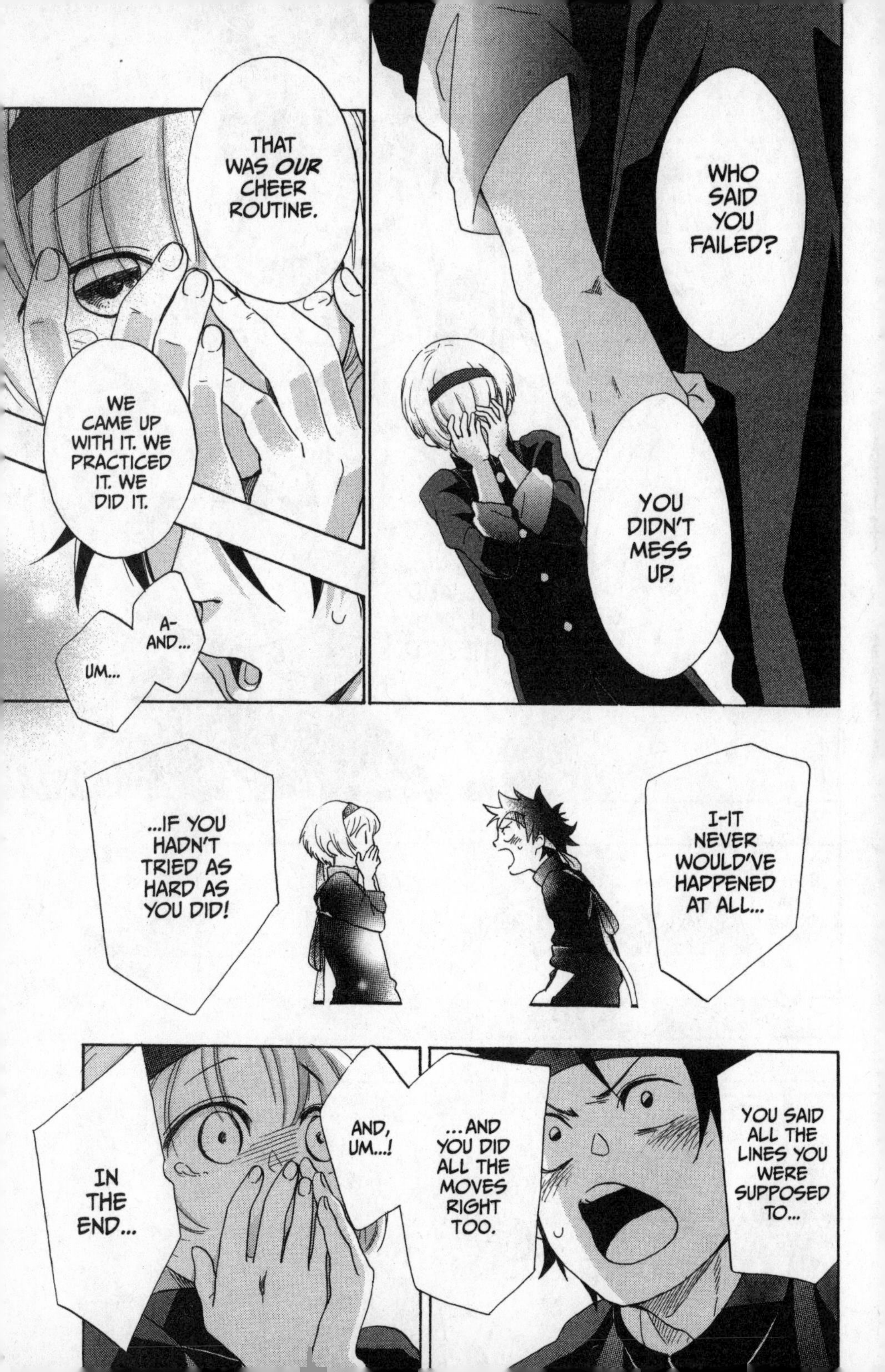
WHO SAID YOU FAILED?
YOU DIDN'T MESS UP.
THAT WAS OUR CHEER ROUTINE.
WE CAME UP WITH IT. WE PRACTICED IT. WE DID IT.
A- AND...
UM...
I-IT NEVER WOULD'VE HAPPENED AT ALL...
...IF YOU HADN'T TRIED AS HARD AS YOU DID!
YOU SAID ALL THE LINES YOU WERE SUPPOSED TO...
...AND YOU DID ALL THE MOVES RIGHT TOO.
AND, UM...!
IN THE END...

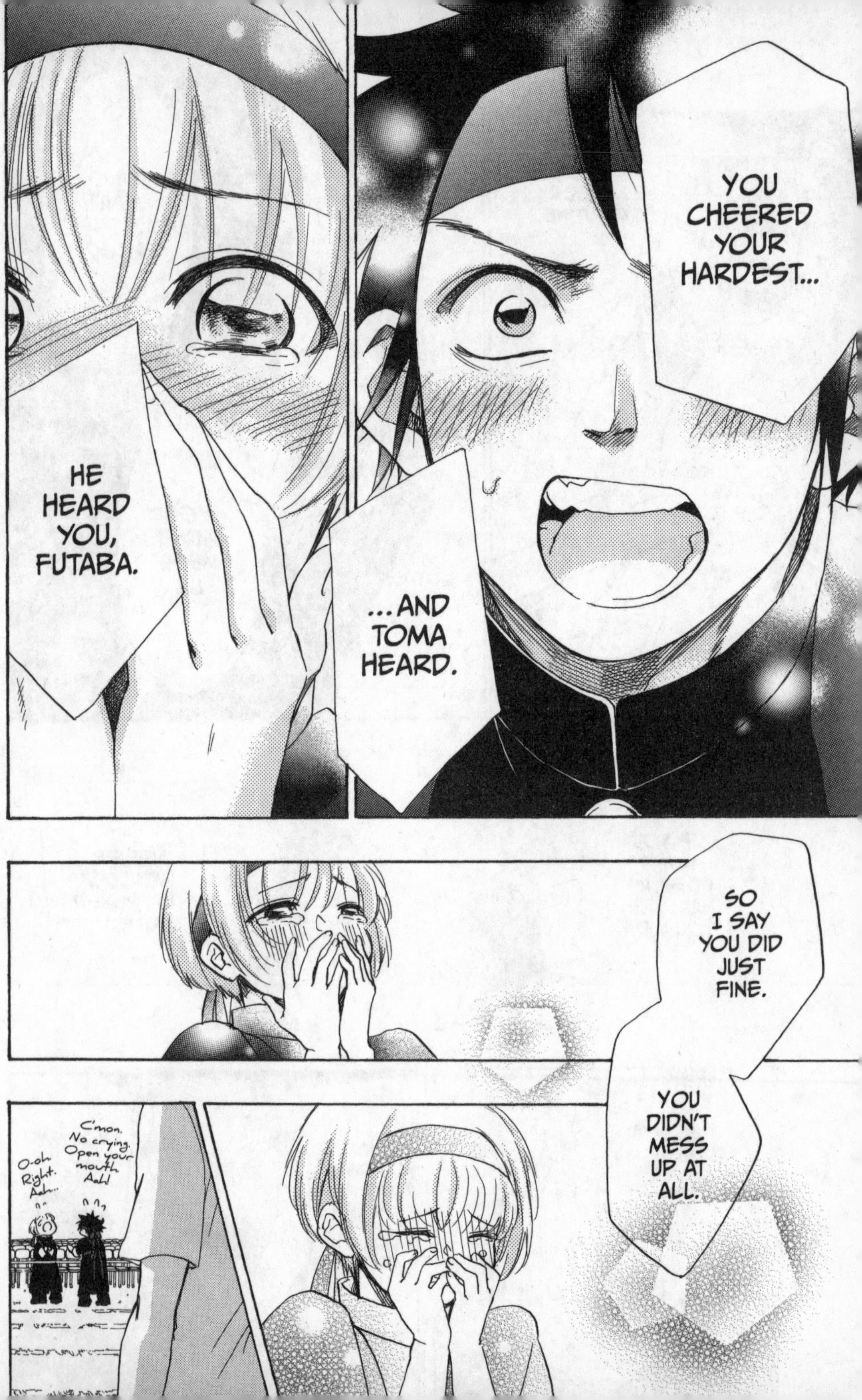
YOU CHEERED YOUR HARDEST...
...AND TOMA HEARD.
HE HEARD YOU, FUTABA.
SO I SAY YOU DID JUST FINE.
YOU DIDN'T MESS UP AT ALL.
C'mon. No crying. Open your mouth. Aah!
O-oh. Right. Aah...

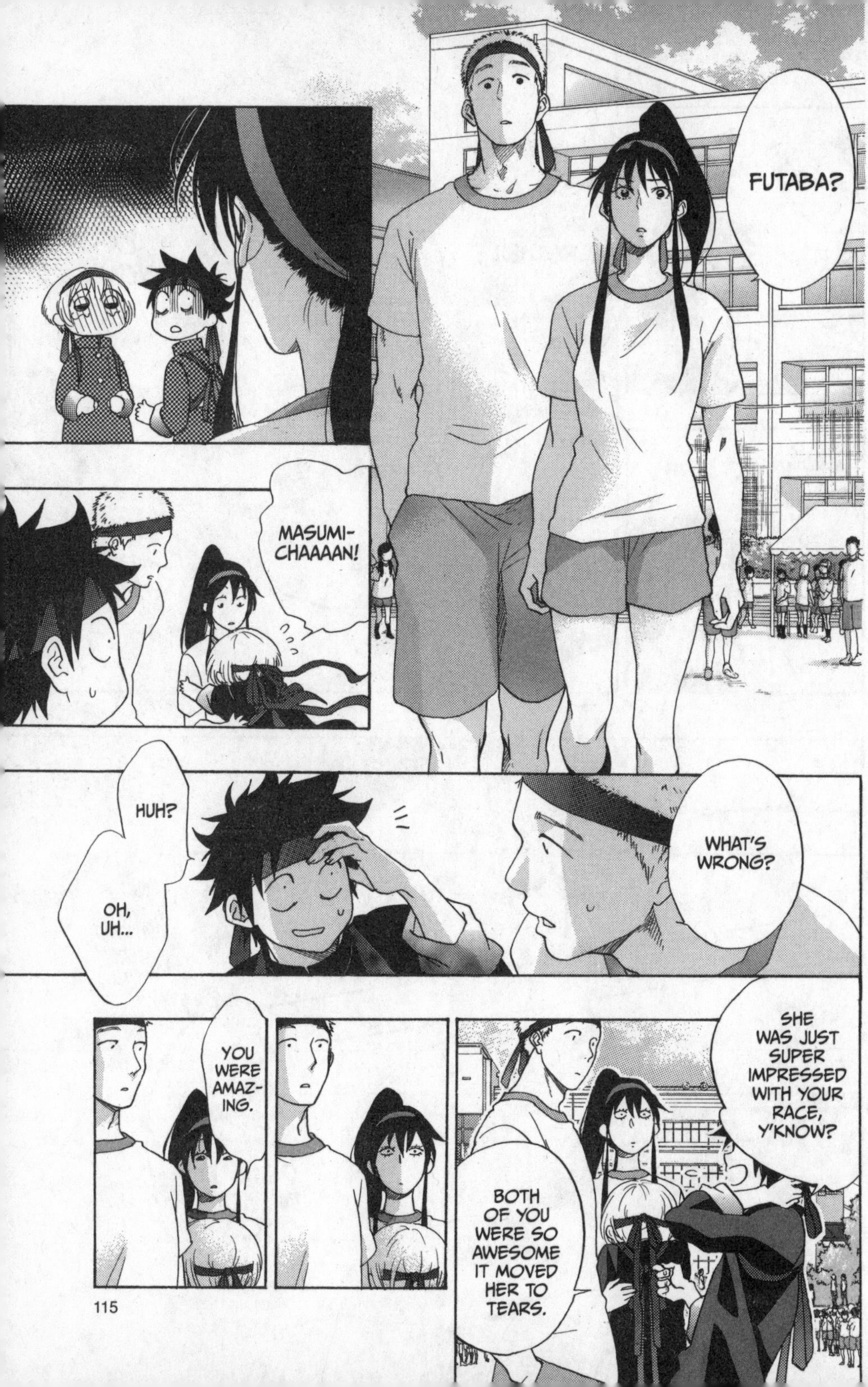
FUTABA?
MASUMI-CHAAAAN!
WHAT'S WRONG?
HUH?
OH, UH...
SHE WAS JUST SUPER IMPRESSED WITH YOUR RACE, Y'KNOW?
BOTH OF YOU WERE SO AWESOME IT MOVED HER TO TEARS.
YOU WERE AMAZ-ING.

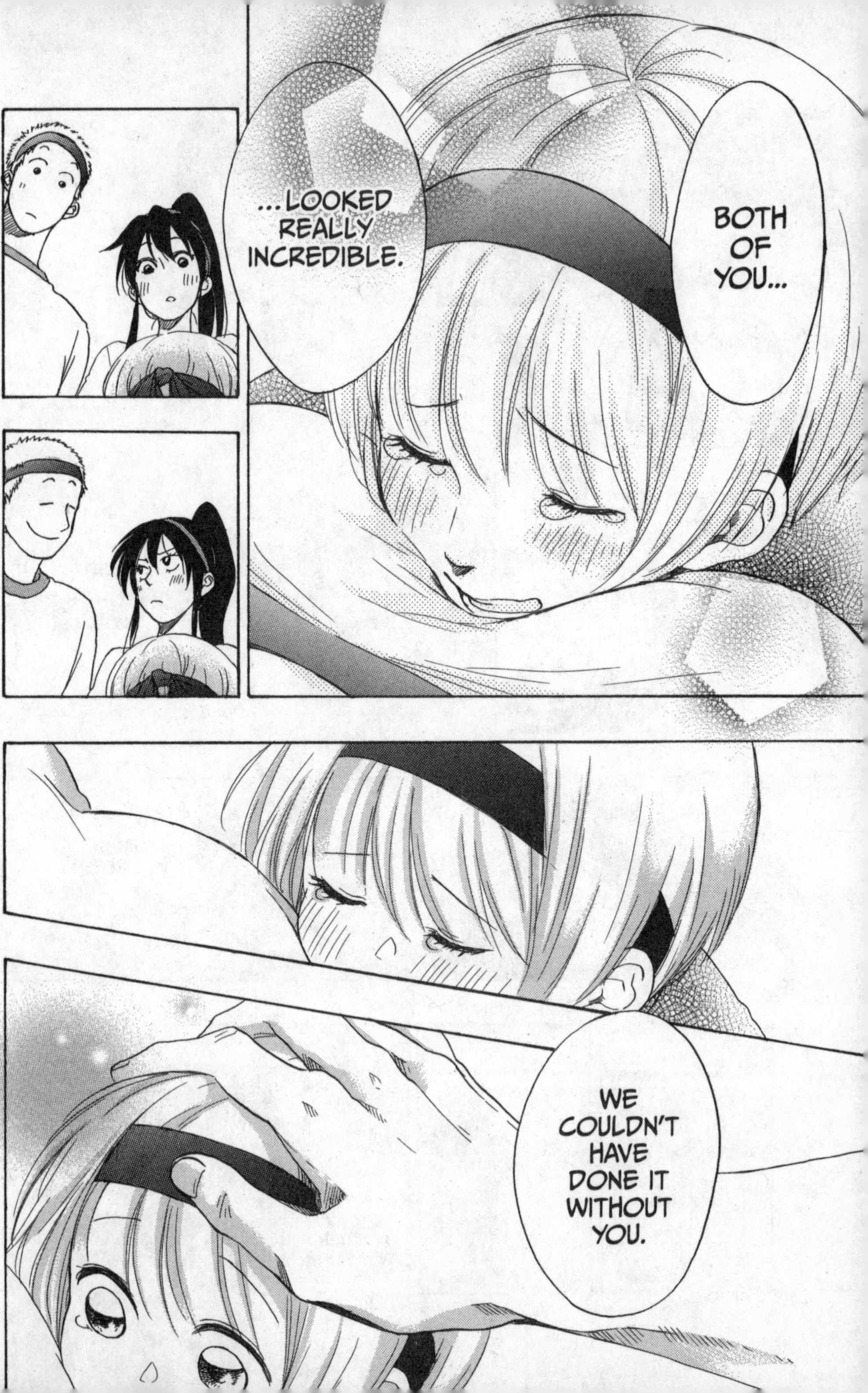
BOTH OF YOU...
...LOOKED REALLY INCREDIBLE.
WE COULDN'T HAVE DONE IT WITHOUT YOU.

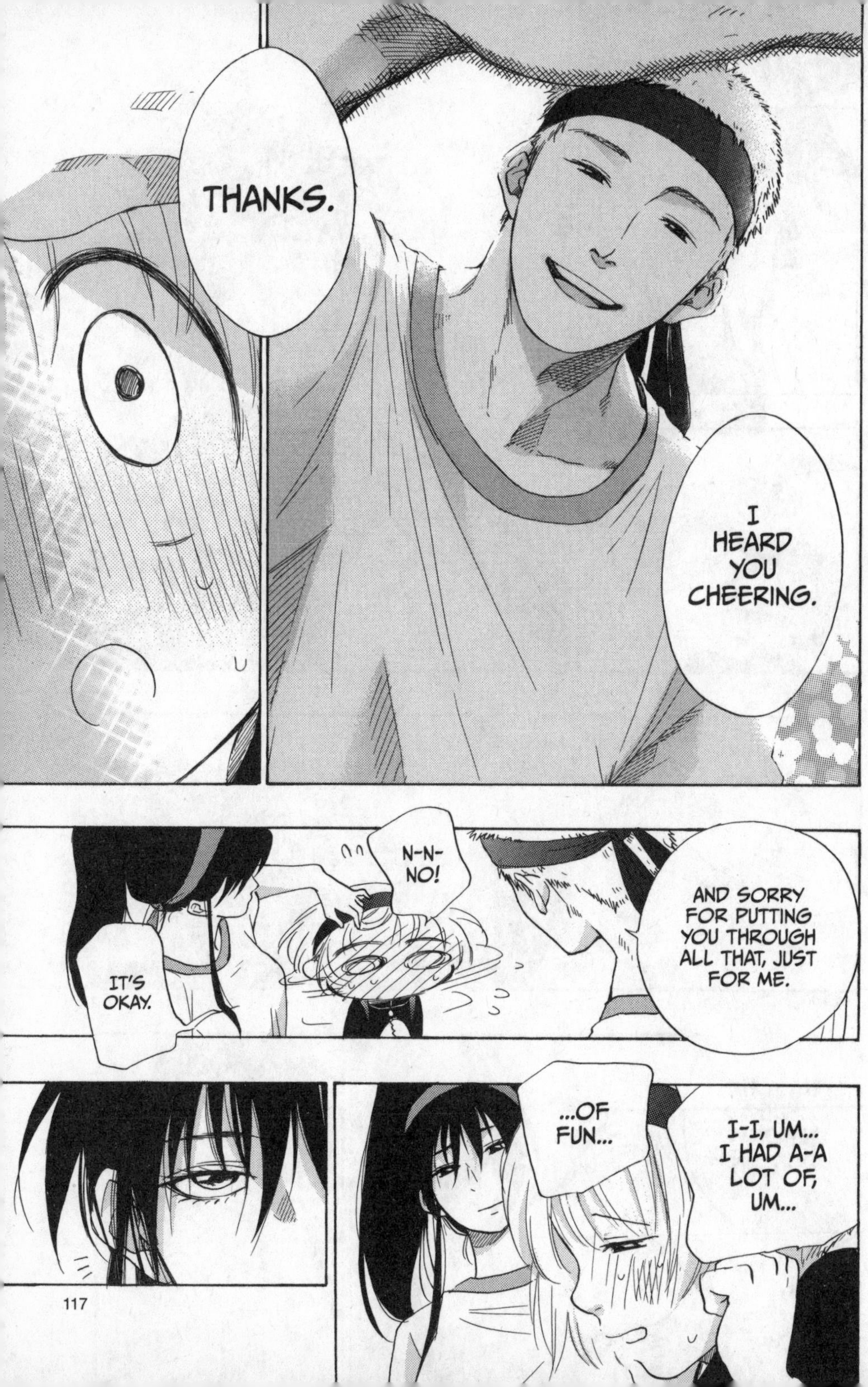
THANKS.
I HEARD YOU CHEERING.
AND SORRY FOR PUTTING YOU THROUGH ALL THAT, JUST FOR ME.
N-N-NO!
IT'S OKAY.
I-I, UM... I HAD A-A LOT OF, UM...
...OF FUN...

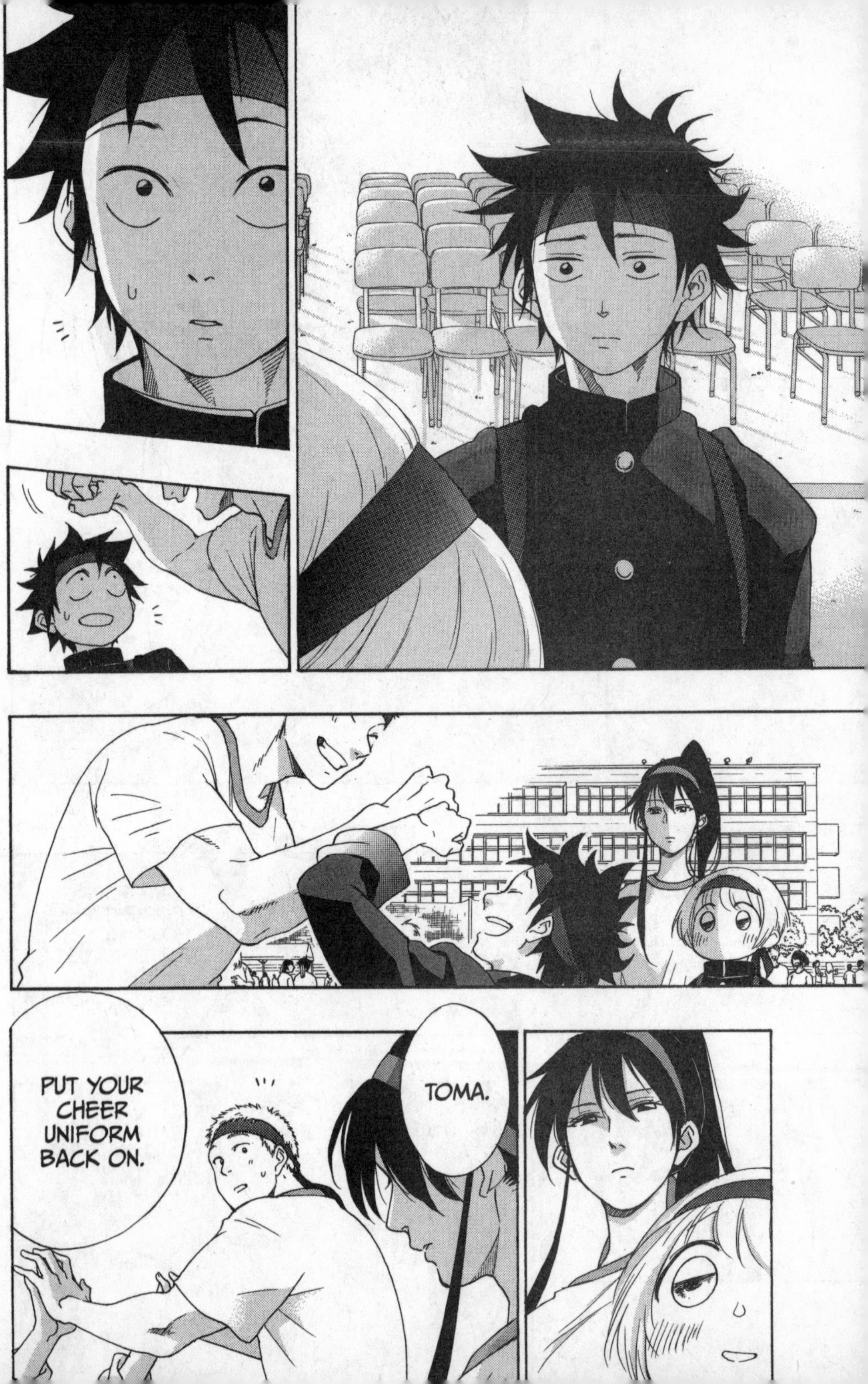

TOMA.
PUT YOUR CHEER UNIFORM BACK ON.

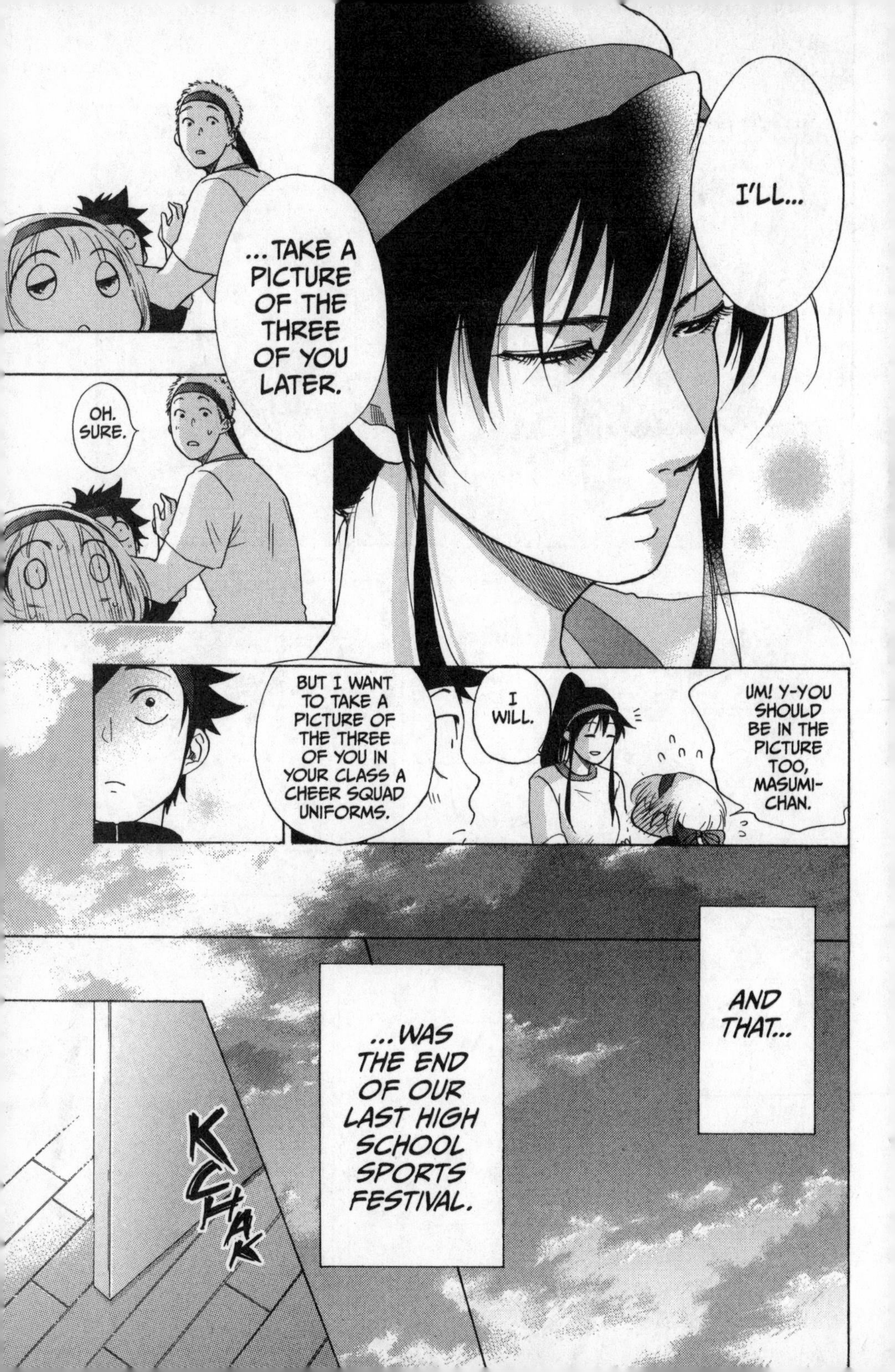

I'LL...
...TAKE A PICTURE OF THE THREE OF YOU LATER.
OH. SURE.
UM! Y-YOU SHOULD BE IN THE PICTURE TOO, MASUMI-CHAN.
I WILL.
BUT I WANT TO TAKE A PICTURE OF THE THREE OF YOU IN YOUR CLASS A CHEER SQUAD UNIFORMS.
AND THAT...
...WAS THE END OF OUR LAST HIGH SCHOOL SPORTS FESTIVAL.
KCHAK

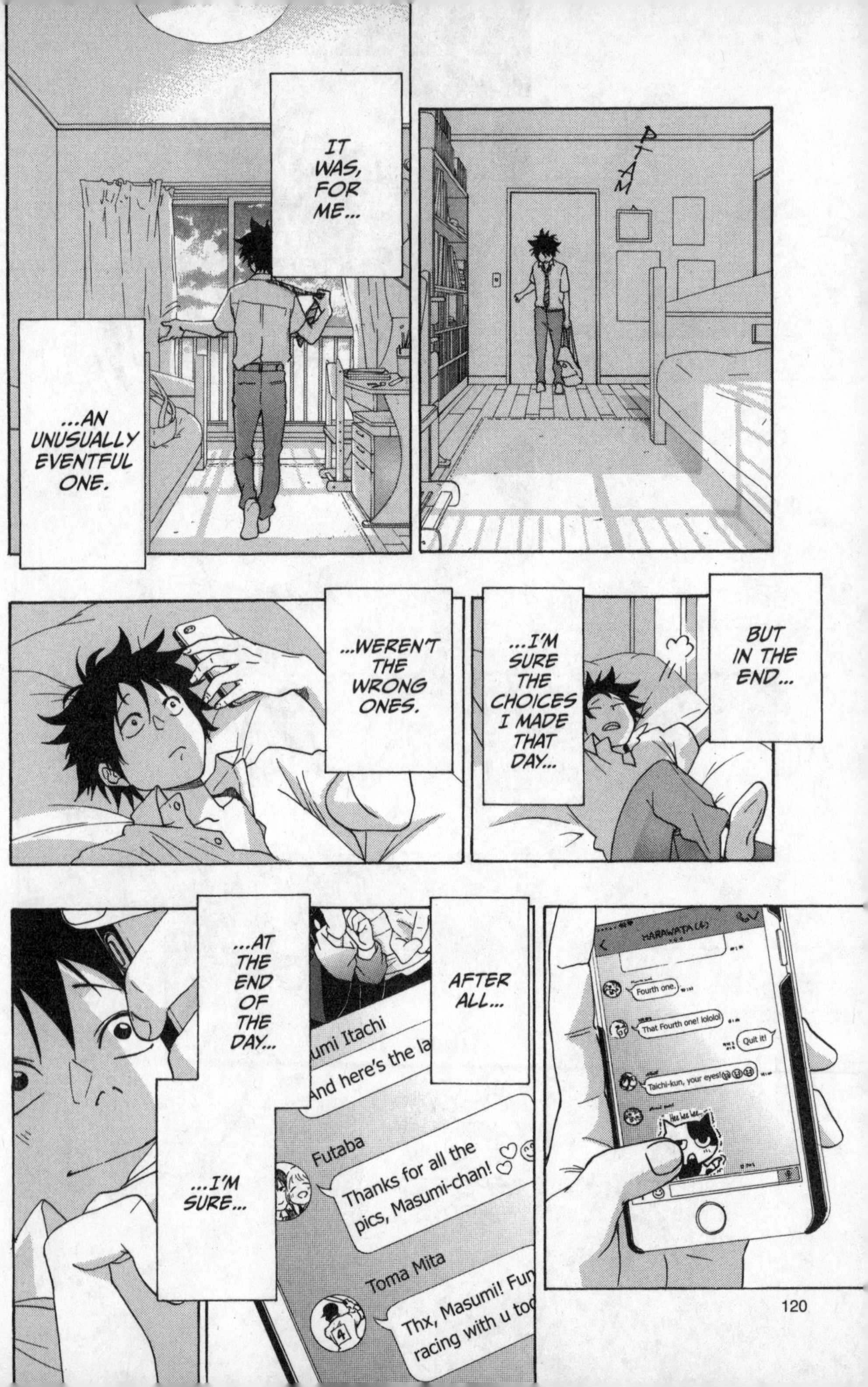
PTAM
IT WAS, FOR ME...
...AN UNUSUALLY EVENTFUL ONE.
BUT IN THE END...
...I'M SURE THE CHOICES I MADE THAT DAY...
...WEREN'T THE WRONG ONES.
Fourth one.
That Fourth one! lololol
Quit it!
Taichi-kun, your eyes!
AFTER ALL...
...AT THE END OF THE DAY...
umi Itachi
And here's the la
Futaba
Thanks for all the pics, Masumi-chan!
Toma Mita
Thx, Masumi! Fun racing with u to
...I'M SURE...

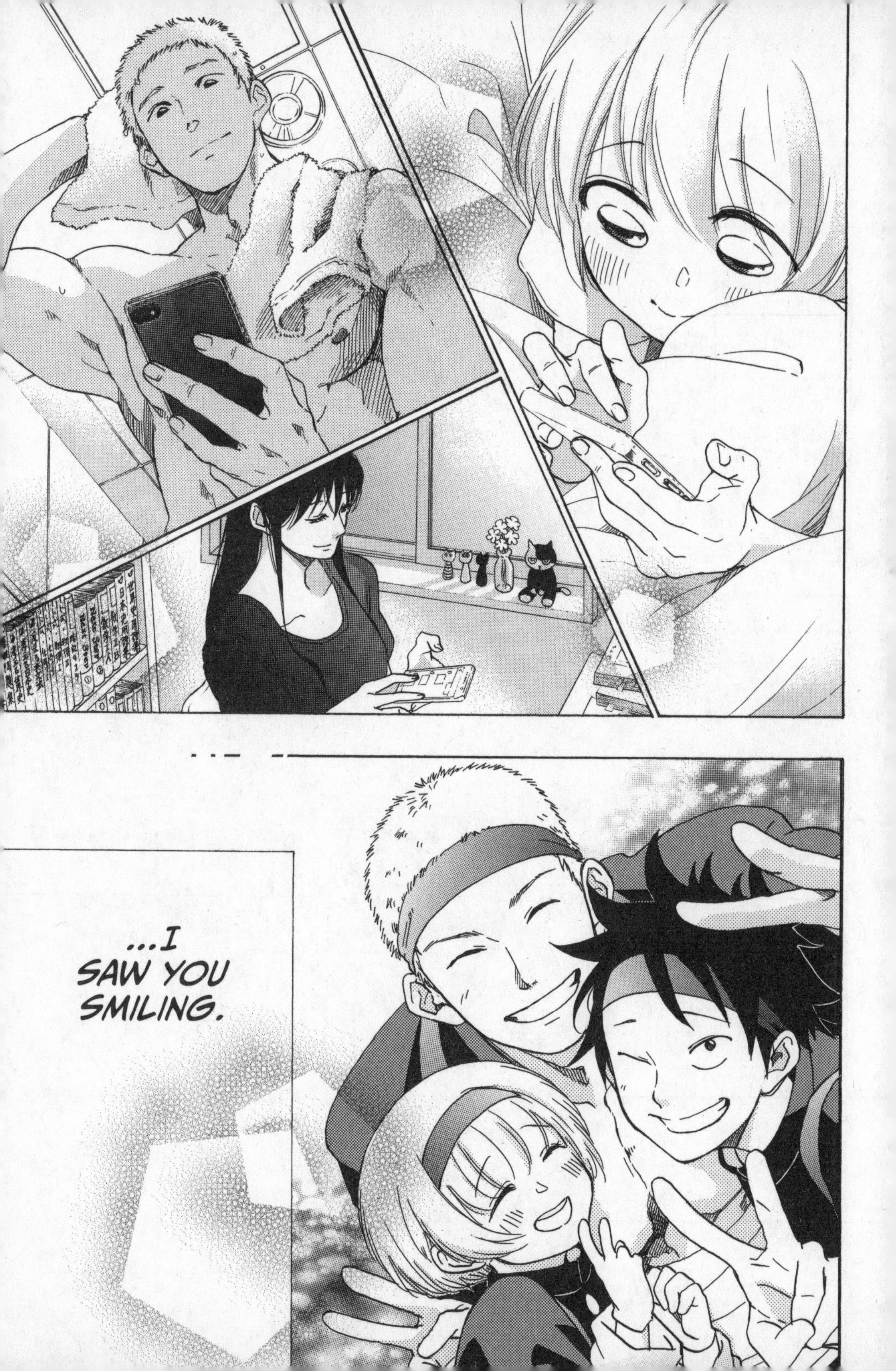
...I SAW YOU SMILING.

The final score at the
end of the festival

The winner was class 3-A. They
pulled a come-from-behind victory
with their win in the relay.

Woo!

CHAPTER 10

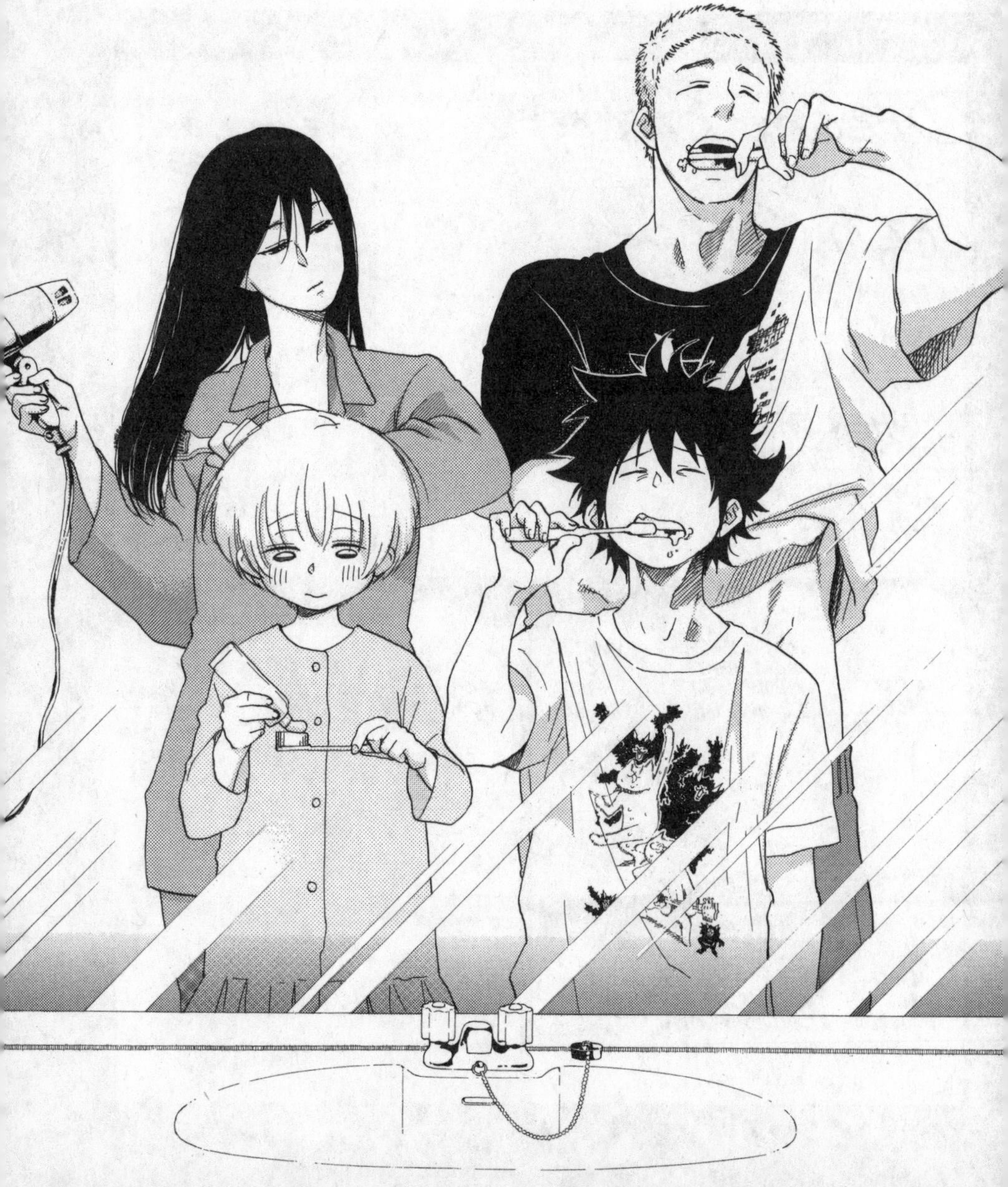

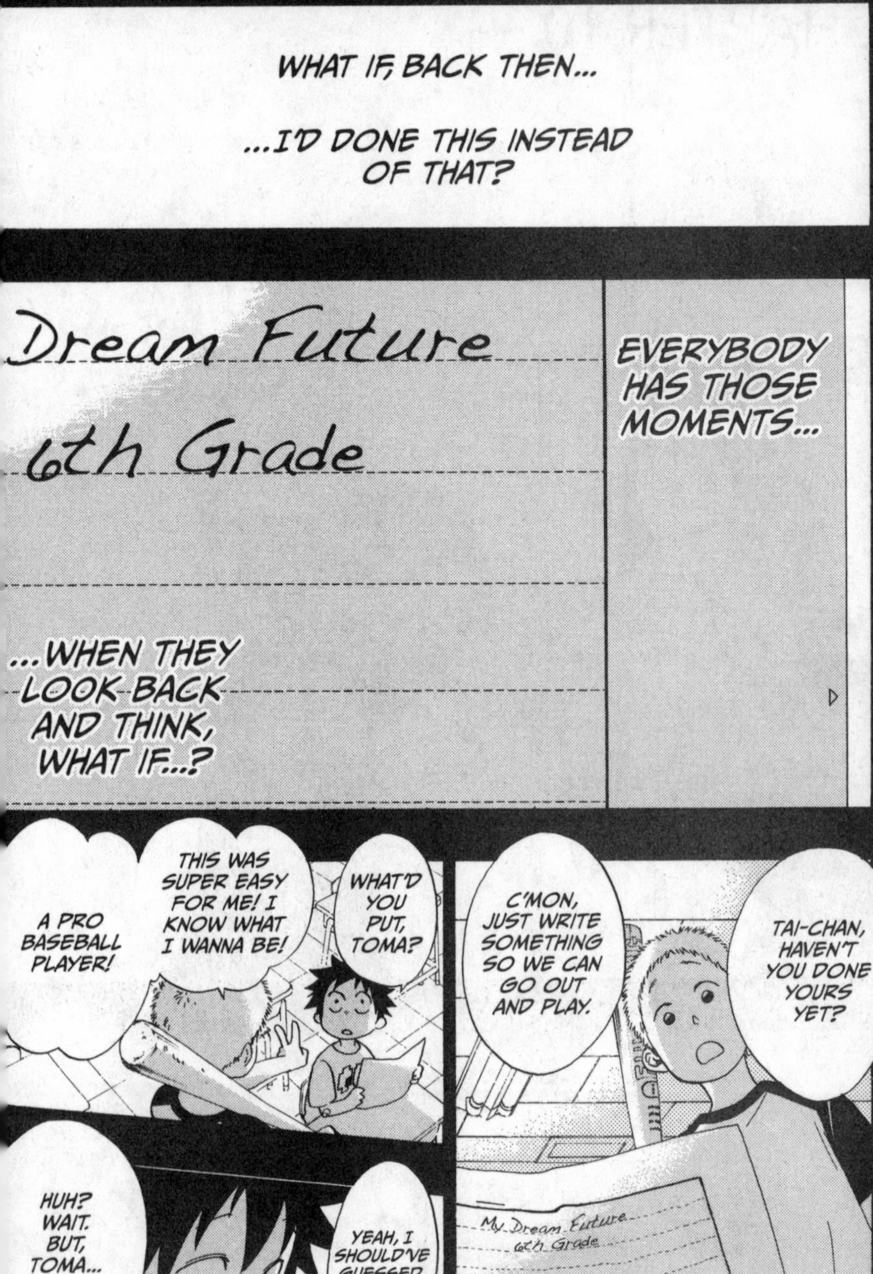
WHAT IF, BACK THEN...
...I'D DONE THIS INSTEAD OF THAT?
EVERYBODY HAS THOSE MOMENTS...
Dream Future
6th Grade
...WHEN THEY LOOK BACK AND THINK, WHAT IF...?
TAI-CHAN, HAVEN'T YOU DONE YOURS YET?
C'MON, JUST WRITE SOMETHING SO WE CAN GO OUT AND PLAY.
My Dream Future
6th Grade
WHAT'D YOU PUT, TOMA?
THIS WAS SUPER EASY FOR ME! I KNOW WHAT I WANNA BE!
A PRO BASEBALL PLAYER!
YEAH, I SHOULD'VE GUESSED.
HUH? WAIT. BUT, TOMA...

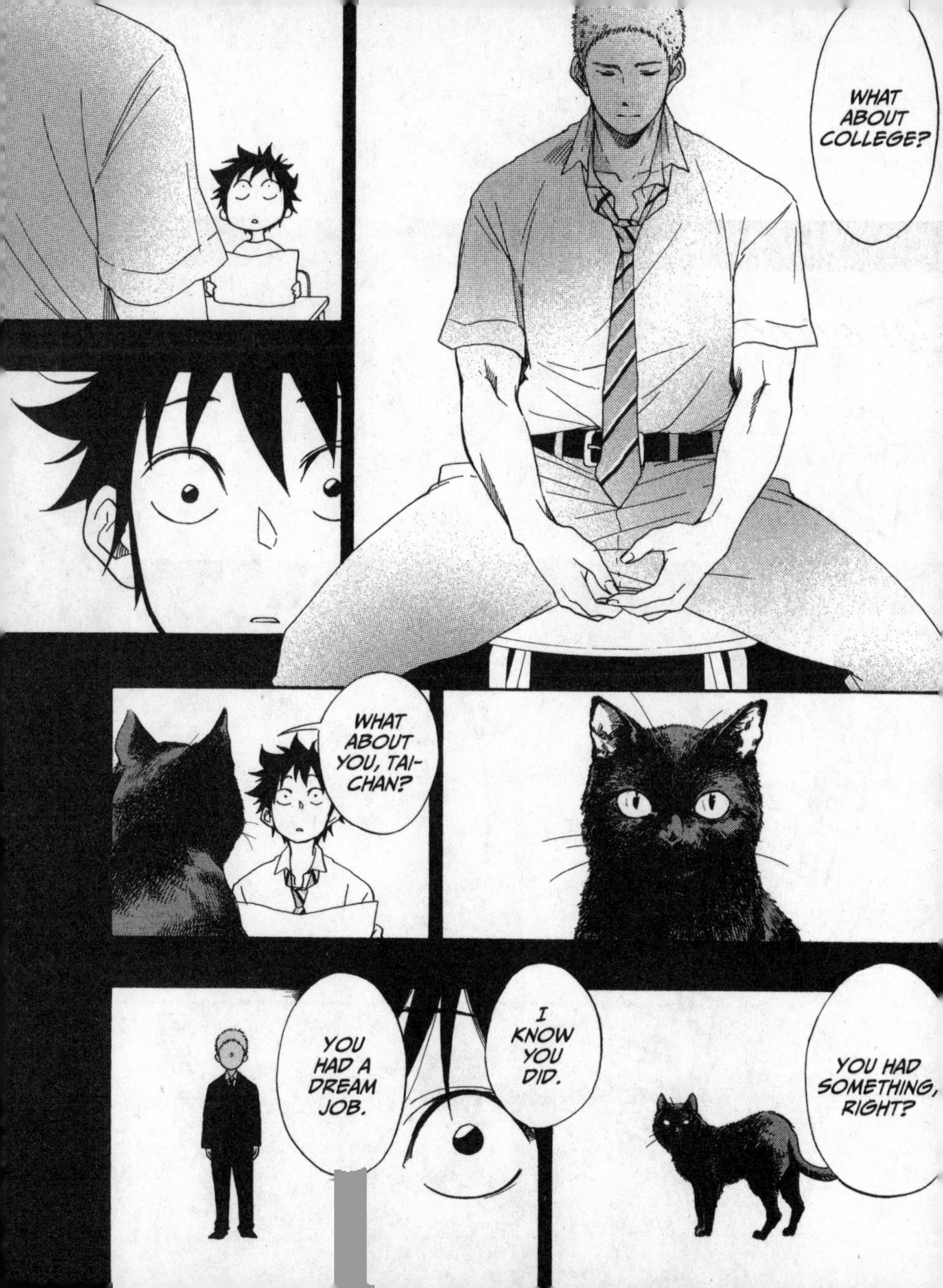
WHAT ABOUT COLLEGE?
WHAT ABOUT YOU, TAI-CHAN?
YOU HAD SOMETHING, RIGHT?
I KNOW YOU DID.
YOU HAD A DREAM JOB.

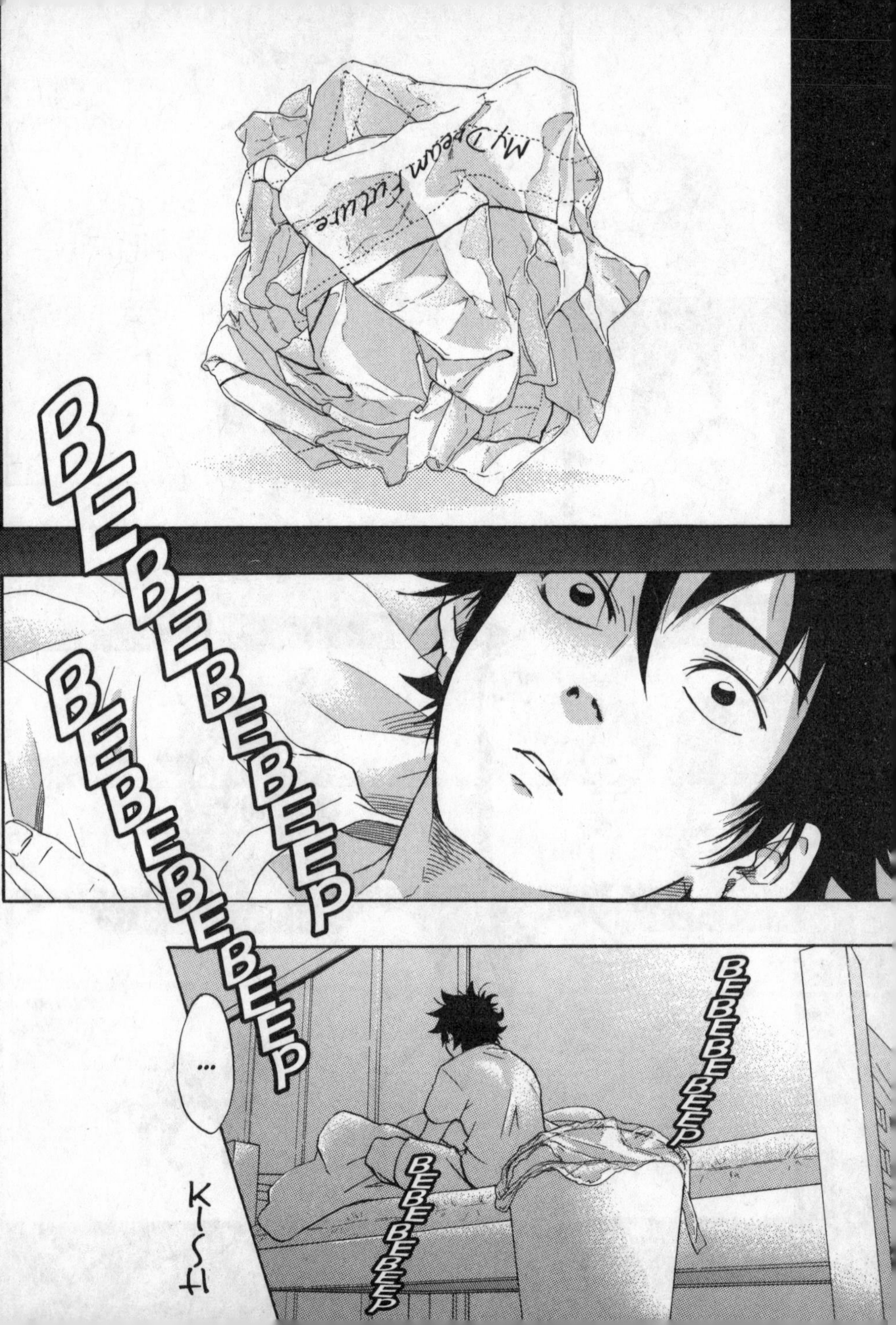
My Dream Future
BEBEBEBEEP
BEBEBEBEBEEP
BEBEBEBEEP
BEBEBEBEEP
...
KISH

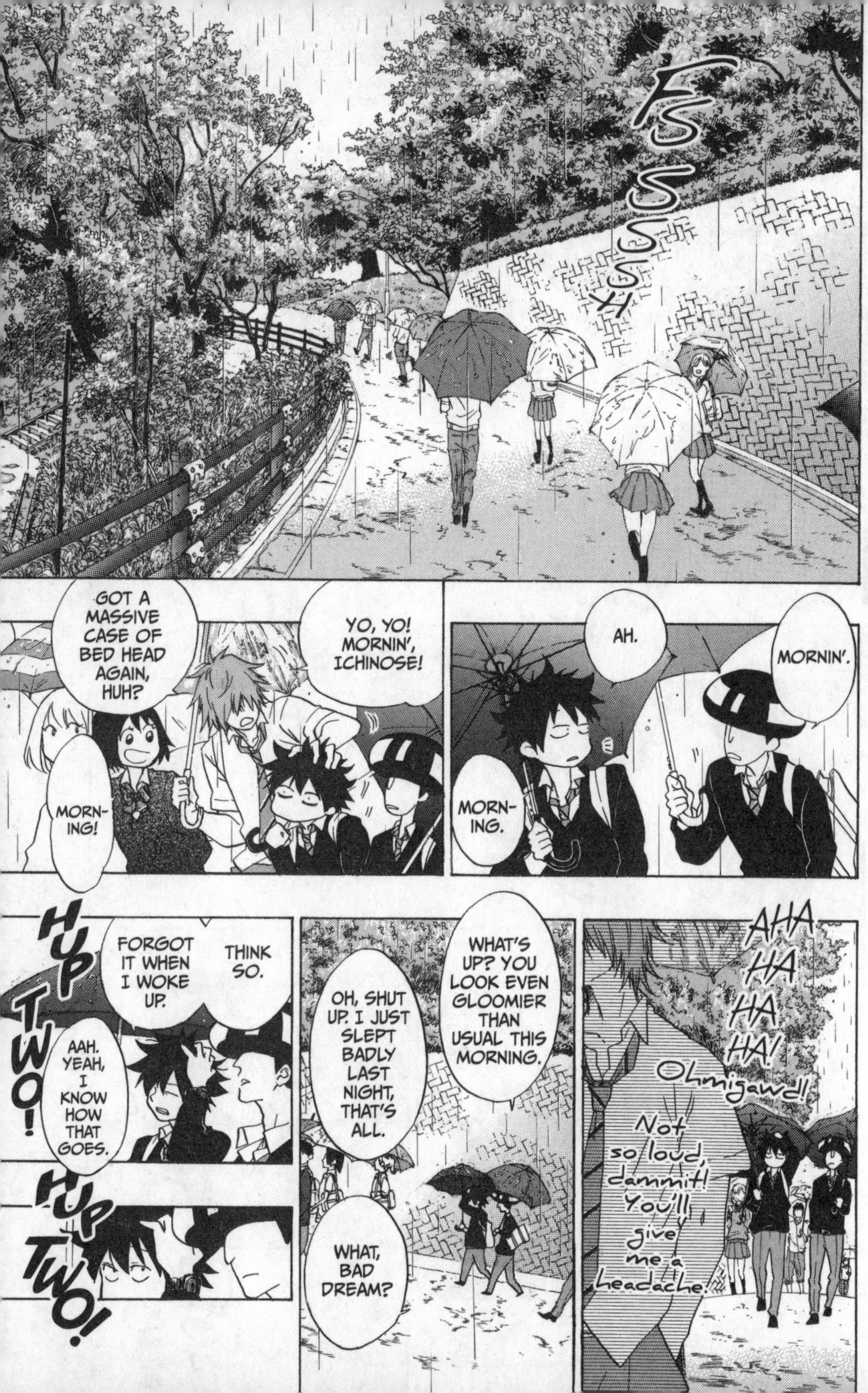
FSSSSH
MORNIN'.
AH.
MORNING.
YO, YO! MORNIN', ICHINOSE!
GOT A MASSIVE CASE OF BED HEAD AGAIN, HUH?
MORNING!
AHA HA HA HA!
Ohmigawd!
Not so loud, dammit! You'll give me a headache.
WHAT'S UP? YOU LOOK EVEN GLOOMIER THAN USUAL THIS MORNING.
OH, SHUT UP. I JUST SLEPT BADLY LAST NIGHT, THAT'S ALL.
WHAT, BAD DREAM?
THINK SO.
FORGOT IT WHEN I WOKE UP.
AAH. YEAH, I KNOW HOW THAT GOES.
HUP TWO!
HUP TWO!

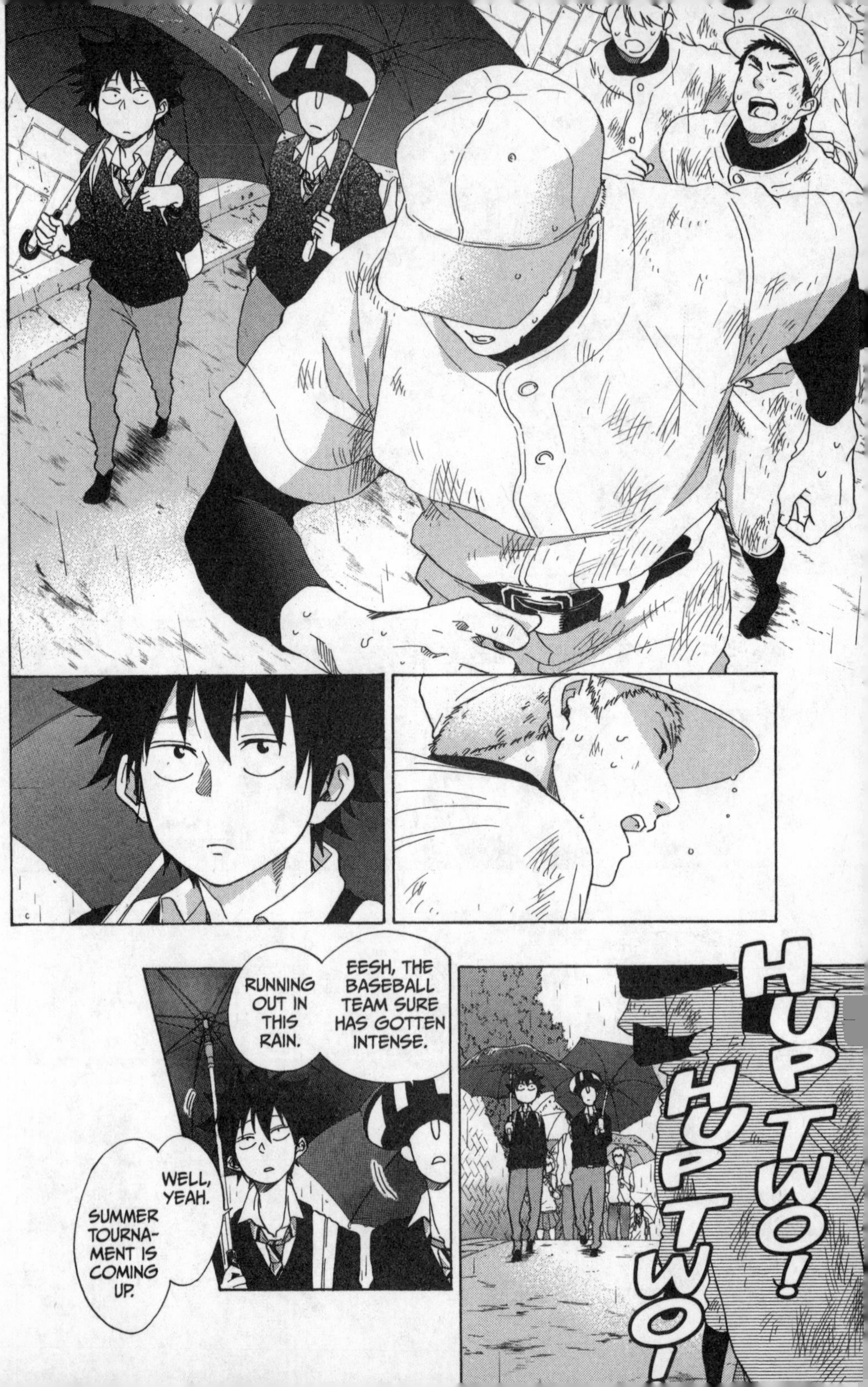
HUP TWO! HUP TWO!
EESH, THE BASEBALL TEAM SURE HAS GOTTEN INTENSE.
RUNNING OUT IN THIS RAIN.
WELL, YEAH.
SUMMER TOURNAMENT IS COMING UP.

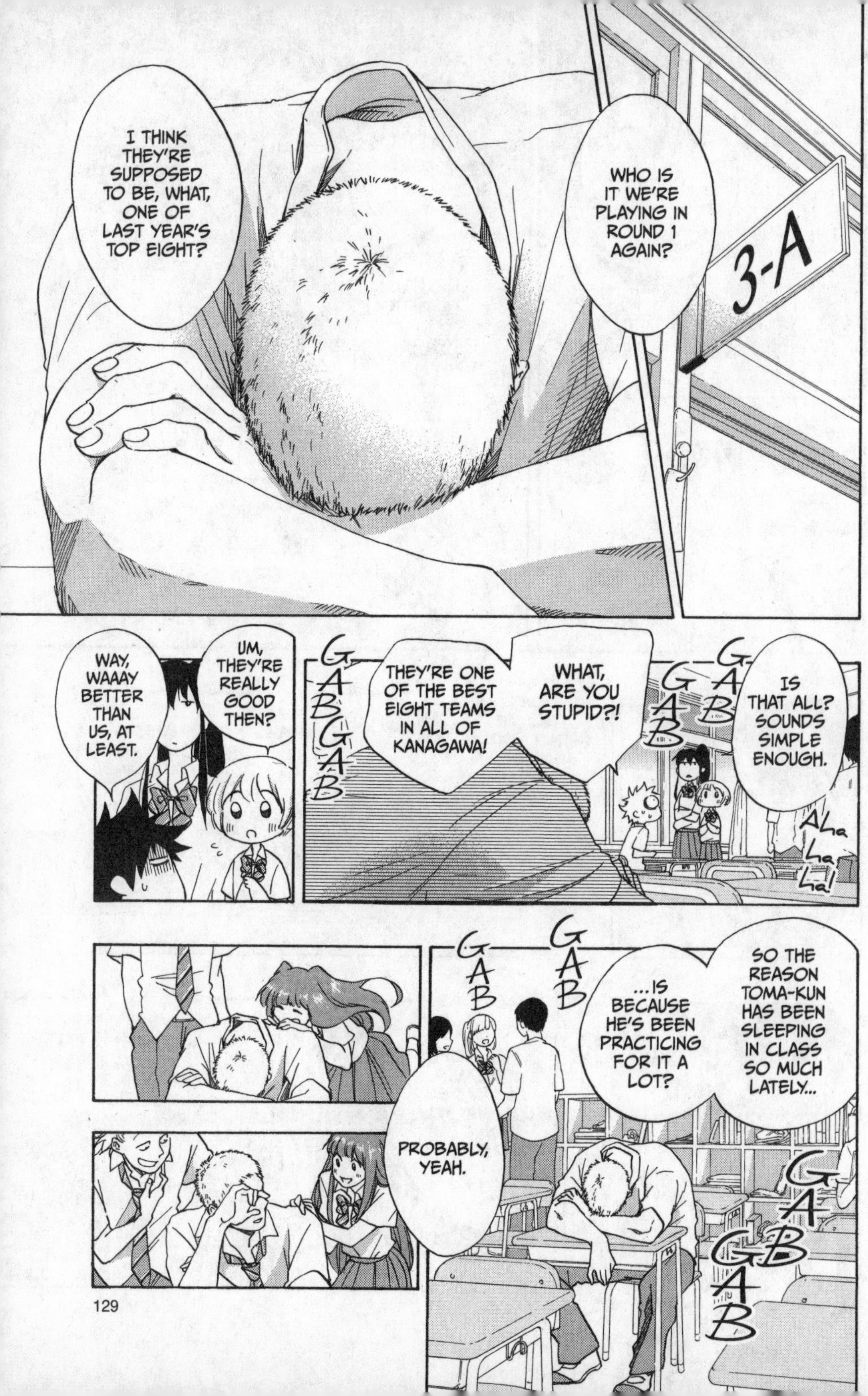
WHO IS IT WE'RE PLAYING IN ROUND 1 AGAIN?
3-A
I THINK THEY'RE SUPPOSED TO BE, WHAT, ONE OF LAST YEAR'S TOP EIGHT?
IS THAT ALL? SOUNDS SIMPLE ENOUGH.
GAB GAB
AHA HA HA!
WHAT, ARE YOU STUPID?!
THEY'RE ONE OF THE BEST EIGHT TEAMS IN ALL OF KANAGAWA!
GAB GAB
UM, THEY'RE REALLY GOOD THEN?
WAY, WAAAY BETTER THAN US, AT LEAST.
SO THE REASON TOMA-KUN HAS BEEN SLEEPING IN CLASS SO MUCH LATELY...
...IS BECAUSE HE'S BEEN PRACTICING FOR IT A LOT?
GAB GAB
PROBABLY, YEAH.
GAB GAB
GAB GAB

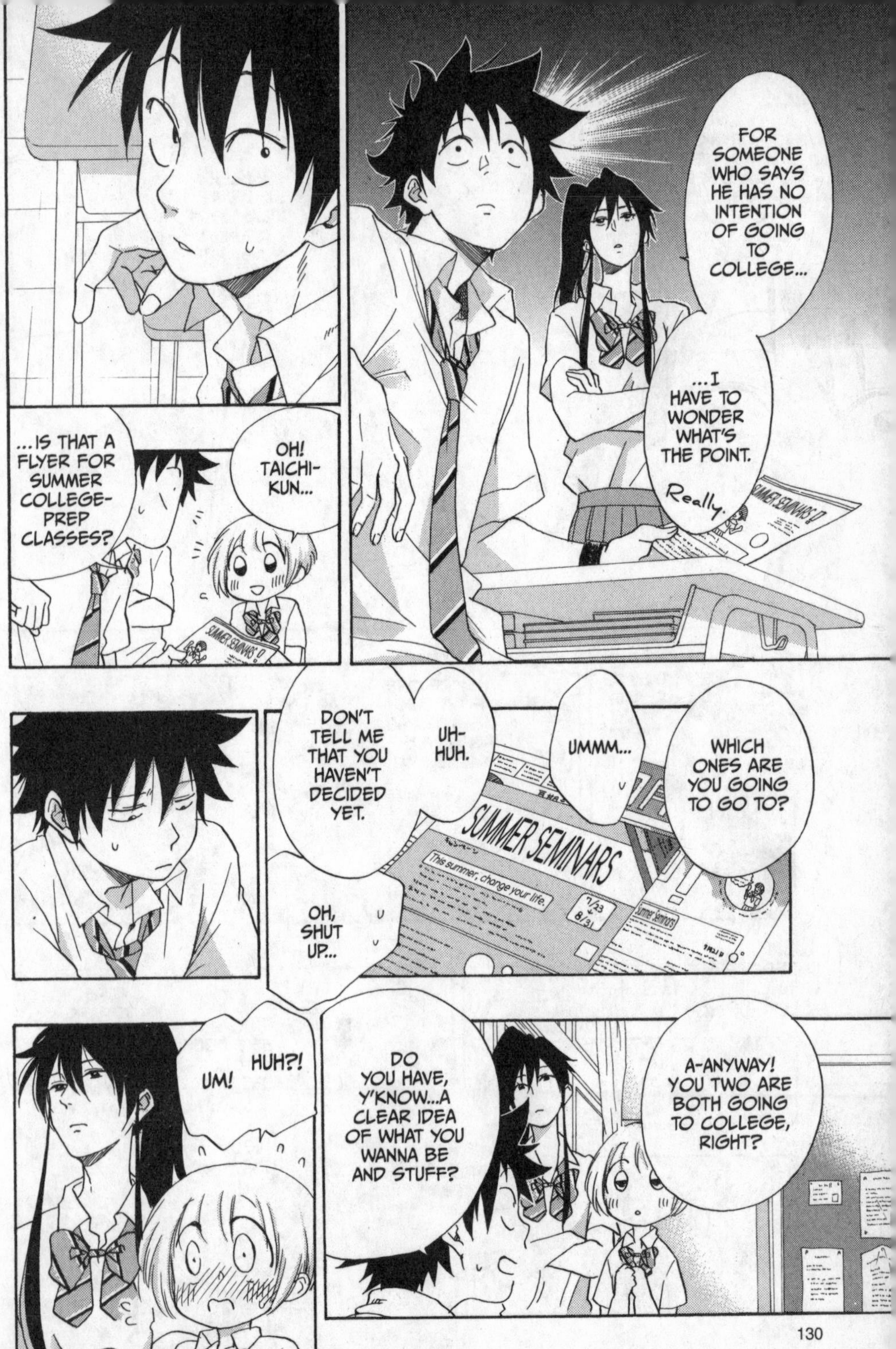
FOR SOMEONE WHO SAYS HE HAS NO INTENTION OF GOING TO COLLEGE...
...I HAVE TO WONDER WHAT'S THE POINT.
Really.
SUMMER SEMINARS!!
OH! TAICHI-KUN...
...IS THAT A FLYER FOR SUMMER COLLEGE-PREP CLASSES?
SUMMER SEMINARS!
WHICH ONES ARE YOU GOING TO GO TO?
UMMM...
UH-HUH.
DON'T TELL ME THAT YOU HAVEN'T DECIDED YET.
SUMMER SEMINARS
This summer, change your life.
7/23 ↓ 8/31
Summer Seminars
OH, SHUT UP...
A-ANYWAY! YOU TWO ARE BOTH GOING TO COLLEGE, RIGHT?
DO YOU HAVE, Y'KNOW...A CLEAR IDEA OF WHAT YOU WANNA BE AND STUFF?
HUH?!
UM!

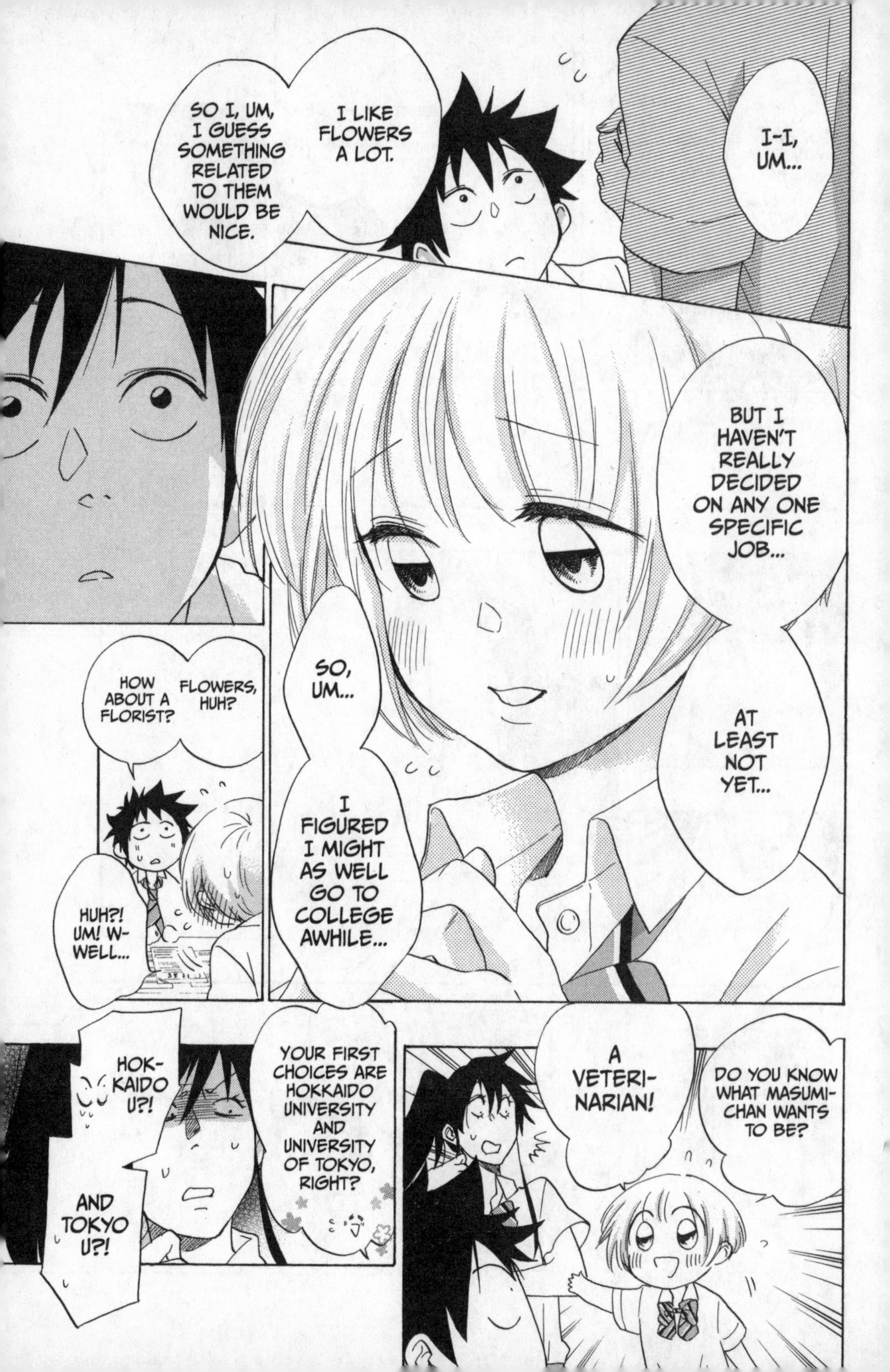
I-I, UM...
I LIKE FLOWERS A LOT.
SO I, UM, I GUESS SOMETHING RELATED TO THEM WOULD BE NICE.
BUT I HAVEN'T REALLY DECIDED ON ANY ONE SPECIFIC JOB...
AT LEAST NOT YET...
SO, UM...
I FIGURED I MIGHT AS WELL GO TO COLLEGE AWHILE...
FLOWERS, HUH?
HOW ABOUT A FLORIST?
HUH?! UM! W-WELL...
DO YOU KNOW WHAT MASUMI-CHAN WANTS TO BE?
A VETERINARIAN!
YOUR FIRST CHOICES ARE HOKKAIDO UNIVERSITY AND UNIVERSITY OF TOKYO, RIGHT?
HOK-KAIDO U?!
AND TOKYO U?!

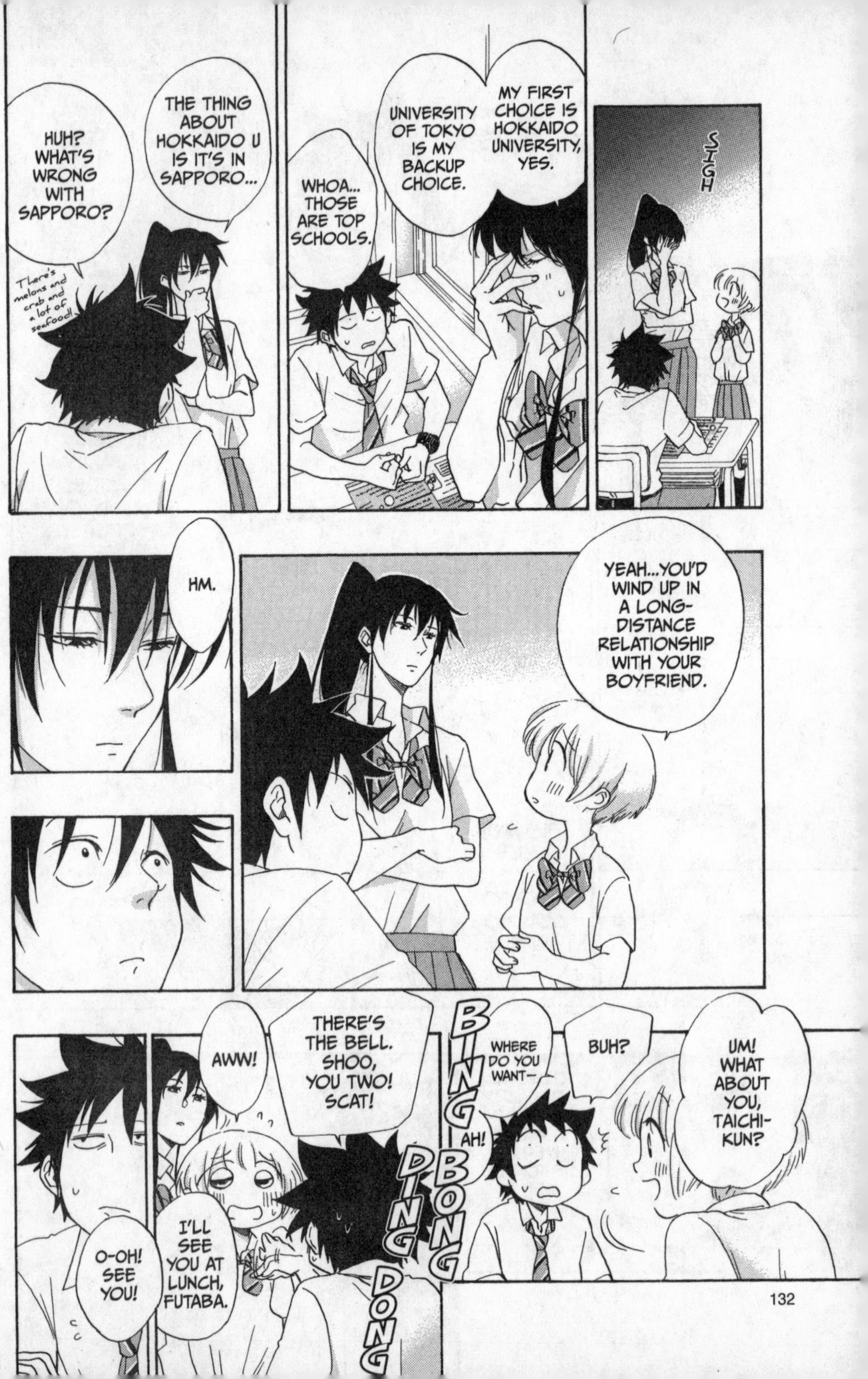
SIGH
MY FIRST CHOICE IS HOKKAIDO UNIVERSITY, YES.
UNIVERSITY OF TOKYO IS MY BACKUP CHOICE.
WHOA... THOSE ARE TOP SCHOOLS.
THE THING ABOUT HOKKAIDO U IS IT'S IN SAPPORO...
HUH? WHAT'S WRONG WITH SAPPORO?
There's melons and crab and a lot of seafood!
YEAH...YOU'D WIND UP IN A LONG-DISTANCE RELATIONSHIP WITH YOUR BOYFRIEND.
HM.
UM! WHAT ABOUT YOU, TAICHI-KUN?
BUH?
WHERE DO YOU WANT—
AH!
BING BONG
DING DONG
THERE'S THE BELL. SHOO, YOU TWO! SCAT!
AWW!
I'LL SEE YOU AT LUNCH, FUTABA.
O-OH! SEE YOU!

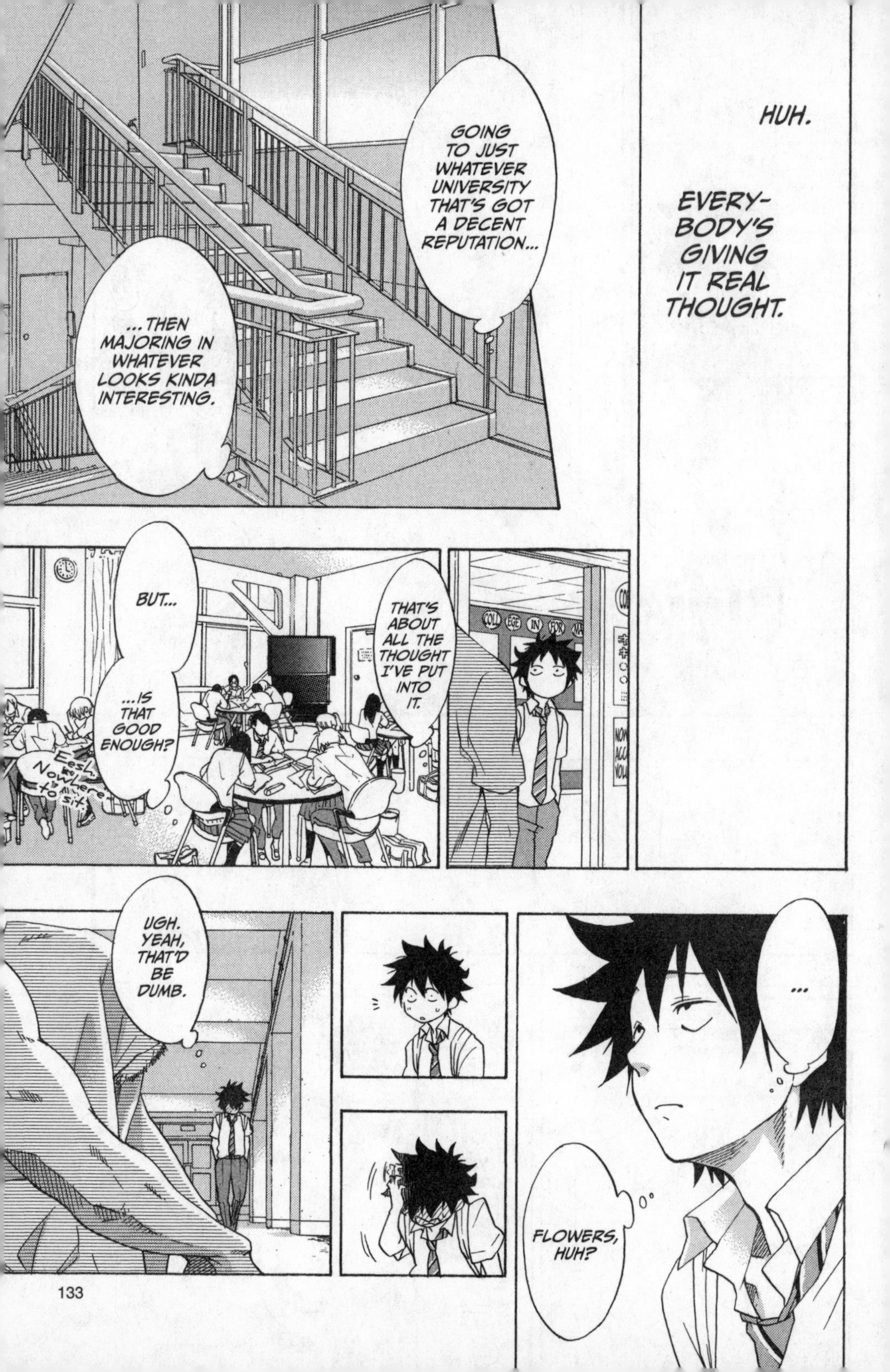
HUH.
EVERY-BODY'S GIVING IT REAL THOUGHT.
GOING TO JUST WHATEVER UNIVERSITY THAT'S GOT A DECENT REPUTATION...
...THEN MAJORING IN WHATEVER LOOKS KINDA INTERESTING.
THAT'S ABOUT ALL THE THOUGHT I'VE PUT INTO IT.
BUT...
...IS THAT GOOD ENOUGH?
Eesh, Nowhere to sit
...
FLOWERS, HUH?
UGH. YEAH, THAT'D BE DUMB.

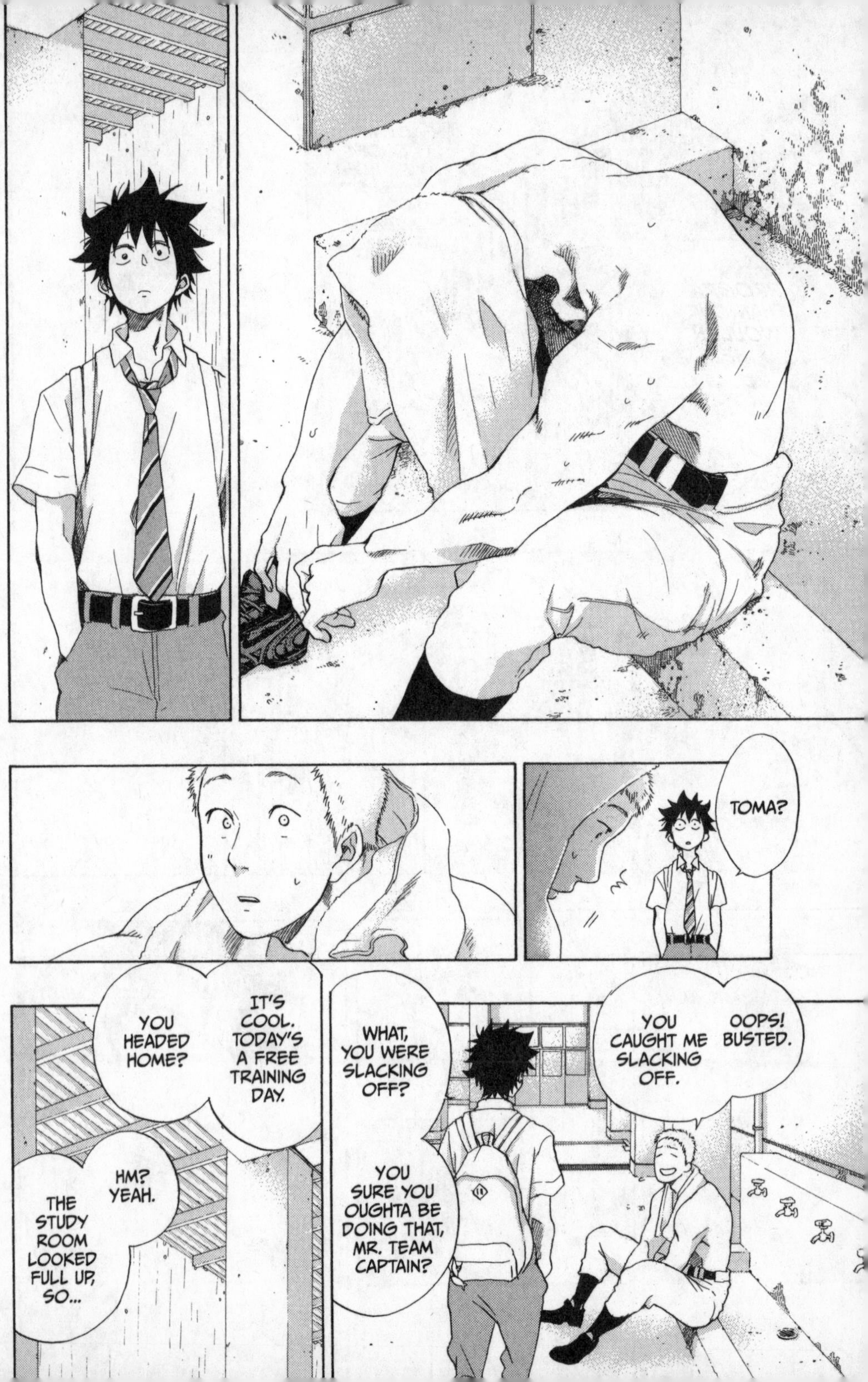
TOMA?
OOPS! BUSTED.
YOU CAUGHT ME SLACKING OFF.
WHAT, YOU WERE SLACKING OFF?
YOU SURE YOU OUGHTA BE DOING THAT, MR. TEAM CAPTAIN?
IT'S COOL. TODAY'S A FREE TRAINING DAY.
YOU HEADED HOME?
HM? YEAH.
THE STUDY ROOM LOOKED FULL UP, SO...

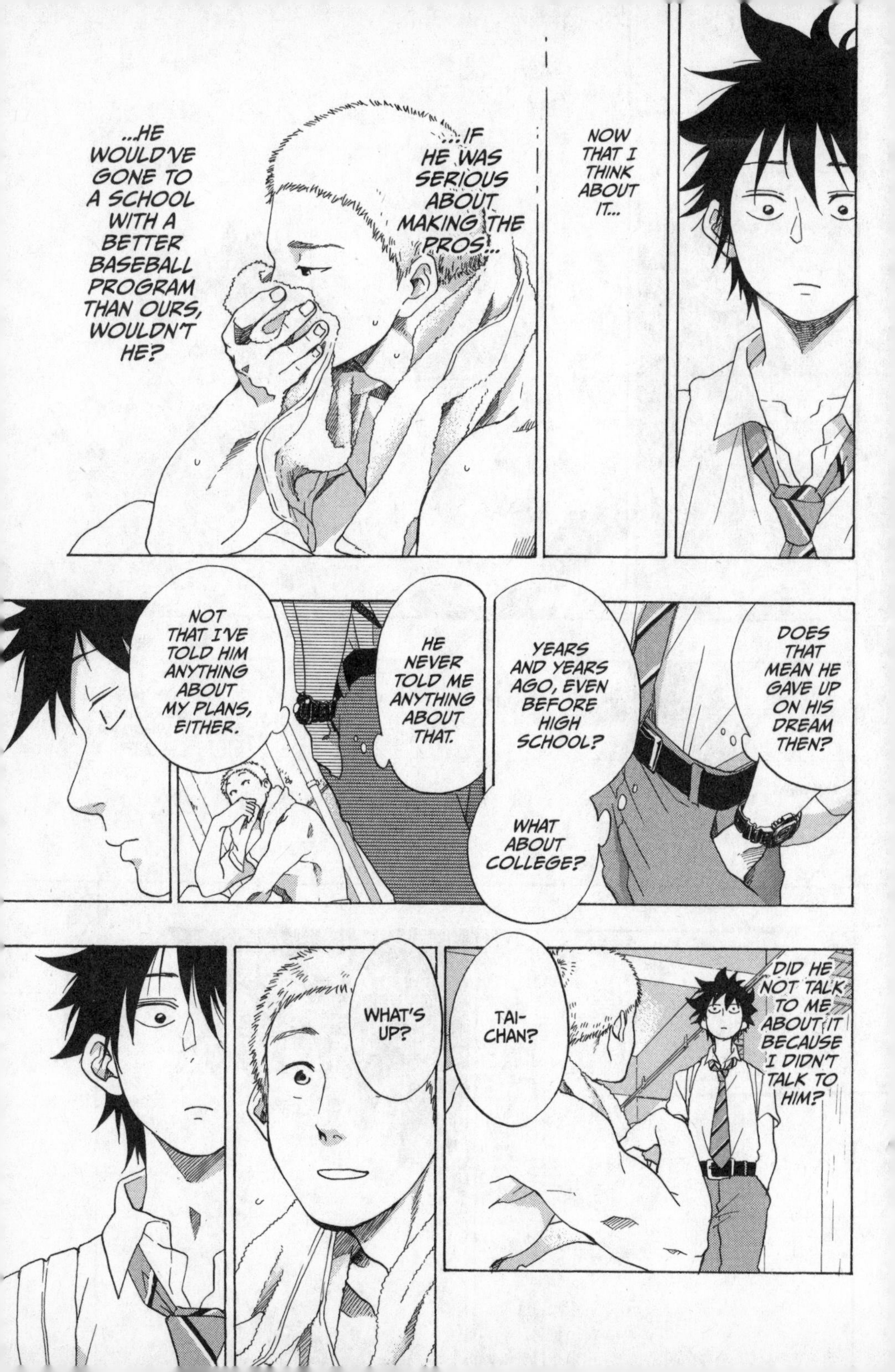
NOW THAT I THINK ABOUT IT...
...IF HE WAS SERIOUS ABOUT MAKING THE PROS...
...HE WOULD'VE GONE TO A SCHOOL WITH A BETTER BASEBALL PROGRAM THAN OURS, WOULDN'T HE?
DOES THAT MEAN HE GAVE UP ON HIS DREAM THEN?
YEARS AND YEARS AGO, EVEN BEFORE HIGH SCHOOL?
WHAT ABOUT COLLEGE?
HE NEVER TOLD ME ANYTHING ABOUT THAT.
NOT THAT I'VE TOLD HIM ANYTHING ABOUT MY PLANS, EITHER.
DID HE NOT TALK TO ME ABOUT IT BECAUSE I DIDN'T TALK TO HIM?
TAI-CHAN?
WHAT'S UP?

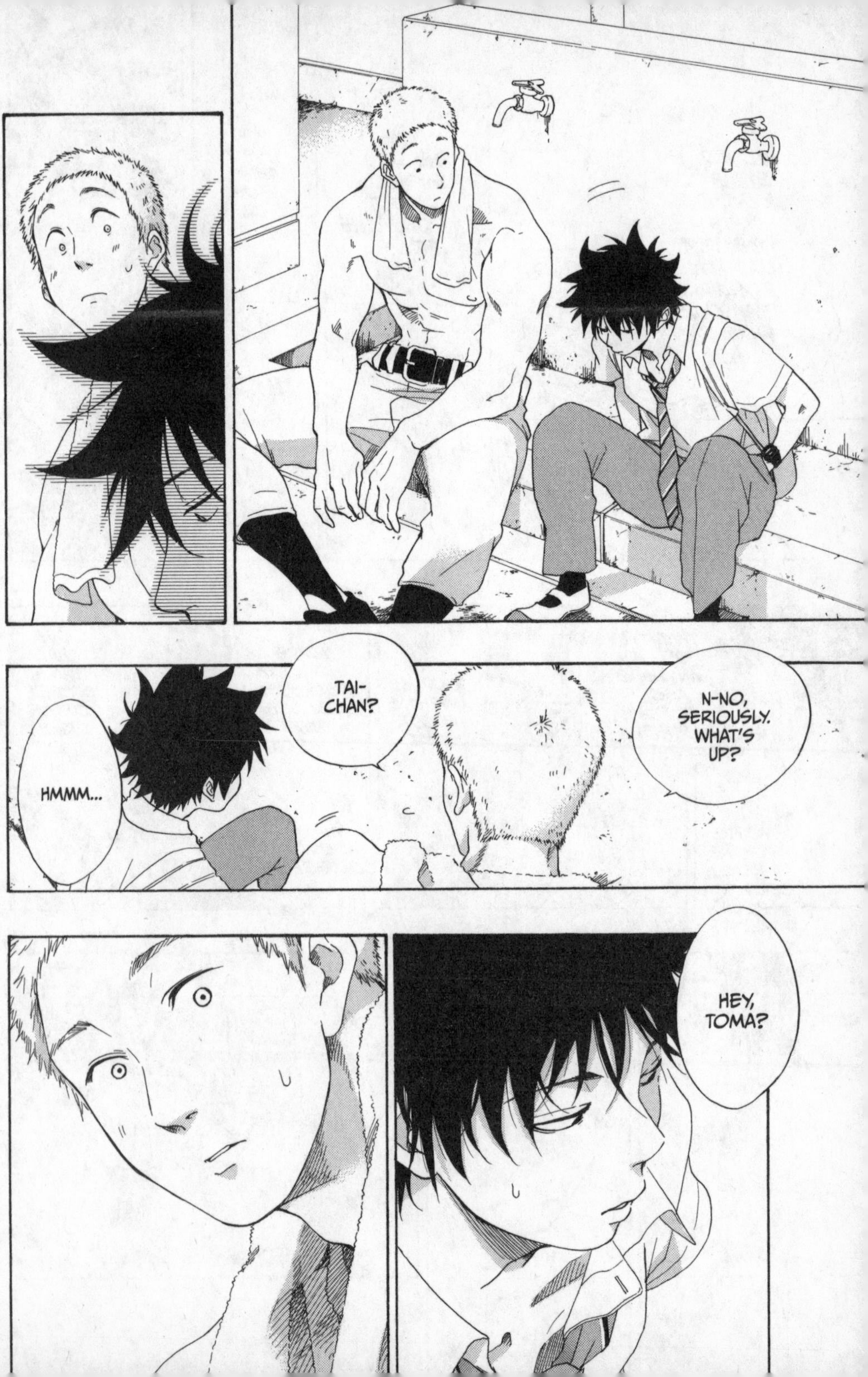
N-NO, SERIOUSLY. WHAT'S UP?
TAI-CHAN?
HMMM...
HEY, TOMA?

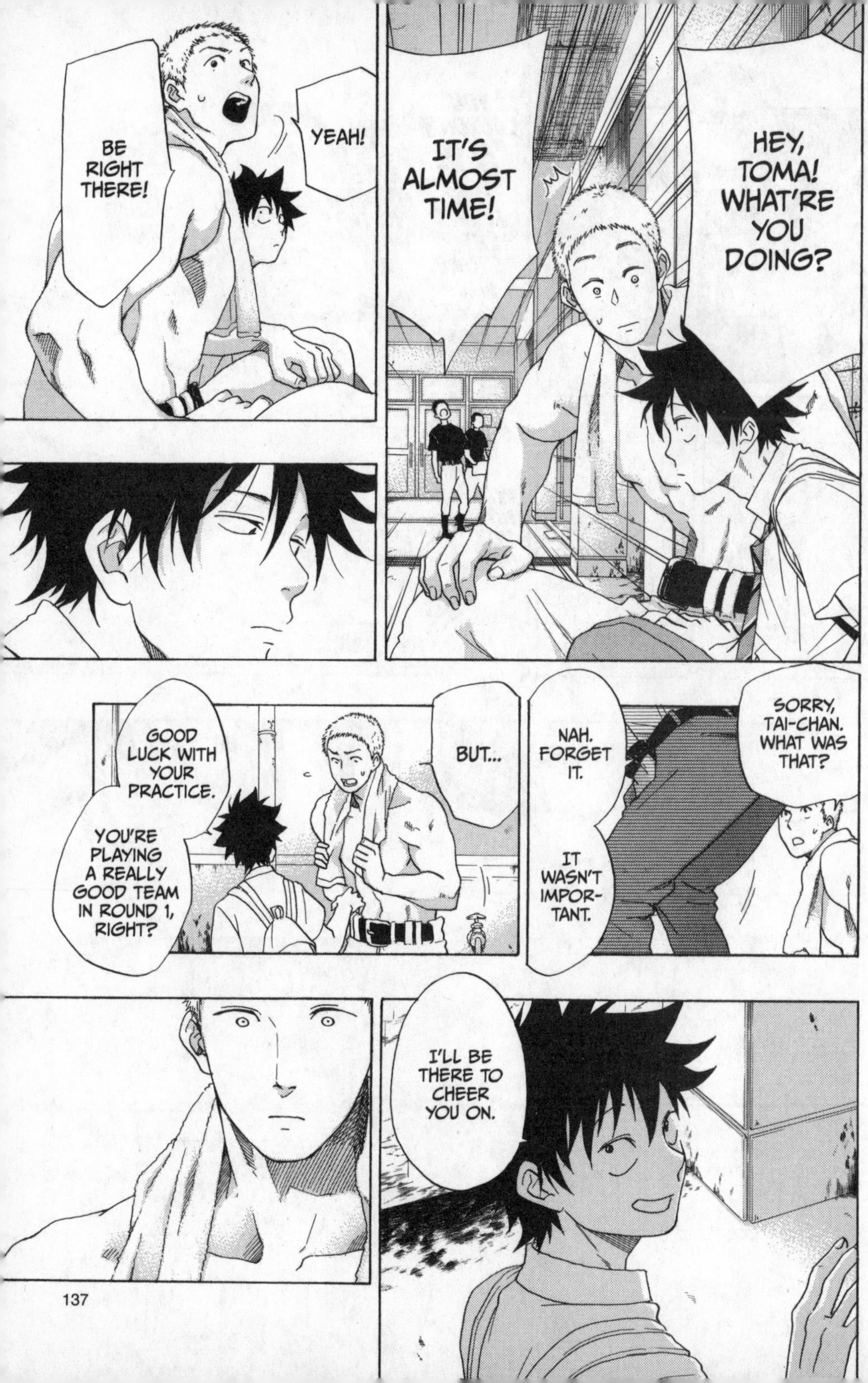
HEY, TOMA! WHAT'RE YOU DOING?
IT'S ALMOST TIME!
YEAH!
BE RIGHT THERE!
SORRY, TAI-CHAN. WHAT WAS THAT?
NAH. FORGET IT.
IT WASN'T IMPOR-TANT.
BUT...
GOOD LUCK WITH YOUR PRACTICE.
YOU'RE PLAYING A REALLY GOOD TEAM IN ROUND 1, RIGHT?
I'LL BE THERE TO CHEER YOU ON.

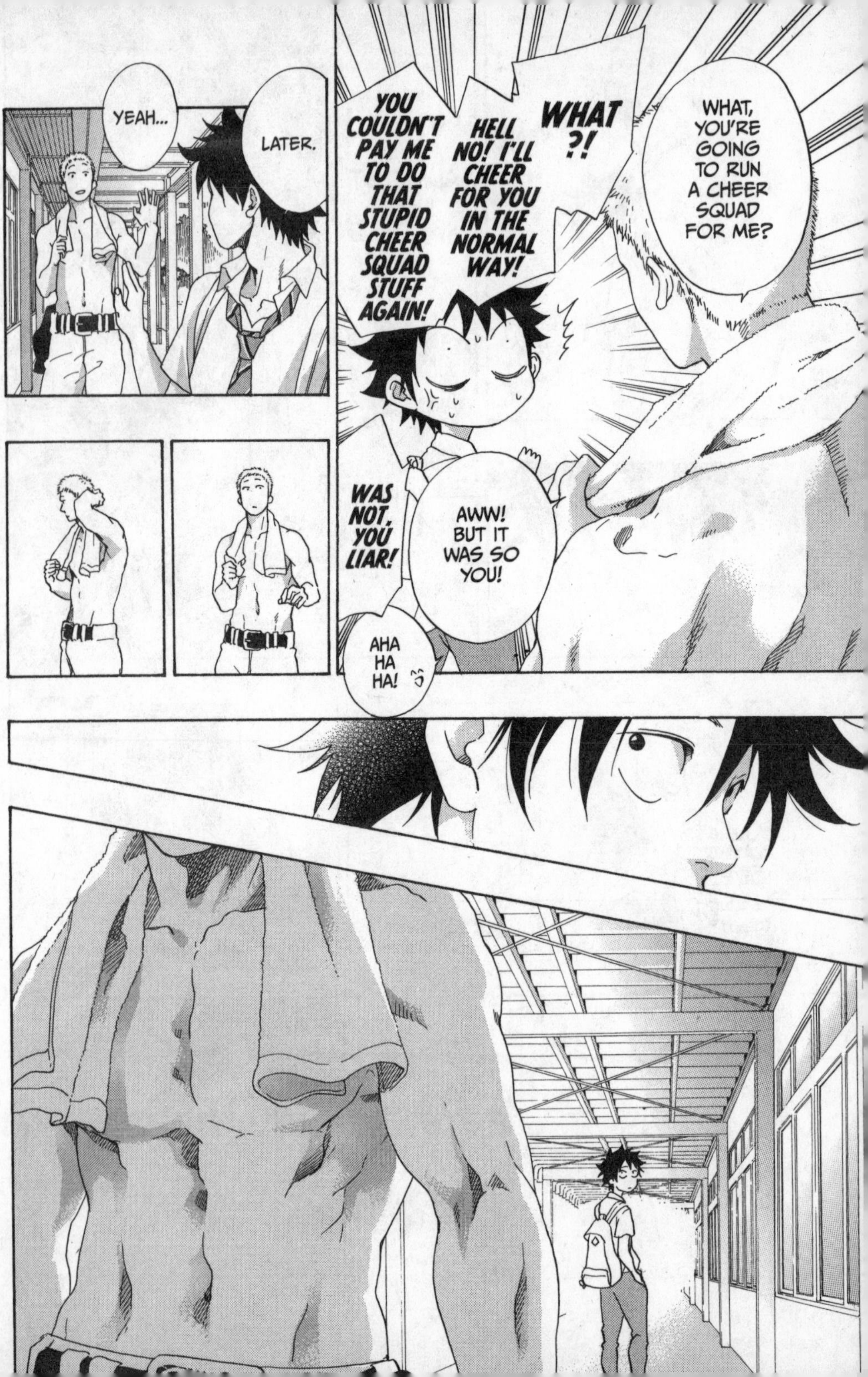
WHAT, YOU'RE GOING TO RUN A CHEER SQUAD FOR ME?
WHAT?!
HELL NO! I'LL CHEER FOR YOU IN THE NORMAL WAY!
YOU COULDN'T PAY ME TO DO THAT STUPID CHEER SQUAD STUFF AGAIN!
AWW! BUT IT WAS SO YOU!
WAS NOT, YOU LIAR!
AHA HA HA!
LATER.
YEAH...

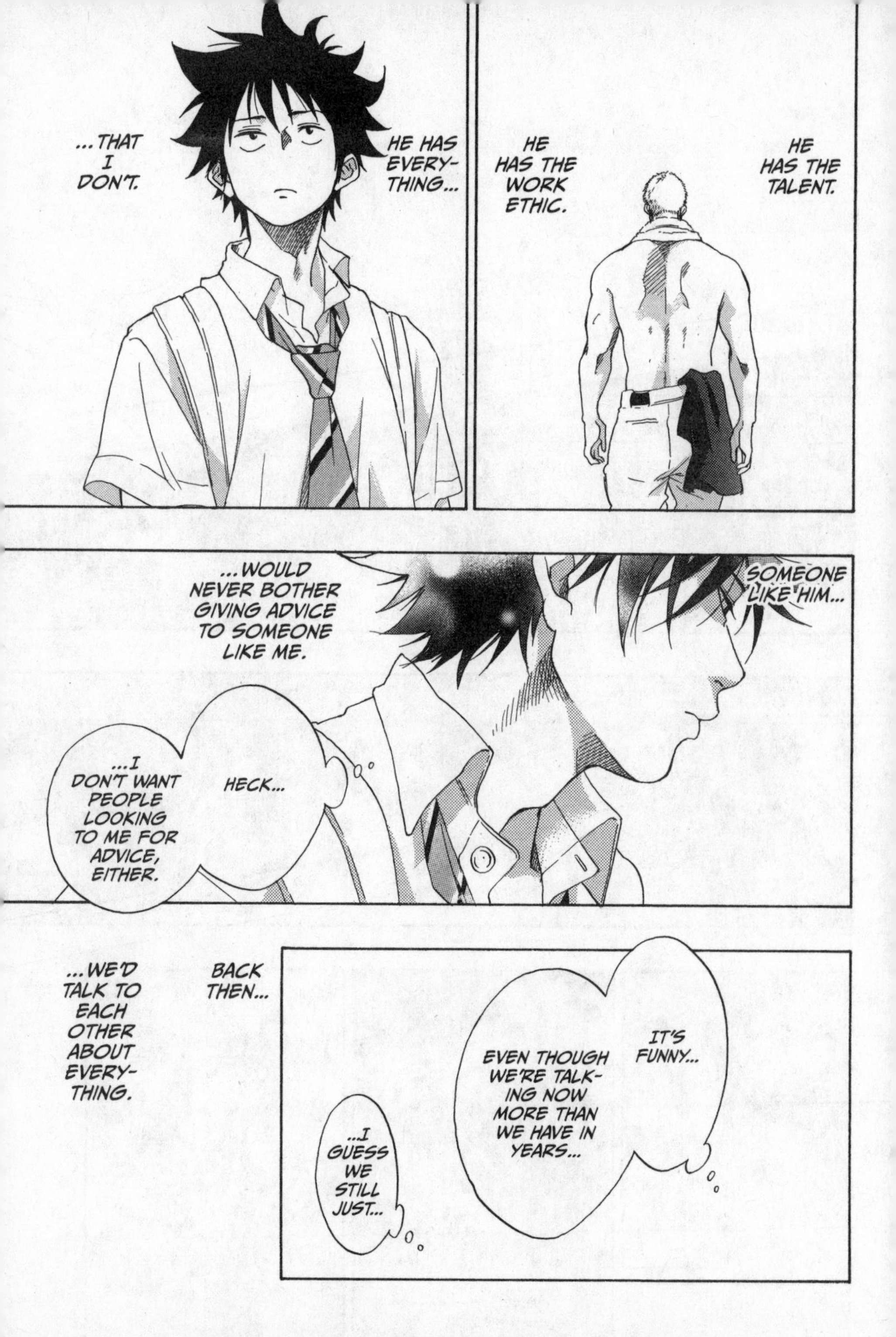
HE HAS THE TALENT.
HE HAS THE WORK ETHIC.
HE HAS EVERYTHING...
...THAT I DON'T.
SOMEONE LIKE HIM...
...WOULD NEVER BOTHER GIVING ADVICE TO SOMEONE LIKE ME.
HECK...
...I DON'T WANT PEOPLE LOOKING TO ME FOR ADVICE, EITHER.
IT'S FUNNY...
EVEN THOUGH WE'RE TALKING NOW MORE THAN WE HAVE IN YEARS...
...I GUESS WE STILL JUST...
BACK THEN...
...WE'D TALK TO EACH OTHER ABOUT EVERYTHING.

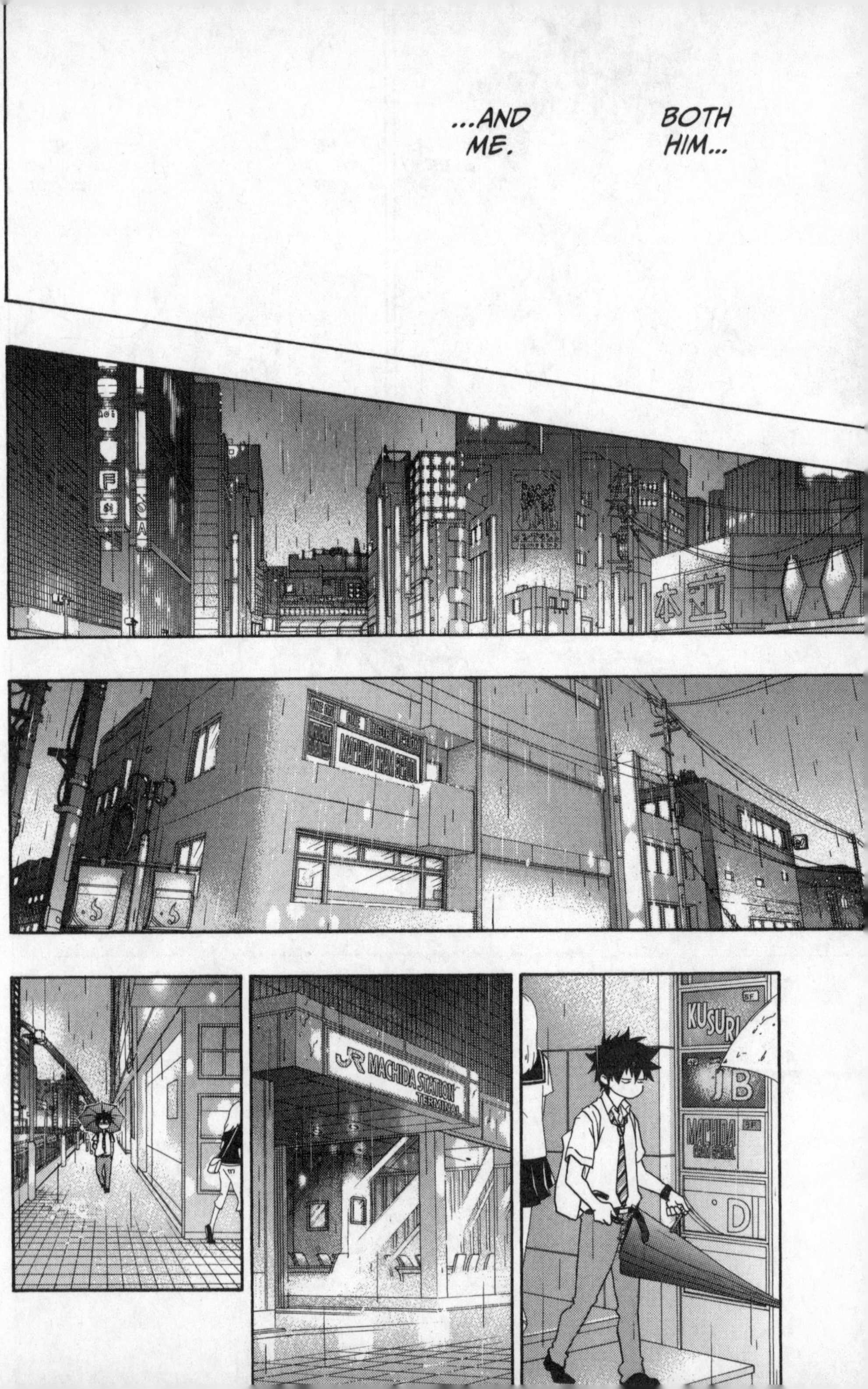
BOTH HIM...
...AND ME.
KUSURI
JB
D
JR MACHIDA STATION TERMINAL

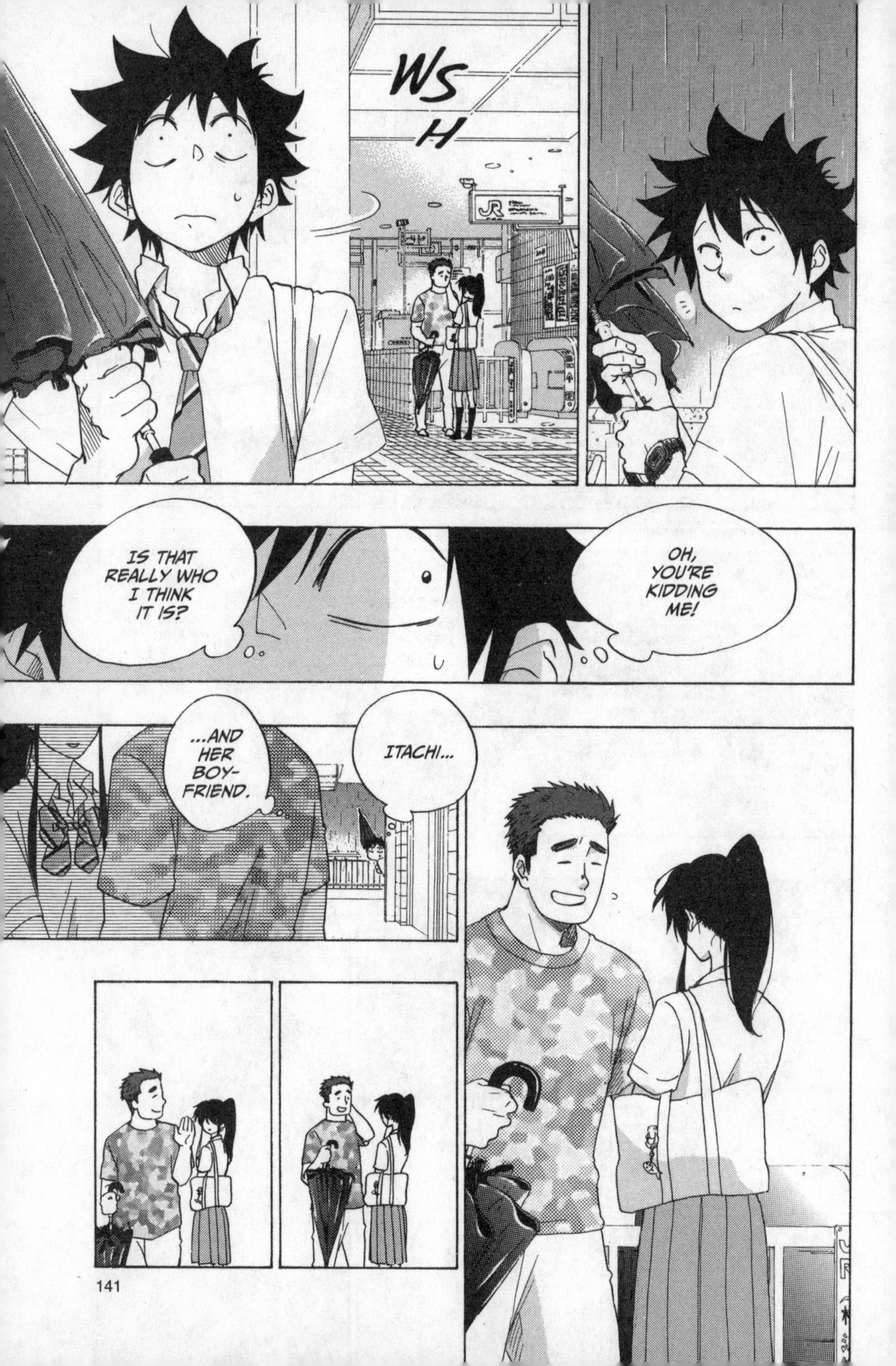
WSH
OH, YOU'RE KIDDING ME!
IS THAT REALLY WHO I THINK IT IS?
ITACHI...
...AND HER BOY-FRIEND.

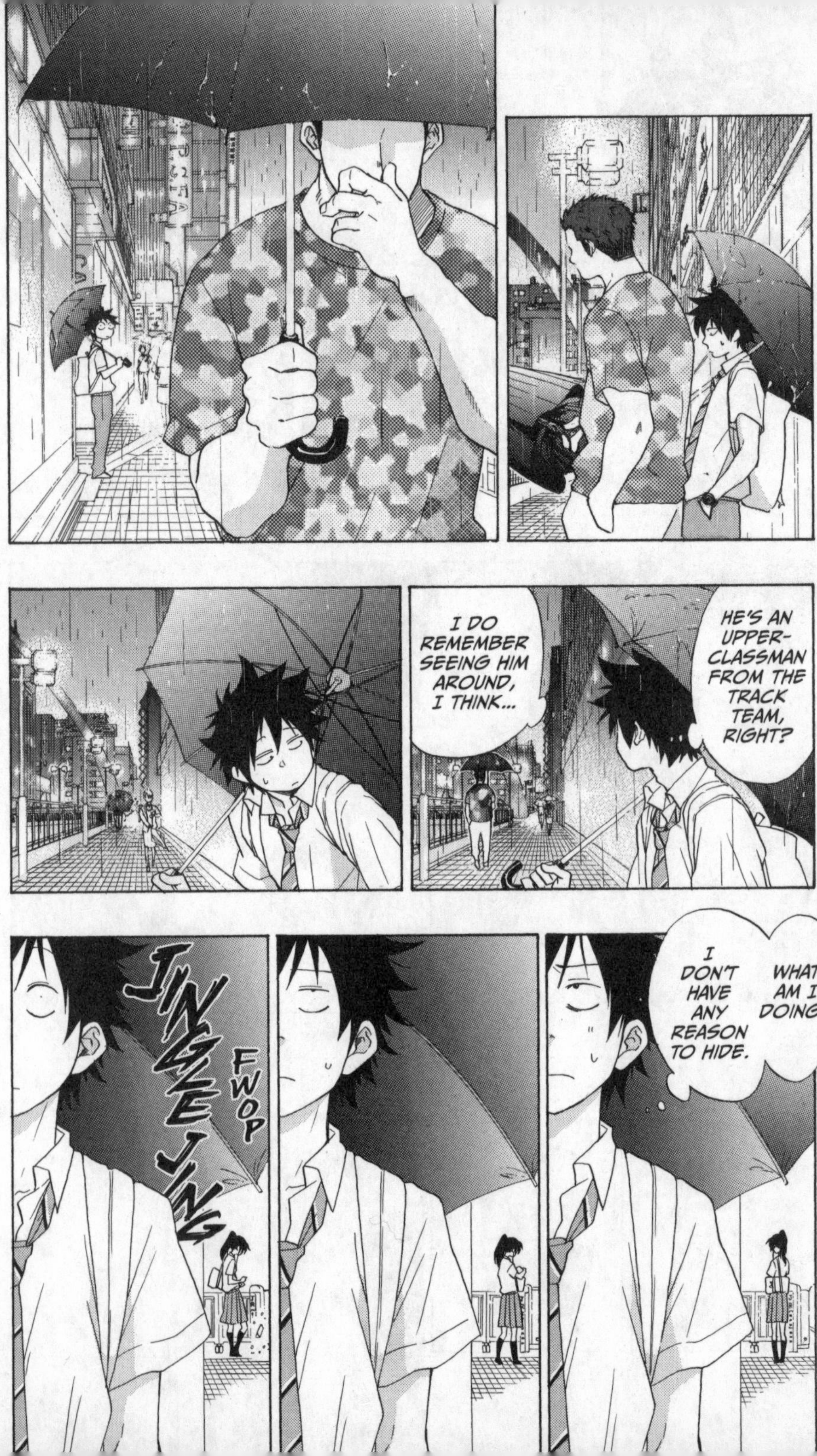

HE'S AN UPPER-CLASSMAN FROM THE TRACK TEAM, RIGHT?
I DO REMEMBER SEEING HIM AROUND, I THINK...
WHAT AM I DOING?
I DON'T HAVE ANY REASON TO HIDE.
FWOP
JINGLE JING

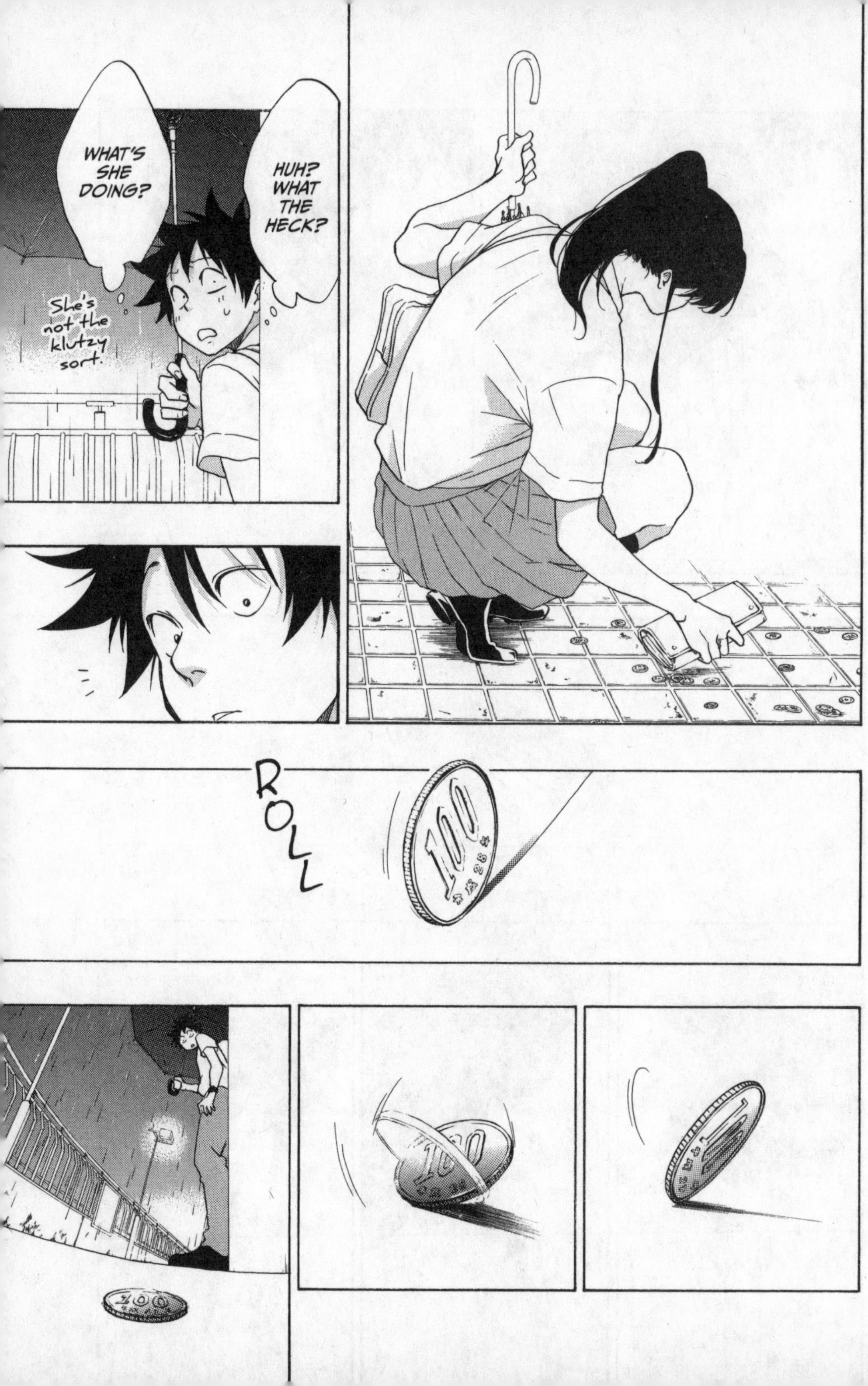
HUH? WHAT THE HECK?
WHAT'S SHE DOING?
She's not the klutzy sort.
ROLL

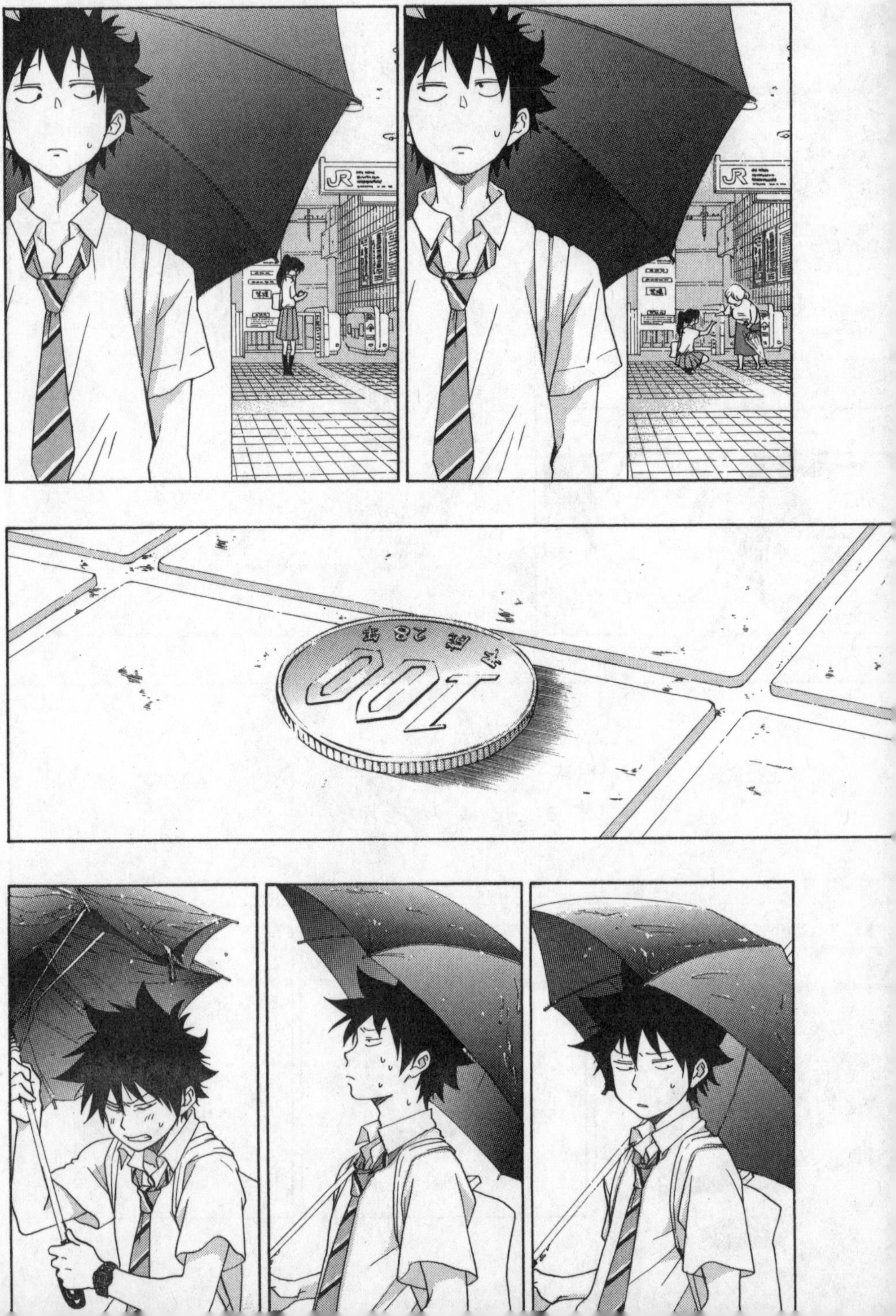
JR
JR
平成28年
100

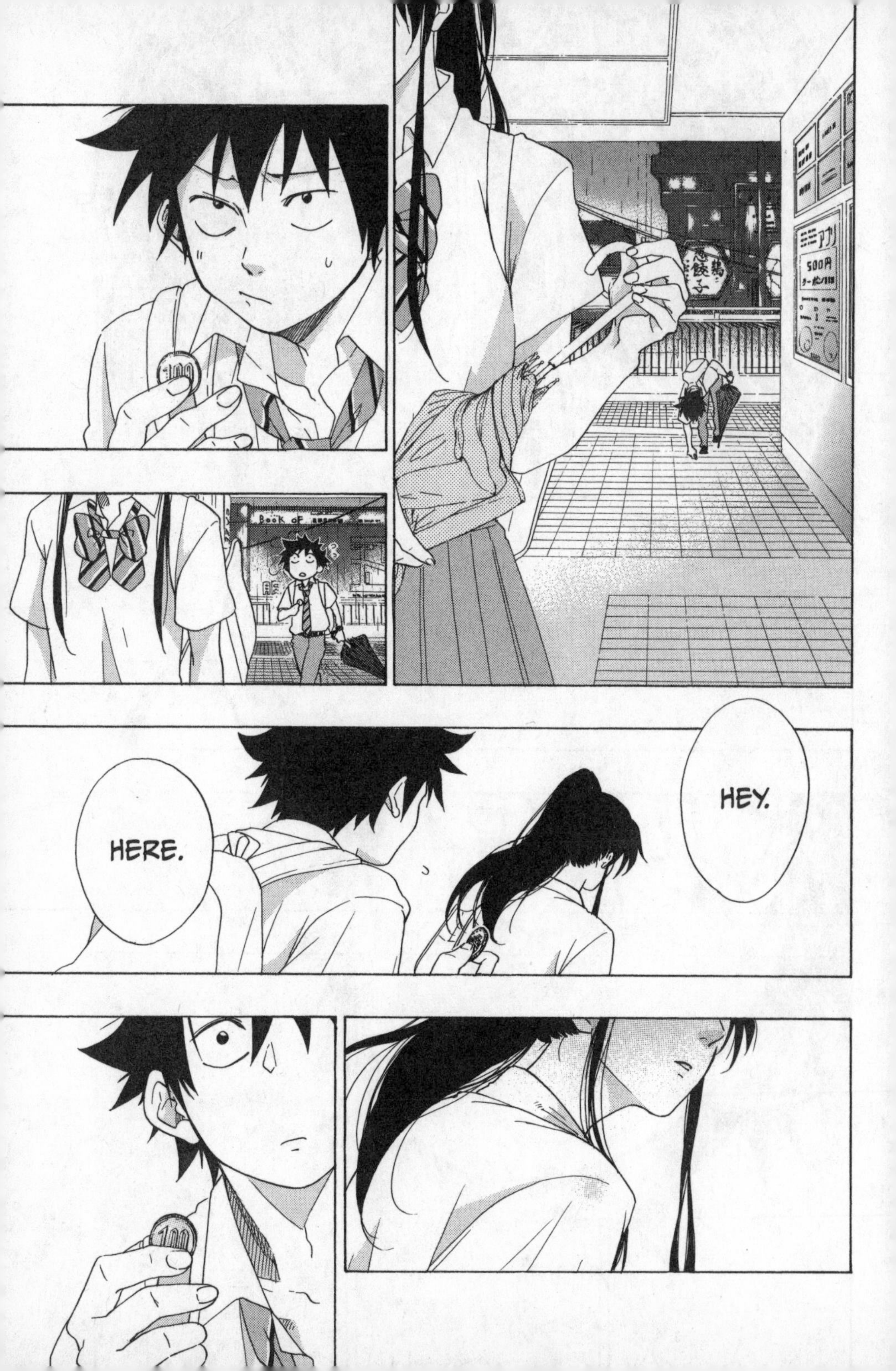
HEY.
HERE.

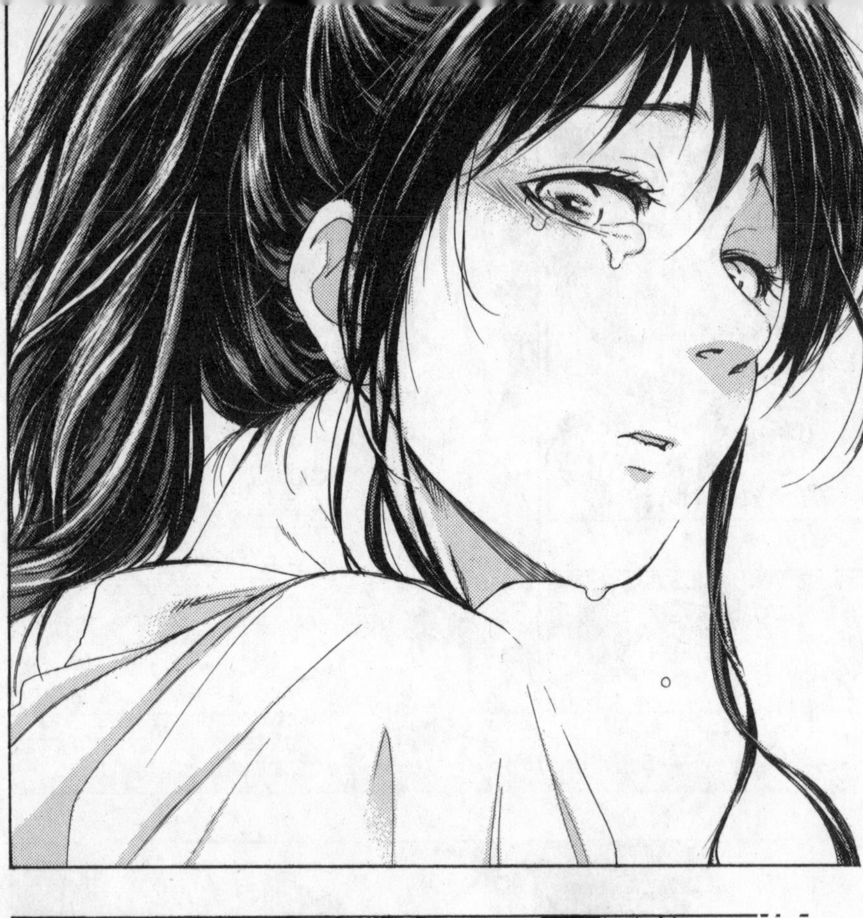

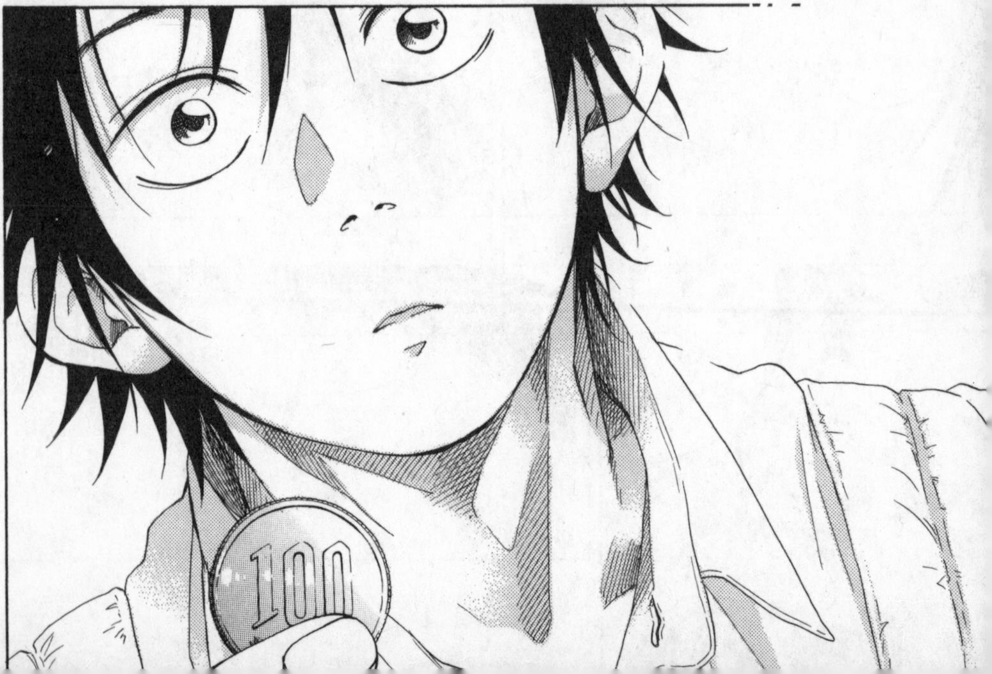
100

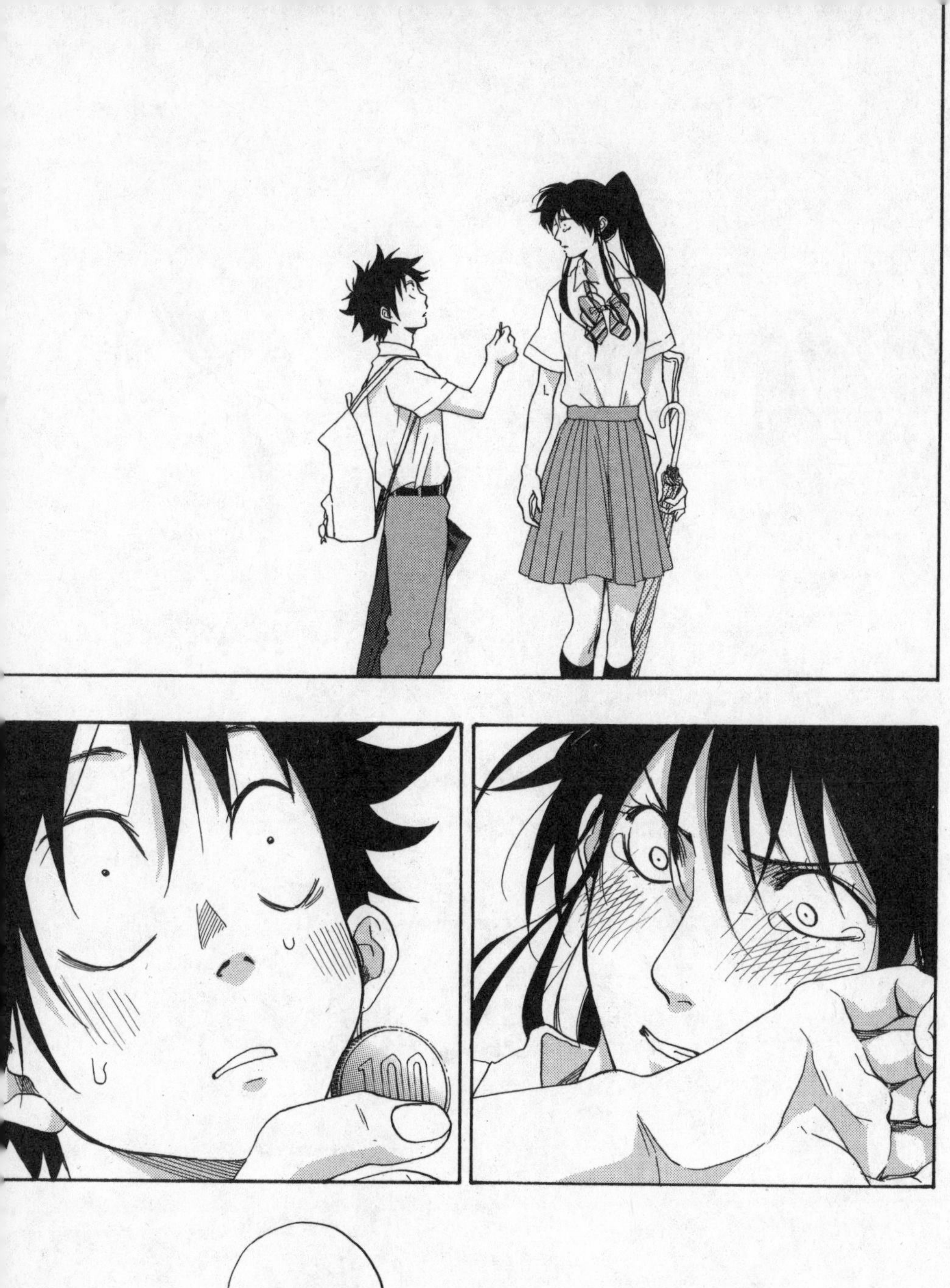
HUH?

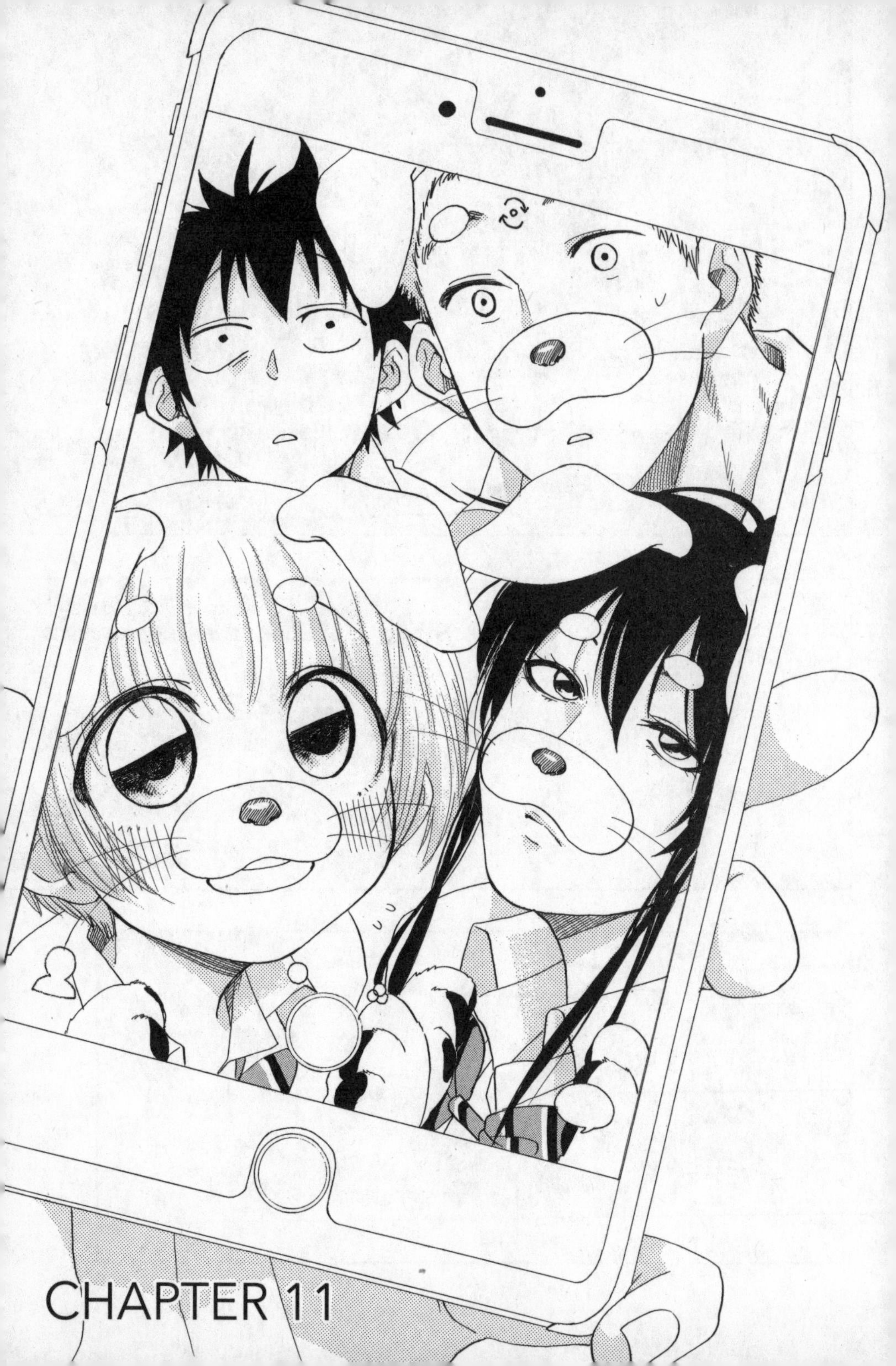

CHAPTER 11

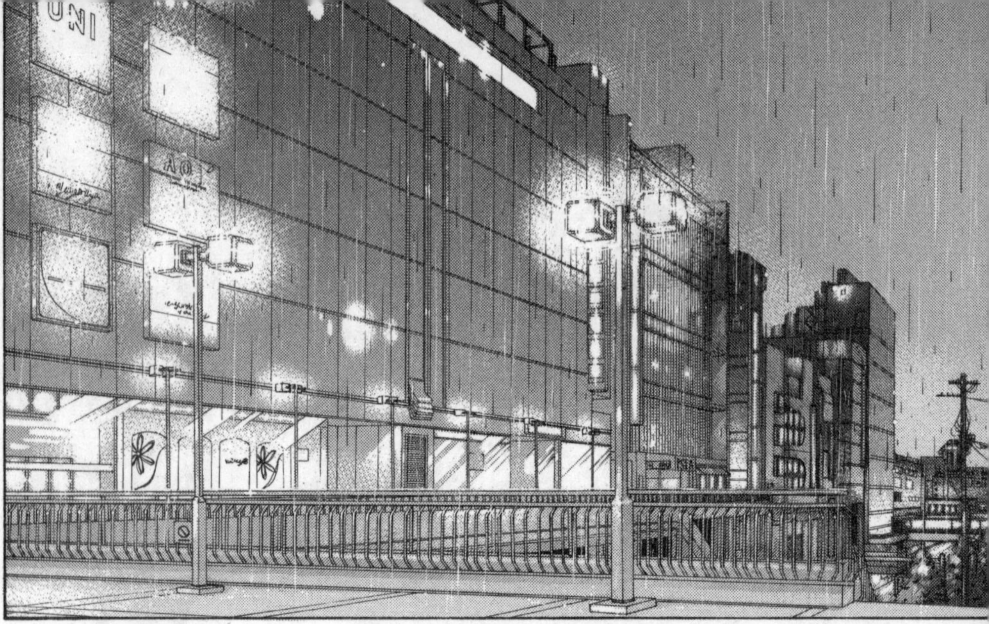
UNI
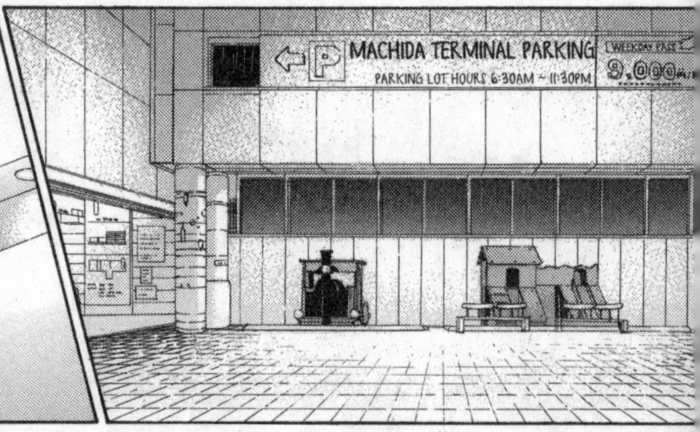
MACHIDA TERMINAL PARKING
PARKING LOT HOURS 6:30AM ~ 11:30PM
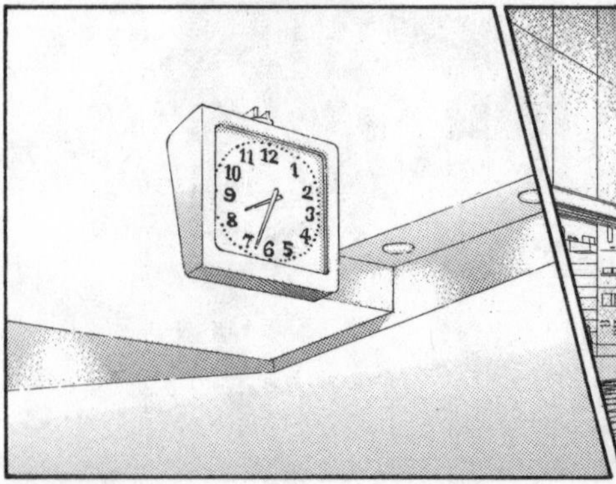
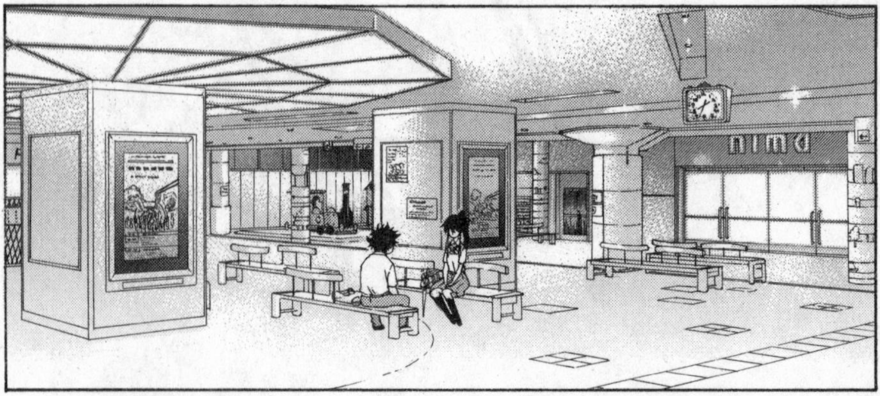

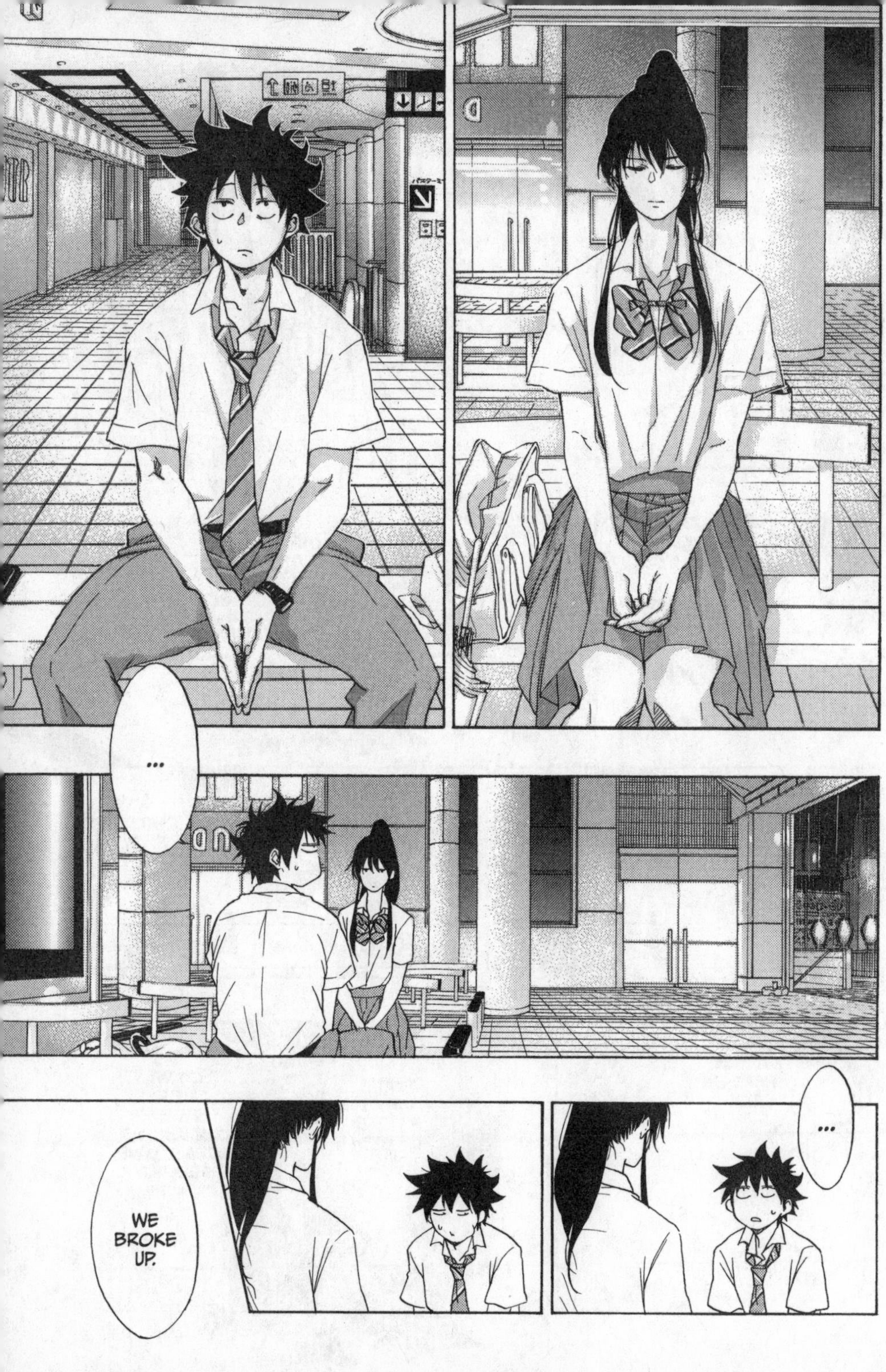
...
...
WE BROKE UP.

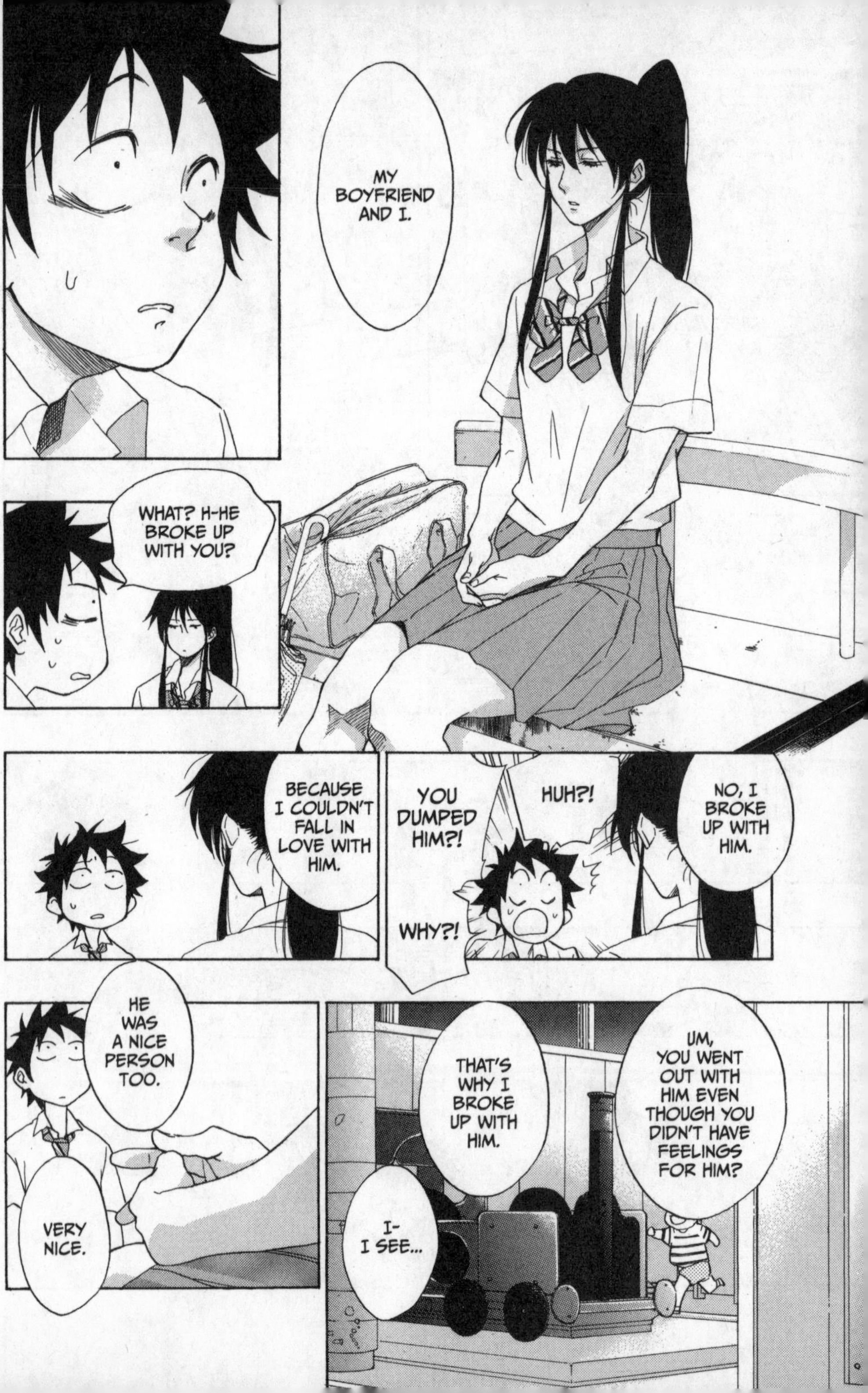
MY BOYFRIEND AND I.
WHAT? H-HE BROKE UP WITH YOU?
NO, I BROKE UP WITH HIM.
HUH?!
YOU DUMPED HIM?!
WHY?!
BECAUSE I COULDN'T FALL IN LOVE WITH HIM.
UM, YOU WENT OUT WITH HIM EVEN THOUGH YOU DIDN'T HAVE FEELINGS FOR HIM?
THAT'S WHY I BROKE UP WITH HIM.
I- I SEE...
HE WAS A NICE PERSON TOO.
VERY NICE.

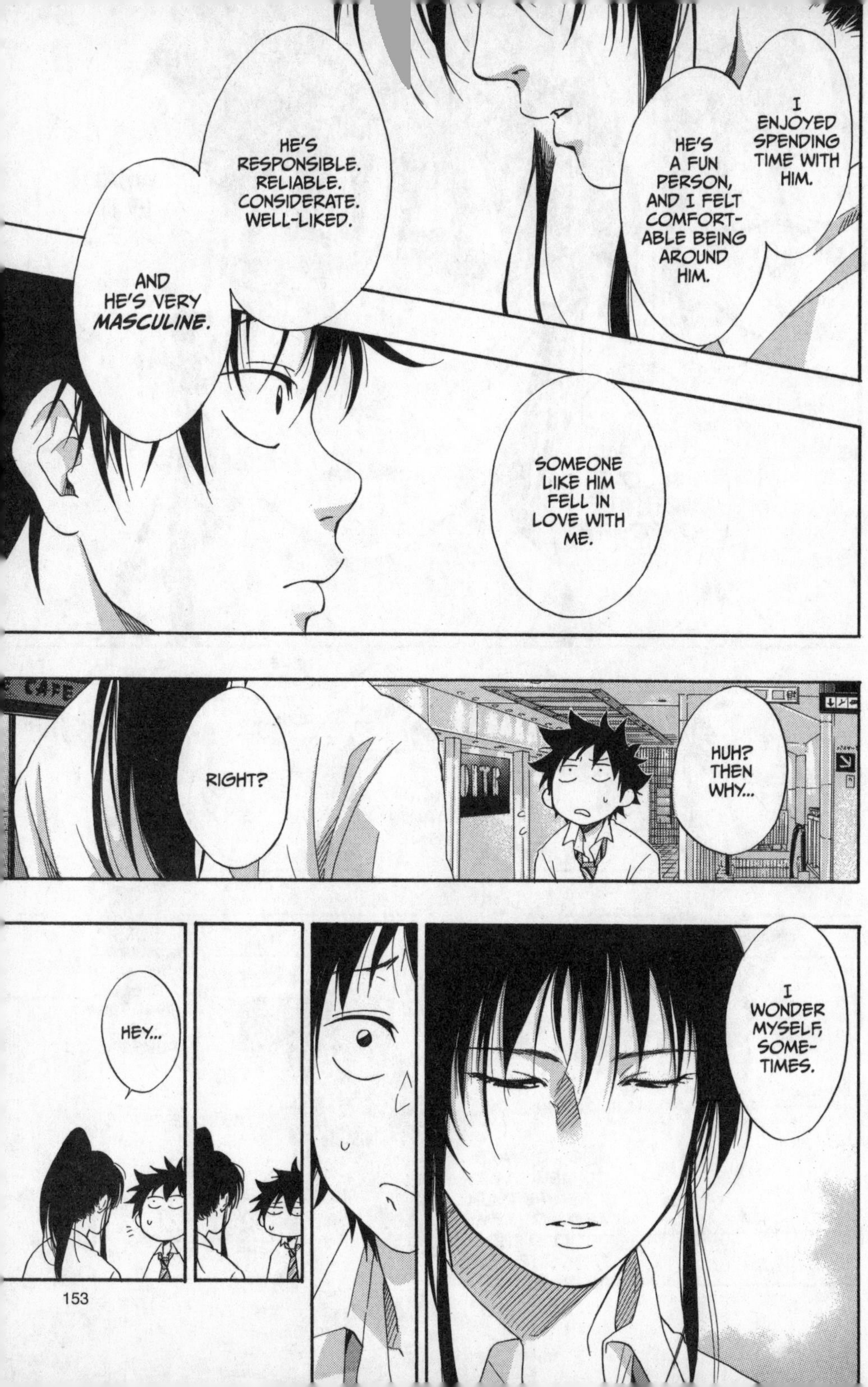
I ENJOYED SPENDING TIME WITH HIM.
HE'S A FUN PERSON, AND I FELT COMFORTABLE BEING AROUND HIM.
HE'S RESPONSIBLE. RELIABLE. CONSIDERATE. WELL-LIKED.
AND HE'S VERY *MASCULINE.*
SOMEONE LIKE HIM FELL IN LOVE WITH ME.
HUH? THEN WHY...
RIGHT?
I WONDER MYSELF, SOMETIMES.
HEY...

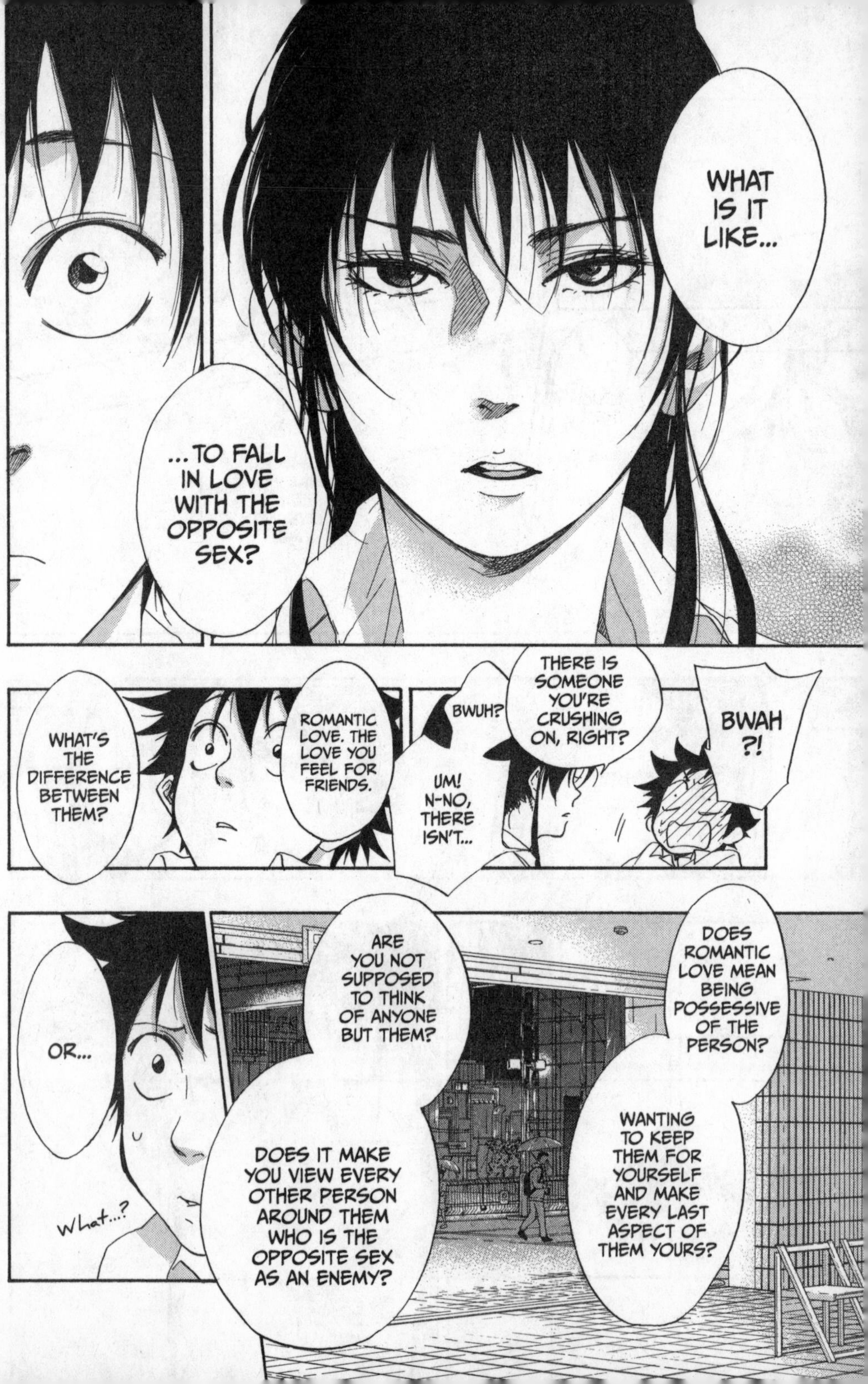
WHAT IS IT LIKE...
...TO FALL IN LOVE WITH THE OPPOSITE SEX?
THERE IS SOMEONE YOU'RE CRUSHING ON, RIGHT?
BWAH ?!
BWUH?
UM! N-NO, THERE ISN'T...
ROMANTIC LOVE. THE LOVE YOU FEEL FOR FRIENDS.
WHAT'S THE DIFFERENCE BETWEEN THEM?
DOES ROMANTIC LOVE MEAN BEING POSSESSIVE OF THE PERSON?
WANTING TO KEEP THEM FOR YOURSELF AND MAKE EVERY LAST ASPECT OF THEM YOURS?
ARE YOU NOT SUPPOSED TO THINK OF ANYONE BUT THEM?
DOES IT MAKE YOU VIEW EVERY OTHER PERSON AROUND THEM WHO IS THE OPPOSITE SEX AS AN ENEMY?
OR...
What...?

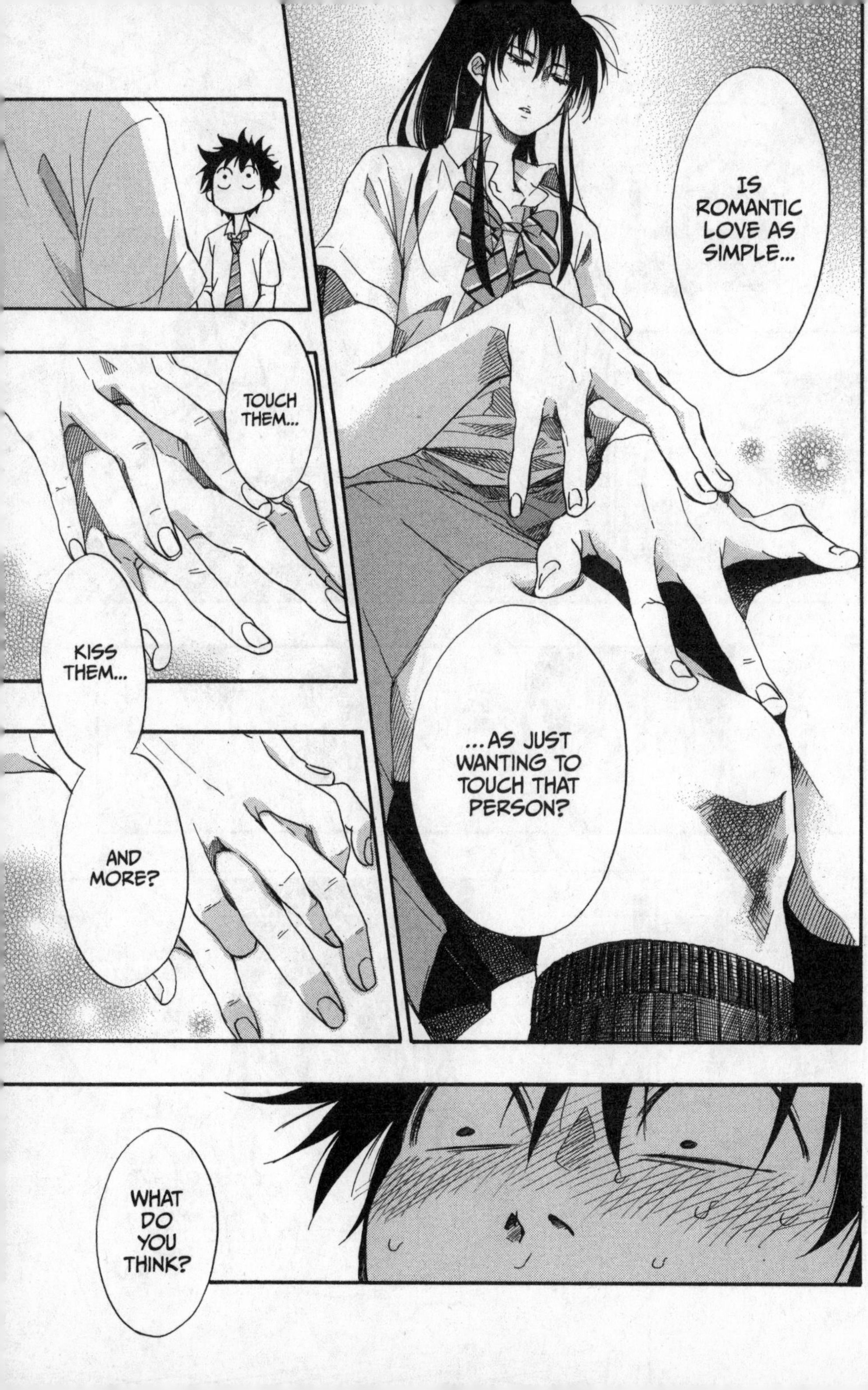
IS ROMANTIC LOVE AS SIMPLE...
...AS JUST WANTING TO TOUCH THAT PERSON?
TOUCH THEM...
KISS THEM...
AND MORE?
WHAT DO YOU THINK?

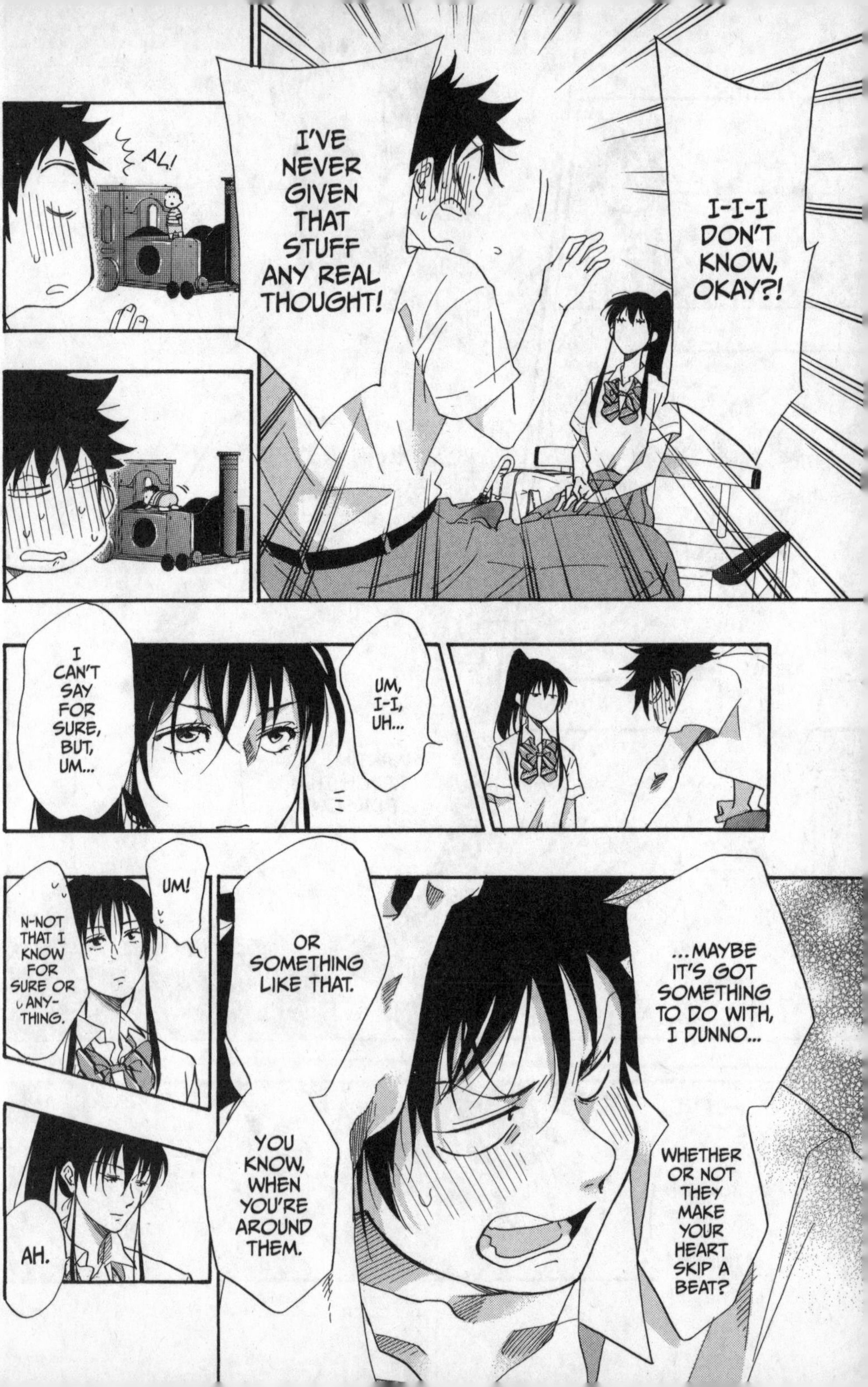
I-I-I DON'T KNOW, OKAY?!
I'VE NEVER GIVEN THAT STUFF ANY REAL THOUGHT!
AH!
UM, I-I, UH...
I CAN'T SAY FOR SURE, BUT, UM...
...MAYBE IT'S GOT SOMETHING TO DO WITH, I DUNNO...
WHETHER OR NOT THEY MAKE YOUR HEART SKIP A BEAT?
YOU KNOW, WHEN YOU'RE AROUND THEM.
OR SOMETHING LIKE THAT.
UM!
N-NOT THAT I KNOW FOR SURE OR ANYTHING.
AH.

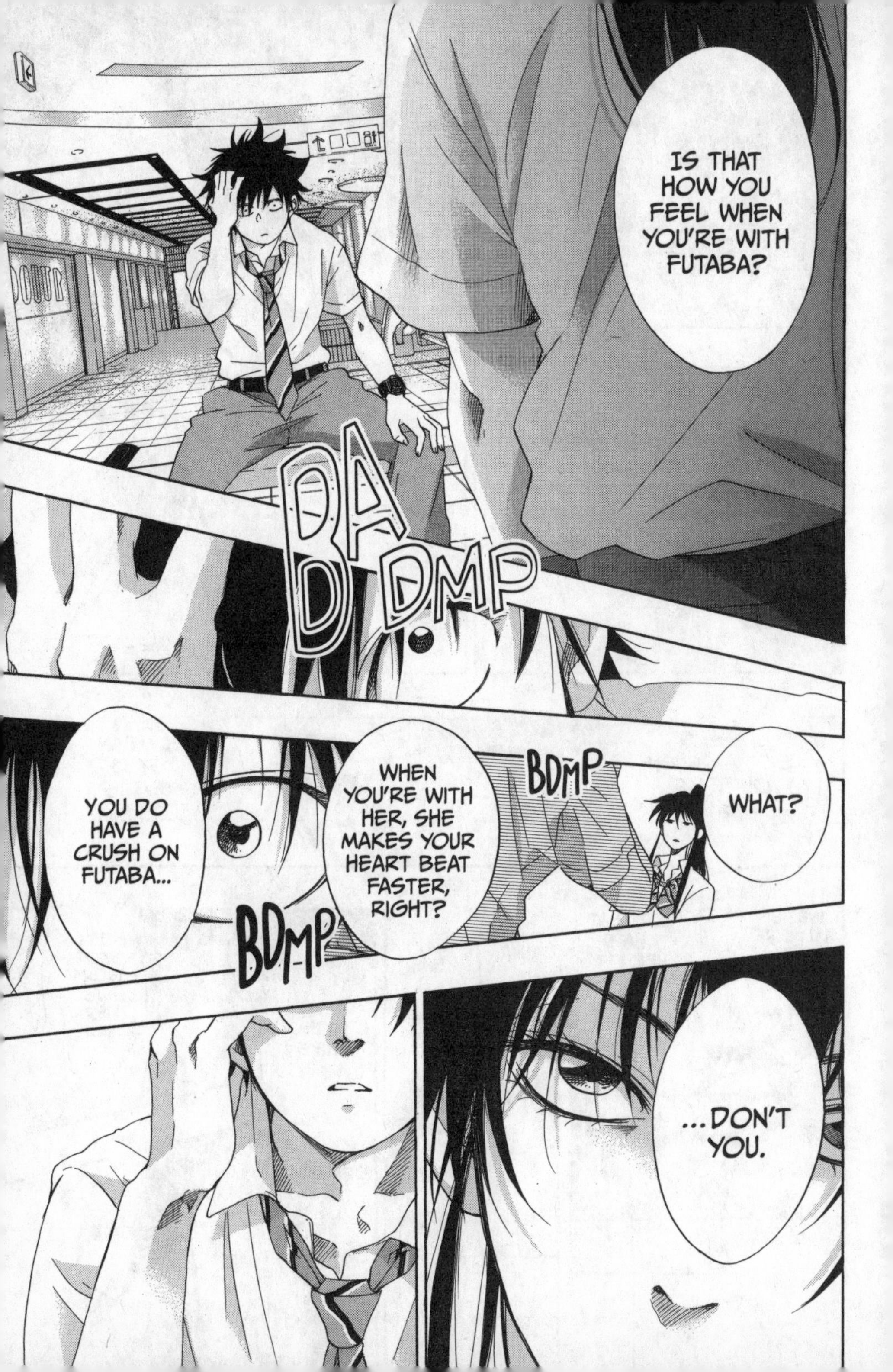
IS THAT HOW YOU FEEL WHEN YOU'RE WITH FUTABA?
DA DDMP
WHAT?
BDMP
WHEN YOU'RE WITH HER, SHE MAKES YOUR HEART BEAT FASTER, RIGHT?
BDMP
YOU DO HAVE A CRUSH ON FUTABA...
...DON'T YOU.

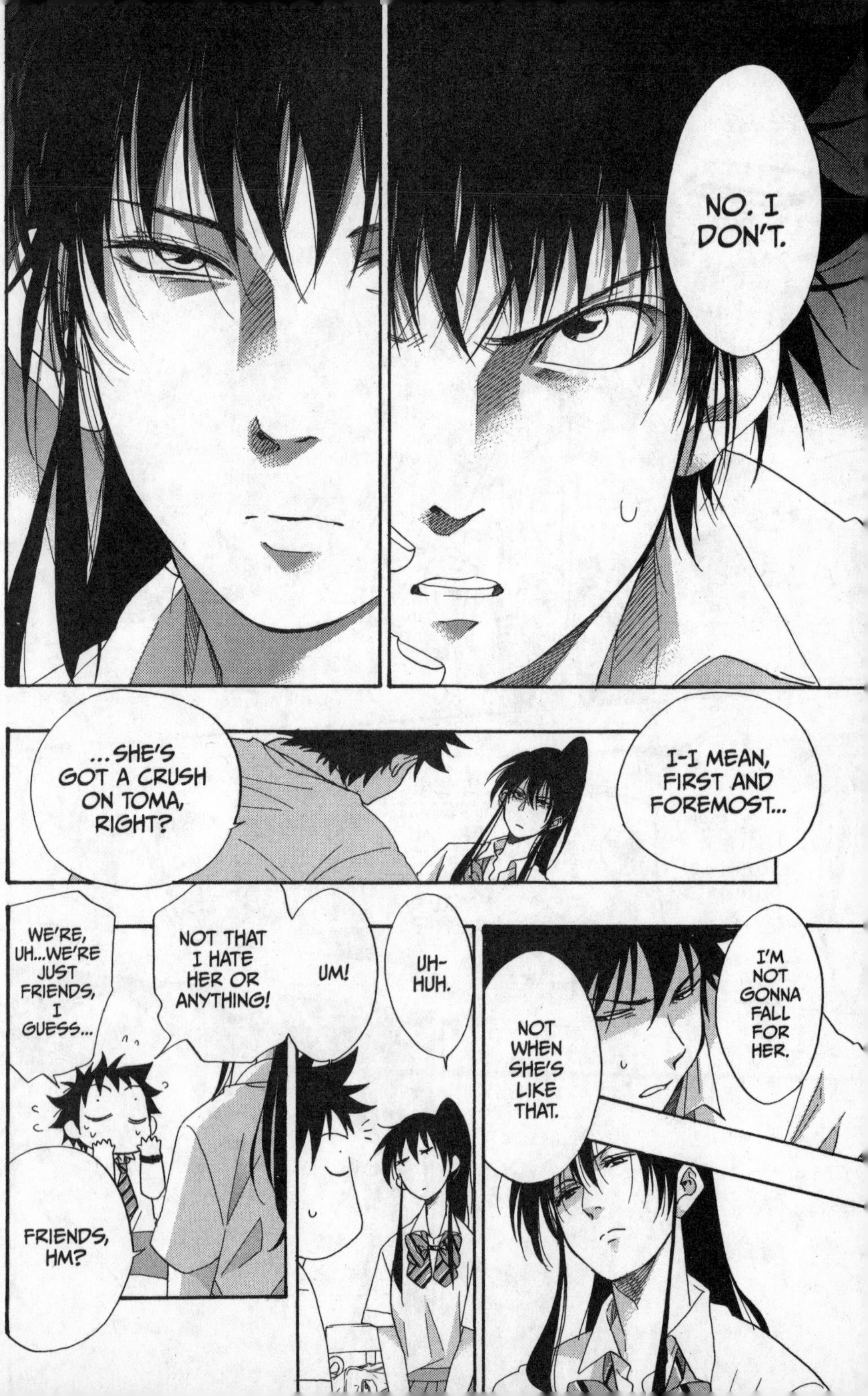
NO. I DON'T.
I-I MEAN, FIRST AND FOREMOST...
...SHE'S GOT A CRUSH ON TOMA, RIGHT?
I'M NOT GONNA FALL FOR HER.
NOT WHEN SHE'S LIKE THAT.
UH-HUH.
UM!
NOT THAT I HATE HER OR ANYTHING!
WE'RE, UH...WE'RE JUST FRIENDS, I GUESS...
FRIENDS, HM?

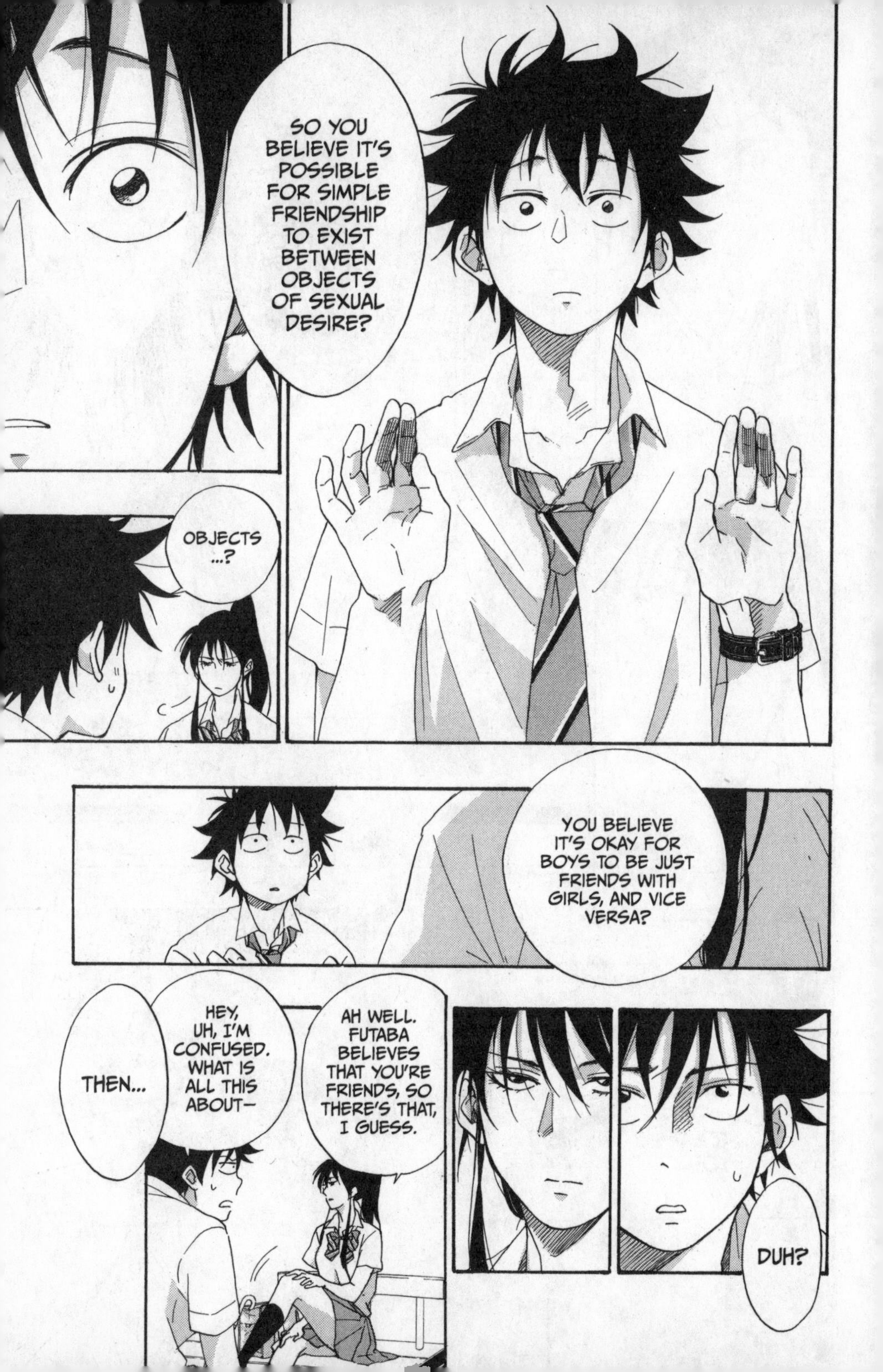

SO YOU BELIEVE IT'S POSSIBLE FOR SIMPLE FRIENDSHIP TO EXIST BETWEEN OBJECTS OF SEXUAL DESIRE?
OBJECTS ...?
YOU BELIEVE IT'S OKAY FOR BOYS TO BE JUST FRIENDS WITH GIRLS, AND VICE VERSA?
DUH?
AH WELL. FUTABA BELIEVES THAT YOU'RE FRIENDS, SO THERE'S THAT, I GUESS.
HEY, UH, I'M CONFUSED. WHAT IS ALL THIS ABOUT—
THEN...

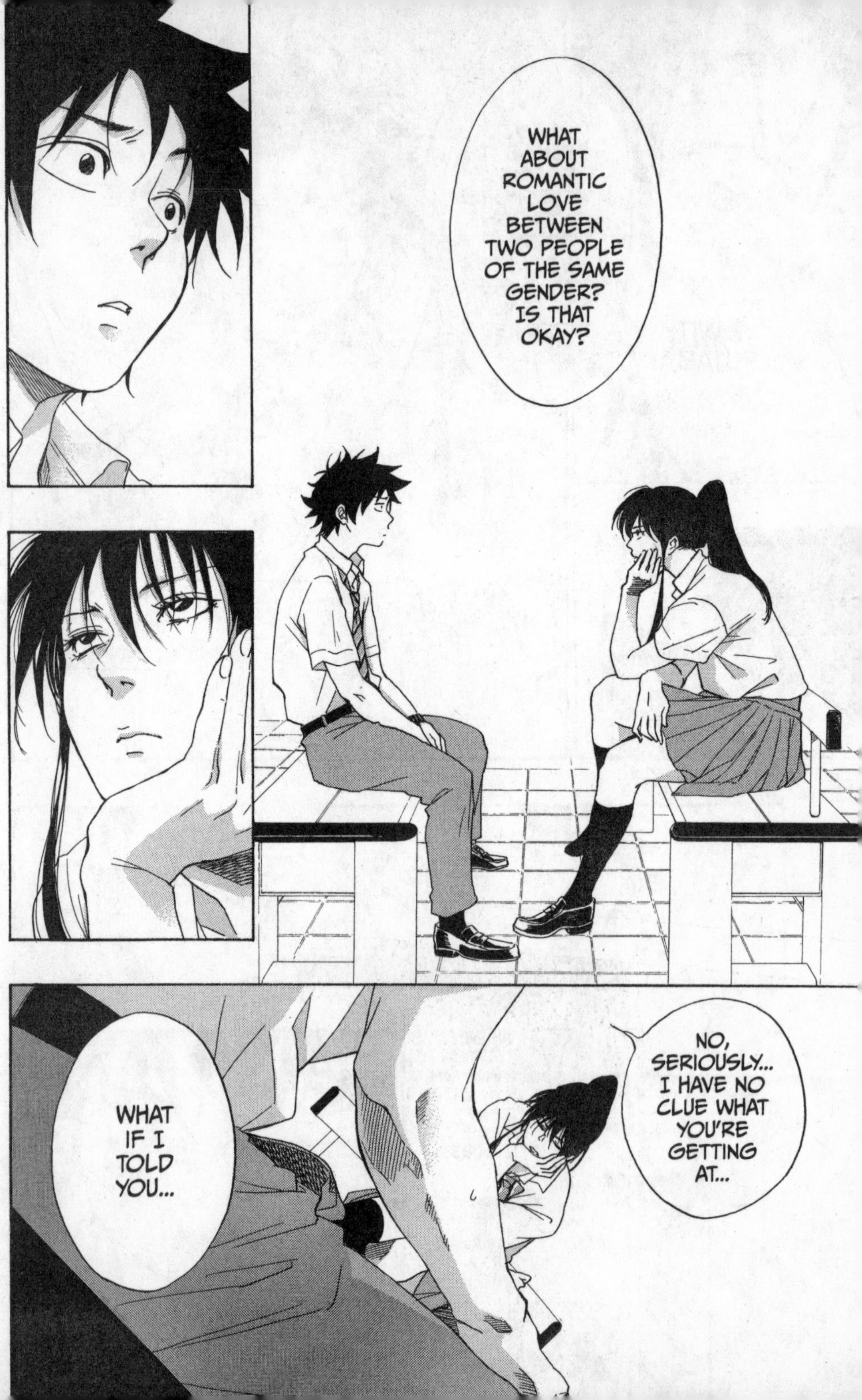
WHAT ABOUT ROMANTIC LOVE BETWEEN TWO PEOPLE OF THE SAME GENDER? IS THAT OKAY?
NO, SERIOUSLY... I HAVE NO CLUE WHAT YOU'RE GETTING AT...
WHAT IF I TOLD YOU...

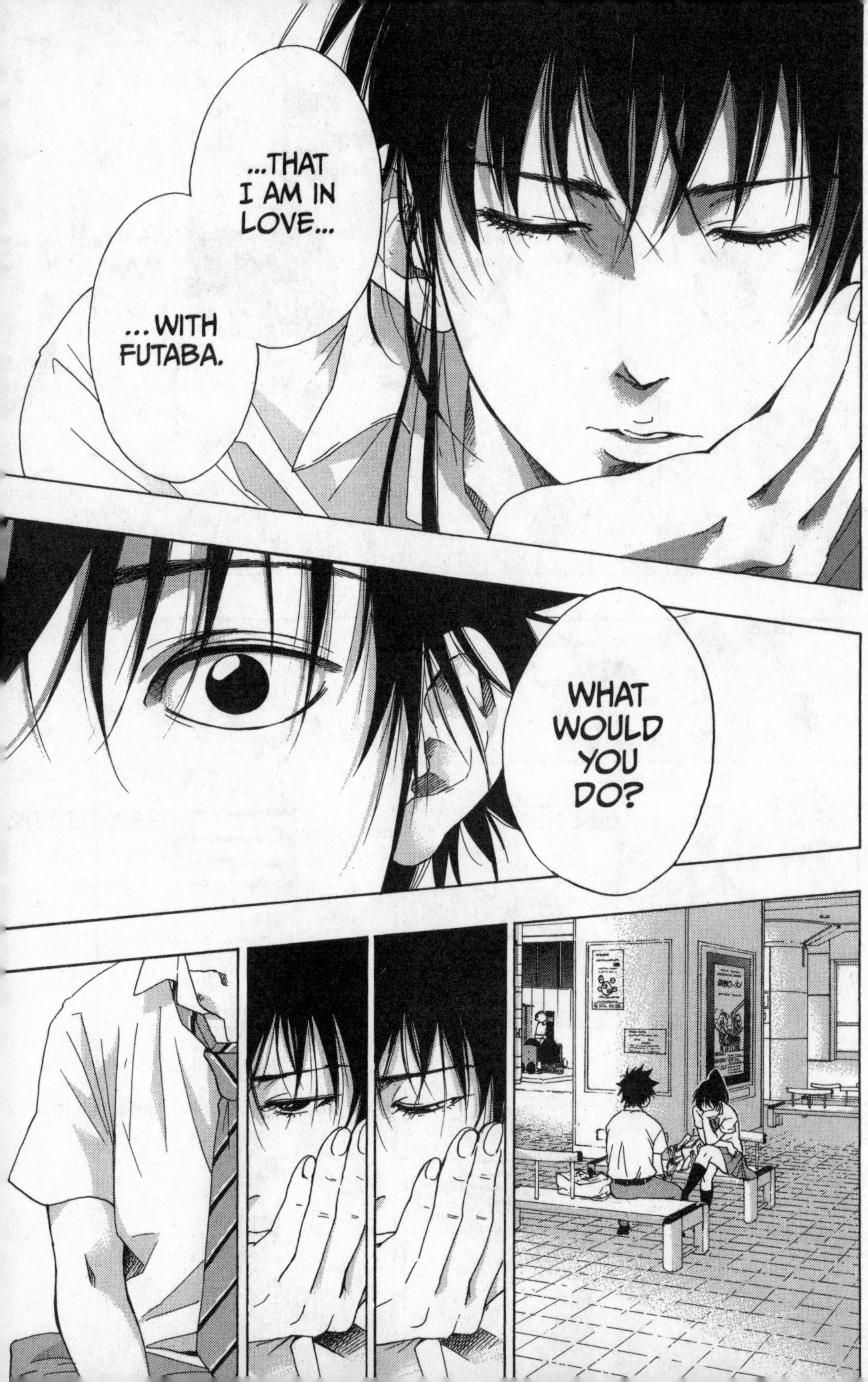
...THAT I AM IN LOVE...
...WITH FUTABA.
WHAT WOULD YOU DO?

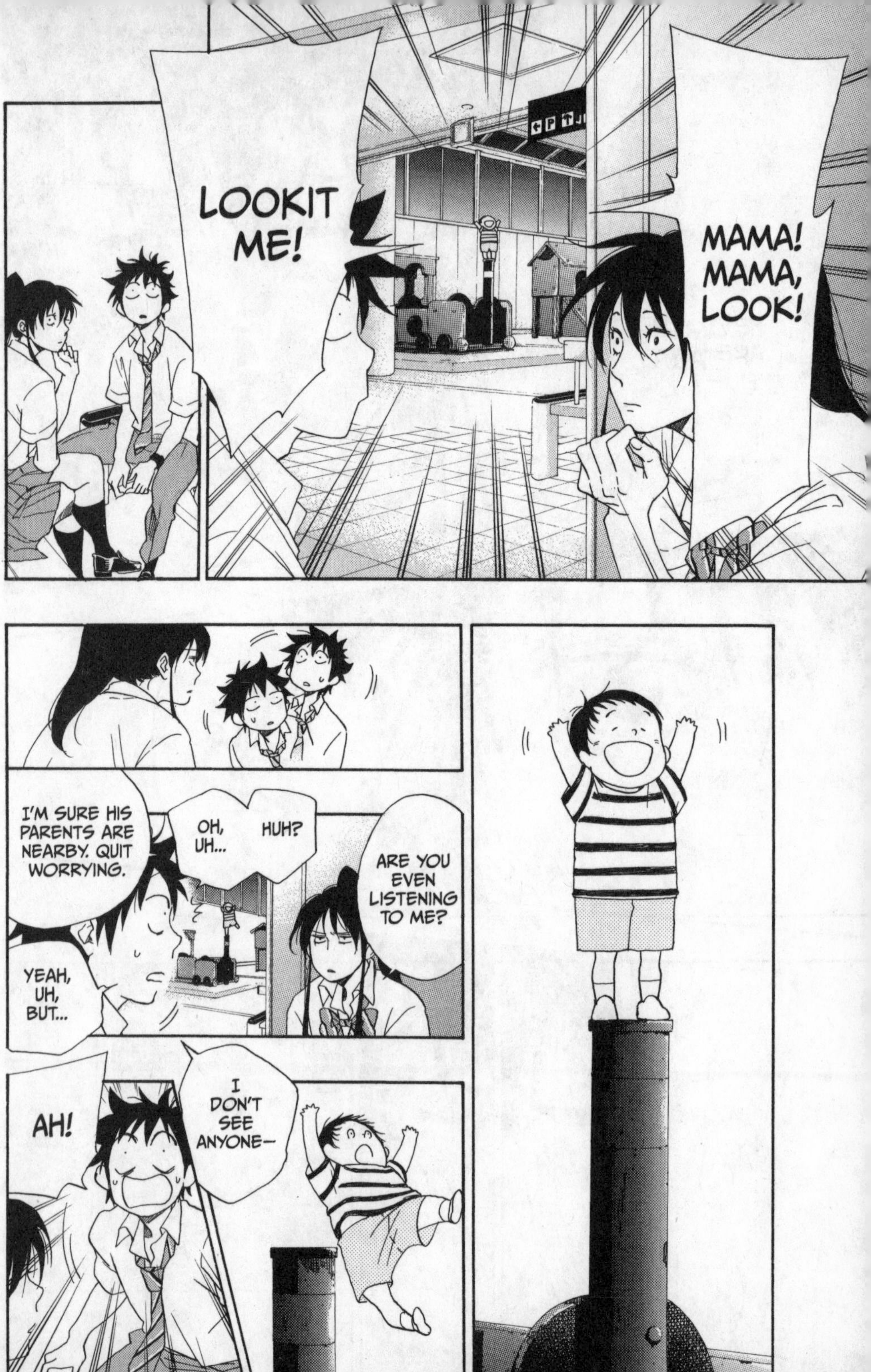
MAMA! MAMA, LOOK!
LOOKIT ME!
ARE YOU EVEN LISTENING TO ME?
HUH?
OH, UH...
I'M SURE HIS PARENTS ARE NEARBY. QUIT WORRYING.
YEAH, UH, BUT...
I DON'T SEE ANYONE—
AH!

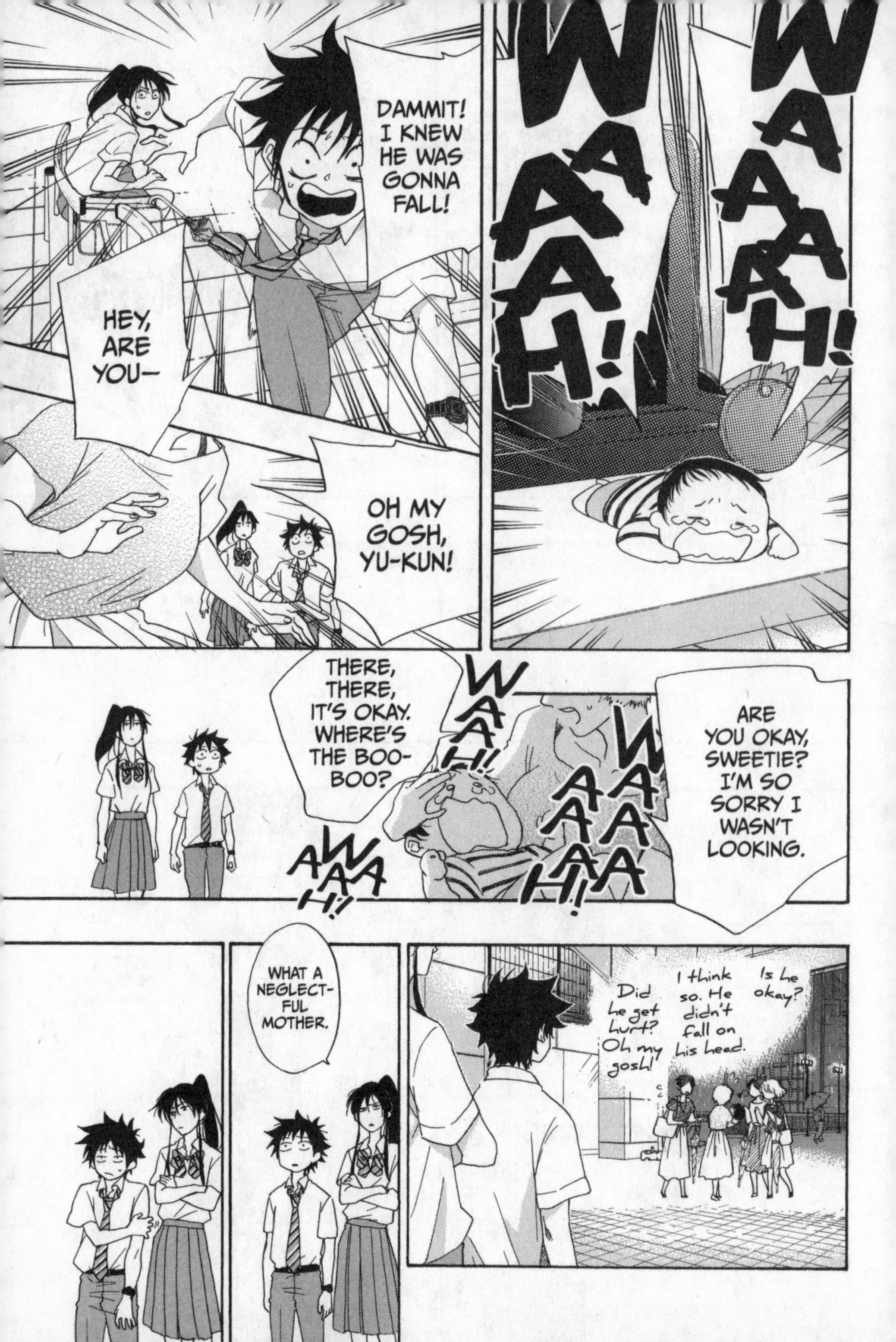
WAAAAH!
WAAAH!
DAMMIT! I KNEW HE WAS GONNA FALL!
HEY, ARE YOU—
OH MY GOSH, YU-KUN!
ARE YOU OKAY, SWEETIE? I'M SO SORRY I WASN'T LOOKING.
WAAAAAH!
THERE, THERE, IT'S OKAY. WHERE'S THE BOO-BOO?
WAAH!!
AWAAH!!
Is he okay?
I think so. He didn't fall on his head.
Did he get hurt? Oh my gosh!
WHAT A NEGLECT-FUL MOTHER.

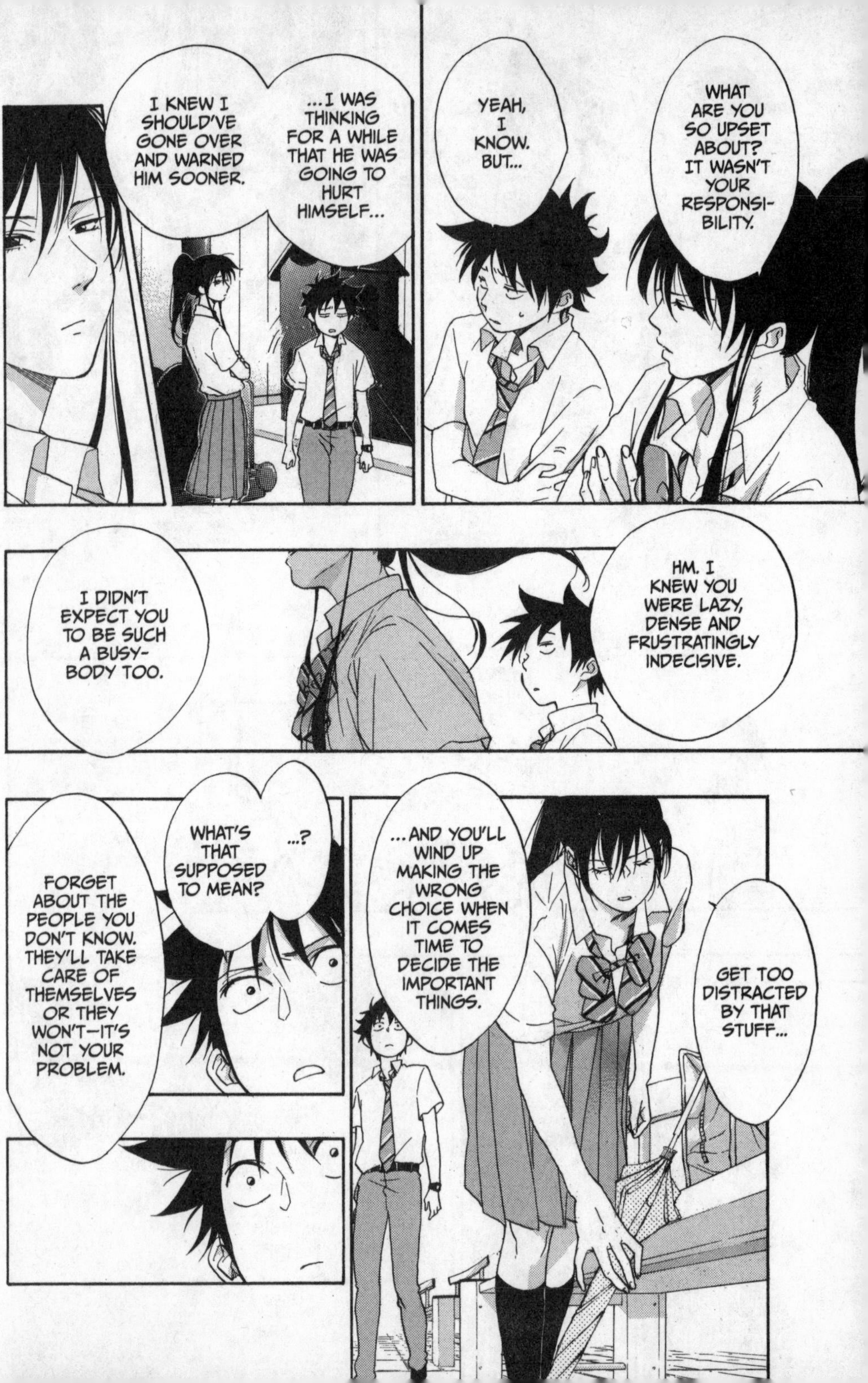
WHAT ARE YOU SO UPSET ABOUT? IT WASN'T YOUR RESPONSIBILITY.
YEAH, I KNOW. BUT...
...I WAS THINKING FOR A WHILE THAT HE WAS GOING TO HURT HIMSELF...
I KNEW I SHOULD'VE GONE OVER AND WARNED HIM SOONER.
HM. I KNEW YOU WERE LAZY, DENSE AND FRUSTRATINGLY INDECISIVE.
I DIDN'T EXPECT YOU TO BE SUCH A BUSY-BODY TOO.
GET TOO DISTRACTED BY THAT STUFF...
...AND YOU'LL WIND UP MAKING THE WRONG CHOICE WHEN IT COMES TIME TO DECIDE THE IMPORTANT THINGS.
...?
WHAT'S THAT SUPPOSED TO MEAN?
FORGET ABOUT THE PEOPLE YOU DON'T KNOW. THEY'LL TAKE CARE OF THEMSELVES OR THEY WON'T—IT'S NOT YOUR PROBLEM.

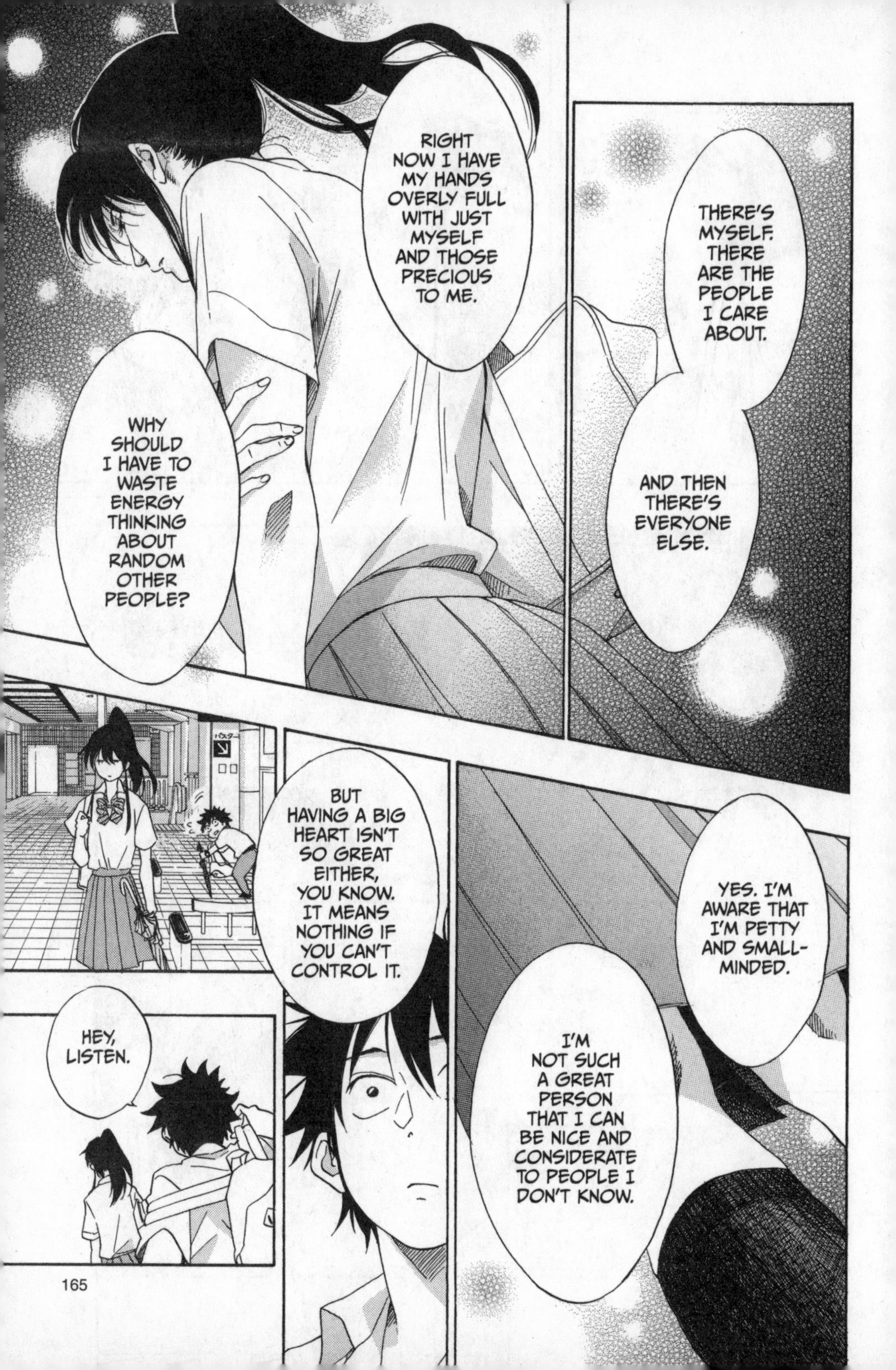
THERE'S MYSELF. THERE ARE THE PEOPLE I CARE ABOUT.
AND THEN THERE'S EVERYONE ELSE.
RIGHT NOW I HAVE MY HANDS OVERLY FULL WITH JUST MYSELF AND THOSE PRECIOUS TO ME.
WHY SHOULD I HAVE TO WASTE ENERGY THINKING ABOUT RANDOM OTHER PEOPLE?
YES. I'M AWARE THAT I'M PETTY AND SMALL-MINDED.
I'M NOT SUCH A GREAT PERSON THAT I CAN BE NICE AND CONSIDERATE TO PEOPLE I DON'T KNOW.
BUT HAVING A BIG HEART ISN'T SO GREAT EITHER, YOU KNOW. IT MEANS NOTHING IF YOU CAN'T CONTROL IT.
HEY, LISTEN.

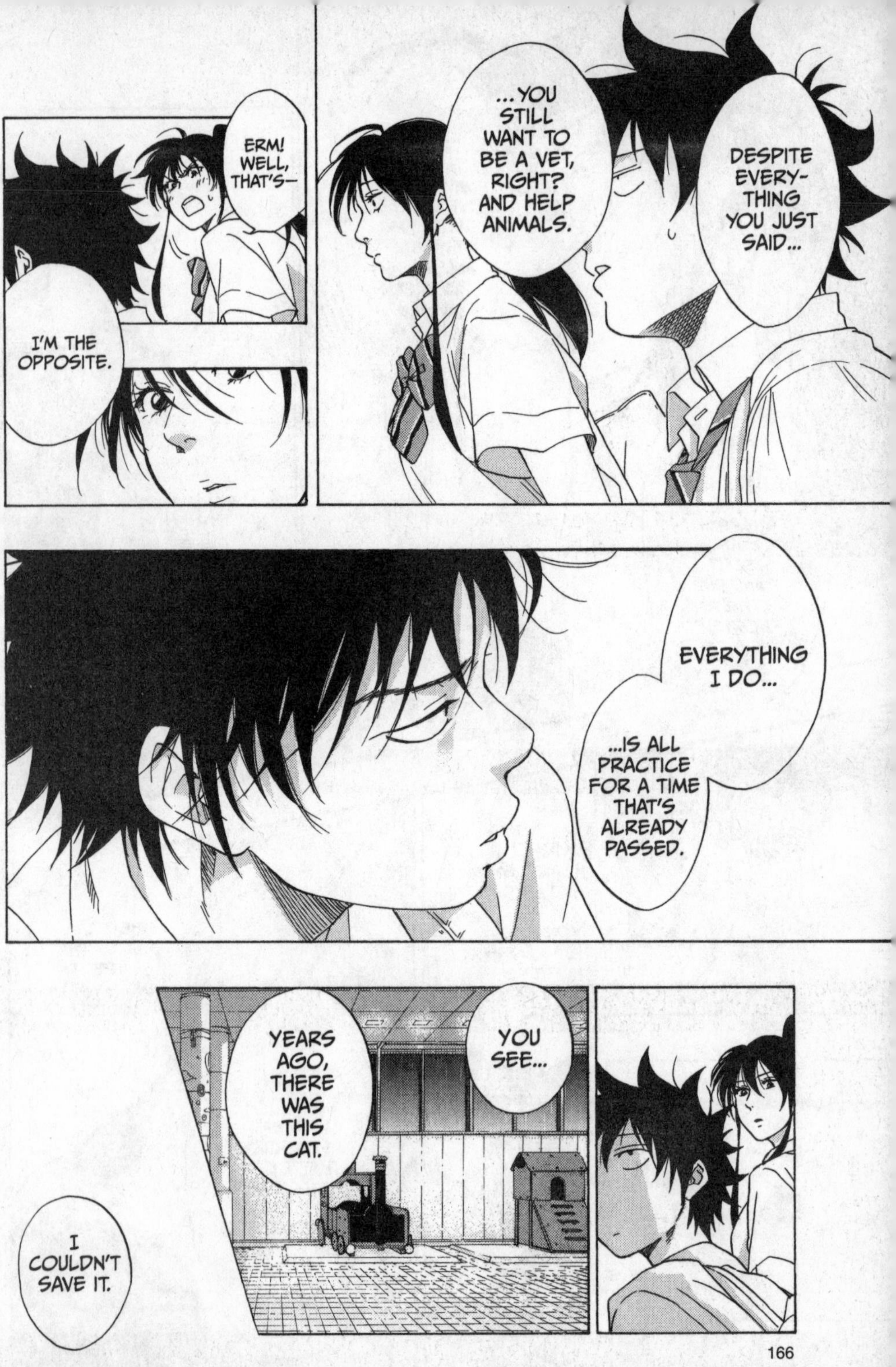
DESPITE EVERY-THING YOU JUST SAID...
...YOU STILL WANT TO BE A VET, RIGHT? AND HELP ANIMALS.
ERM! WELL, THAT'S—
I'M THE OPPOSITE.
EVERYTHING I DO...
...IS ALL PRACTICE FOR A TIME THAT'S ALREADY PASSED.
YOU SEE...
YEARS AGO, THERE WAS THIS CAT.
I COULDN'T SAVE IT.

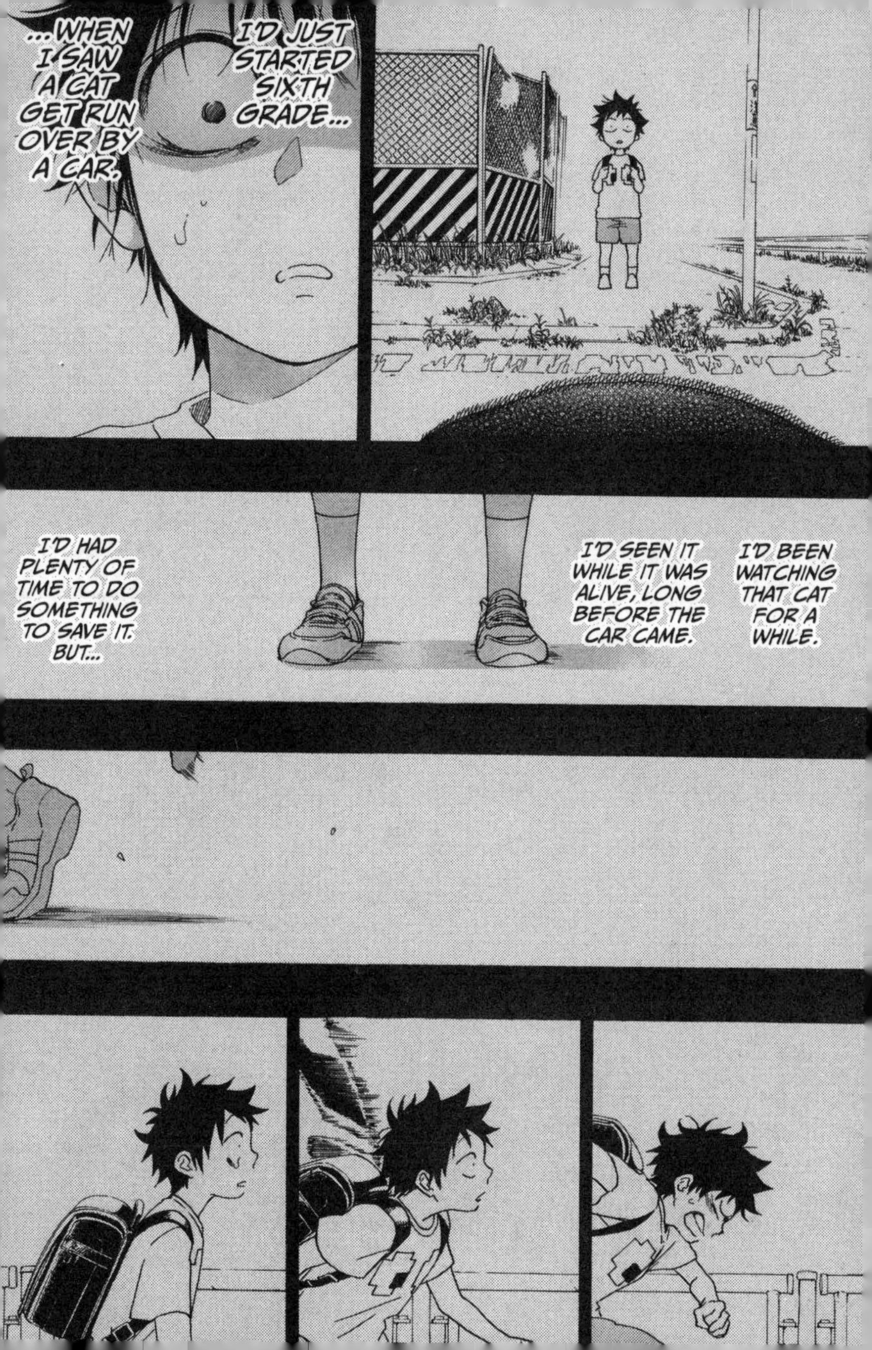
I'D JUST STARTED SIXTH GRADE...
...WHEN I SAW A CAT GET RUN OVER BY A CAR.
I'D BEEN WATCHING THAT CAT FOR A WHILE.
I'D SEEN IT WHILE IT WAS ALIVE, LONG BEFORE THE CAR CAME.
I'D HAD PLENTY OF TIME TO DO SOMETHING TO SAVE IT. BUT...

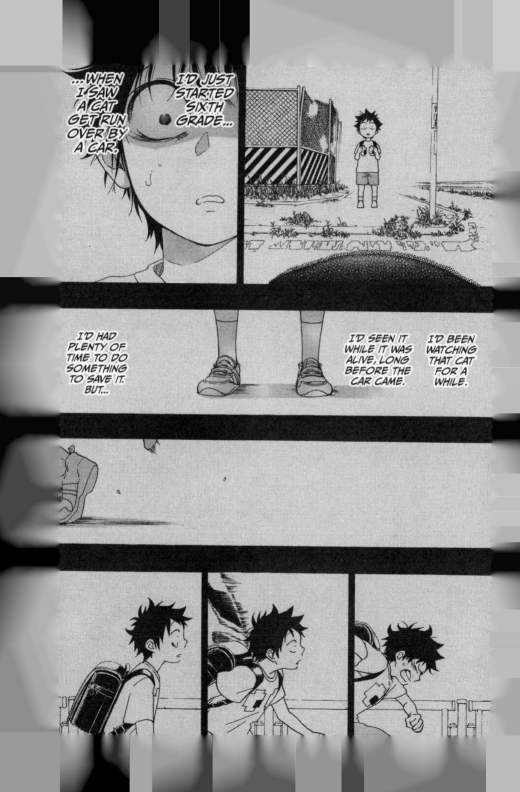

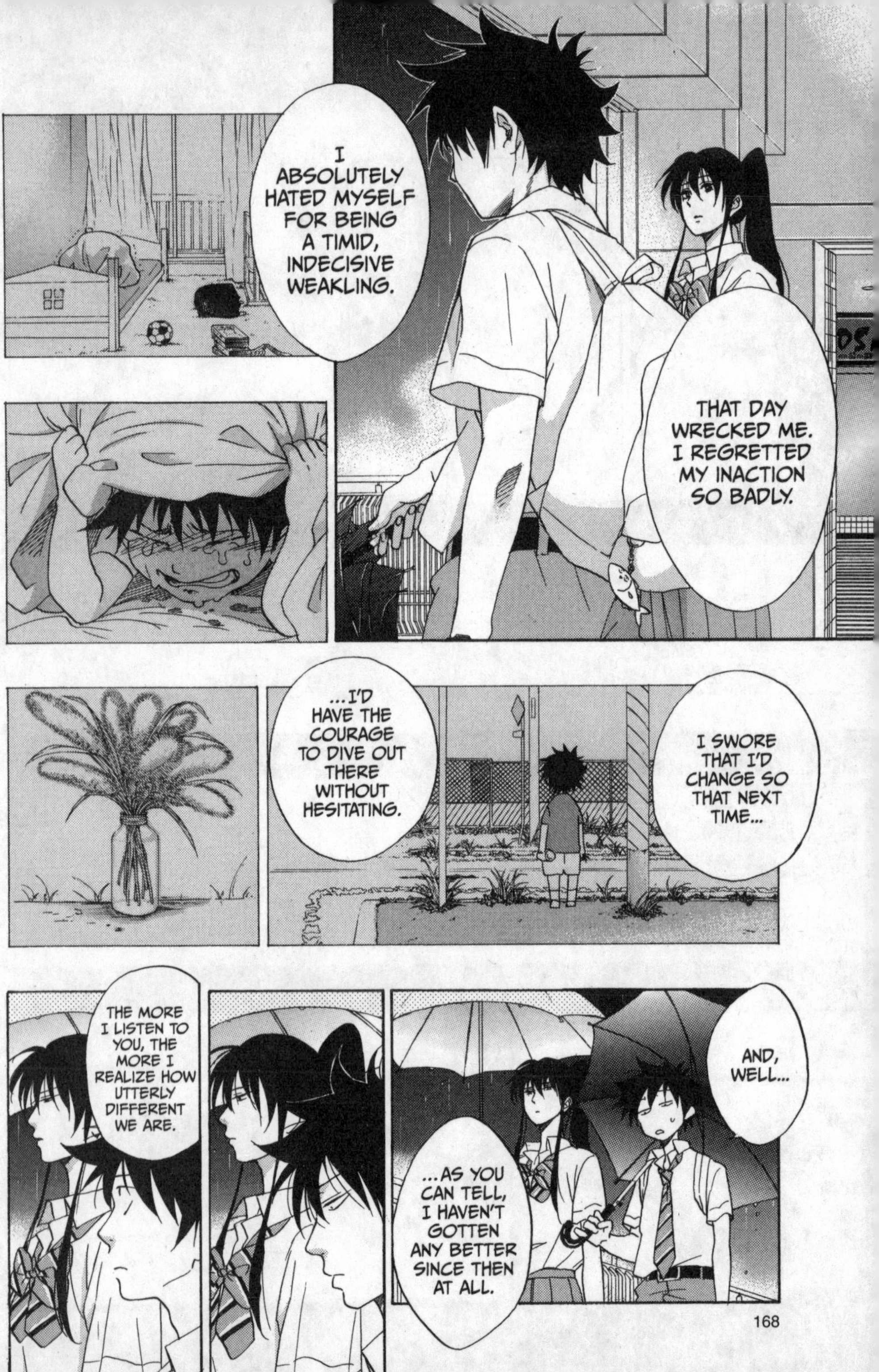
THAT DAY WRECKED ME. I REGRETTED MY INACTION SO BADLY.
I ABSOLUTELY HATED MYSELF FOR BEING A TIMID, INDECISIVE WEAKLING.
I SWORE THAT I'D CHANGE SO THAT NEXT TIME...
...I'D HAVE THE COURAGE TO DIVE OUT THERE WITHOUT HESITATING.
AND, WELL...
...AS YOU CAN TELL, I HAVEN'T GOTTEN ANY BETTER SINCE THEN AT ALL.
THE MORE I LISTEN TO YOU, THE MORE I REALIZE HOW UTTERLY DIFFERENT WE ARE.

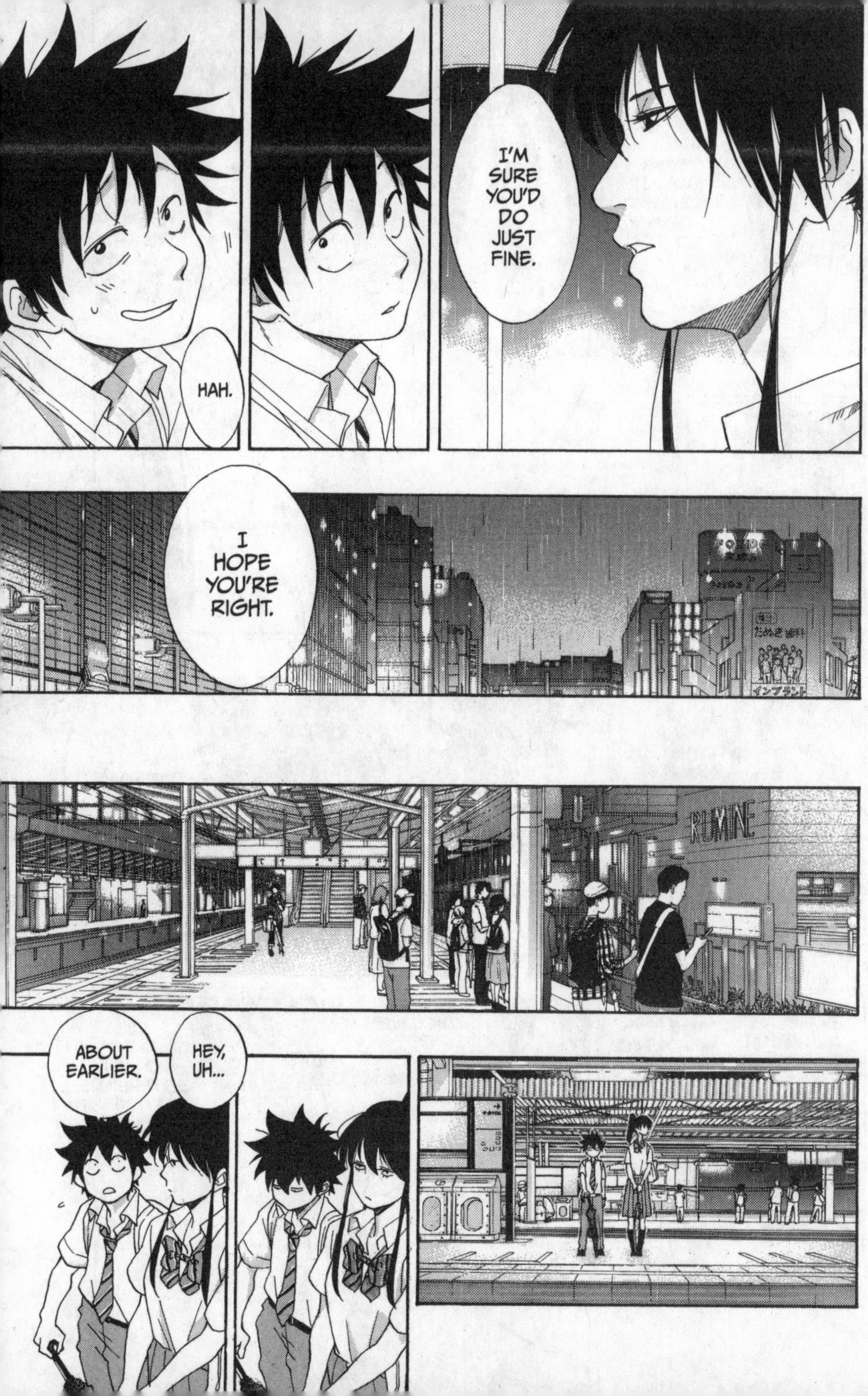
I'M SURE YOU'D DO JUST FINE.
HAH.
I HOPE YOU'RE RIGHT.
インプラント
RUMINE
HEY, UH...
ABOUT EARLIER.

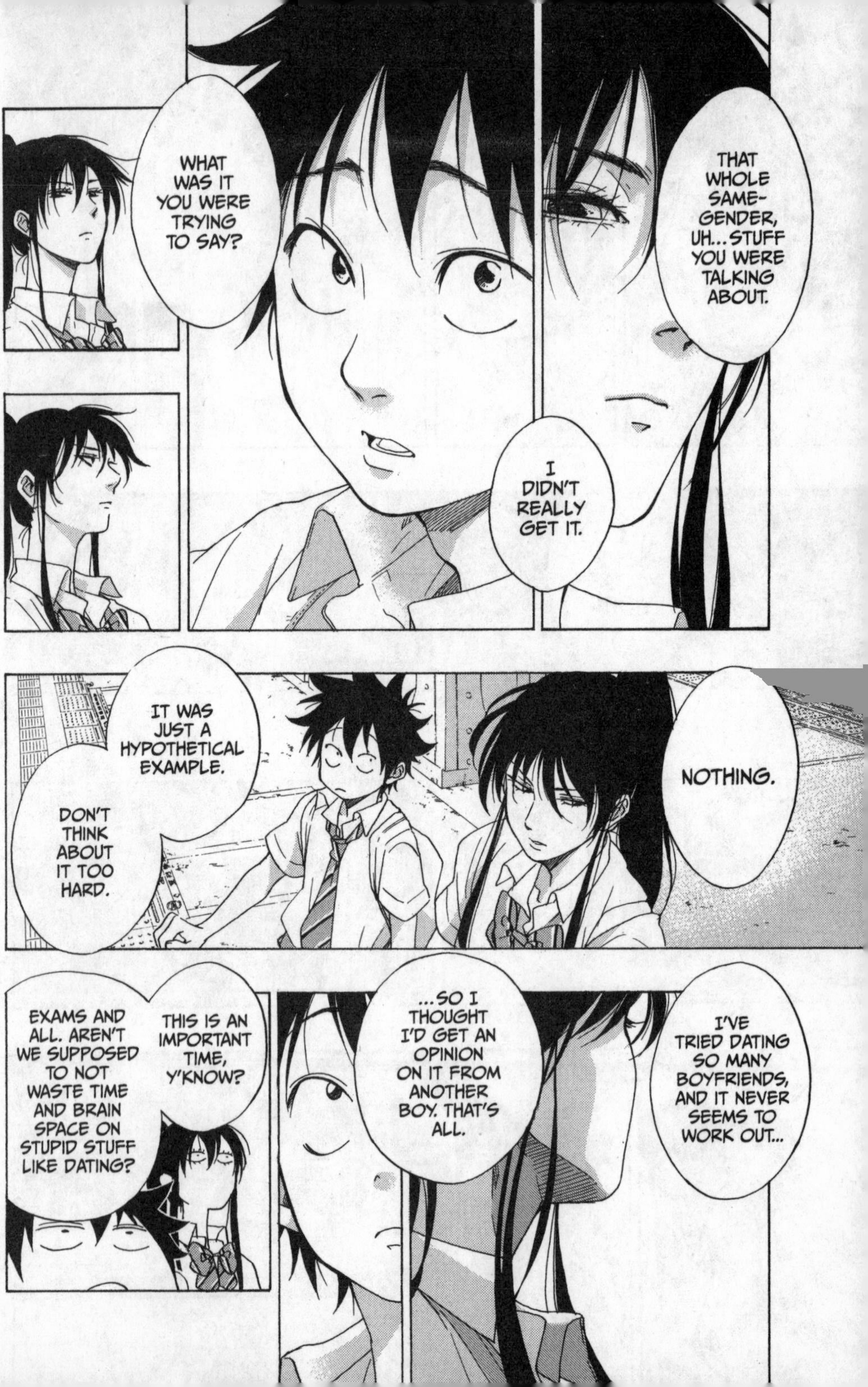
THAT WHOLE SAME-GENDER, UH... STUFF YOU WERE TALKING ABOUT.
I DIDN'T REALLY GET IT.
WHAT WAS IT YOU WERE TRYING TO SAY?
NOTHING.
IT WAS JUST A HYPOTHETICAL EXAMPLE.
DON'T THINK ABOUT IT TOO HARD.
I'VE TRIED DATING SO MANY BOYFRIENDS, AND IT NEVER SEEMS TO WORK OUT...
...SO I THOUGHT I'D GET AN OPINION ON IT FROM ANOTHER BOY. THAT'S ALL.
THIS IS AN IMPORTANT TIME, Y'KNOW?
EXAMS AND ALL. AREN'T WE SUPPOSED TO NOT WASTE TIME AND BRAIN SPACE ON STUPID STUFF LIKE DATING?

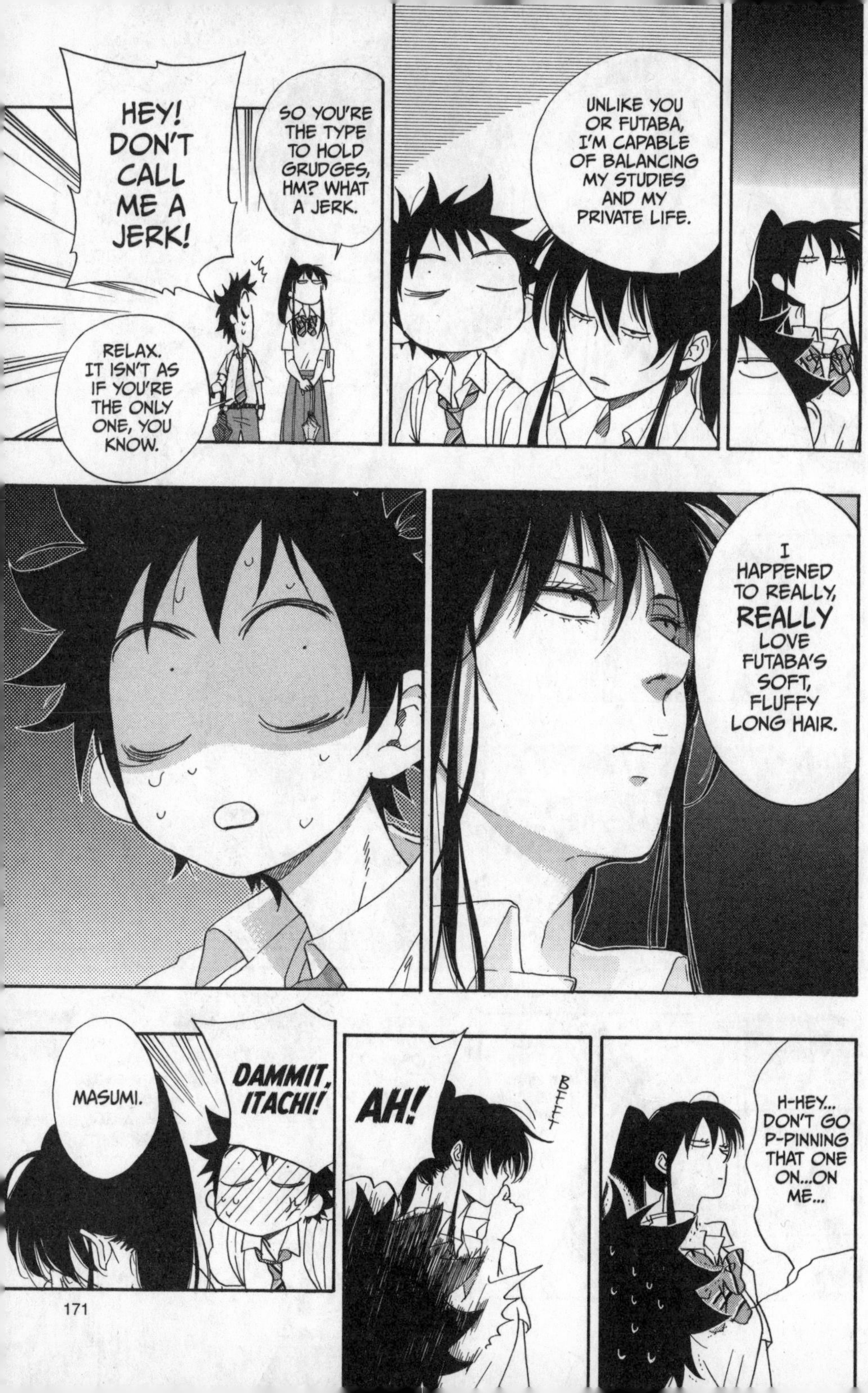
UNLIKE YOU OR FUTABA, I'M CAPABLE OF BALANCING MY STUDIES AND MY PRIVATE LIFE.
SO YOU'RE THE TYPE TO HOLD GRUDGES, HM? WHAT A JERK.
HEY! DON'T CALL ME A JERK!
RELAX. IT ISN'T AS IF YOU'RE THE ONLY ONE, YOU KNOW.
I HAPPENED TO REALLY, REALLY LOVE FUTABA'S SOFT, FLUFFY LONG HAIR.
H-HEY... DON'T GO P-PINNING THAT ONE ON...ON ME...
BFFT
AH!
DAMMIT, ITACHI!
MASUMI.

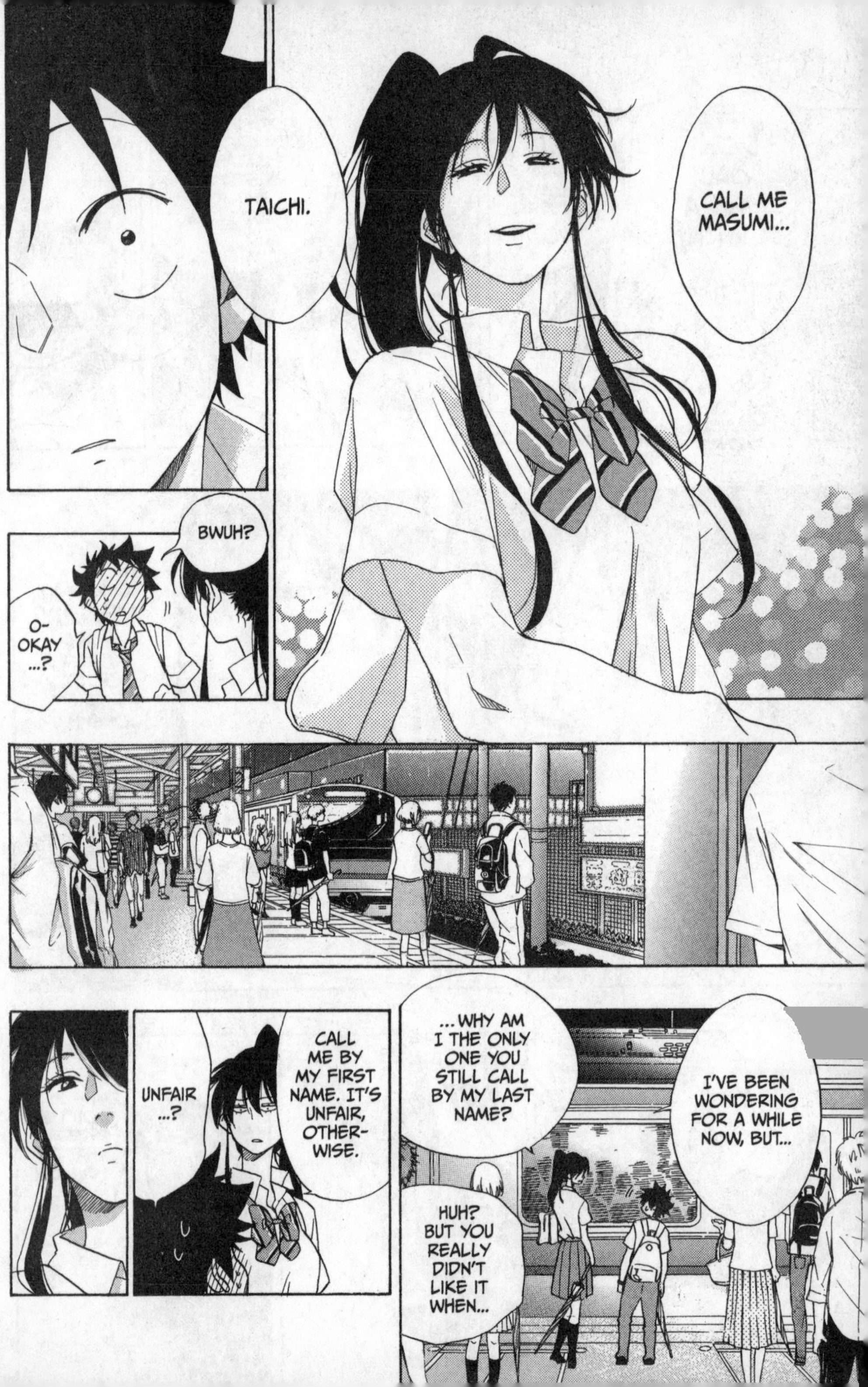
CALL ME MASUMI...
TAICHI.
BWUH?
O- OKAY ...?
I'VE BEEN WONDERING FOR A WHILE NOW, BUT...
...WHY AM I THE ONLY ONE YOU STILL CALL BY MY LAST NAME?
HUH? BUT YOU REALLY DIDN'T LIKE IT WHEN...
CALL ME BY MY FIRST NAME. IT'S UNFAIR, OTHER- WISE.
UNFAIR ...?

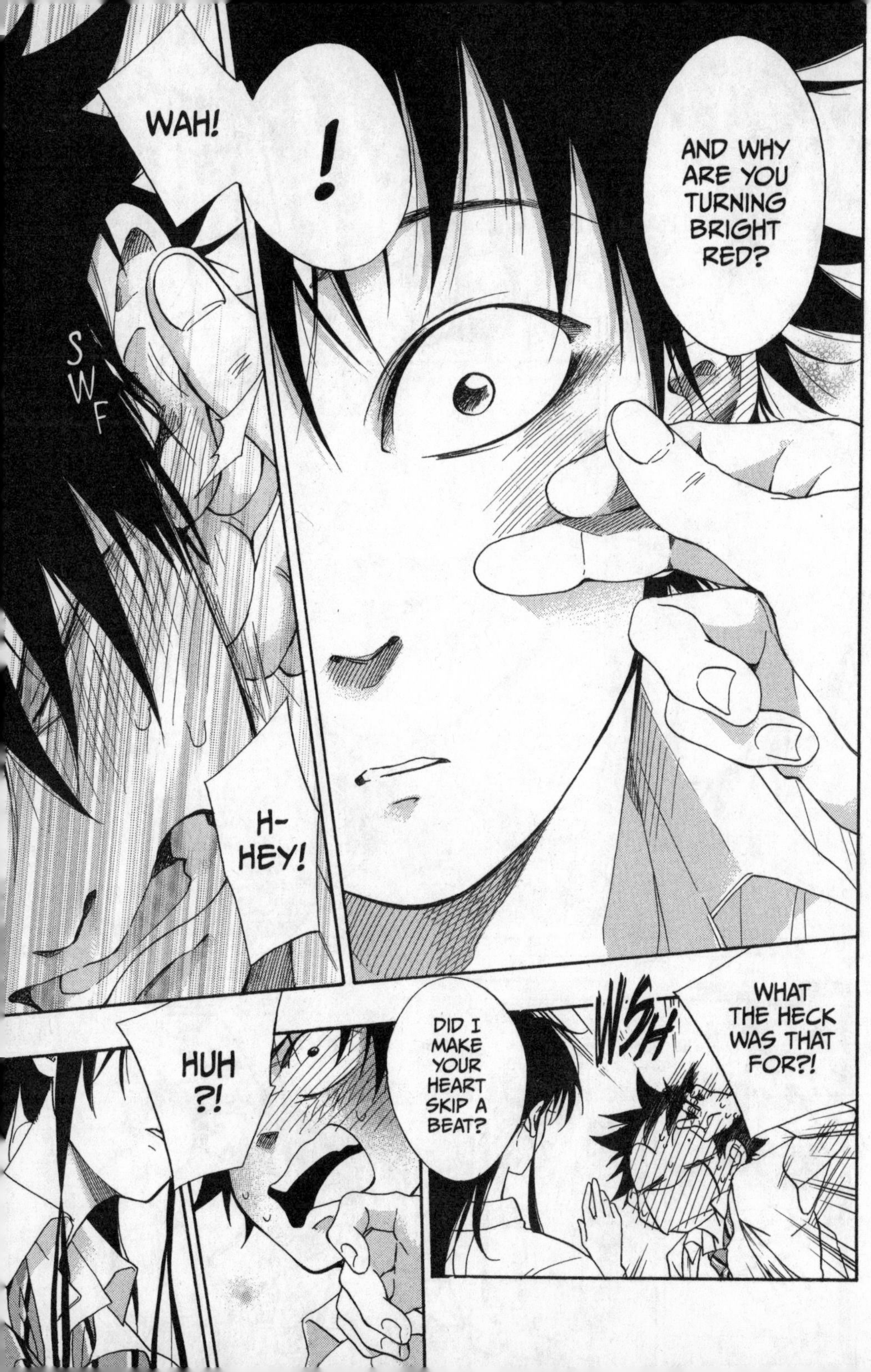
AND WHY ARE YOU TURNING BRIGHT RED?
!
WAH!
SWF
H-HEY!
WHAT THE HECK WAS THAT FOR?!
WSH
DID I MAKE YOUR HEART SKIP A BEAT?
HUH ?!

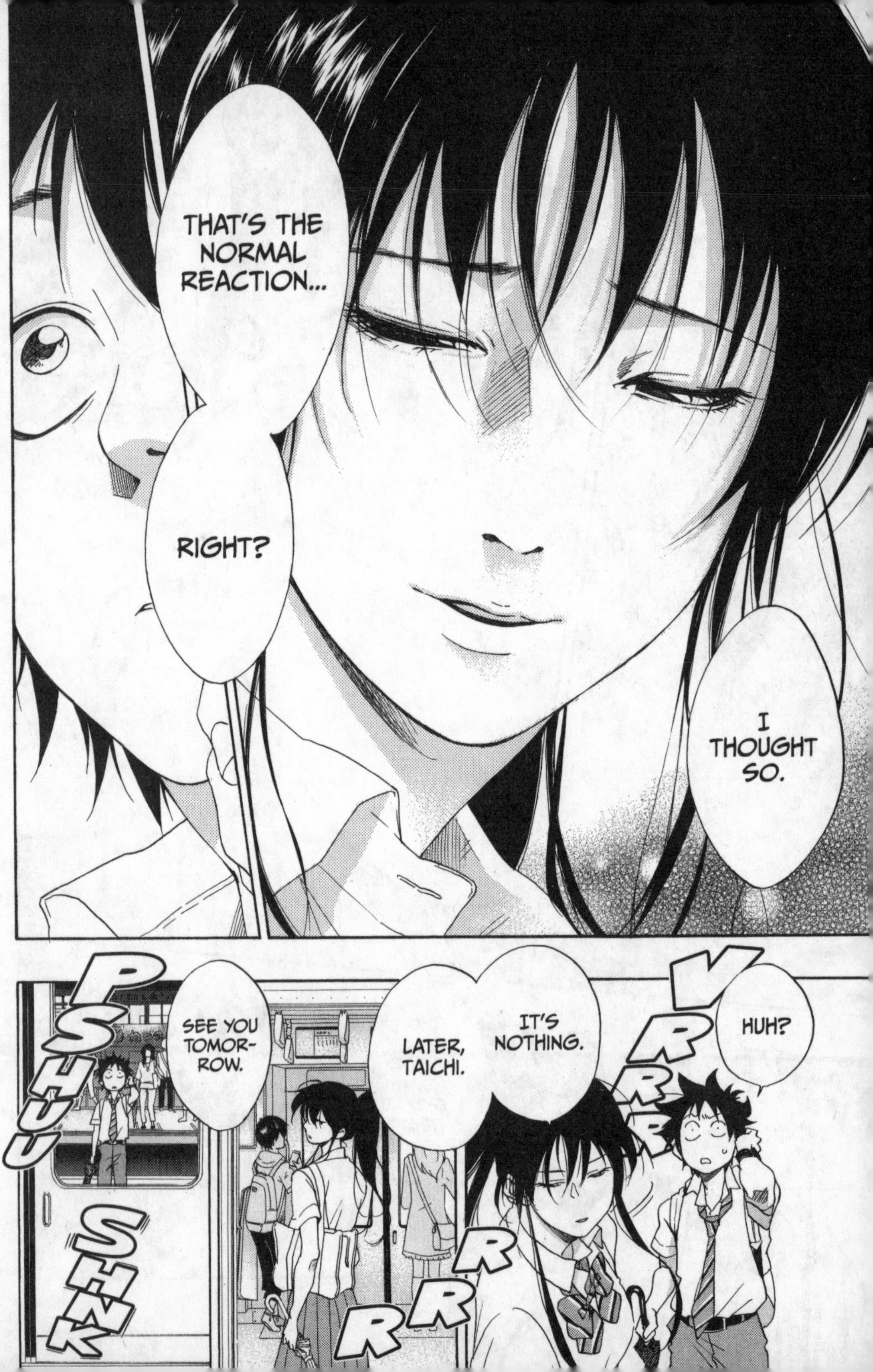
I THOUGHT SO.
THAT'S THE NORMAL REACTION...
RIGHT?
VRRR
HUH?
IT'S NOTHING.
LATER, TAICHI.
RRR
SEE YOU TOMOR-ROW.
PSHUU
SHNK

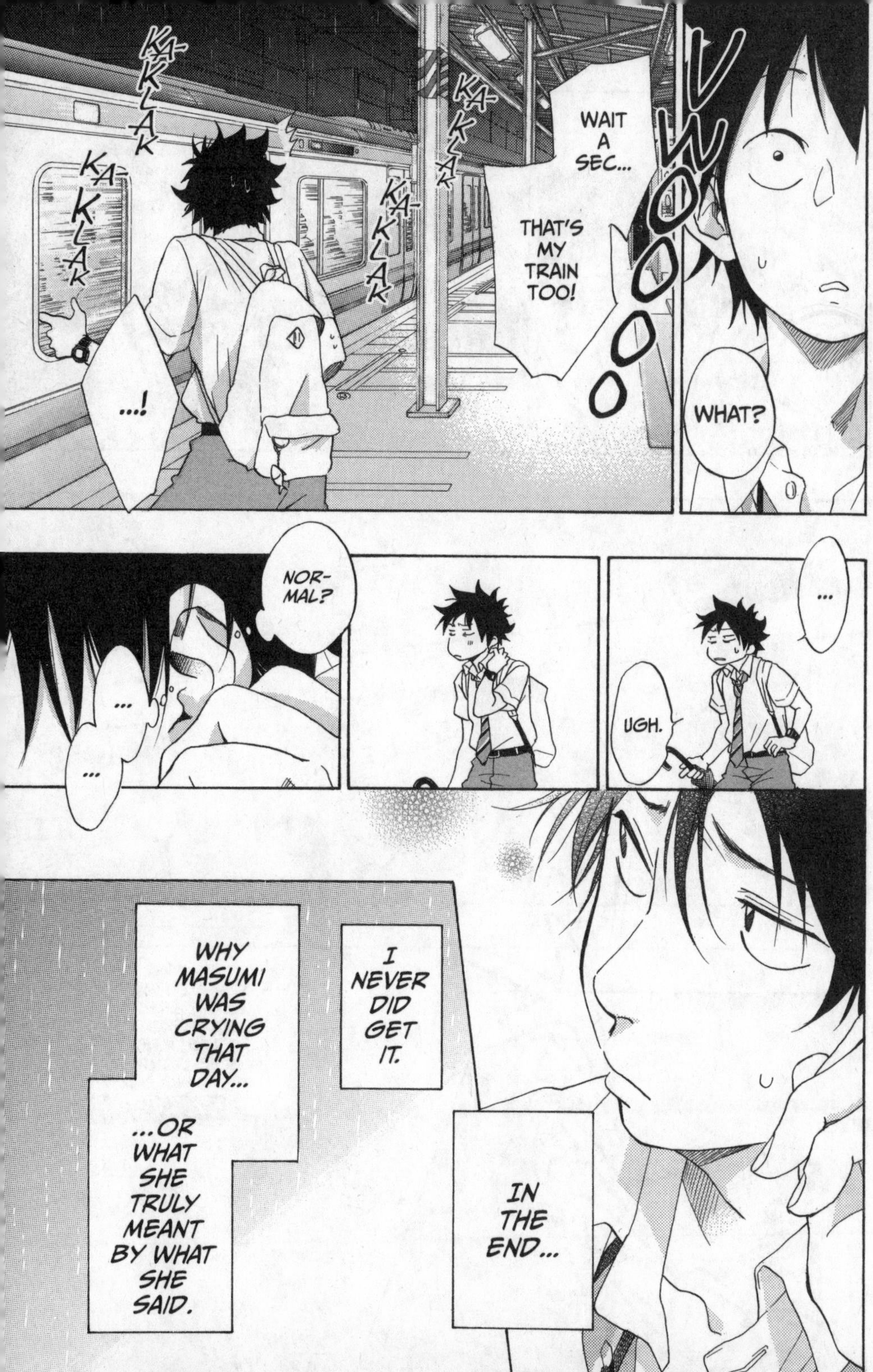
VWOOOOOO
WHAT?
WAIT A SEC...
THAT'S MY TRAIN TOO!
KA-KLAK
KA-KLAK
KA-KLAK
KA-KLAK
...!
...
UGH.
NOR-MAL?
...
...
IN THE END...
I NEVER DID GET IT.
WHY MASUMI WAS CRYING THAT DAY...
...OR WHAT SHE TRULY MEANT BY WHAT SHE SAID.

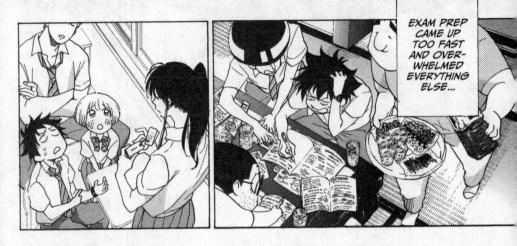

EXAM PREP CAME UP TOO FAST AND OVER-WHELMED EVERYTHING ELSE...

...ALL OTHER CONCERNS COMPLETELY FORGOTTEN IN FAVOR OF STUDYING AND PRACTICE TESTS.

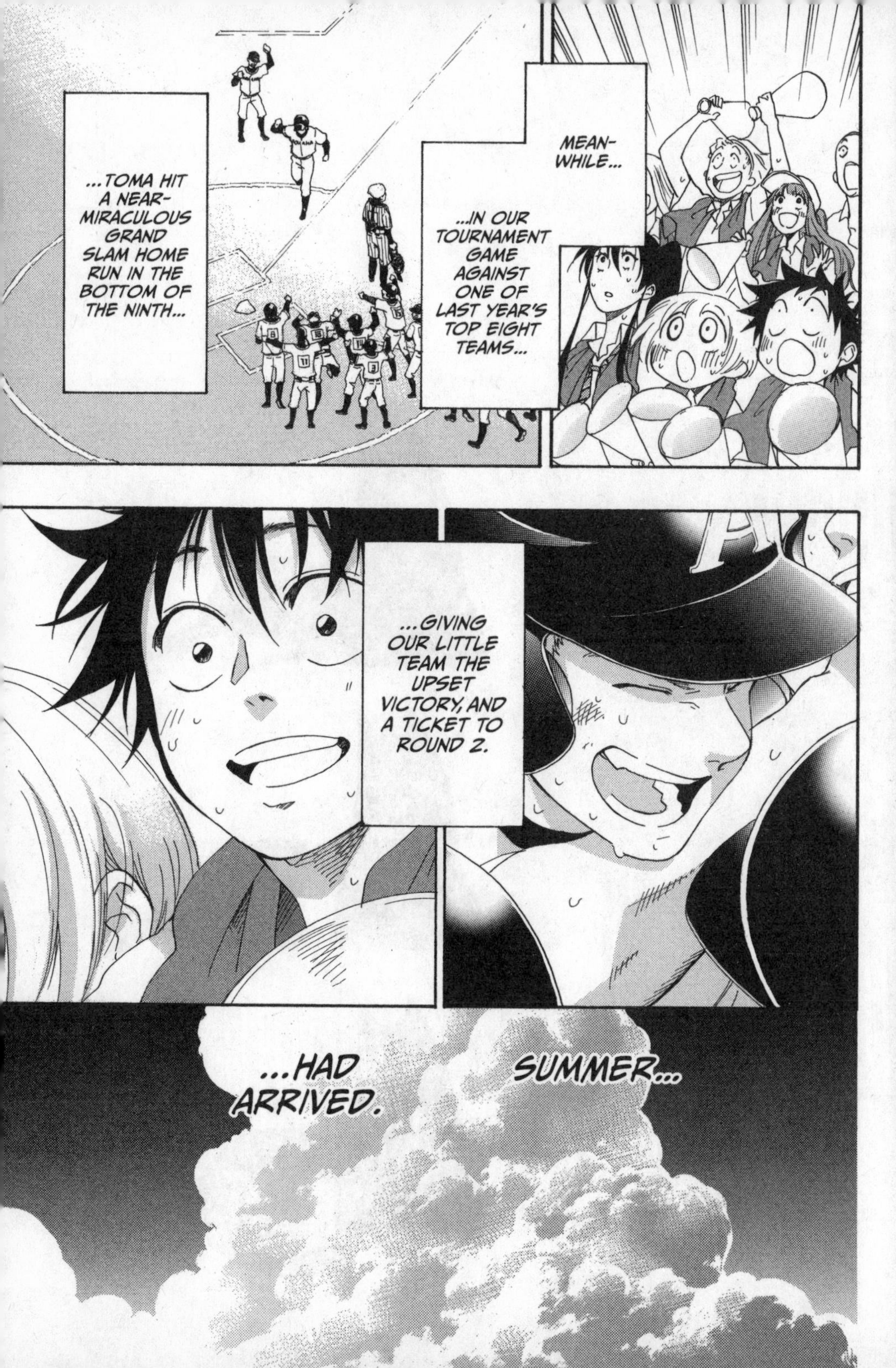
MEAN-WHILE...
...IN OUR TOURNAMENT GAME AGAINST ONE OF LAST YEAR'S TOP EIGHT TEAMS...
...TOMA HIT A NEAR-MIRACULOUS GRAND SLAM HOME RUN IN THE BOTTOM OF THE NINTH...
...GIVING OUR LITTLE TEAM THE UPSET VICTORY, AND A TICKET TO ROUND 2.
SUMMER...
...HAD ARRIVED.

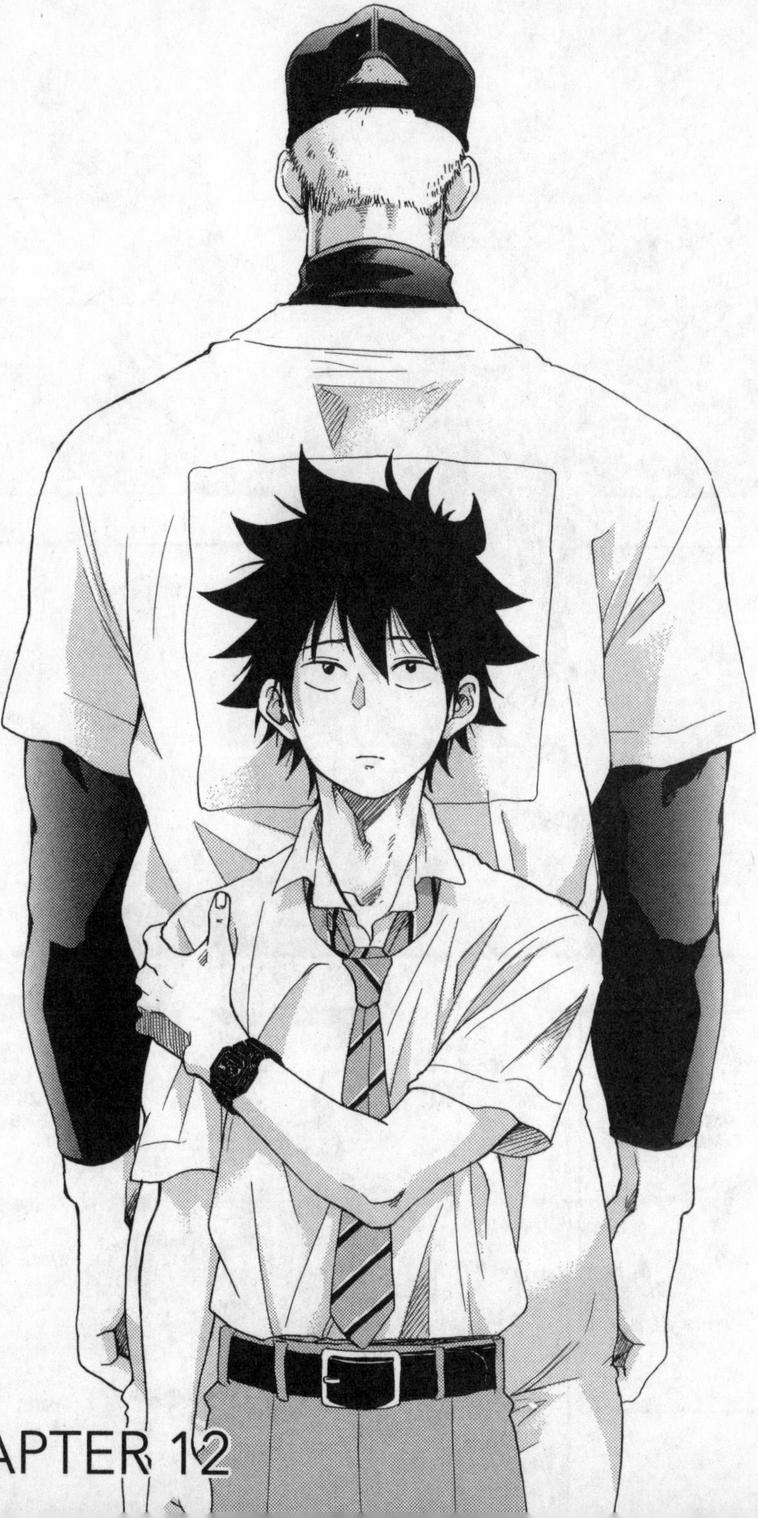

CHAPTER 12

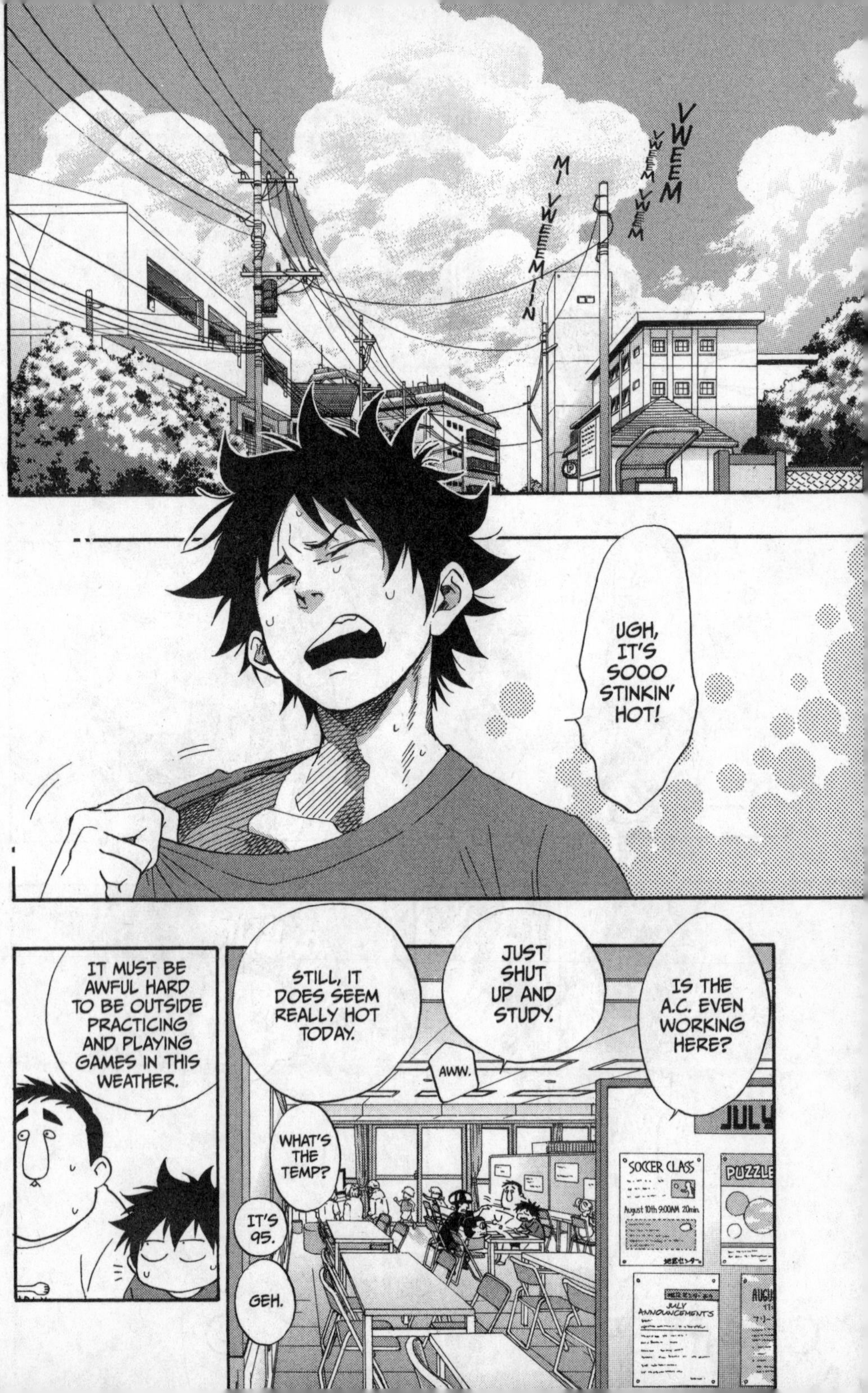
VWEEEM
VWEEM VWEEM
MI VWEEMIN
UGH, IT'S SOOO STINKIN' HOT!
IS THE A.C. EVEN WORKING HERE?
JUST SHUT UP AND STUDY.
AWW.
STILL, IT DOES SEEM REALLY HOT TODAY.
WHAT'S THE TEMP?
IT'S 95.
GEH.
JULY
SOCCER CLASS
August 10th 9:00AM 20min.
PUZZLE
JULY ANNOUNCEMENTS
IT MUST BE AWFUL HARD TO BE OUTSIDE PRACTICING AND PLAYING GAMES IN THIS WEATHER.

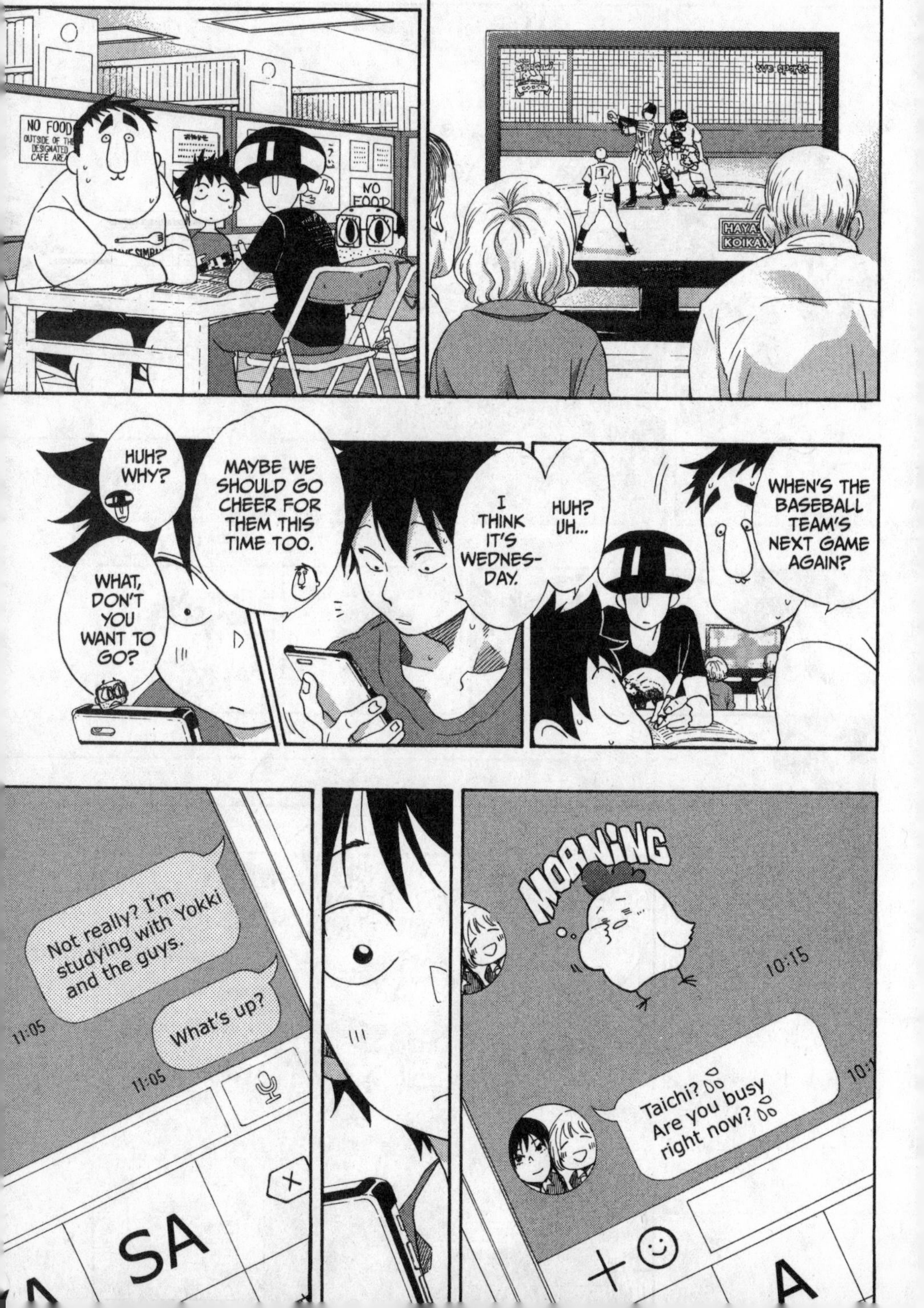
tve sports
NO FOOD OUTSIDE OF THE DESIGNATED CAFÉ AREA
NO FOOD
WHEN'S THE BASEBALL TEAM'S NEXT GAME AGAIN?
HUH? UH...
I THINK IT'S WEDNES-DAY.
MAYBE WE SHOULD GO CHEER FOR THEM THIS TIME TOO.
HUH? WHY?
WHAT, DON'T YOU WANT TO GO?
MORNING
10:15
Taichi? Are you busy right now?
Not really? I'm studying with Yokki and the guys.
11:05
What's up?
11:05
SA

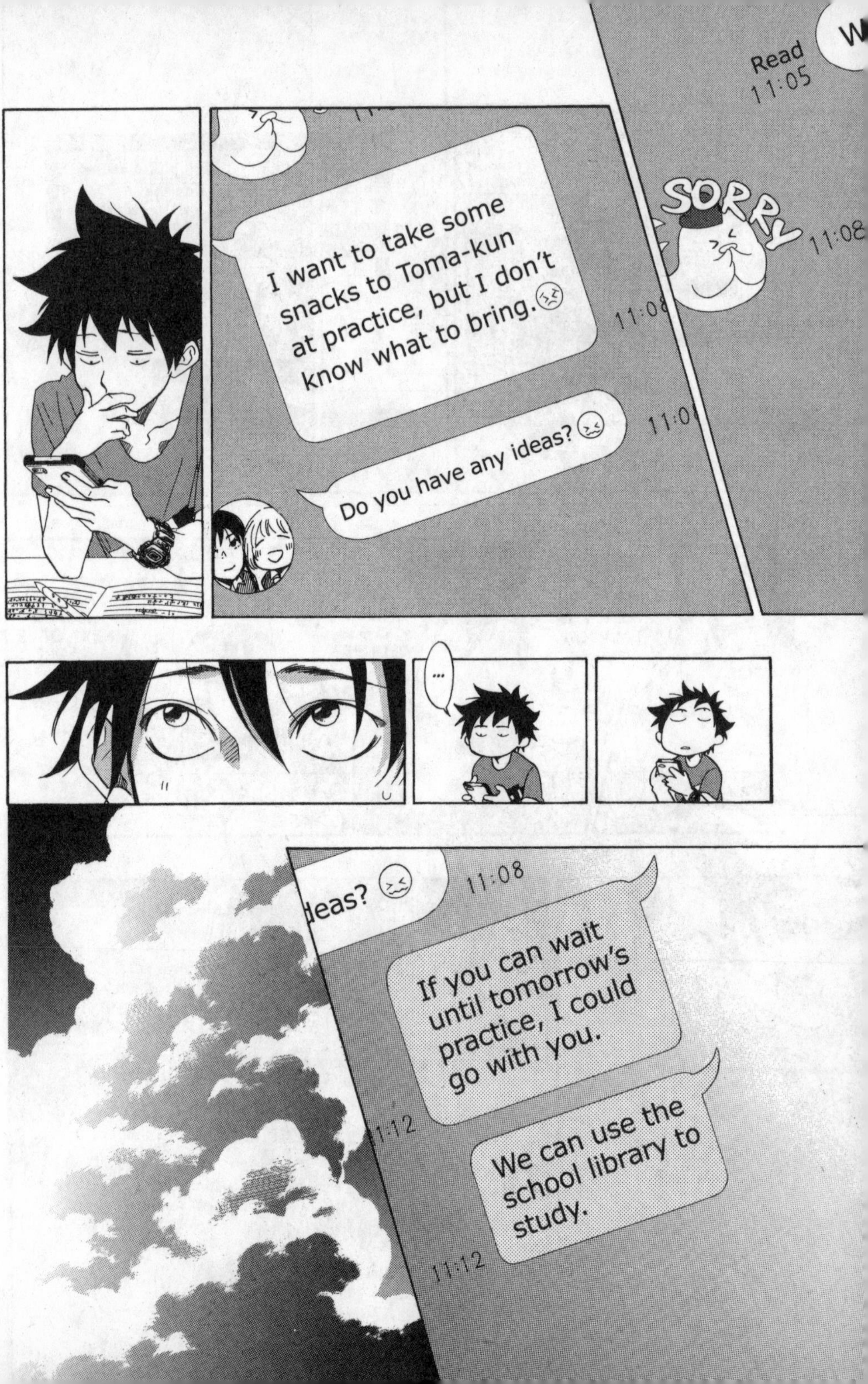
Read
11:05
SORRY
11:08
I want to take some snacks to Toma-kun at practice, but I don't know what to bring.
11:08
Do you have any ideas?
...
ideas?
11:08
If you can wait until tomorrow's practice, I could go with you.
11:12
We can use the school library to study.
11:12

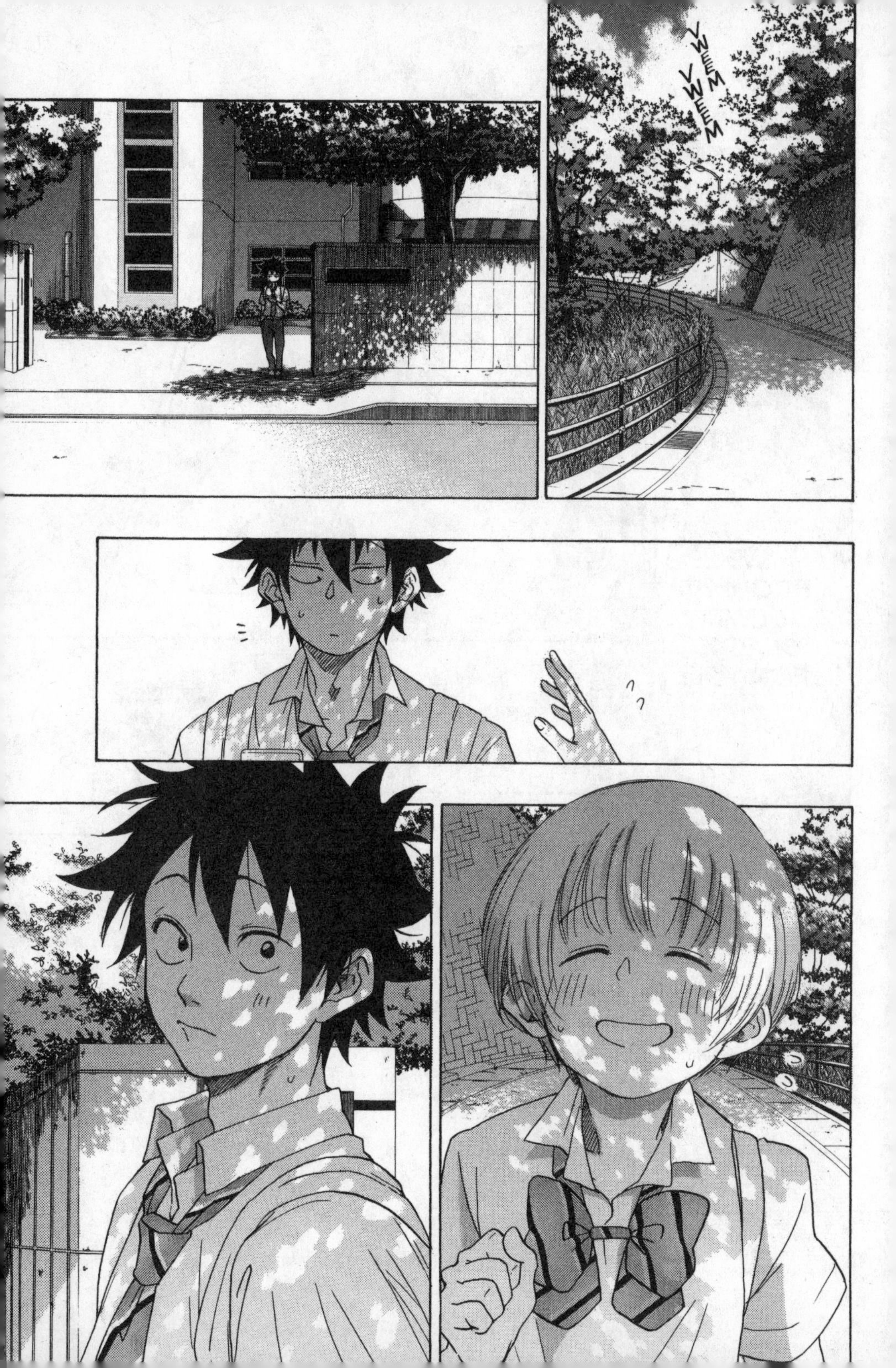
VWEEM
VWEEM

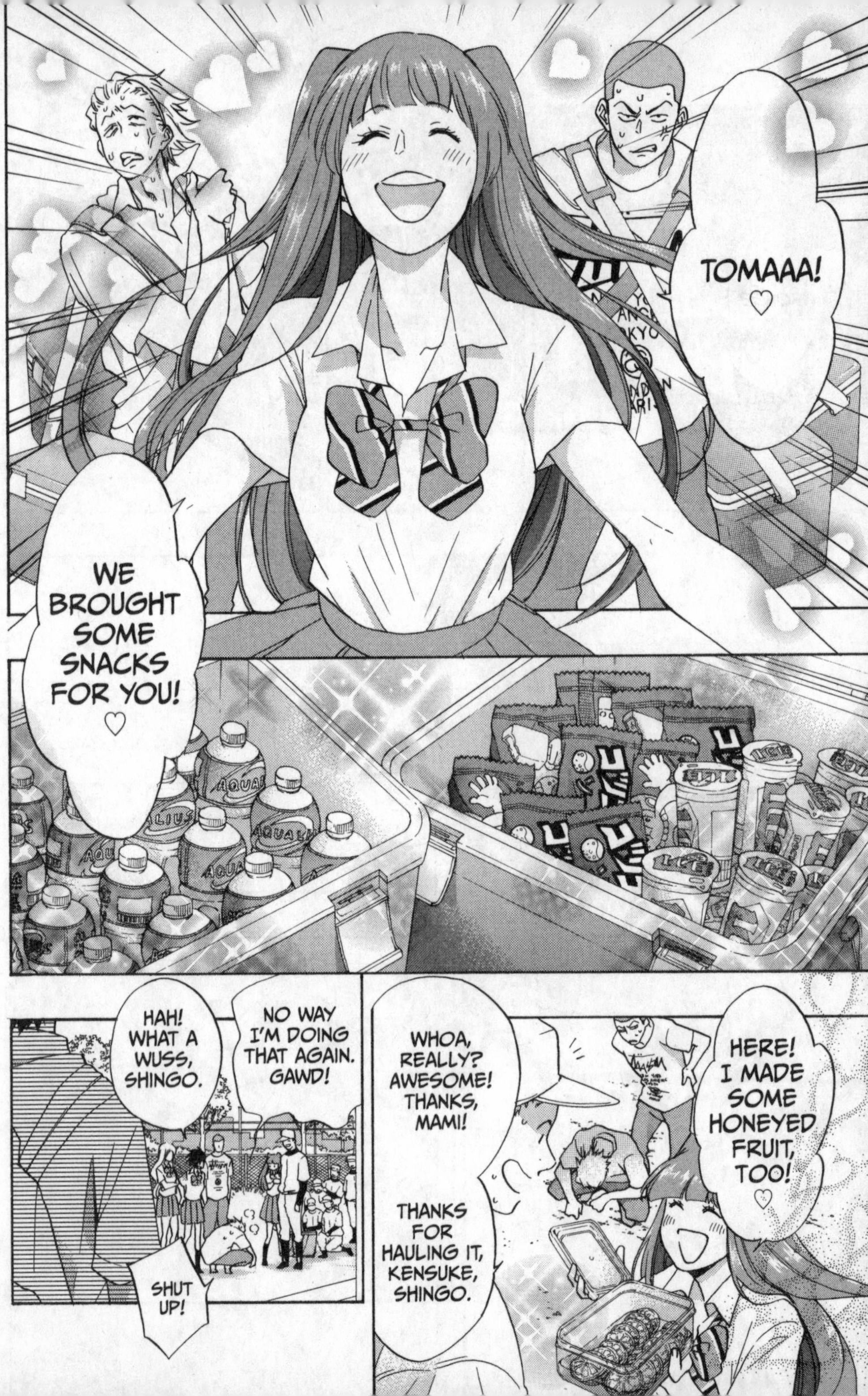
TOMAAA! ♡
WE BROUGHT SOME SNACKS FOR YOU! ♡
HERE! I MADE SOME HONEYED FRUIT, TOO! ♡
WHOA, REALLY? AWESOME! THANKS, MAMI!
THANKS FOR HAULING IT, KENSUKE, SHINGO.
NO WAY I'M DOING THAT AGAIN. GAWD!
HAH! WHAT A WUSS, SHINGO.
SHUT UP!

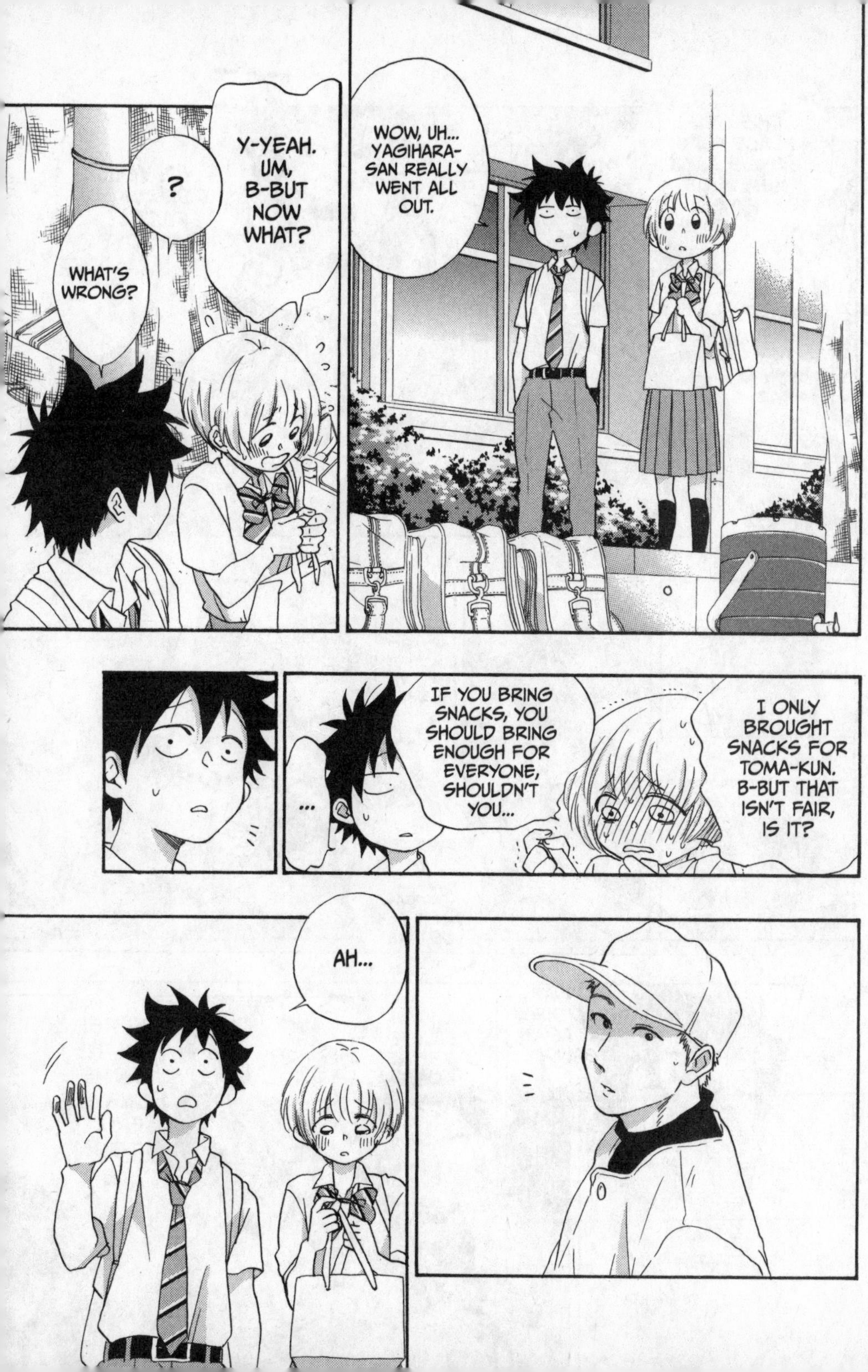
WOW, UH... YAGIHARA-SAN REALLY WENT ALL OUT.
Y-YEAH. UM, B-BUT NOW WHAT?
?
WHAT'S WRONG?
I ONLY BROUGHT SNACKS FOR TOMA-KUN. B-BUT THAT ISN'T FAIR, IS IT?
IF YOU BRING SNACKS, YOU SHOULD BRING ENOUGH FOR EVERYONE, SHOULDN'T YOU...
...
AH...

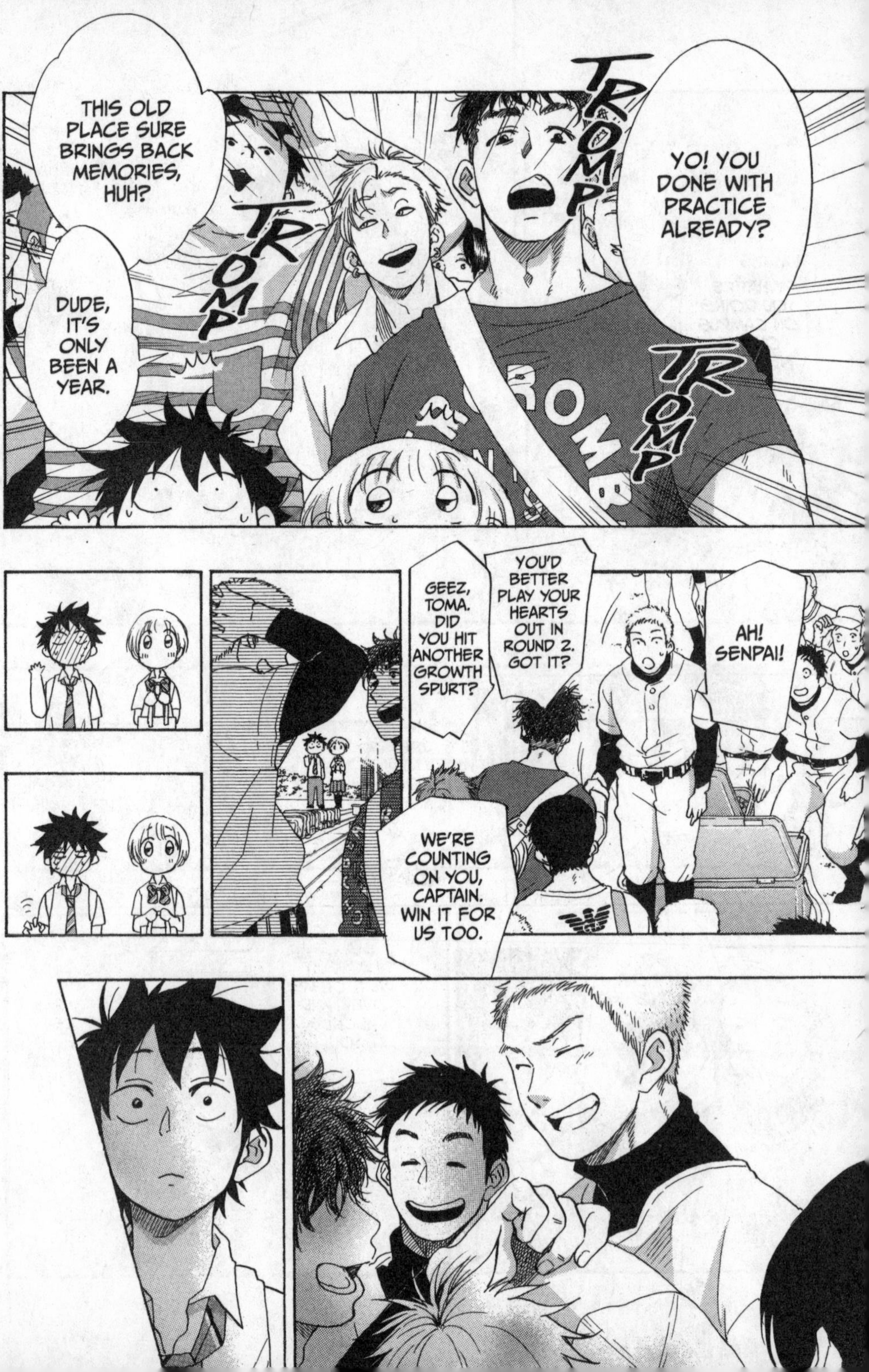
YO! YOU DONE WITH PRACTICE ALREADY?
TROMP
TROMP
TROMP
TROMP
THIS OLD PLACE SURE BRINGS BACK MEMORIES, HUH?
DUDE, IT'S ONLY BEEN A YEAR.
AH! SENPAI!
YOU'D BETTER PLAY YOUR HEARTS OUT IN ROUND 2. GOT IT?
GEEZ, TOMA. DID YOU HIT ANOTHER GROWTH SPURT?
WE'RE COUNTING ON YOU, CAPTAIN. WIN IT FOR US TOO.

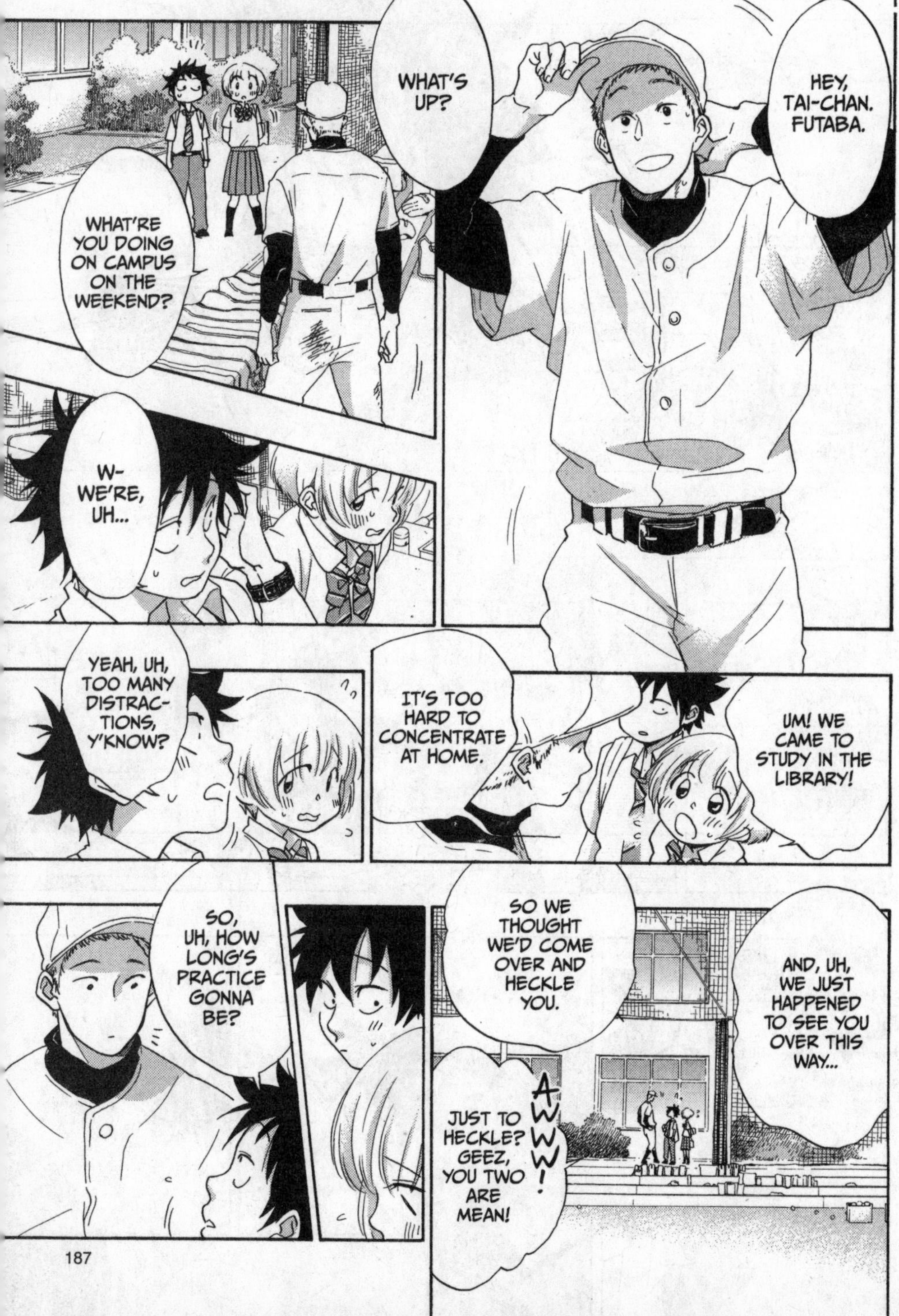
HEY, TAI-CHAN. FUTABA.
WHAT'S UP?
WHAT'RE YOU DOING ON CAMPUS ON THE WEEKEND?
W-WE'RE, UH...
UM! WE CAME TO STUDY IN THE LIBRARY!
IT'S TOO HARD TO CONCENTRATE AT HOME.
YEAH, UH, TOO MANY DISTRACTIONS, Y'KNOW?
AND, UH, WE JUST HAPPENED TO SEE YOU OVER THIS WAY...
SO WE THOUGHT WE'D COME OVER AND HECKLE YOU.
AWWW!
JUST TO HECKLE? GEEZ, YOU TWO ARE MEAN!
SO, UH, HOW LONG'S PRACTICE GONNA BE?

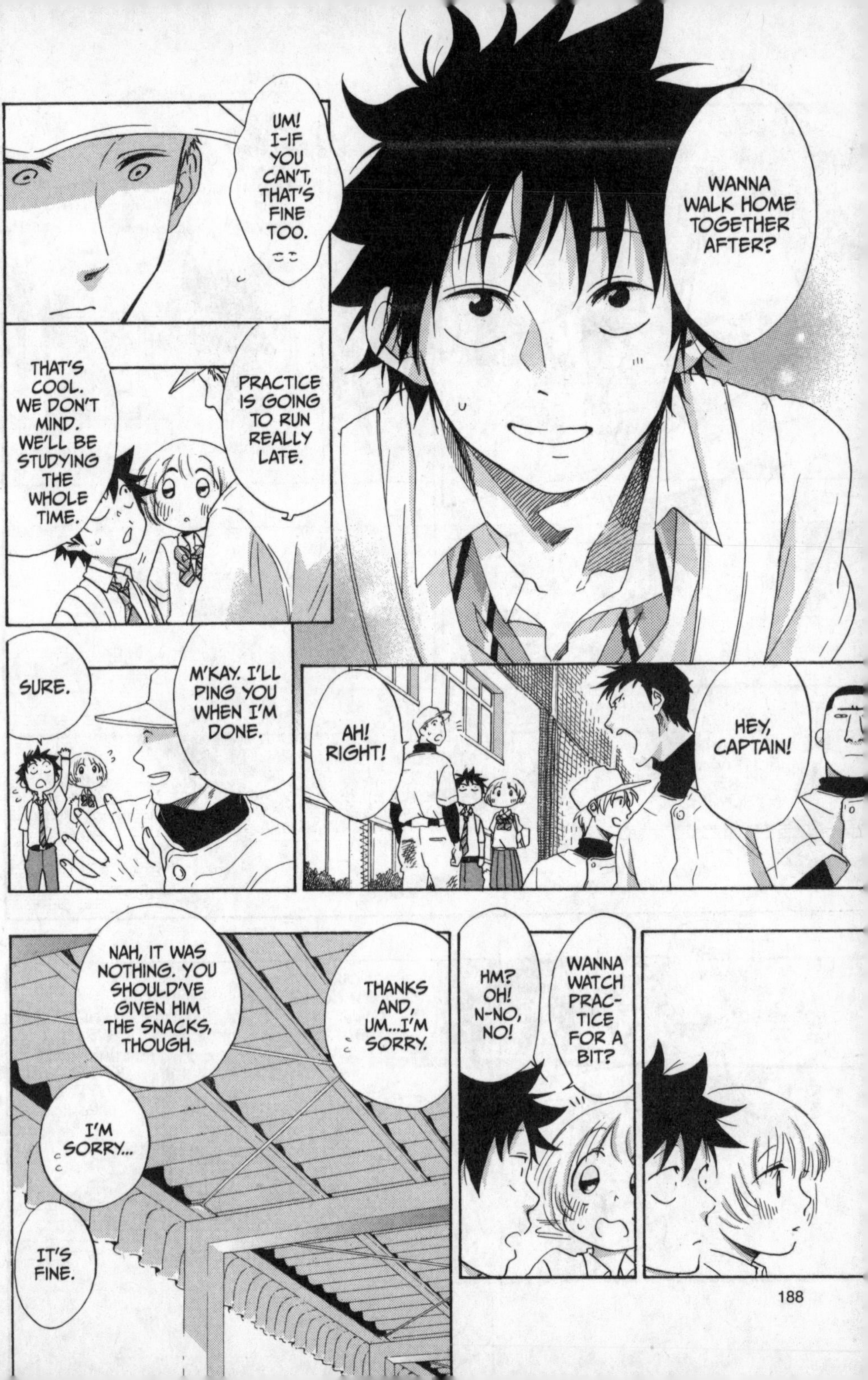
WANNA WALK HOME TOGETHER AFTER?
UM! I-IF YOU CAN'T, THAT'S FINE TOO.
PRACTICE IS GOING TO RUN REALLY LATE.
THAT'S COOL. WE DON'T MIND. WE'LL BE STUDYING THE WHOLE TIME.
HEY, CAPTAIN!
AH! RIGHT!
M'KAY. I'LL PING YOU WHEN I'M DONE.
SURE.
WANNA WATCH PRAC-TICE FOR A BIT?
HM? OH! N-NO, NO!
THANKS AND, UM...I'M SORRY.
NAH, IT WAS NOTHING. YOU SHOULD'VE GIVEN HIM THE SNACKS, THOUGH.
I'M SORRY...
IT'S FINE.

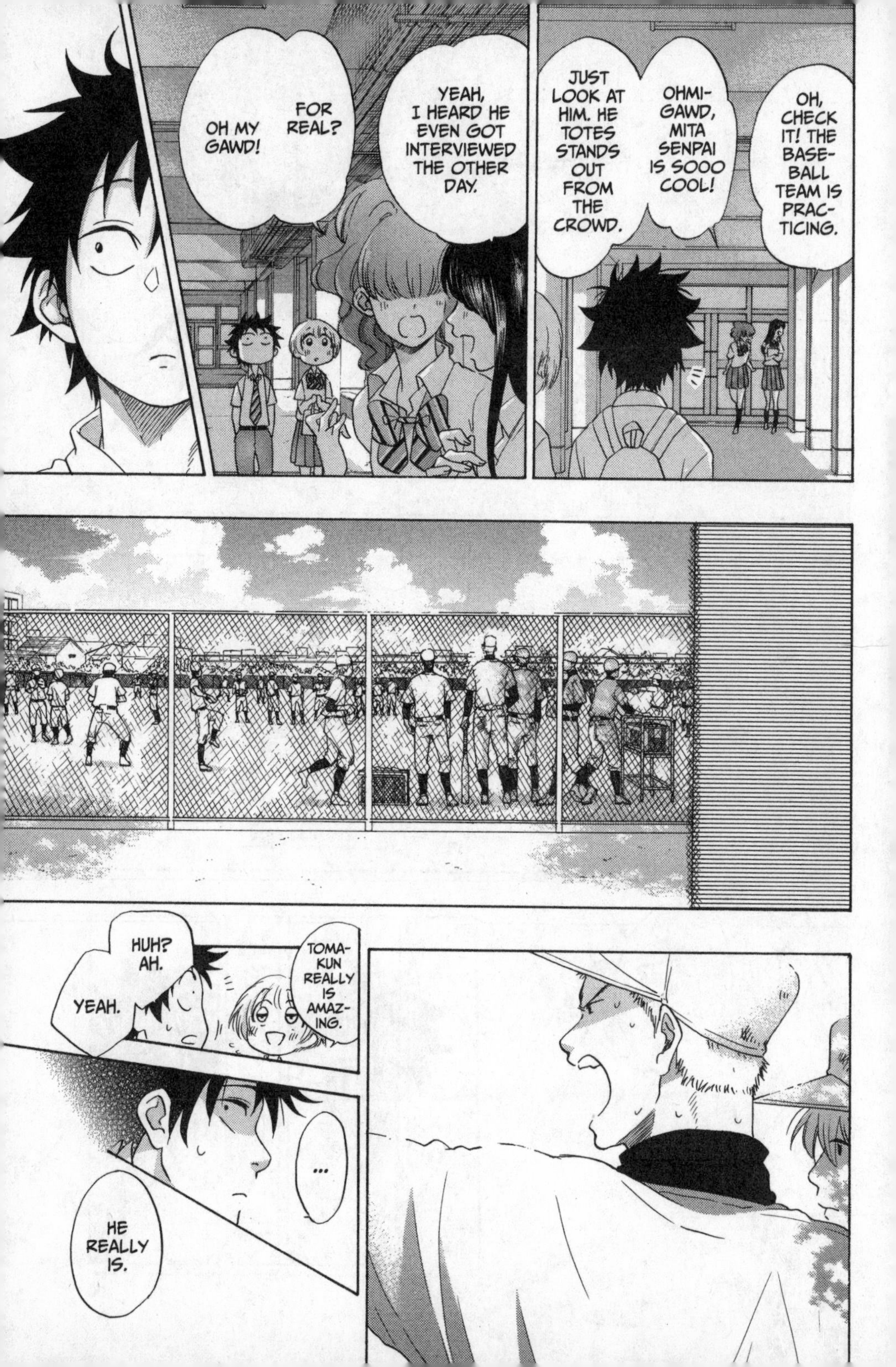
OH, CHECK IT! THE BASE-BALL TEAM IS PRAC-TICING.
OHMI-GAWD, MITA SENPAI IS SOOO COOL!
JUST LOOK AT HIM. HE TOTES STANDS OUT FROM THE CROWD.
YEAH, I HEARD HE EVEN GOT INTERVIEWED THE OTHER DAY.
FOR REAL?
OH MY GAWD!
TOMA-KUN REALLY IS AMAZ-ING.
HUH? AH.
YEAH.
...
HE REALLY IS.

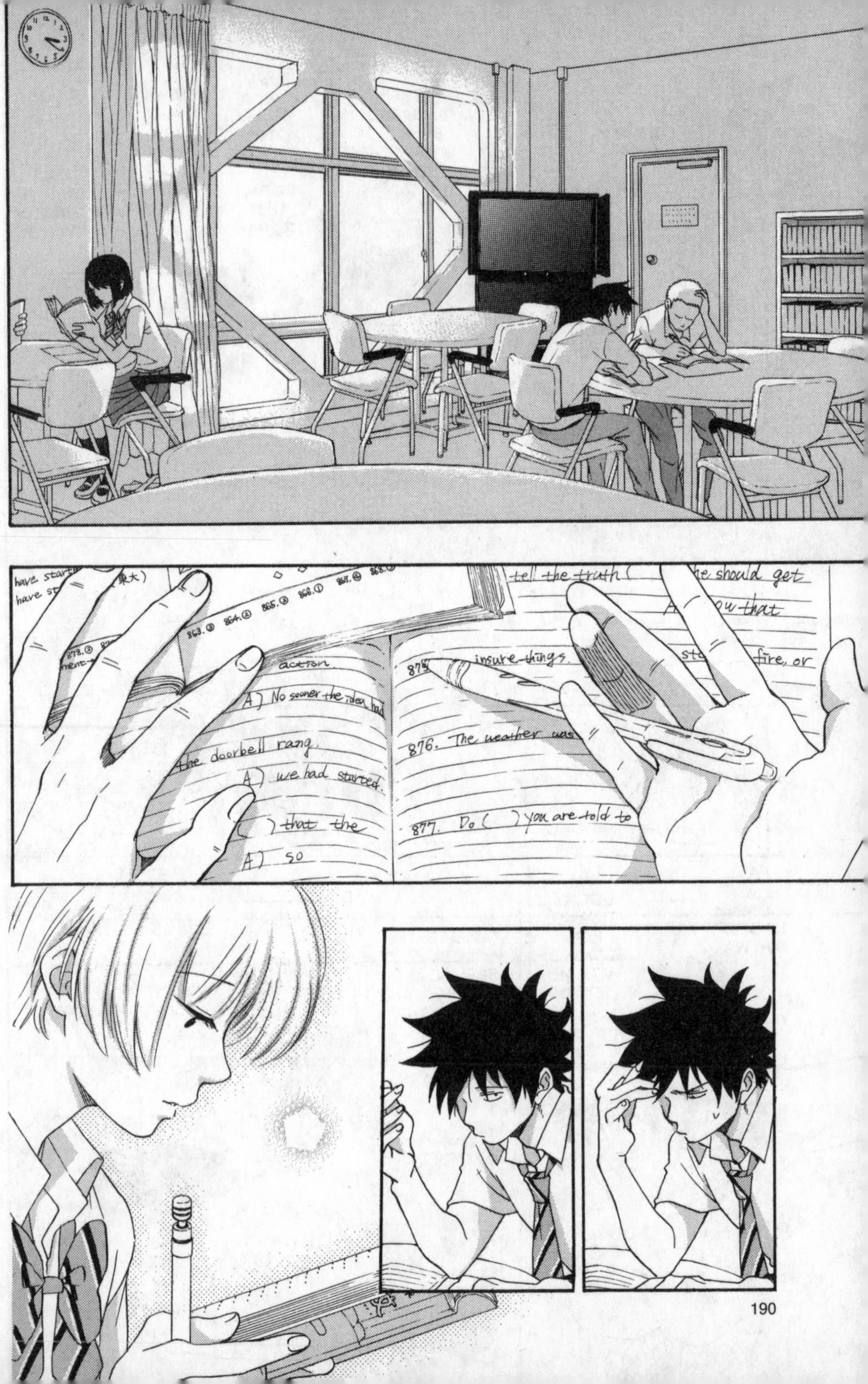
tell the truth
he should get
insure things.
fire, or
action
A) No sooner the idea had
the doorbell rang.
A) we had started.
) that the
A) so
876. The weather was
877. Do ( ) you are told to

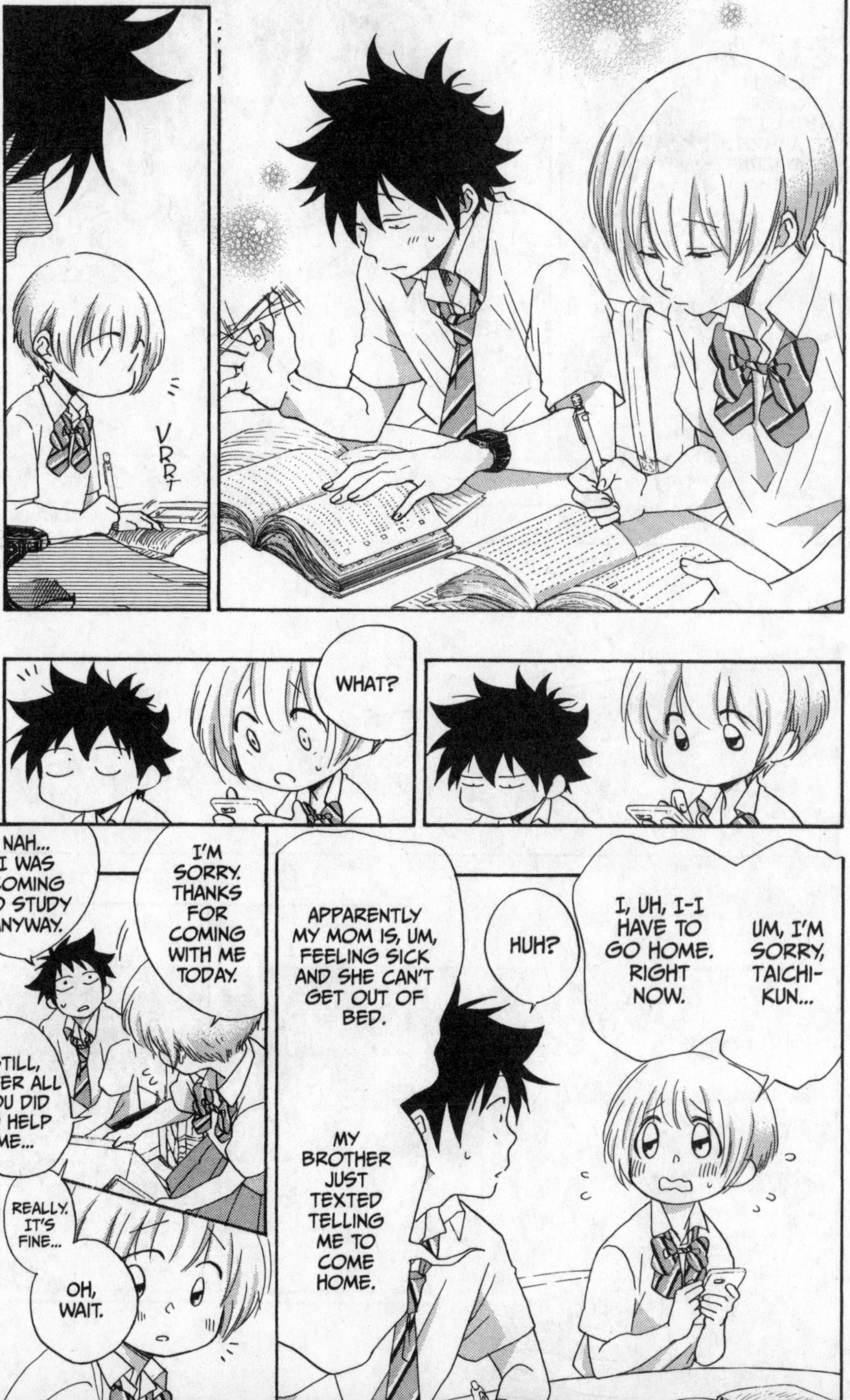
VRRT
WHAT?
UM, I'M SORRY, TAICHI-KUN...
I, UH, I-I HAVE TO GO HOME. RIGHT NOW.
HUH?
APPARENTLY MY MOM IS, UM, FEELING SICK AND SHE CAN'T GET OUT OF BED.
MY BROTHER JUST TEXTED TELLING ME TO COME HOME.
I'M SORRY. THANKS FOR COMING WITH ME TODAY.
NAH... I WAS COMING TO STUDY ANYWAY.
STILL, AFTER ALL YOU DID TO HELP ME...
REALLY. IT'S FINE...
OH, WAIT.

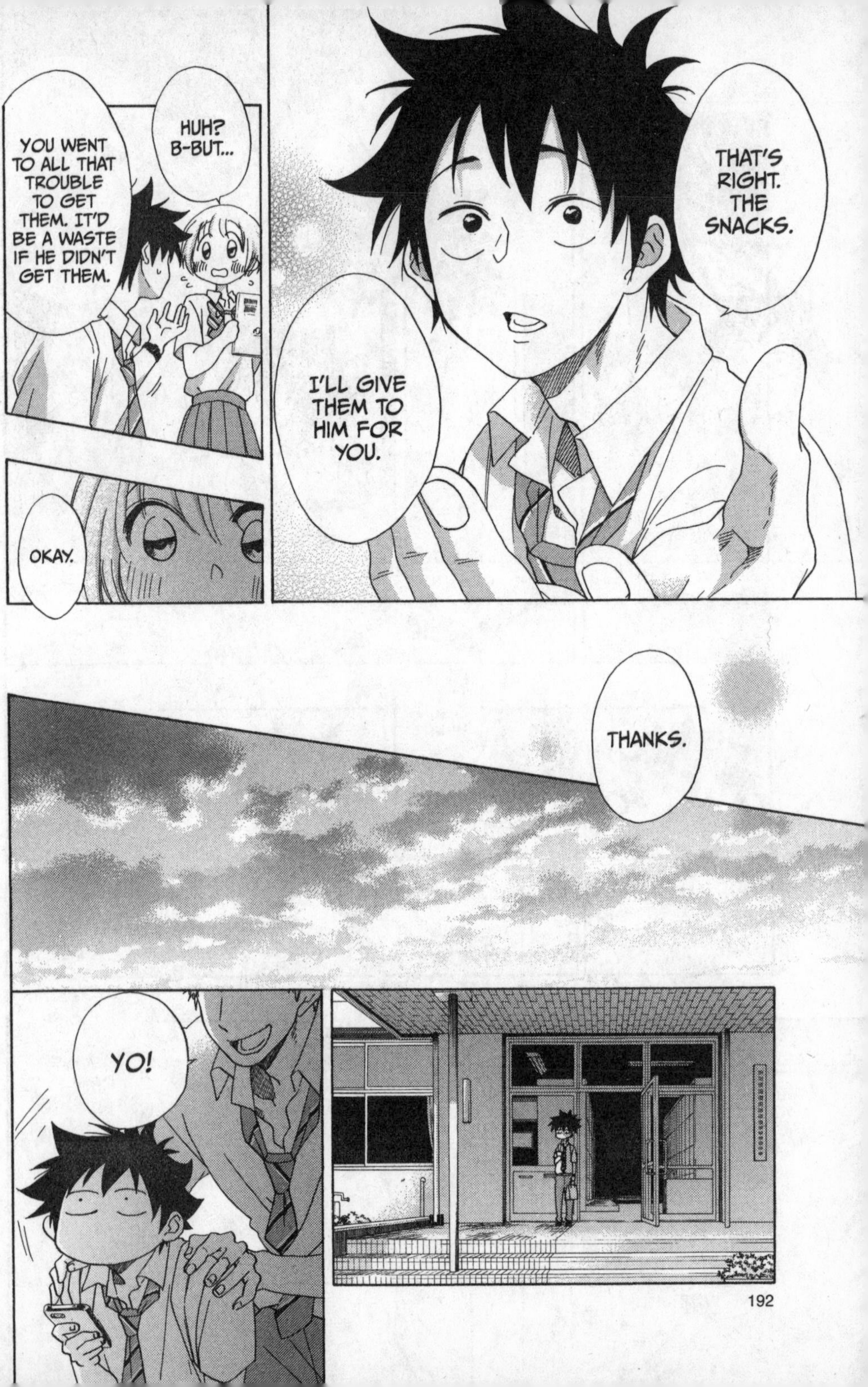
THAT'S RIGHT. THE SNACKS.
I'LL GIVE THEM TO HIM FOR YOU.
HUH? B-BUT...
YOU WENT TO ALL THAT TROUBLE TO GET THEM. IT'D BE A WASTE IF HE DIDN'T GET THEM.
OKAY.
THANKS.
YO!

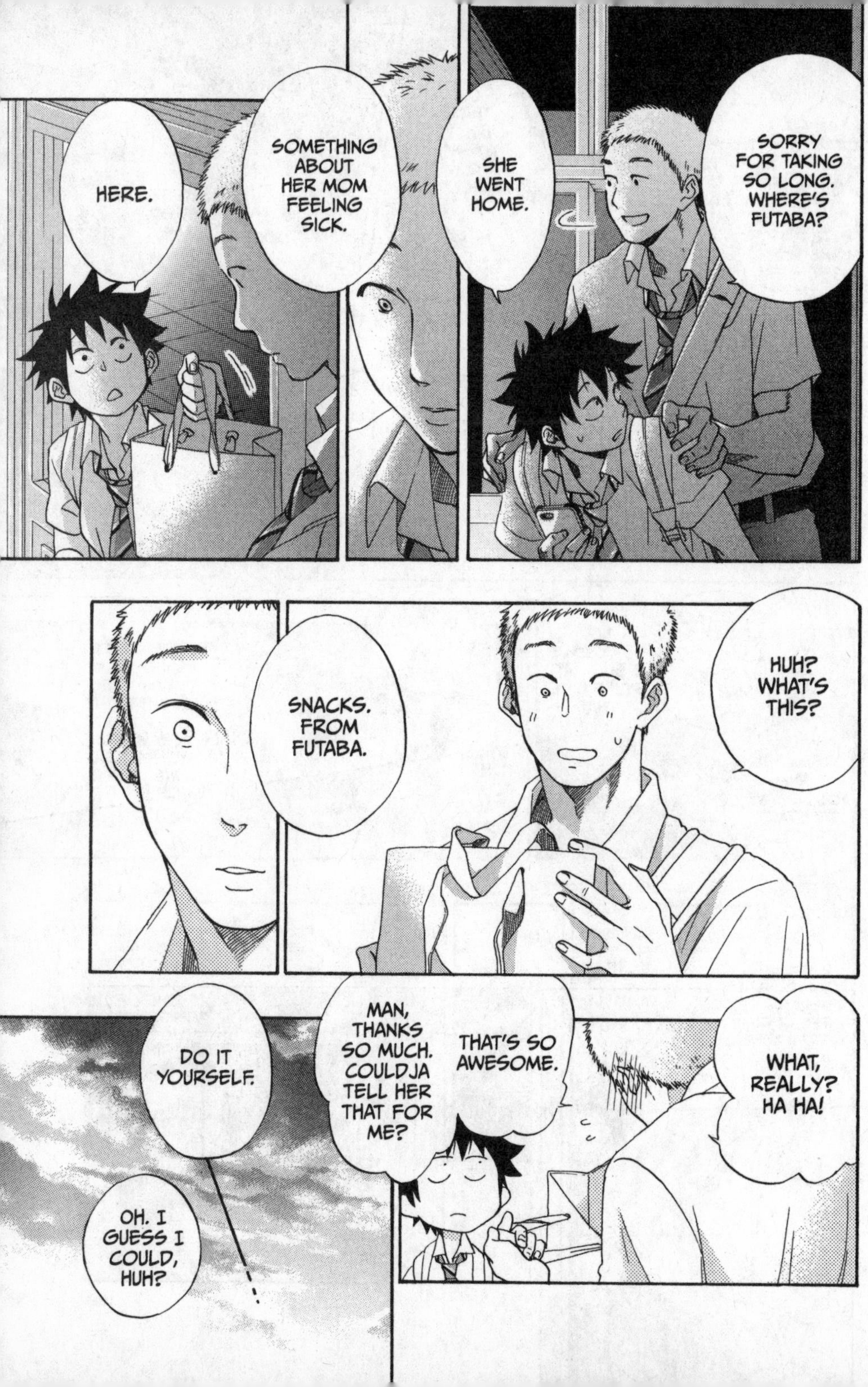
SORRY FOR TAKING SO LONG. WHERE'S FUTABA?
SHE WENT HOME.
SOMETHING ABOUT HER MOM FEELING SICK.
HERE.
HUH? WHAT'S THIS?
SNACKS. FROM FUTABA.
WHAT, REALLY? HA HA!
THAT'S SO AWESOME.
MAN, THANKS SO MUCH. COULDJA TELL HER THAT FOR ME?
DO IT YOURSELF.
OH. I GUESS I COULD, HUH?

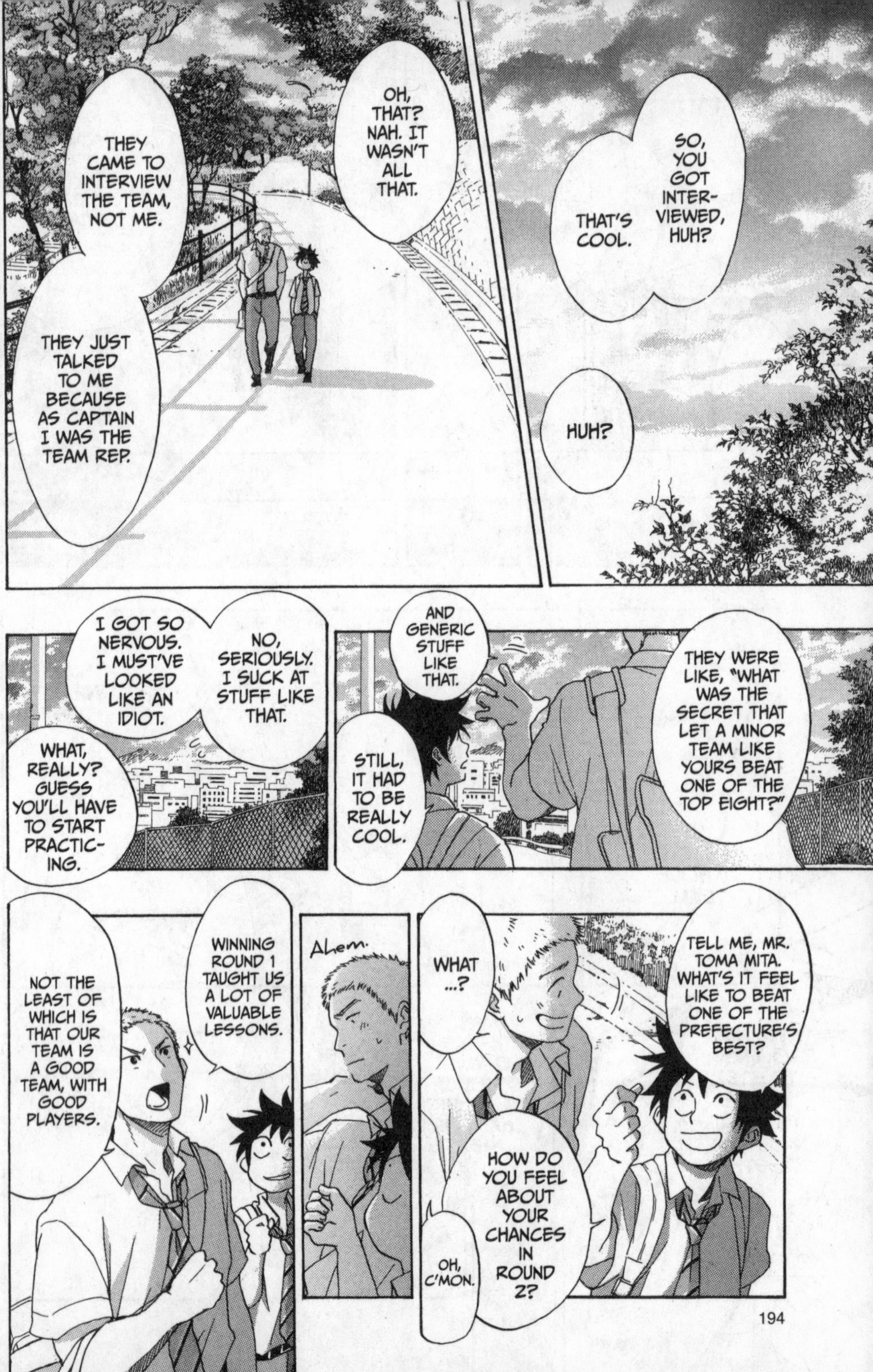
SO, YOU GOT INTER-VIEWED, HUH?
THAT'S COOL.
HUH?
OH, THAT? NAH. IT WASN'T ALL THAT.
THEY CAME TO INTERVIEW THE TEAM, NOT ME.
THEY JUST TALKED TO ME BECAUSE AS CAPTAIN I WAS THE TEAM REP.
THEY WERE LIKE, "WHAT WAS THE SECRET THAT LET A MINOR TEAM LIKE YOURS BEAT ONE OF THE TOP EIGHT?"
AND GENERIC STUFF LIKE THAT.
STILL, IT HAD TO BE REALLY COOL.
NO, SERIOUSLY. I SUCK AT STUFF LIKE THAT.
I GOT SO NERVOUS. I MUST'VE LOOKED LIKE AN IDIOT.
WHAT, REALLY? GUESS YOU'LL HAVE TO START PRACTIC-ING.
TELL ME, MR. TOMA MITA. WHAT'S IT FEEL LIKE TO BEAT ONE OF THE PREFECTURE'S BEST?
WHAT ...?
HOW DO YOU FEEL ABOUT YOUR CHANCES IN ROUND 2?
OH, C'MON.
Ahem.
WINNING ROUND 1 TAUGHT US A LOT OF VALUABLE LESSONS.
NOT THE LEAST OF WHICH IS THAT OUR TEAM IS A GOOD TEAM, WITH GOOD PLAYERS.

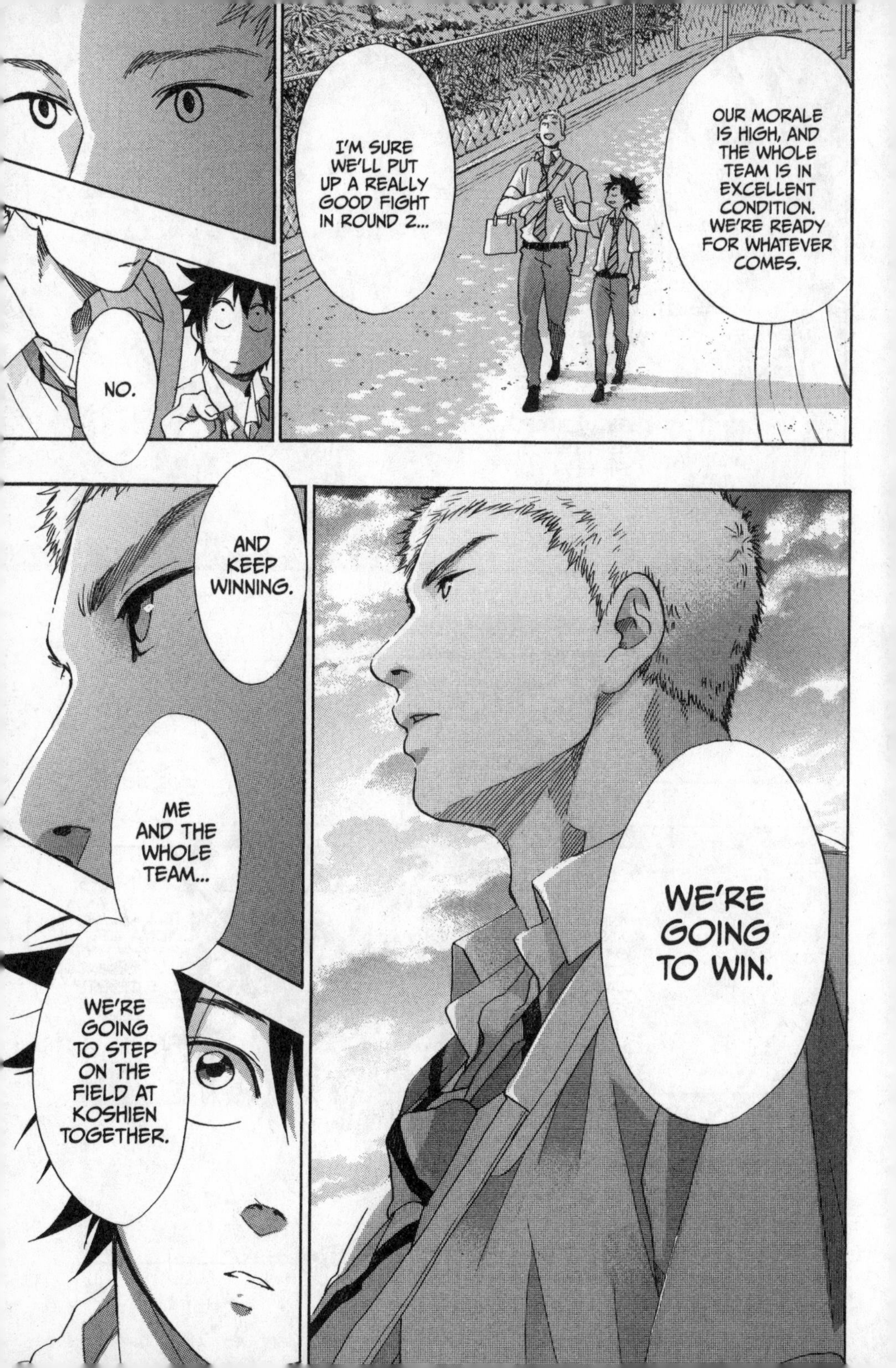
OUR MORALE IS HIGH, AND THE WHOLE TEAM IS IN EXCELLENT CONDITION. WE'RE READY FOR WHATEVER COMES.
I'M SURE WE'LL PUT UP A REALLY GOOD FIGHT IN ROUND 2...
NO.
WE'RE GOING TO WIN.
AND KEEP WINNING.
ME AND THE WHOLE TEAM...
WE'RE GOING TO STEP ON THE FIELD AT KOSHIEN TOGETHER.

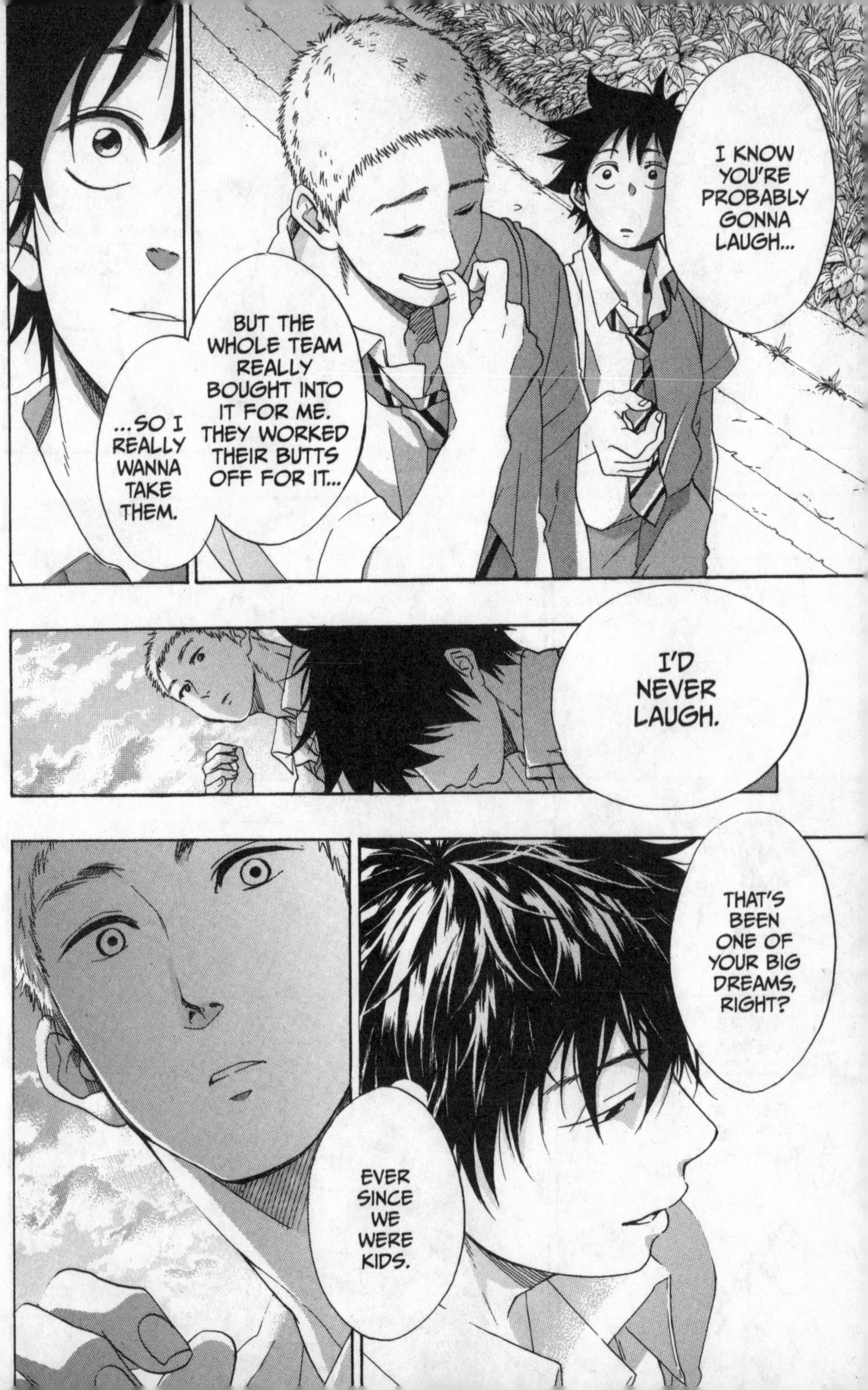
I KNOW YOU'RE PROBABLY GONNA LAUGH...
BUT THE WHOLE TEAM REALLY BOUGHT INTO IT FOR ME. THEY WORKED THEIR BUTTS OFF FOR IT...
...SO I REALLY WANNA TAKE THEM.
I'D NEVER LAUGH.
THAT'S BEEN ONE OF YOUR BIG DREAMS, RIGHT?
EVER SINCE WE WERE KIDS.

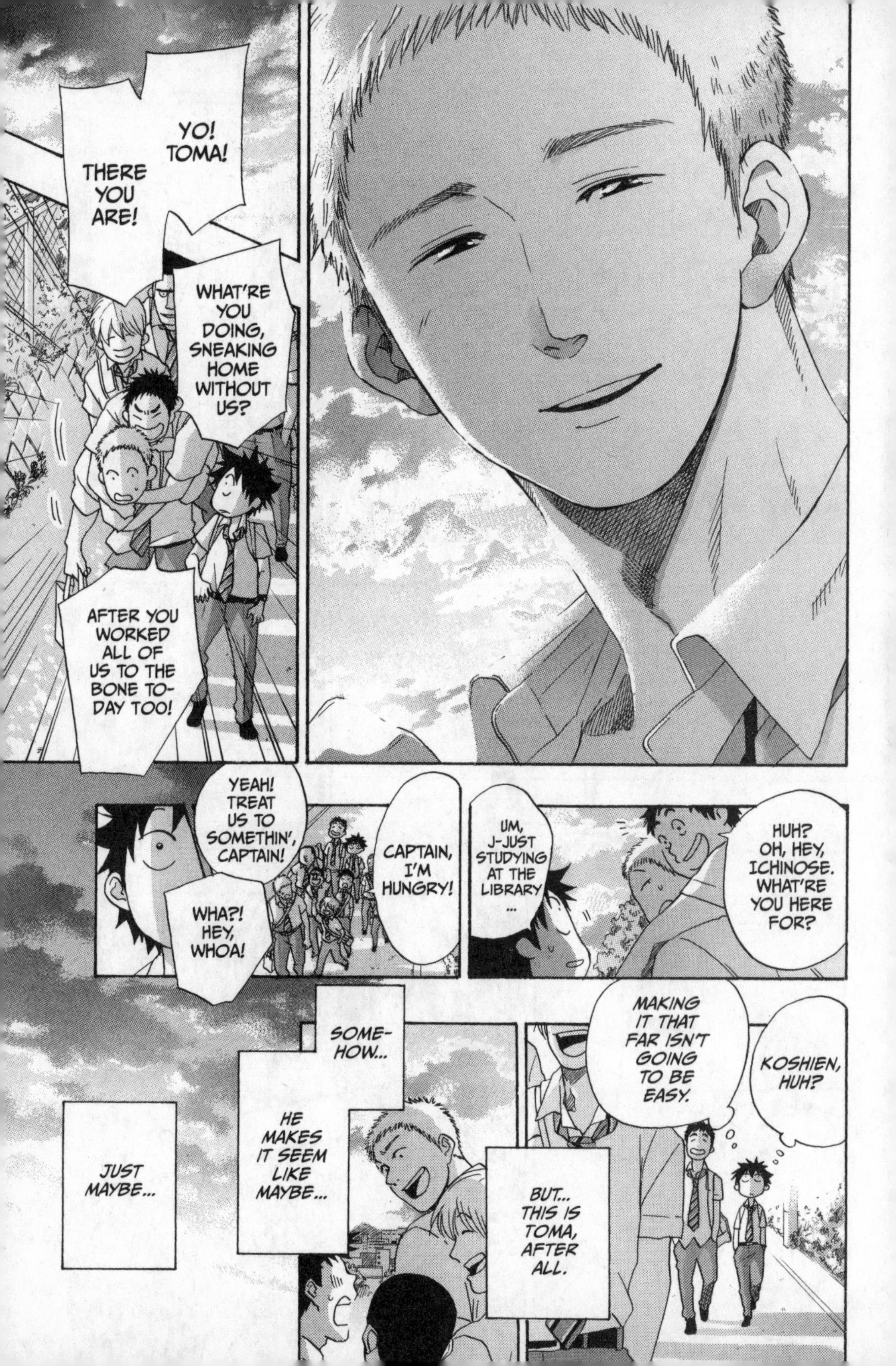

YO! TOMA!
THERE YOU ARE!
WHAT'RE YOU DOING, SNEAKING HOME WITHOUT US?
AFTER YOU WORKED ALL OF US TO THE BONE TO-DAY TOO!
HUH? OH, HEY, ICHINOSE. WHAT'RE YOU HERE FOR?
UM, J-JUST STUDYING AT THE LIBRARY ...
CAPTAIN, I'M HUNGRY!
YEAH! TREAT US TO SOMETHIN', CAPTAIN!
WHA?! HEY, WHOA!
KOSHIEN, HUH?
MAKING IT THAT FAR ISN'T GOING TO BE EASY.
BUT... THIS IS TOMA, AFTER ALL.
SOME-HOW...
HE MAKES IT SEEM LIKE MAYBE...
JUST MAYBE...

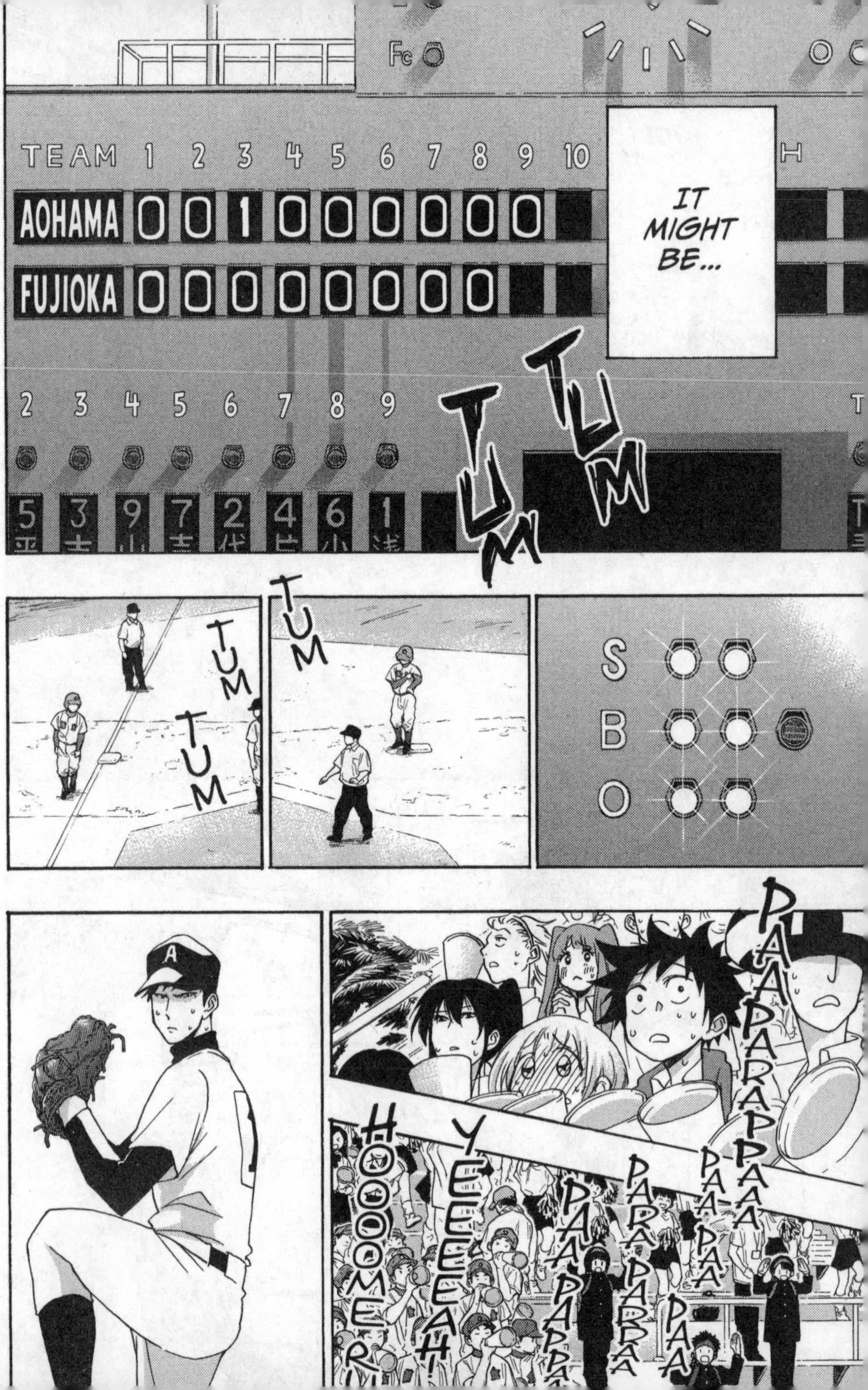
TEAM 1 2 3 4 5 6 7 8 9 10 H
AOHAMA 0 0 1 0 0 0 0 0 0
FUJIOKA 0 0 0 0 0 0 0 0
IT MIGHT BE...
TUM TUM
S B O
TUM
TUM TUM
TUM
PAAPARAPPAPAAA
PAA-PAPAA
PAA
PARAPARPAA
PAAPAPA
YEEEEEEAH!
HOOOOOOMER

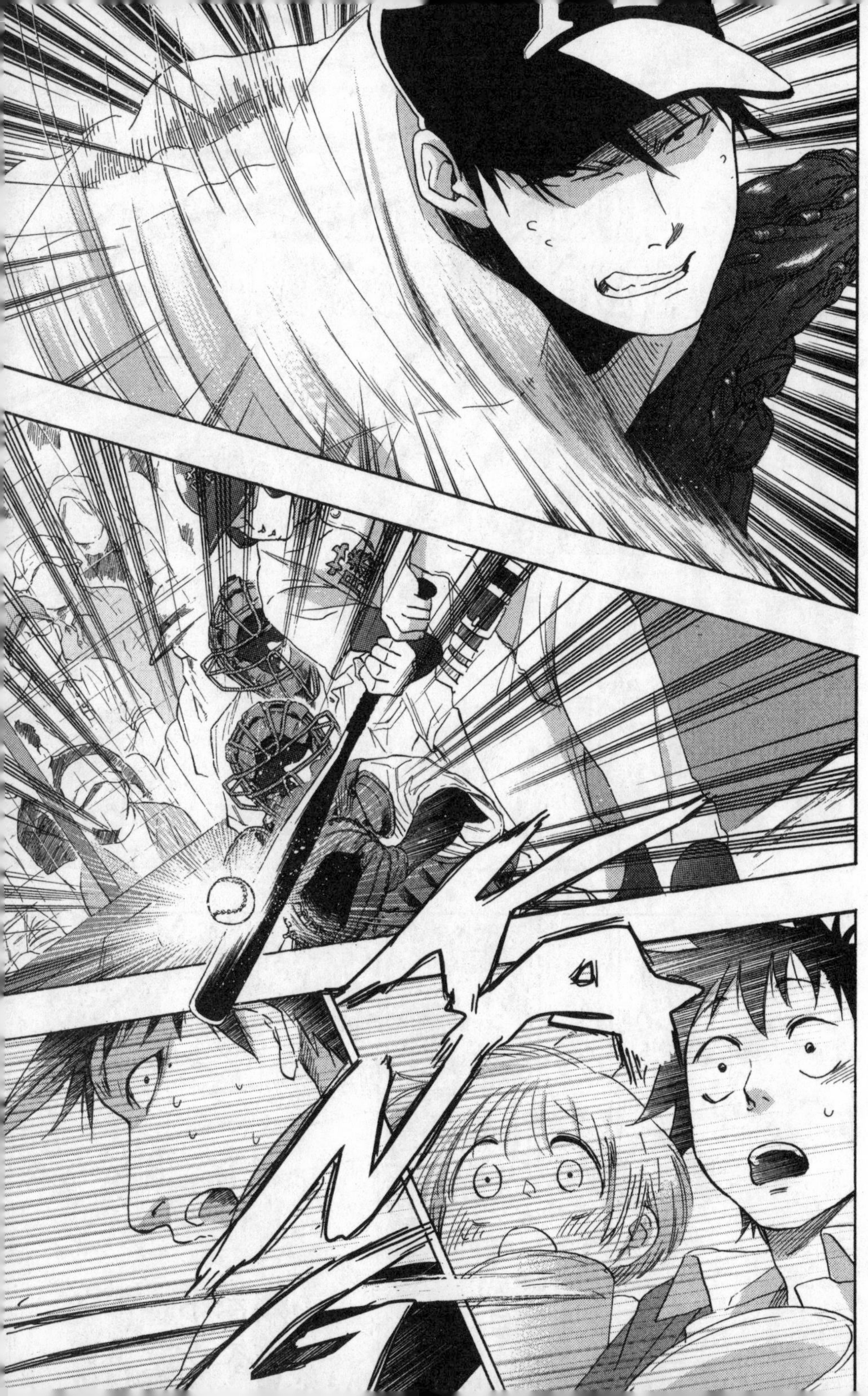

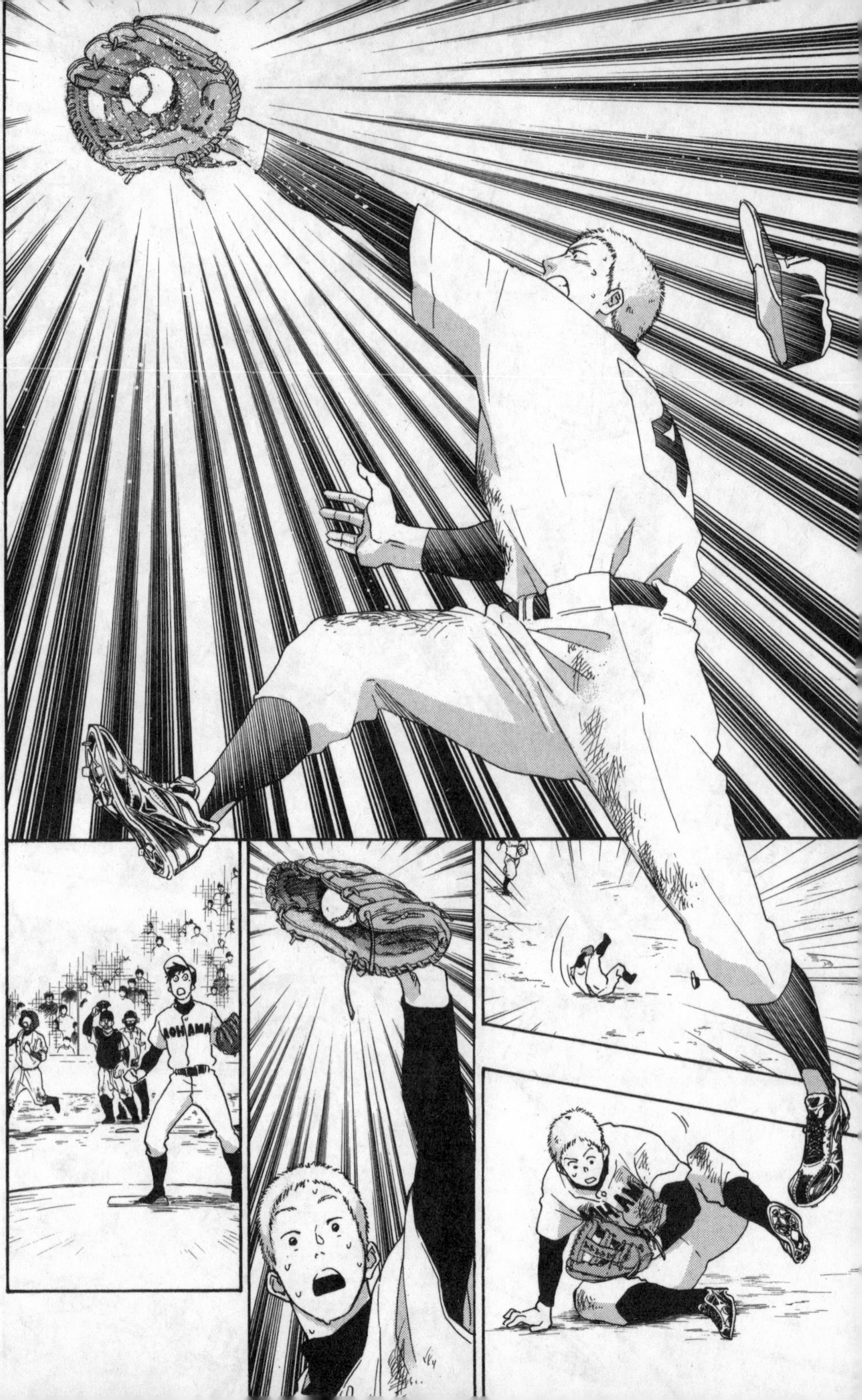
AOHAMA

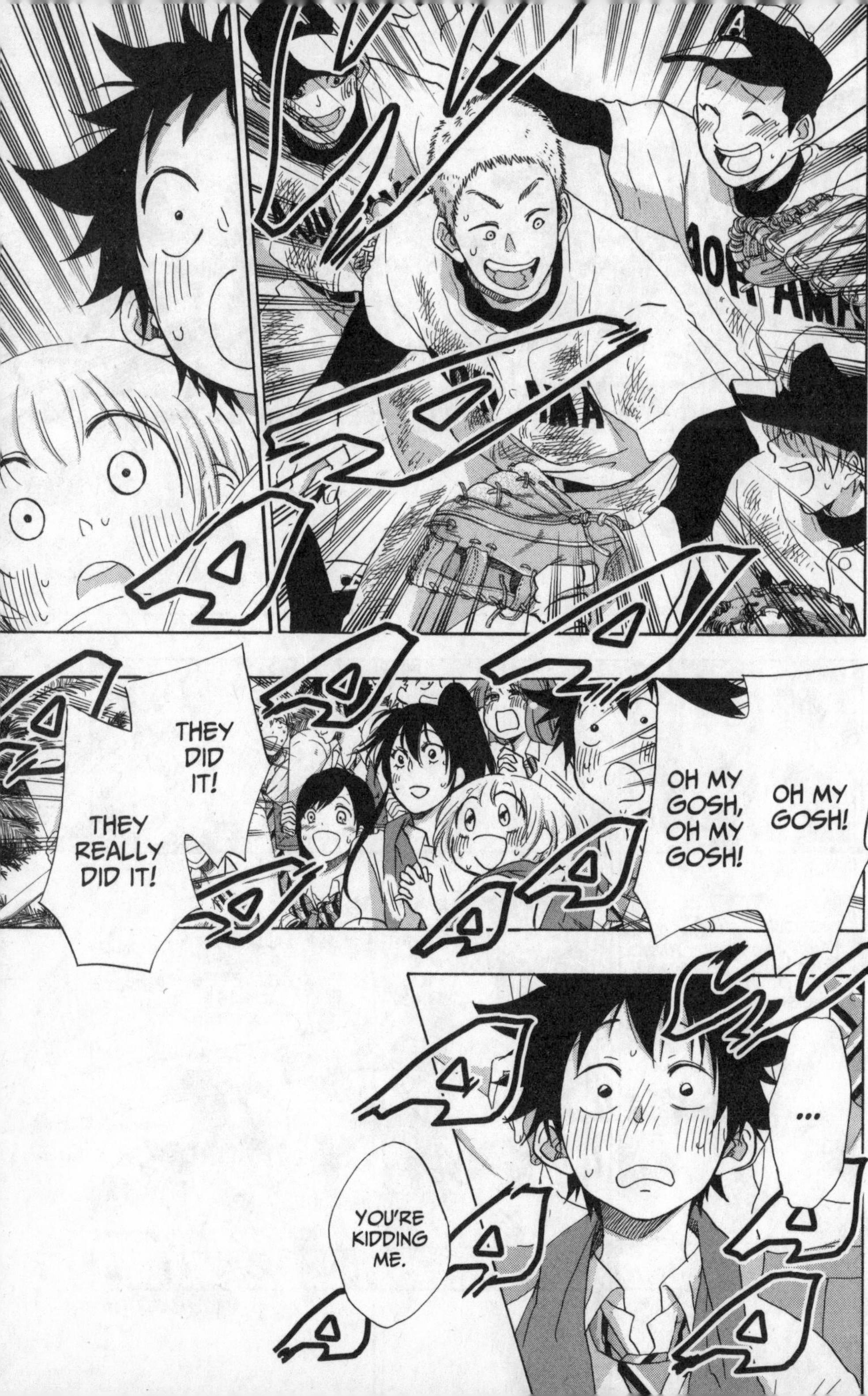

OH MY GOSH!
OH MY GOSH, OH MY GOSH!
THEY DID IT!
THEY REALLY DID IT!
...
YOU'RE KIDDING ME.

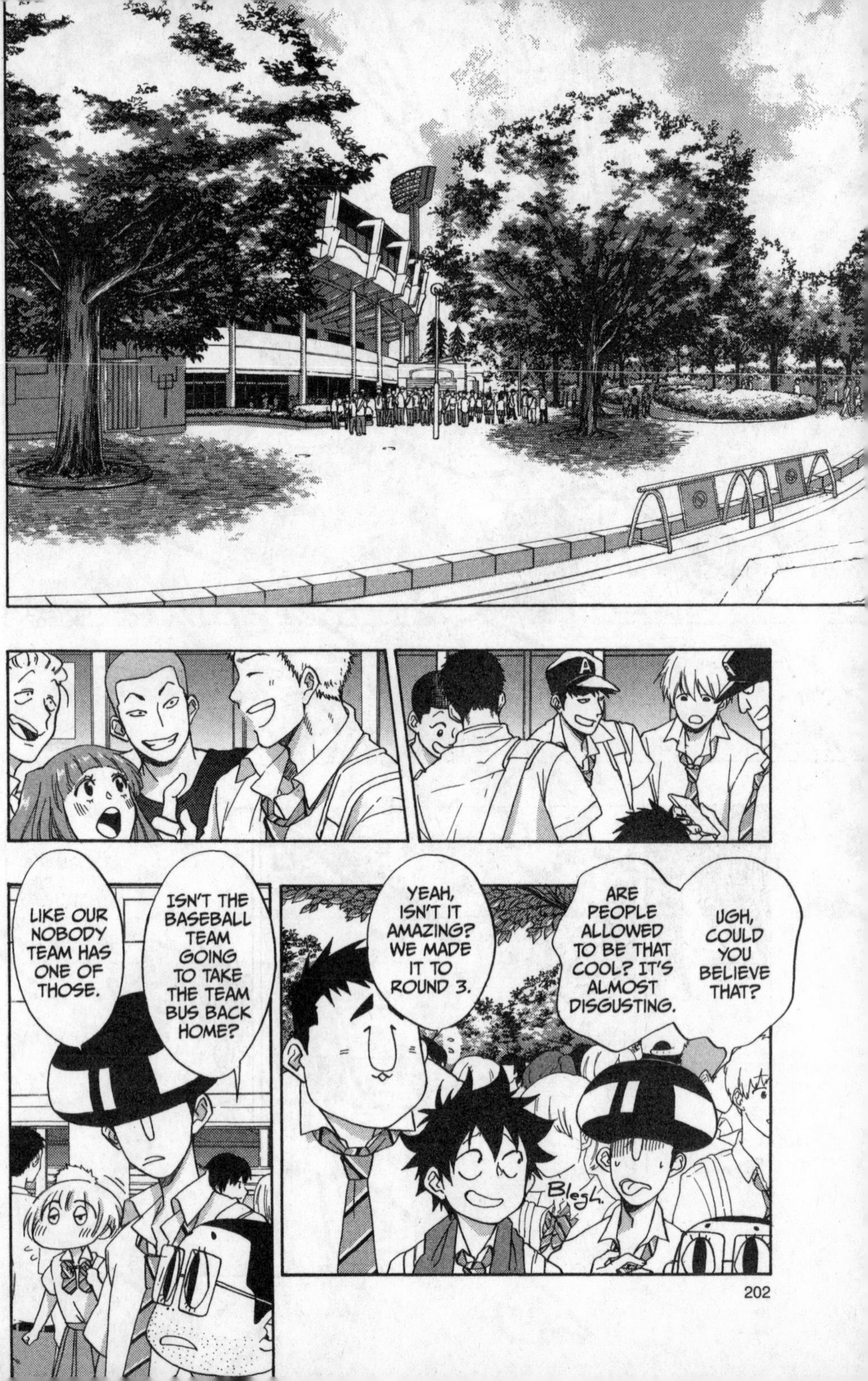
UGH, COULD YOU BELIEVE THAT?
ARE PEOPLE ALLOWED TO BE THAT COOL? IT'S ALMOST DISGUSTING.
YEAH, ISN'T IT AMAZING? WE MADE IT TO ROUND 3.
Blegh.
ISN'T THE BASEBALL TEAM GOING TO TAKE THE TEAM BUS BACK HOME?
LIKE OUR NOBODY TEAM HAS ONE OF THOSE.

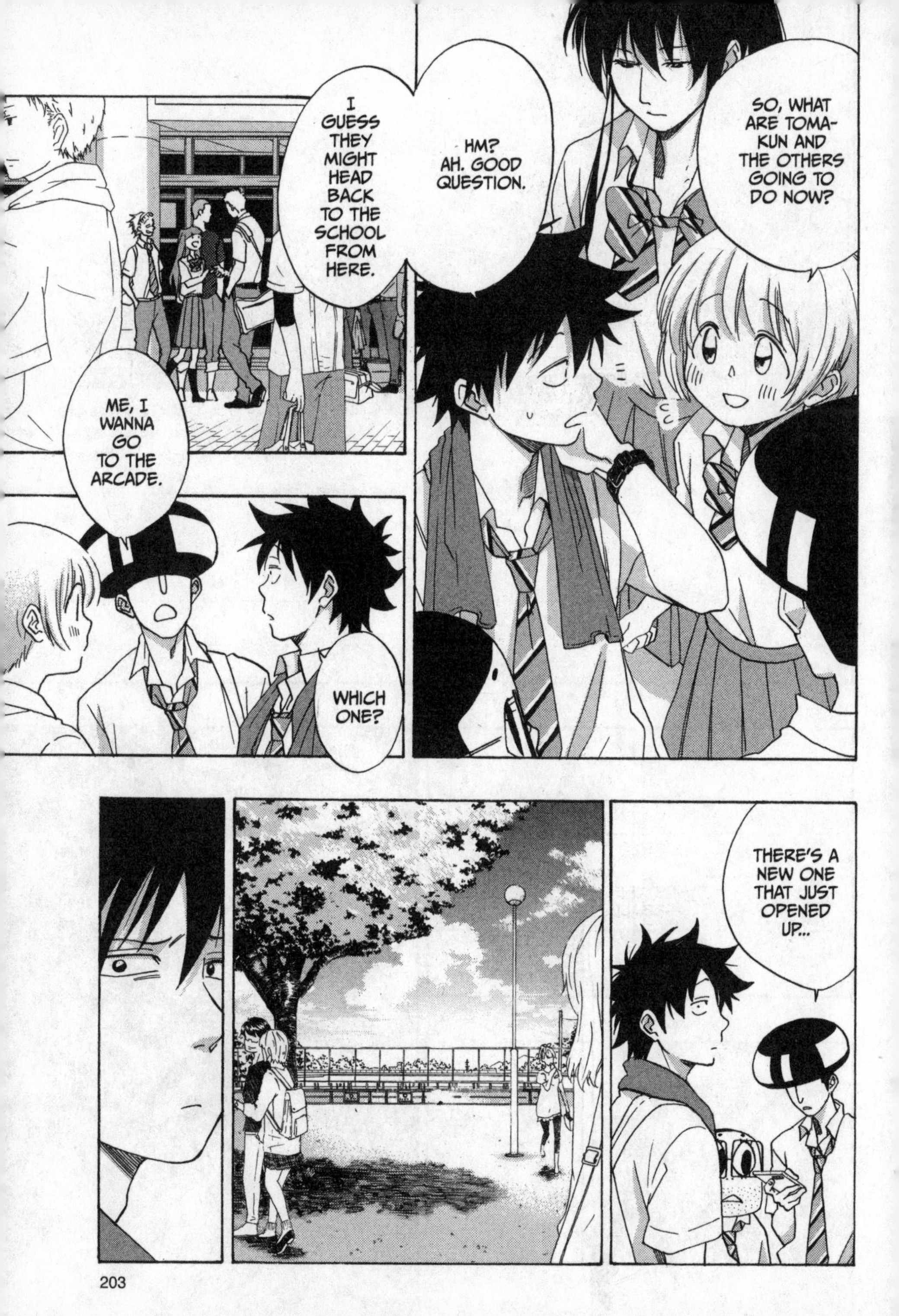
SO, WHAT ARE TOMA-KUN AND THE OTHERS GOING TO DO NOW?
HM? AH. GOOD QUESTION.
I GUESS THEY MIGHT HEAD BACK TO THE SCHOOL FROM HERE.
ME, I WANNA GO TO THE ARCADE.
WHICH ONE?
THERE'S A NEW ONE THAT JUST OPENED UP...

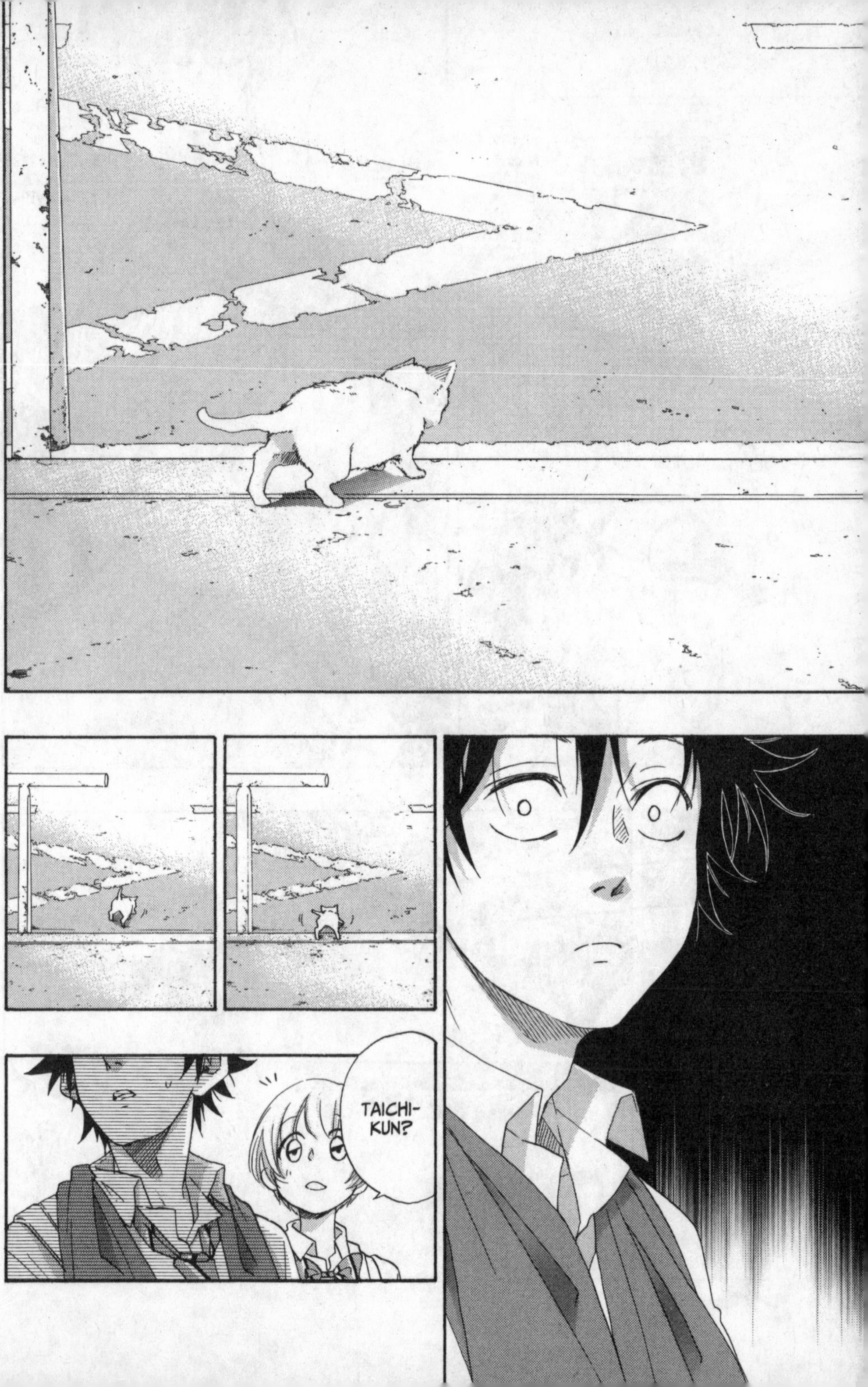
TAICHI-
KUN?

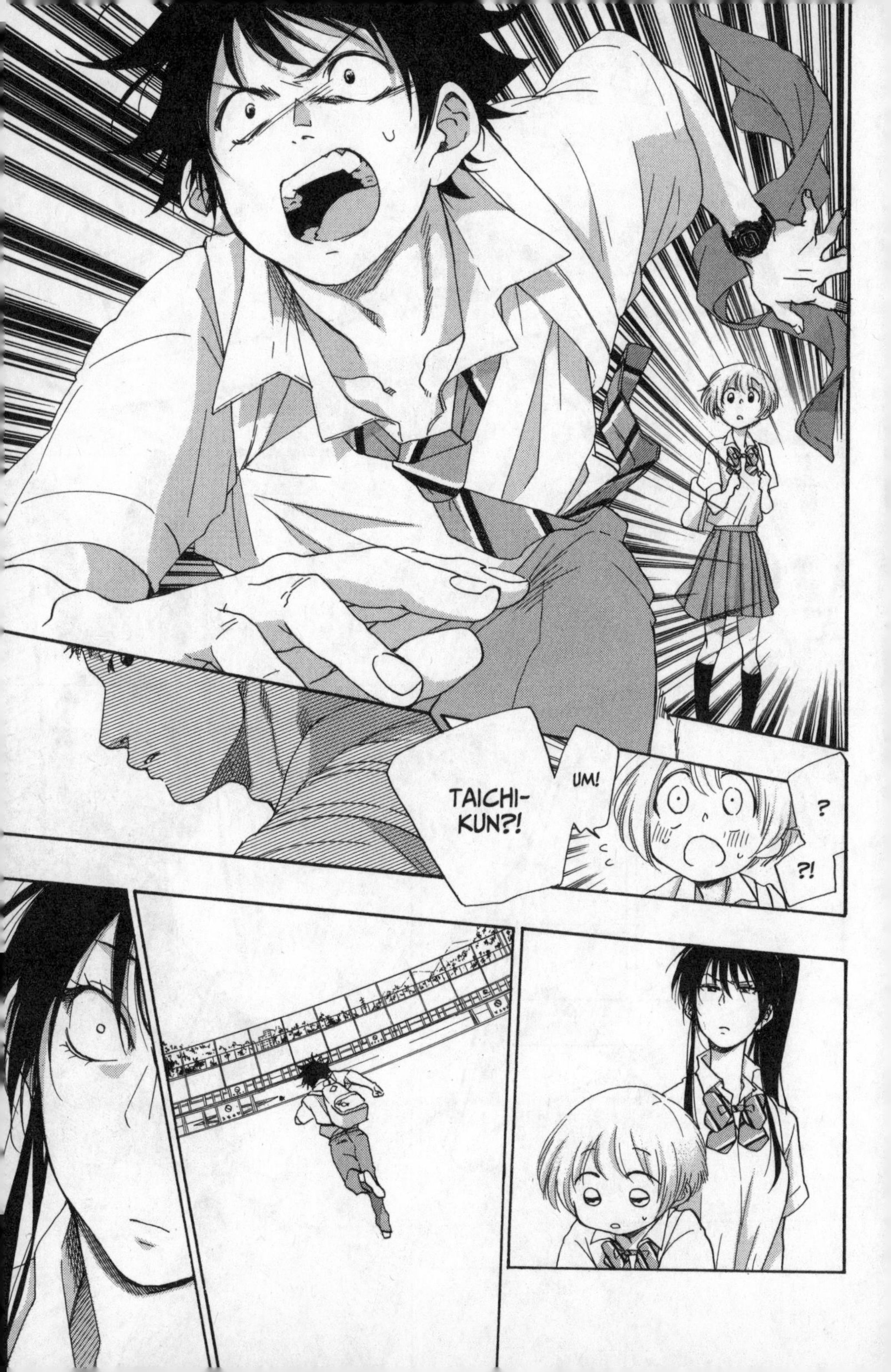
?
?!
UM!
TAICHI-KUN?!

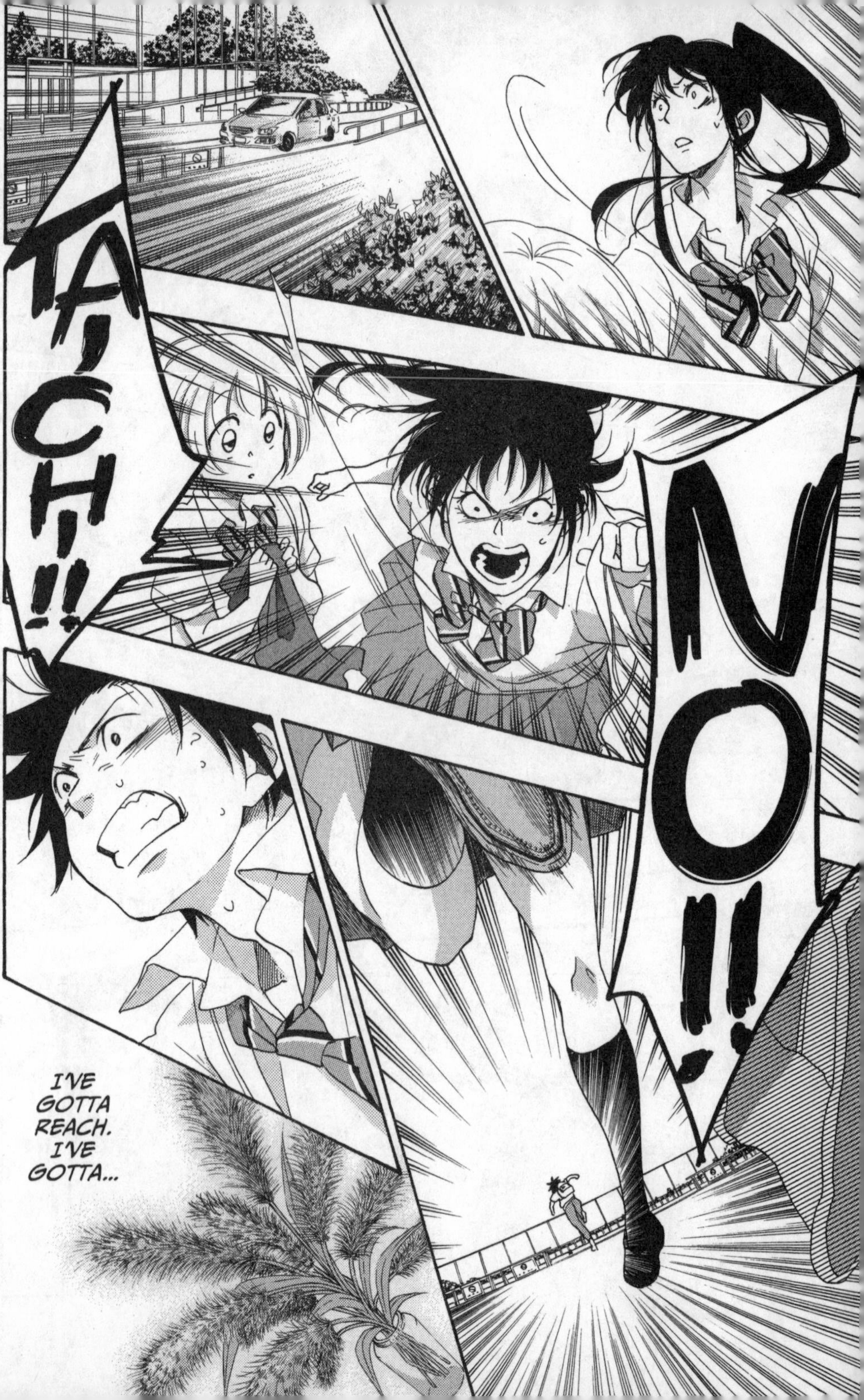
NO!!
TACHI!!
I'VE GOTTA REACH. I'VE GOTTA...

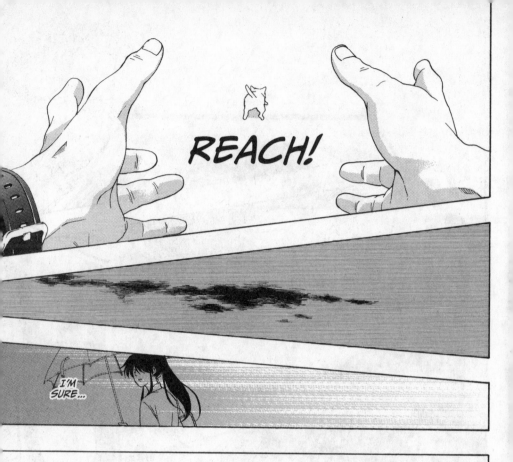

REACH!

I'M SURE...

...YOU'D DO JUST FINE.

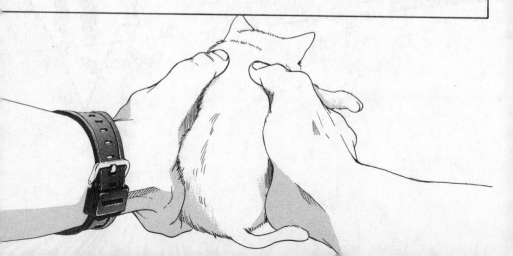

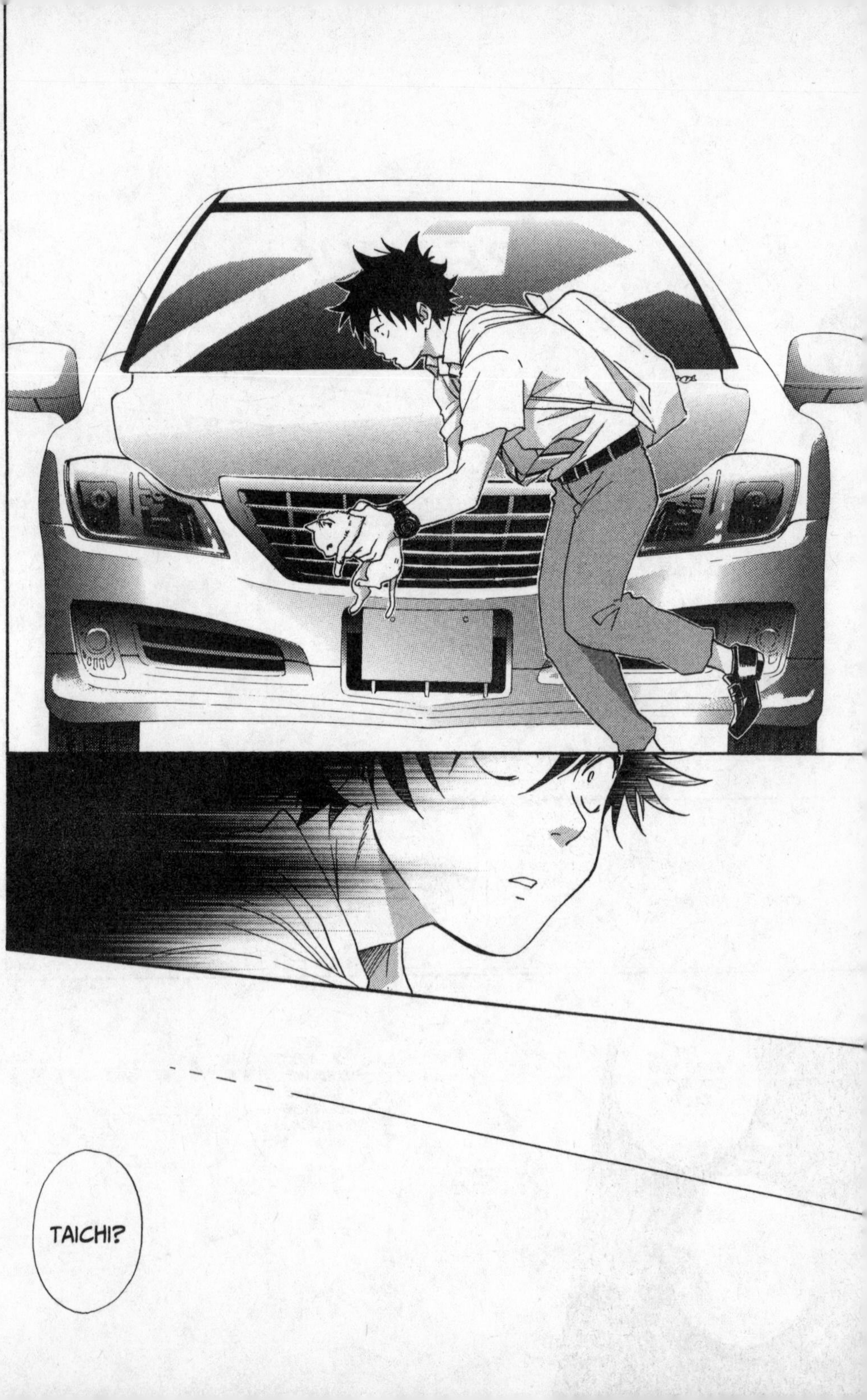
TAICHI?

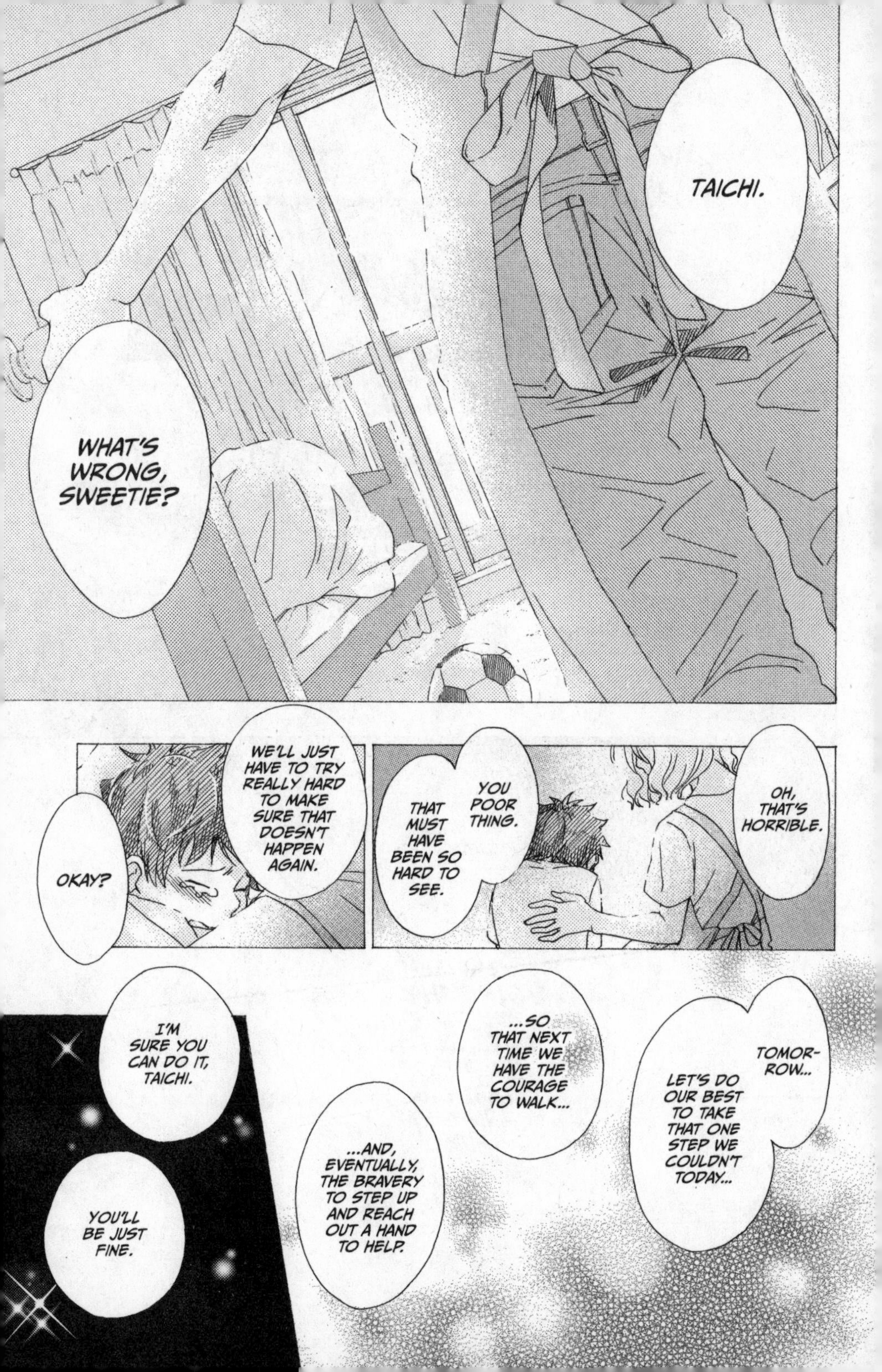
TAICHI.
WHAT'S WRONG, SWEETIE?
OH, THAT'S HORRIBLE.
YOU POOR THING.
THAT MUST HAVE BEEN SO HARD TO SEE.
WE'LL JUST HAVE TO TRY REALLY HARD TO MAKE SURE THAT DOESN'T HAPPEN AGAIN.
OKAY?
TOMOR-ROW...
LET'S DO OUR BEST TO TAKE THAT ONE STEP WE COULDN'T TODAY...
...SO THAT NEXT TIME WE HAVE THE COURAGE TO WALK...
...AND, EVENTUALLY, THE BRAVERY TO STEP UP AND REACH OUT A HAND TO HELP.
I'M SURE YOU CAN DO IT, TAICHI.
YOU'LL BE JUST FINE.

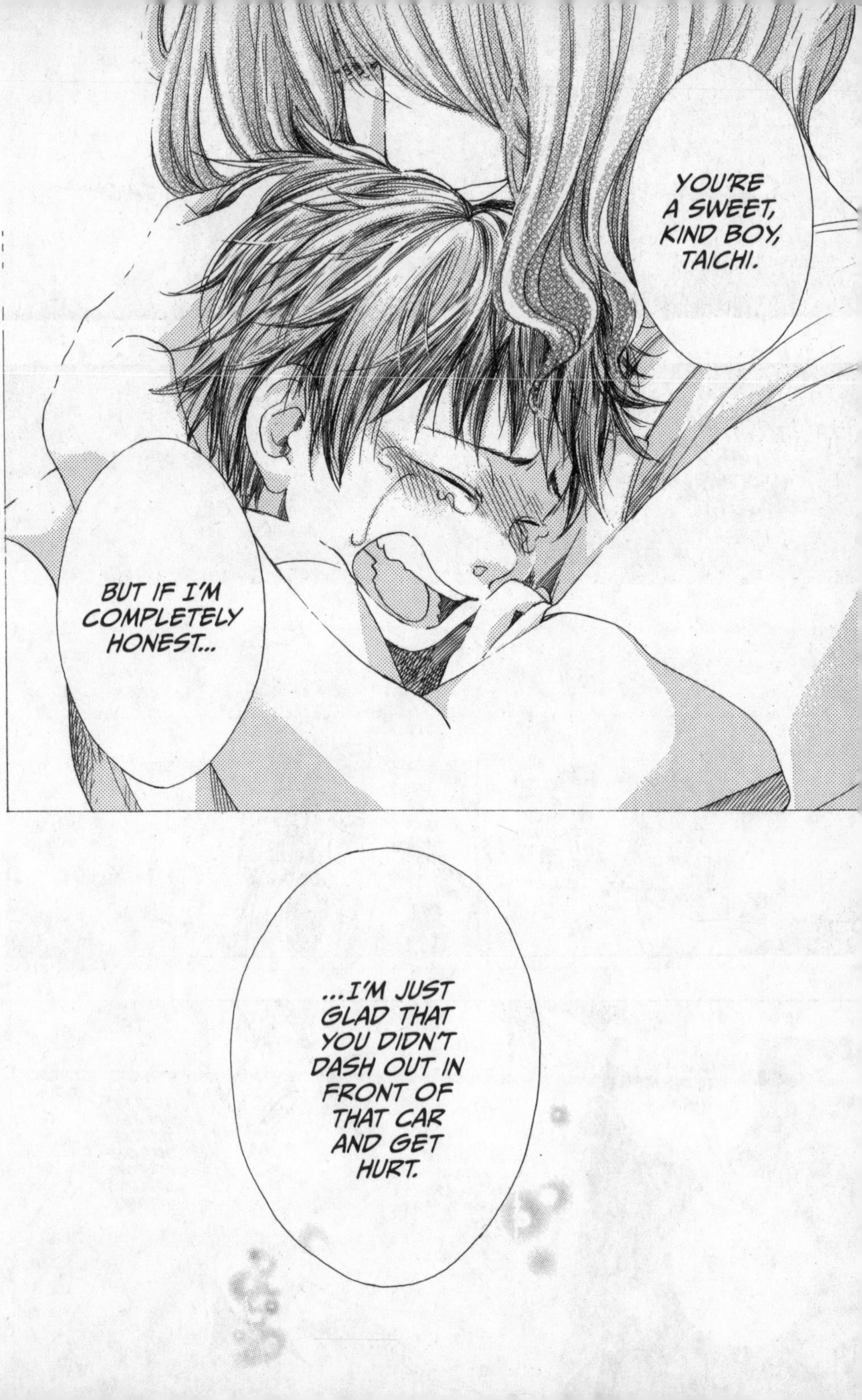
YOU'RE A SWEET, KIND BOY, TAICHI.
BUT IF I'M COMPLETELY HONEST...
...I'M JUST GLAD THAT YOU DIDN'T DASH OUT IN FRONT OF THAT CAR AND GET HURT.

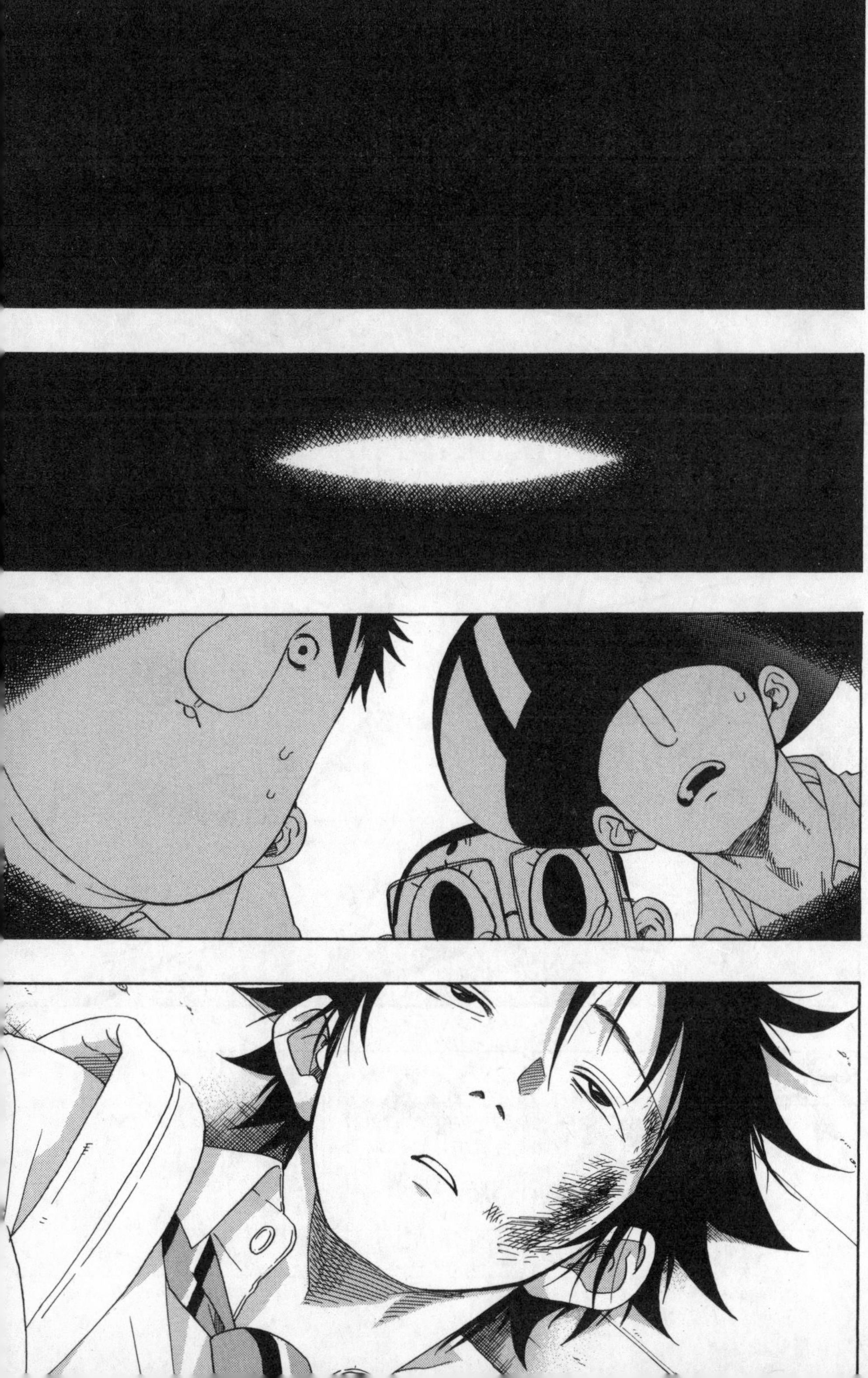

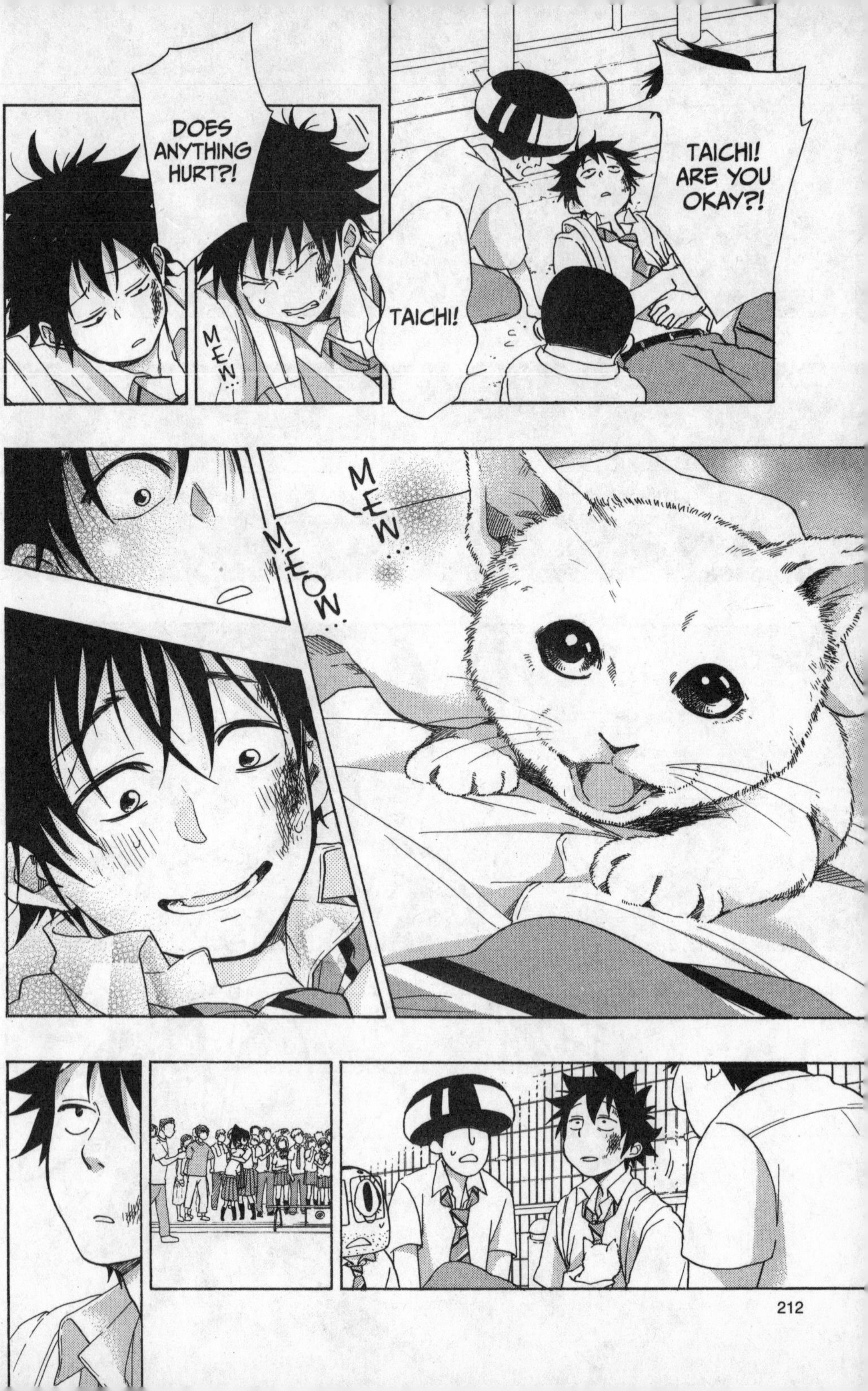
TAICHI! ARE YOU OKAY?!
TAICHI!
DOES ANYTHING HURT?!
MEW...
MEW...
MEOW...

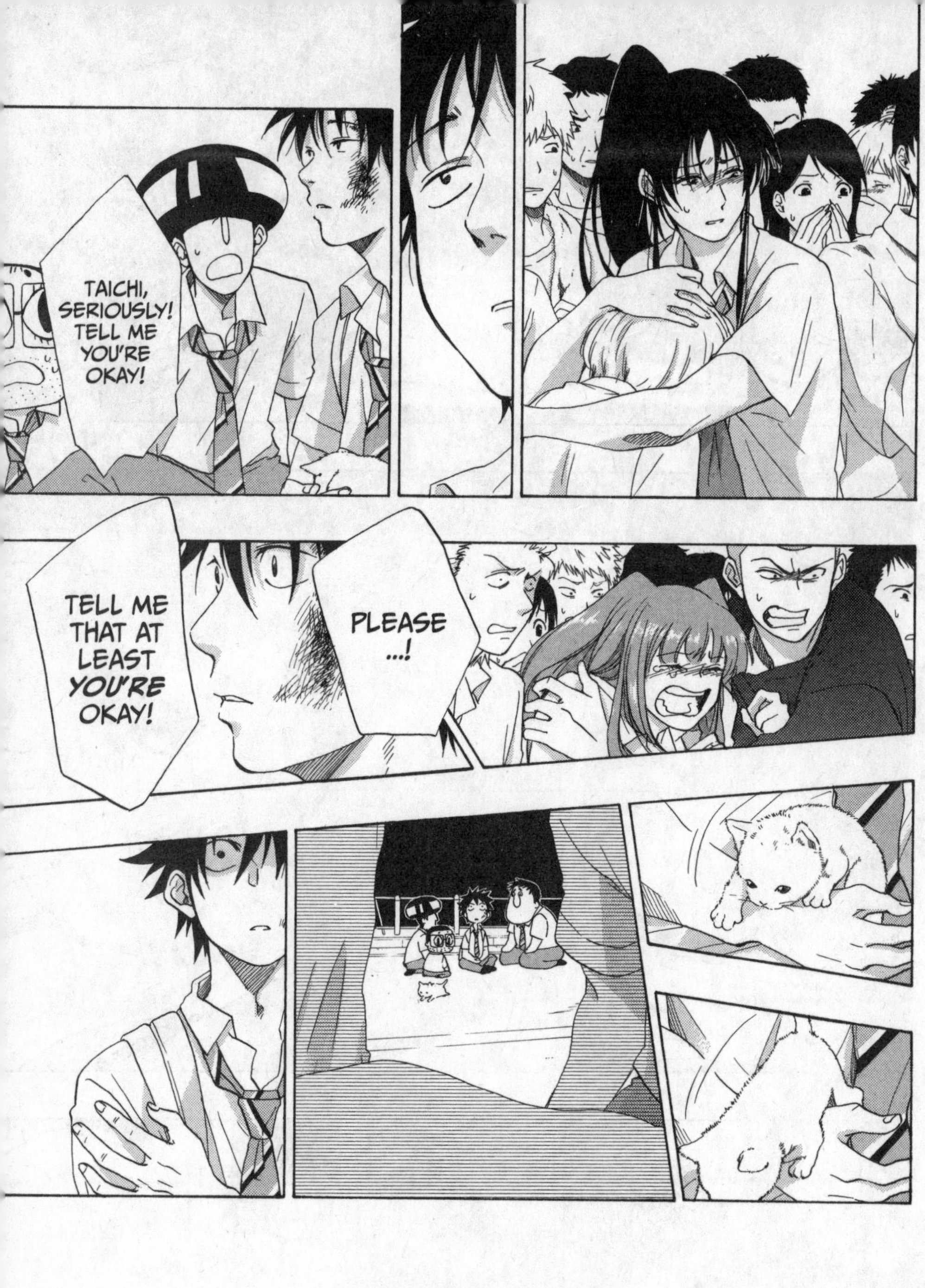
TAICHI, SERIOUSLY! TELL ME YOU'RE OKAY!
PLEASE ...!
TELL ME THAT AT LEAST *YOU'RE* OKAY!

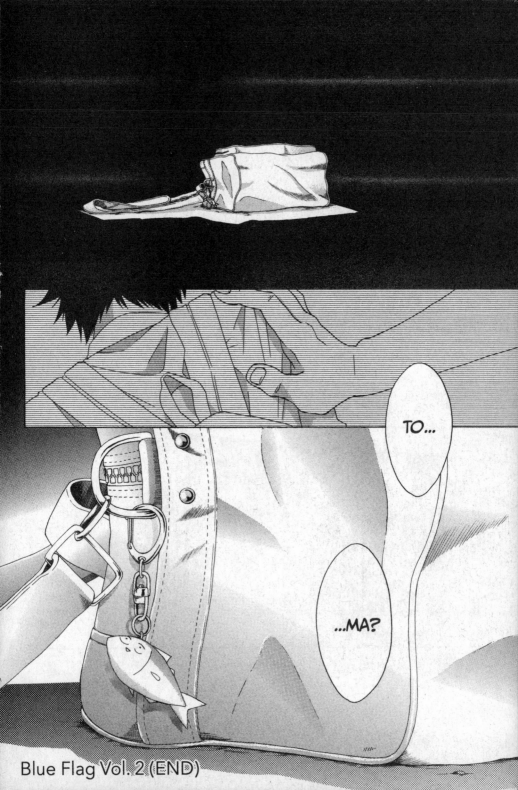

TO...

...MA?

Blue Flag Vol. 2 (END)

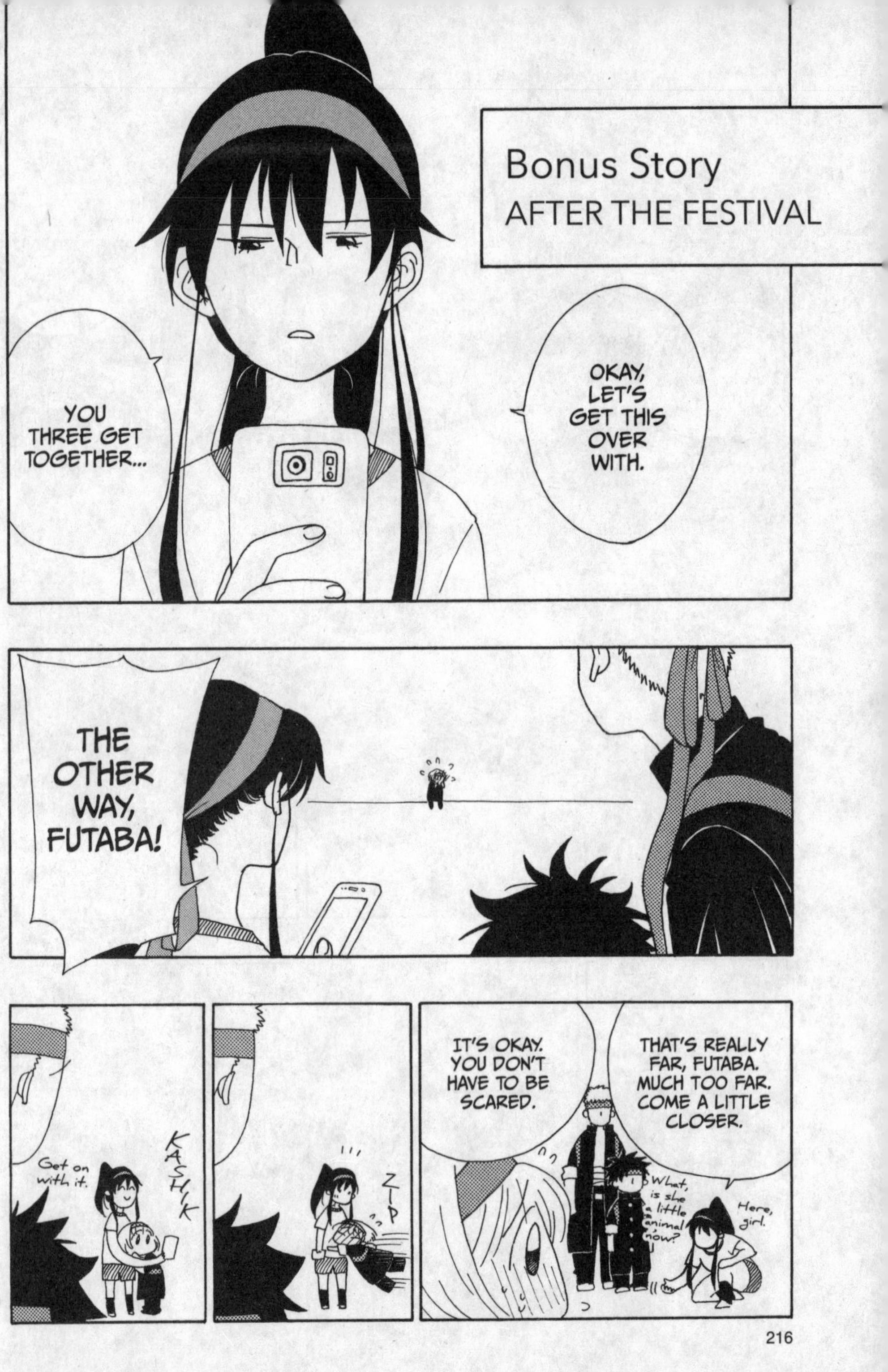
Bonus Story
AFTER THE FESTIVAL
OKAY, LET'S GET THIS OVER WITH.
YOU THREE GET TOGETHER...
THE OTHER WAY, FUTABA!
THAT'S REALLY FAR, FUTABA. MUCH TOO FAR. COME A LITTLE CLOSER.
IT'S OKAY. YOU DON'T HAVE TO BE SCARED.
Here, girl.
What, is she a little animal now?
ZIP
KASHIK
Get on with it.

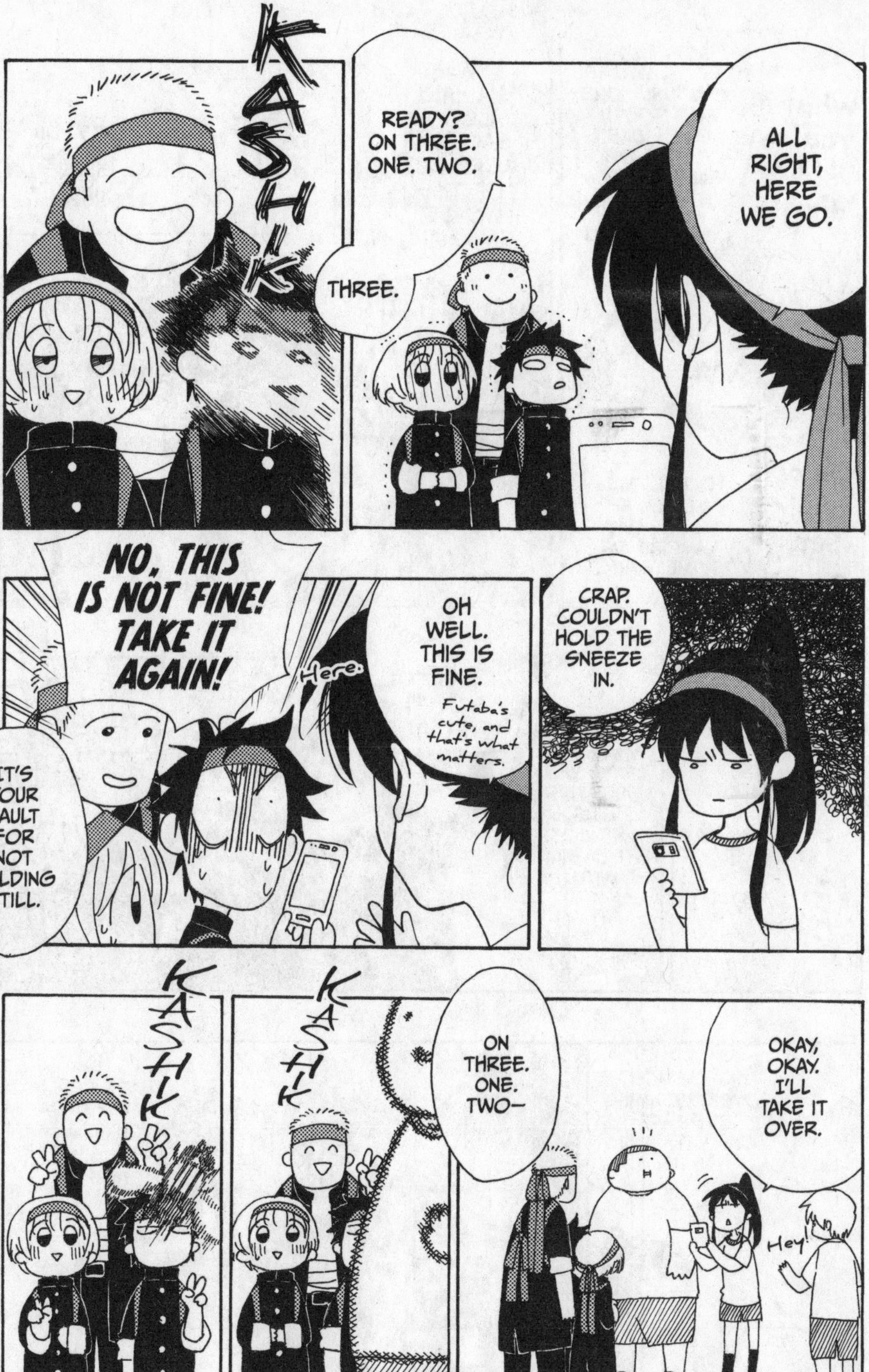
ALL RIGHT, HERE WE GO.
READY? ON THREE. ONE. TWO.
THREE.
KASHIK
CRAP. COULDN'T HOLD THE SNEEZE IN.
OH WELL. THIS IS FINE.
Futaba's cute, and that's what matters.
Here.
NO, THIS IS NOT FINE! TAKE IT AGAIN!
IT'S YOUR FAULT FOR NOT HOLDING STILL.
OKAY, OKAY. I'LL TAKE IT OVER.
Hey!
ON THREE. ONE. TWO—
KASHIK
KASHIK

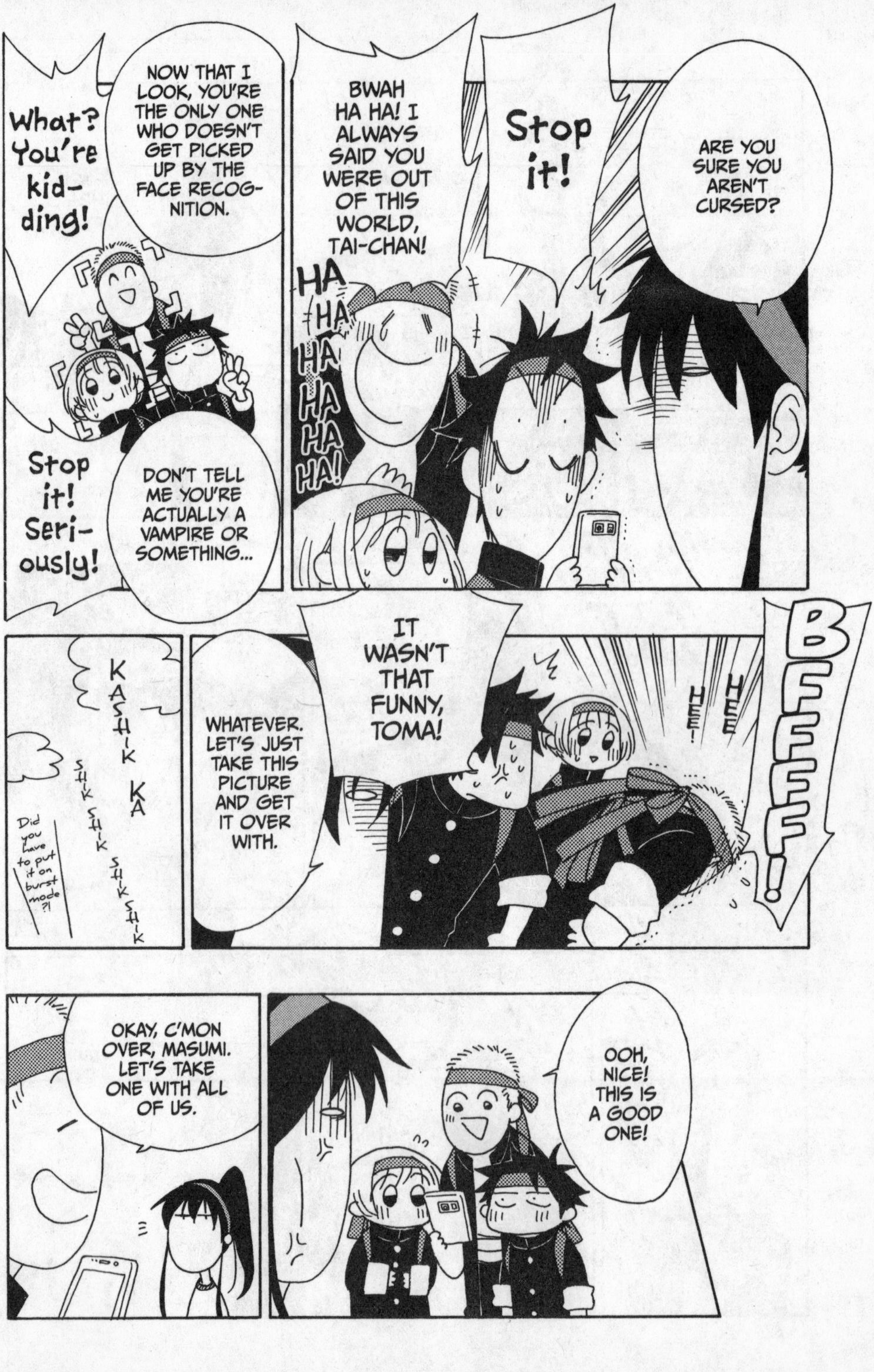

ARE YOU SURE YOU AREN'T CURSED?
Stop it!
BWAH HA HA! I ALWAYS SAID YOU WERE OUT OF THIS WORLD, TAI-CHAN!
HA HA HA HA HA HA HA!
NOW THAT I LOOK, YOU'RE THE ONLY ONE WHO DOESN'T GET PICKED UP BY THE FACE RECOGNITION.
What? You're kidding!
DON'T TELL ME YOU'RE ACTUALLY A VAMPIRE OR SOMETHING...
Stop it! Seriously!
BFFFF!
HEE HEE!
IT WASN'T THAT FUNNY, TOMA!
WHATEVER. LET'S JUST TAKE THIS PICTURE AND GET IT OVER WITH.
KASHIK KA
SHIK SHIK SHIK SHIK
Did you have to put it on burst mode?!
OOH, NICE! THIS IS A GOOD ONE!
OKAY, C'MON OVER, MASUMI. LET'S TAKE ONE WITH ALL OF US.

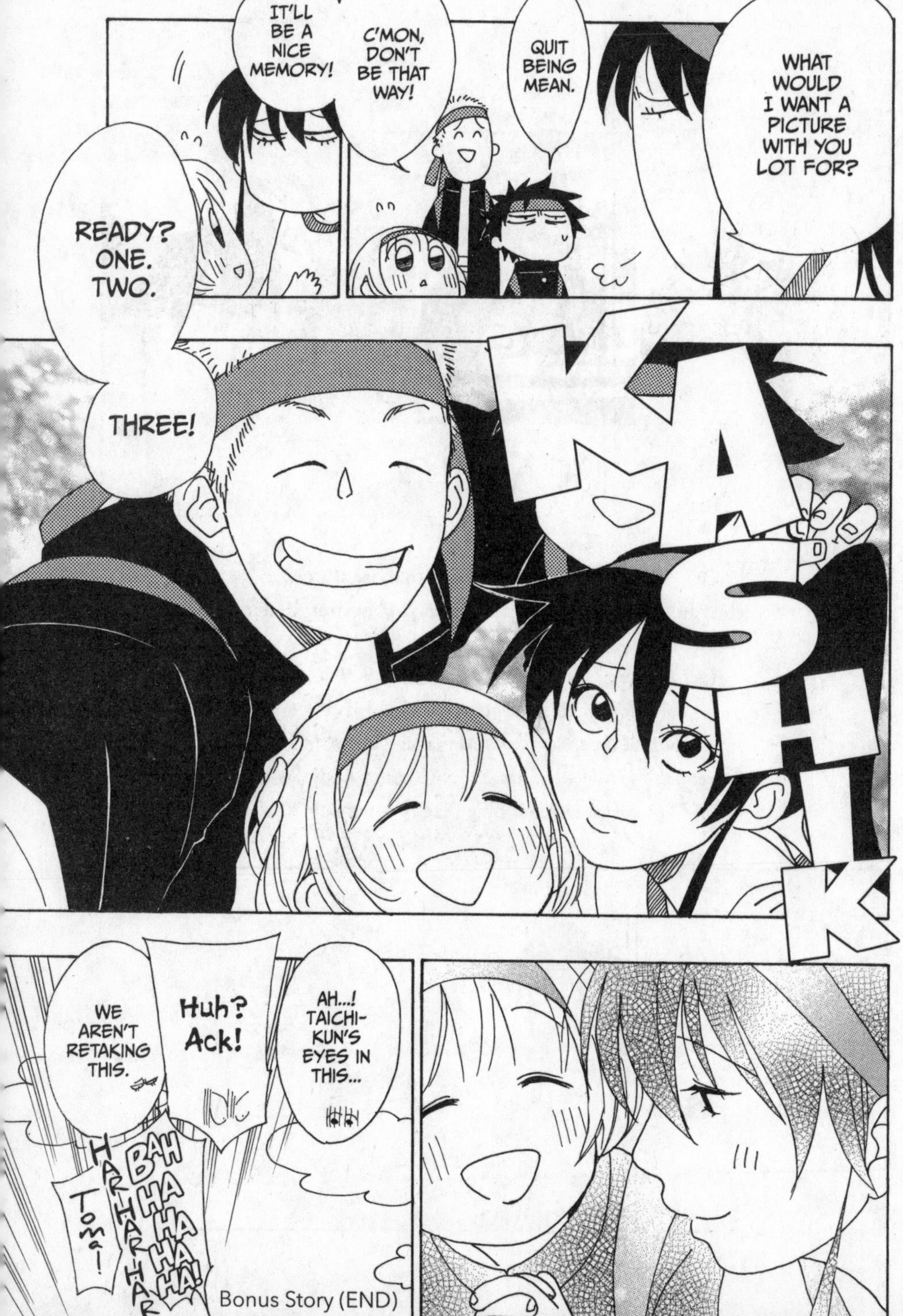
WHAT WOULD I WANT A PICTURE WITH YOU LOT FOR?
QUIT BEING MEAN.
C'MON, DON'T BE THAT WAY!
IT'LL BE A NICE MEMORY!
READY? ONE. TWO.
THREE!
KASHIK
AH...! TAICHI-KUN'S EYES IN THIS...
Huh? Ack!
WE AREN'T RETAKING THIS.
BAH HA HA HA HA HA!
HAR HAR HAR HAR
Toma!

Bonus Story (END)

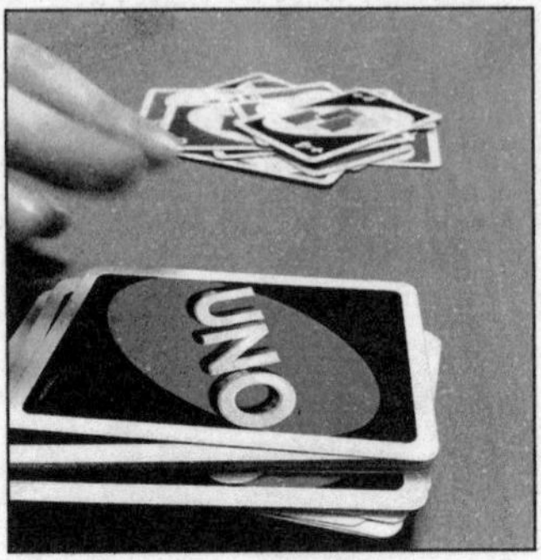
UNO

KAITO

One of the things I look forward to most at work is the game of Uno the staff and I always play after dinner.

KAITO began his manga career at the age of 20, when his one-shot "Happy Magi" debuted in Weekly Shonen Jump. *He published the series* Cross Manage *in 2012. In 2015, he returned to* Weekly Shonen Jump *with* Buddy Strike. *KAITO started work on* Blue Flag *in* Jump+ *in 2017.*